PREFACE

With the recent dramatic discoveries of fossils and footprints in Ethiopia, we now know that our ancestors walked erect some 4 million years ago. Hands, no longer required for locomotion, took on some of the tasks that the mouth had performed, such as carrying and fighting. In turn, it became possible for the mouth to form increasingly complex signals for communicative purposes, leading ultimately to the sounds of speech.

Stone tools date back more than 2 million years. Since that time, the human brain has more than doubled in size and has evolved into the most complicated and powerful piece of machinery known. The mental life and social structure of early humans elaborated symbiotically with the development of the brain, stimulating its growth and drawing on its increasing powers.

Fire was brought under control some 500,000 years ago; organized hunting probably took place much earlier. Microscopic analysis of stone implements 200,000 years old suggests that their makers were right-handed; this observation may link up with the fact that language too is significantly lateralized to the left brain. The first evidence we have of the transition into a distinctly human type of consciousness dates from 50,000 years ago: cave paintings, primitive sculpture, and flower burials.

We may never be able to determine exactly where along this corridor of time language emerged. In all likelihood, its development was a long and gradual process, and the rate must have been importantly influenced by cultural advances as well as by population density. Certainly by 10,000 years ago, language must have evolved close to the rich and subtle system that we have today. By then, there existed the first agricultural societies, with their extensive need for intricate communications and planning. Very soon thereafter came the earliest precursors of writing, which could have derived in the catalytic presence of a well-developed system of speech.

In human life today, language is everywhere. We study the teachings of Confucius and Jesus through languages that were used 2,000 years ago, and we communicate with computers through languages designed anew each day. Society is maintained, for better or worse, largely by means of language. Our inner selves are clearly dominated by language as well, as it helps us remember, plan, and carry out the day's activities. We experience language even during sleep, occasionally talking out loud.

Inescapably, each of us is at once the beneficiary of language, for access to social experiences accumulated through millennia, and its victim, for the lure to confuse saying for doing and to mistake words for real feelings and actual things. This intricate weaving of language into the innermost fabric of human existence has led scholars to question the name of our species, *Homo sapiens*, suggested by Linnaeus some 200 years ago. Would not *Homo loquens* be more appropriate?

Language means different things to different people. It has been likened to a symphony to be played, a cipher to be analyzed, a weapon to control others, a bond to be shared, and a window to the mind or perhaps a large part of the mind itself. As in the parable of the blind men who tried to understand the elephant simply by touching only one of its various parts, language is not any of these things singly. Rather, it must be seen from a composite of all these different perspectives.

The readings collected here reflect the multiple disciplines from which a true understanding of language must ultimately be derived. In the first section, on human language and animal communication, language is considered within an evolutionary framework. In the second section, several specific languages are discussed, including some writing systems. The last section, language as biological and social behavior, deals with how language is organized in our heads and how it is used in daily life.

It is in the nature of this kind of anthology that some parts will be more dated than others. This is remedied somewhat by the list of suggested readings that follows my introduction to each section. My hope is that readers will be sufficiently stimulated by the articles here to go on to the more recent and more technical literature, and perhaps even add their own talents to the exciting current investigations into the many facets of human communication.

September 1981   William S-Y. Wang

Readings from
SCIENTIFIC AMERICAN

HUMAN COMMUNICATION

Language and Its Psychobiological Bases

With Introductions by
William S-Y. Wang
University of California, Berkeley

 W. H. Freeman and Company
San Francisco

Most of the SCIENTIFIC AMERICAN articles in *Human Communication* are available as separate Offprints. For a complete list of articles now available as Offprints, write to W. H. Freeman and Company, 660 Market Street, San Francisco, California 94104.

Library of Congress Cataloging in Publication Data

Main entry under title:

Human communication.

Includes bibliographies and index.
    1. Language and languages—Addresses, essays, lectures.   I. Wang, William S-Y., 1933–
II. Scientific American.
P106.H79   1982   400   81–17436
ISBN 0–7167–1387–X   AACR2
ISBN 0–7167–1388–8 (pbk.)

Printed in the United States of America

1 2 3 4 5 6 7 8 9 0   KP   0 8 9 8 7 6 5 4 3 2

CONTENTS

Note on cross-references to SCIENTIFIC AMERICAN *articles*: Articles included in this book are referred to by title and page number; articles not included in this book but available as Offprints are referred to by title and offprint number; articles not included in this book and not available as Offprints are referred to by title and date of publication.

Some of the earliest records of human communication were pictorial, rather than linguistic, for example, the cave paintings of southern Europe that date back 40,000 years. In the painting above, due to the unique properties of the Chinese script, art and language blend harmoniously into each other. The artist's seal is at the bottom left. He was Zeng Yan-dong of the Qing dynasty (1644–1911). From the collection of Liu Mao-zhi, Shanghai.

I

HUMAN LANGUAGE
AND ANIMAL
COMMUNICATION

I HUMAN LANGUAGE AND ANIMAL COMMUNICATION

INTRODUCTION

Alfred Russell Wallace, the codiscoverer of the theory of evolution with Charles Darwin, is sometimes credited with being the first to see clearly the vital distinction between biological evolution and cultural evolution. It makes all the difference, of course, whether our bodies change to meet the needs of the environment or whether we change the environment to suit us instead. Cultural evolution proceeds at a much quicker pace, and can develop in infinitely more directions. Of the countless species that biological evolution has produced on this planet, we are the only species that has developed culture to any significant degree. The key to this development is language.

Other species communicate, to be sure, but in ways drastically more limiting than the language we use. In his comparison of the various systems of communication, "The Origin of Speech," Charles F. Hockett pioneered an approach that uses "design features." These features allow us to see more clearly how human speech has a basically distinct logical design from, say, the dance of the stickleback fish or the repertory of calls of the gibbon.

One feature that may be unique to language is "duality of patterning." Although each language has thousands of words to form infinitely numerous sentences, the words are themselves formed of a very small inventory of sounds. This feature makes possible mapping an immensely complex cognitive world onto a simple set of no more than several dozen motor gestures. The expressive power of language lies in part in the large number of possibilities in which these gestures may be sequenced.

It has long been known that social insects can communicate a surprising amount of data concerning a food source. A bee, with a brain that is miniscule compared to ours, can nevertheless provide reliable information regarding the location and quantity of nectar a good distance away from the hive. Through decades of painstaking research, Karl von Frisch and his colleagues succeeded in "cracking the code" of the bee dance. The system apparently makes use of some rather advanced design features that are not present in the communicative behavior of most higher species, i.e., semanticity, displacement, and productivity. In the article included here, "Dialects in the Language of the Bees," von Frisch adds some observations on how different species of bees vary in their "dialects," giving us a valuable perspective on the evolution of this fascinating communicative system.

Another area of animal behavior that has considerable interest for understanding the evolutionary context of human speech is birdsong. Some species of birds need to sing frequently for purposes of claiming territory and attracting sexual partners. Several striking parallels have been observed between their songs and human speech; for example, young birds go through a stage of "subsong" much as human infants go through "babbling." Neurally, the singing seems to be controlled in one side of the bird's brain, paralleling the lateralization of speech in the left hemisphere for most humans.

Furthermore, song learning appears to be maturationally timed, perhaps in a way that is analogous to the "critical period" that has been posited for the child's learning of speech. If a young bird is deprived of hearing the proper songs during that period, then those songs will never be learned properly. Likewise, it has been widely noted that the earlier a language is learned— and puberty seems to be an important milestone in the schedule—the more perfect is the mastery.

Some birds, like the parrot, are famous for their ability to imitate sounds. There are species of birds for which this ability is an important part of their reproductive strategy. They deposit their eggs in the nests of other species. The eggs are then incubated and the hatchlings raised by the host. "Mimicry in Parasitic Birds," by Jürgen Nicolai, describes one such species, the African widow bird, which has an especially well-developed capacity for song mimicry.

The last article in this section, "Teaching Language to an Ape," deals with our closest relative—the chimpanzee. It has been estimated that the human line diverged from that of the chimpanzee as recently as 10 million years ago. Biochemical analysis reveals that humans and chimpanzees share more than 99% of their genetic material, and are more closely related to each other than, say, the horse and the zebra. If these close relatives did not invent language on their own, perhaps they could learn one of ours. Yet all early attempts to teach the chimpanzee to *speak* were completely unsuccessful.

The realization came in the 1960s that the chimpanzee's limitation could be due more to an inability to produce or perceive speech sounds than to an inadequate cognitive capacity at symbolization. It has been remarked that chess pieces could be made of wood or ivory without changing the nature of the game. And in a limited sense this is also true of language. A variety of techniques was then developed to teach chimpanzees to symbolize in the visual mode—from American Sign Language, to pressing buttons on a computer terminal, to placing plastic chips on a magnetic board. This last technique was used by Ann and David Premack in their attempts to teach linguistic behavior to a chimpanzee.

SUGGESTED FURTHER READING

Books

Bonner, John T. 1980. *The Evolution of Culture in Animals*. Princeton, N.J.: Princeton University Press.

Harnad, Stevan R., Horst D. Steklis, and Jane Lancaster, eds. 1976. *Origins and Evolution of Language and Speech*. Annals of the New York Academy of Sciences, vol. 280.

Hockett, Charles F. 1978. *In Search of Jove's Brow*. (*American Speech*, vol. 4, no. 4.) University: University of Alabama Press.

Sebeok, Thomas A., ed. 1977. *How Animals Communicate*. Bloomington: Indiana University Press.

Smith, W. John. 1977. *The Behavior of Communicating*. Cambridge: Harvard University Press.

Swadesh, Morris. 1981. *The Origin and Diversification of Language*. Hawthorne, N.Y.: Aldine.

Scientific American Articles

Andres, Richard J. "The Origins of Facial Expressions." October 1965.

Esch, Harald. "The Evolution of Bee Language." April 1967. Offprint No. 1071.

Krogh, August. "The Language of the Bees." August 1948. Offprint No. 21.

Frings, Hubert and Mabel. "The Language of Crows." November 1959.

Thorpe, W. H. "The Language of Birds." October 1956. Offprint No. 145.

Wilson, Edward O. "Animal Communication." September 1972. Offprint No. 1258.

Würsig, Bernd. "Dolphins." March 1979. Offprint No. 1424.

THREAT POSTURE of male stickleback is example of nonvocal communication in lower animals. In this picture, made by N. Tinbergen of the University of Oxford, the fish is responding to its mirror image by indicating readiness to fight "intruding" male.

The Origin of Speech

1

by Charles F. Hockett
September 1960

Man is the only animal that can communicate by means of abstract symbols. Yet this ability shares many features with communication in other animals, and has arisen from these more primitive systems

About 50 years ago the Linguistic Society of Paris established a standing rule barring from its sessions papers on the origin of language. This action was a symptom of the times. Speculation about the origin of language had been common throughout the 19th century, but had reached no conclusive results. The whole enterprise in consequence had come to be frowned upon—as futile or crackpot—in respectable linguistic and philological circles. Yet amidst the speculations there were two well-reasoned empirical plans that deserve mention even though their results were negative.

A century ago there were still many corners of the world that had not been visited by European travelers. It was reasonable for the European scholar to suspect that beyond the farthest frontiers there might lurk half-men or man-apes who would be "living fossils" attesting to earlier stages of human evolution. The speech (or quasi-speech) of these men (or quasi-men) might then similarly attest to earlier stages in the evolution of language. The search was vain. Nowhere in the world has there been discovered a language that can validly and meaningfully be called "primitive." Edward Sapir wrote in 1921: "There is no more striking general fact about language than its universality. One may argue as to whether a particular tribe engages in activities that are worthy of the name of religion or of art, but we know of no people that is not possessed of a fully developed language. The lowliest South African Bushman speaks in the forms of a rich symbolic system that is in essence perfectly comparable to the speech of the cultivated Frenchman."

The other empirical hope in the 19th century rested on the comparative meth-od of historical linguistics, the discovery of which was one of the triumphs of the period. Between two languages the resemblances are sometimes so extensive and orderly that they cannot be attributed to chance or to parallel development. The alternative explanation is that the two are divergent descendants of a single earlier language. English, Dutch, German and the Scandinavian languages are related in just this way. The comparative method makes it possible to examine such a group of related languages and to construct, often in surprising detail, a portrayal of the common ancestor, in this case the proto-Germanic language. Direct documentary evidence of proto-Germanic does not exist, yet understanding of its workings exceeds that of many languages spoken today.

There was at first some hope that the comparative method might help determine the origin of language. This hope was rational in a day when it was thought that language might be only a few thousands or tens of thousands of years old, and when it was repeatedly being demonstrated that languages that had been thought to be unrelated were in fact related. By applying the comparative method to all the languages of the world, some earliest reconstructable horizon would be reached. This might not date back so early as the origin of language, but it might bear certain earmarks of primitiveness, and thus it would enable investigators to extrapolate toward the origin. This hope also proved vain. The earliest reconstructable stage for any language family shows all the complexities and flexibilities of the languages of today.

These points had become clear a half-century ago, by the time of the Paris ruling. Scholars cannot really approve of such a prohibition. But in this instance it had the useful result of channeling the energies of investigators toward the gathering of more and better information about languages as they are today. The subsequent progress in understanding the workings of language has been truly remarkable. Various related fields have also made vast strides in the last half-century: zoologists know more about the evolutionary process, anthropologists know more about the nature of culture, and so on. In the light of these developments there need be no apology for reopening the issue of the origins of human speech.

Although the comparative method of linguistics, as has been shown, throws no light on the origin of language, the investigation may be furthered by a comparative method modeled on that of the zoologist. The frame of reference must be such that all languages look alike when viewed through it, but such that within it human language as a whole can be compared with the communicative systems of other animals, especially the other hominoids, man's closest living relatives, the gibbons and great apes. The useful items for this sort of comparison cannot be things such as the word for "sky"; languages have such words, but gibbon calls do not involve words at all. Nor can they be even the signal for "danger," which gibbons do have. Rather, they must be the basic features of design that can be present or absent in any communicative system, whether it be a communicative system of humans, of animals or of machines.

With this sort of comparative method it may be possible to reconstruct the communicative habits of the remote ancestors of the hominoid line, which may be called the protohominoids. The task, then, is to work out the sequence by which that ancestral system became language as the hominids—the man-apes and ancient men—became man.

A set of 13 design-features is presented in the illustration on the opposite page. There is solid empirical justification for the belief that all the languages of the world share every one of them. At first sight some appear so trivial that no one looking just at language would bother to note them. They become worthy of mention only when it is realized that certain animal systems—and certain human systems other than language—lack them.

The first design-feature—the "vocal-auditory channel"—is perhaps the most obvious. There are systems of communication that use other channels; for example, gesture, the dancing of bees or the courtship ritual of the stickleback. The vocal-auditory channel has the advantage—at least for primates—that it leaves much of the body free for other activities that can be carried on at the same time.

The next two design-features—"rapid fading" and "broadcast transmission and directional reception," stemming from the physics of sound—are almost unavoidable consequences of the first. A linguistic signal can be heard by any auditory system within earshot, and the source can normally be localized by binaural direction-finding. The rapid fading of such a signal means that it does not linger for reception at the hearer's convenience. Animal tracks and spoors, on the other hand, persist for a while; so of course do written records, a product of man's extremely recent cultural evolution.

The significance of "interchangeability" and "total feedback" for language becomes clear upon comparison with other systems. In general a speaker of a language can reproduce any linguistic message he can understand, whereas the characteristic courtship motions of the male and female stickleback are different, and neither can act out those appropriate to the other. For that matter in the communication of a human mother and infant neither is apt to transmit the characteristic signals or to manifest the typical responses of the other. Again, the speaker of a language hears, by total feedback, everything of linguistic relevance in what he himself says. In contrast, the male stickleback does not see the colors of his own eye and belly that are crucial in stimulating the female. Feedback is important, since it makes possible the so-called internalization of communicative behavior that

constitutes at least a major portion of "thinking."

The sixth design-feature, "specialization," refers to the fact that the bodily effort and spreading sound waves of speech serve no function except as signals. A dog, panting with his tongue hanging out, is performing a biologically essential activity, since this is how dogs cool themselves off and maintain the proper body temperature. The panting dog incidentally produces sound, and thereby may inform other dogs (or humans) as to where he is and how he feels. But this transmission of information is strictly a side effect. Nor does the dog's panting exhibit the design-feature of "semanticity." It is not a signal meaning that the dog is hot; it is part of being hot. In language, however, a message triggers the particular result it does because there are relatively fixed associations between elements in messages (e.g., words) and recurrent features or situations of the world around us. For example, the English word "salt" means salt, not sugar or pepper. The calls of gibbons also possess semanticity. The gibbon has a danger call, for example, and it does not in principle matter that the meaning of the call is a great deal broader and more vague than, say, the cry of "Fire!"

In a semantic communicative system the ties between meaningful message-elements and their meanings can be arbitrary or nonarbitrary. In language the ties are arbitrary. The word "salt" is not salty nor granular; "dog" is not "canine"; "whale" is a small word for a large object; "microorganism" is the reverse. A picture, on the other hand, looks like what it is a picture of. A bee dances faster if the source of nectar she is reporting is closer, and slower if it is farther away. The design-feature of "arbitrariness" has the disadvantage of being arbitrary, but the great advantage that there is no limit to what can be communicated about.

Human vocal organs can produce a huge variety of sound. But in any one language only a relatively small set of ranges of sound is used, and the differences between these ranges are functionally absolute. The English words "pin" and "bin" are different to the ear only at one point. If a speaker produces a syllable that deviates from the normal pronunciation of "pin" in the direction of that of "bin," he is not producing still a third word, but just saying "pin" (or perhaps "bin") in a noisy way. The hearer compensates if he can, on the basis of context, or else fails to under-

stand. This feature of "discreteness" in the elementary signaling units of a language contrasts with the use of sound effects by way of vocal gesture. There is an effectively continuous scale of degrees to which one may raise his voice as in anger, or lower it to signal confidentiality. Bee-dancing also is continuous rather than discrete.

Man is apparently almost unique in being able to talk about things that are remote in space or time (or both) from where the talking goes on. This feature—"displacement"—seems to be definitely lacking in the vocal signaling of man's closest relatives, though it does occur in bee-dancing.

One of the most important design-features of language is "productivity"; that is, the capacity to say things that have never been said or heard before and yet to be understood by other speakers of the language. If a gibbon makes any vocal sound at all, it is one or another of a small finite repertory of familiar calls. The gibbon call system can be characterized as closed. Language is open, or "productive," in the sense that one can coin new utterances by putting together pieces familiar from old utterances, assembling them by patterns of arrangement also familiar in old utterances.

Human genes carry the capacity to acquire a language, and probably also a strong drive toward such acquisition, but the detailed conventions of any one language are transmitted extragenetically by learning and teaching. To what extent such "traditional transmission" plays a part in gibbon calls or for other mammalian systems of vocal signals is not known, though in some instances the uniformity of the sounds made by a species, wherever the species is found over the world, is so great that genetics must be responsible.

The meaningful elements in any language—"words" in everyday parlance, "morphemes" to the linguist—constitute an enormous stock. Yet they are represented by small arrangements of a relatively very small stock of distinguishable sounds which are in themselves wholly meaningless. This "duality of patterning" is illustrated by the English words

THIRTEEN DESIGN-FEATURES of animal communication, discussed in detail in the text of this article, are symbolized on opposite page. The patterns of the words "pin," "bin," "team" and "meat" were recorded at Bell Telephone Laboratories.

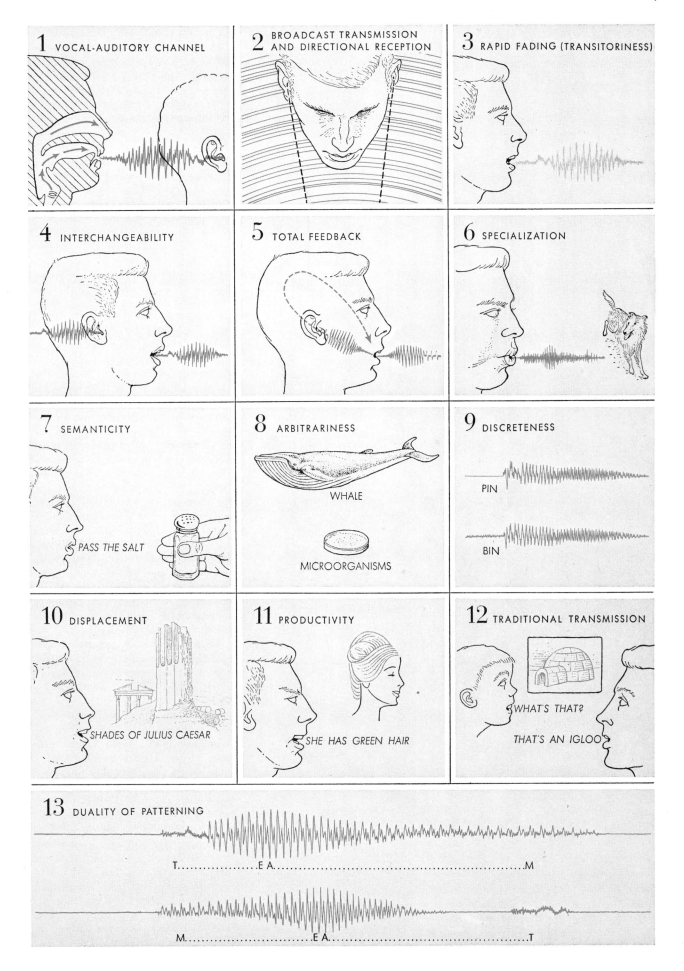

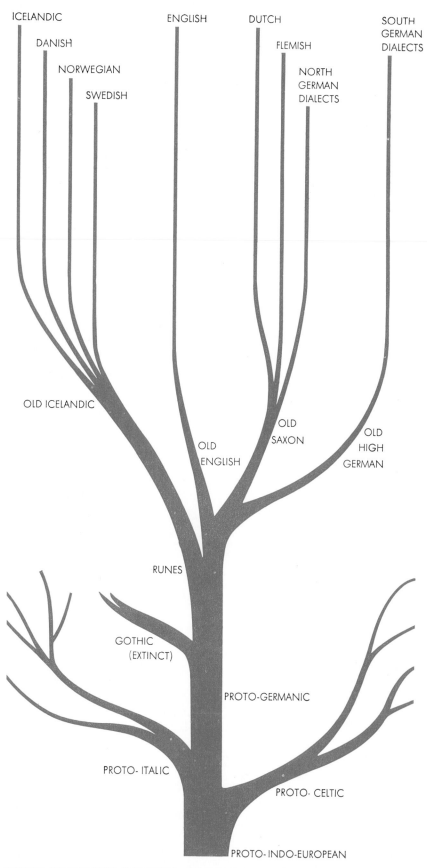

ICELANDIC

DANISH

NORWEGIAN

SWEDISH

ENGLISH

DUTCH

FLEMISH

NORTH
GERMAN
DIALECTS

SOUTH
GERMAN
DIALECTS

OLD ICELANDIC

OLD
ENGLISH

OLD
SAXON

OLD
HIGH
GERMAN

RUNES

GOTHIC
(EXTINCT)

PROTO-GERMANIC

PROTO- ITALIC

PROTO- CELTIC

PROTO-INDO-EUROPEAN

**ORIGIN OF MODERN GERMANIC LANGUAGES, as indicated by this "family tree,"
was proto-Germanic, spoken some 2,700 years ago. Comparison of present-day languages
has provided detailed knowledge of proto-Germanic, although no direct documentary evidence for the language exists. It grew, in turn, from the proto-Indo-European of 5000 B.C.
Historical studies cannot, however, trace origins of language back much further in time.**

"tack," "cat" and "act." They are totally
distinct as to meaning, and yet are composed of just three basic meaningless
sounds in different permutations. Few
animal communicative systems share this
design-feature of language—none among
the other hominoids, and perhaps none
at all.

It should be noted that some of these
13 design-features are not independent. In particular, a system cannot be
either arbitrary or nonarbitrary unless it
is semantic, and it cannot have duality
of patterning unless it is semantic. It
should also be noted that the listing does
not attempt to include all the features
that might be discovered in the communicative behavior of this or that species,
but only those that are clearly important
for language.

It is probably safe to assume that nine
of the 13 features were already present
in the vocal-auditory communication of
the protohominoids—just the nine that
are securely attested for the gibbons and
humans of today. That is, there were a
dozen or so distinct calls, each the appropriate vocal response (or vocal part
of the whole response) to a recurrent
and biologically important type of situation: the discovery of food, the detec-
tion of a predator, sexual interest, need
for maternal care, and so on. The problem of the origin of human speech, then,
is that of trying to determine how such a
system could have developed the four
additional properties of displacement,
productivity and full-blown traditional
transmission. Of course the full story involves a great deal more than communicative behavior alone. The development
must be visualized as occurring in the
context of the evolution of the primate
horde into the primitive society of food-
gatherers and hunters, an integral part,
but a part, of the total evolution of behavior.

It is possible to imagine a closed system developing some degree of productivity, even in the absence of the other
three features. Human speech exhibits a
phenomenon that could have this effect,
the phenomenon of "blending." Sometimes a speaker will hesitate between
two words or phrases, both reasonably
appropriate for the situation in which he
is speaking, and actually say something
that is neither wholly one nor wholly the
other, but a combination of parts of
each. Hesitating between "Don't shout
so loud" and "Don't yell so loud," he
might come out with "Don't shell so
loud." Blending is almost always involved in slips of the tongue, but it may

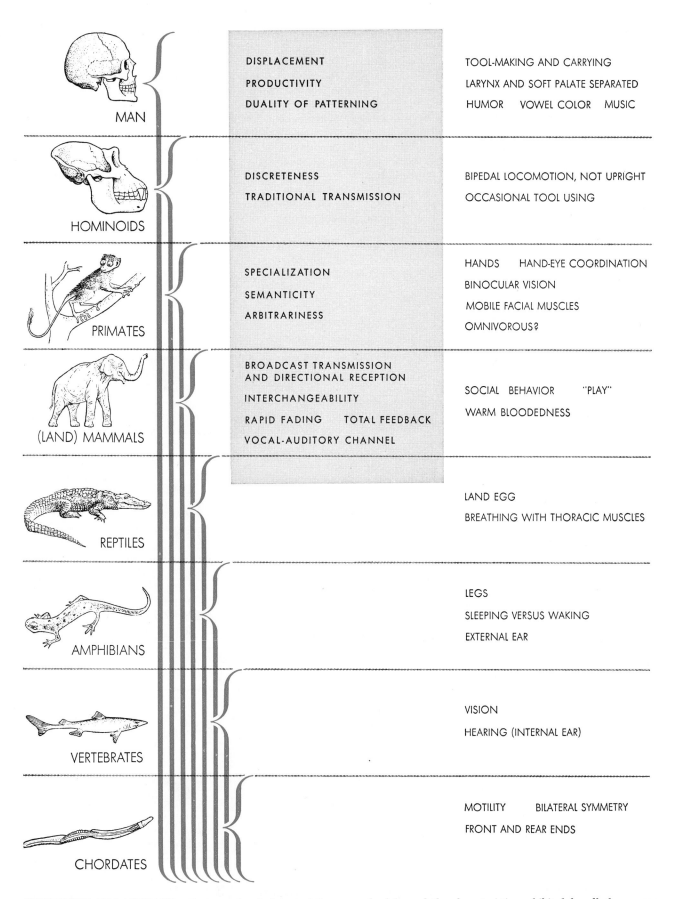

EVOLUTION OF LANGUAGE and some related characteristics are suggested by this classification of chordates. The lowest form of animal in each classification exhibits the features listed at the right of the class. Brackets indicate that each group possesses or has evolved beyond the characteristics exhibited by all the groups below. The 13 design-features of language appear in the colored rectangle. Some but by no means all of the characteristics associated with communication are presented in the column at right.

also be the regular mechanism by which a speaker of a language says something that he has not said before. Anything a speaker says must be either an exact repetition of an utterance he has heard before, or else some blended product of two or more such familiar utterances. Thus even such a smooth and normal sentence as "I tried to get there, but the car broke down" might be produced as a blend, say, of "I tried to get there but couldn't" and "While I was driving down Main Street the car broke down."

Children acquiring the language of their community pass through a stage that is closed in just the way gibbon calls

are. A child may have a repertory of several dozen sentences, each of which, in adult terms, has an internal structure, and yet for the child each may be an indivisible whole. He may also learn new whole utterances from surrounding adults. The child takes the crucial step, however, when he first says something that he has not learned from others. The only way in which the child can possibly do this is by blending two of the whole utterances that he already knows.

In the case of the closed call-system of the gibbons or the protohominoids, there is no source for the addition of new

unitary calls to the repertory except perhaps by occasional imitation of the calls and cries of other species. Even this would not render the system productive, but would merely enlarge it. But blending might occur. Let AB represent the food call and CD the danger call, each a fairly complex phonetic pattern. Suppose a protohominoid encountered food and caught sight of a predator at the same time. If the two stimuli were balanced just right, he might emit the calls ABCD or CDAB in quick sequence, or might even produce AD or CB. Any of these would be a blend. AD, for example, would mean "both food and danger." By

		A SOME GRYLLIDAE AND TETTIGONIIDAE	B BEE DANCING	C STICKLEBACK COURTSHIP	D WESTERN MEADOWLARK SONG
1	THE VOCAL-AUDITORY CHANNEL	AUDITORY, NOT VOCAL	NO	NO	YES
2	BROADCAST TRANSMISSION AND DIRECTIONAL RECEPTION	YES	YES	YES	YES
3	RAPID FADING (TRANSITORINESS)	YES, REPEATED	?	?	YES
4	INTERCHANGEABILITY	LIMITED	LIMITED	NO	?
5	TOTAL FEEDBACK	YES	?	NO	YES
6	SPECIALIZATION	YES?	?	IN PART	YES?
7	SEMANTICITY	NO?	YES	NO	IN PART ?
8	ARBITRARINESS	?	NO		IF SEMANTIC, YES
9	DISCRETENESS	YES?	NO	?	?
10	DISPLACEMENT		YES, ALWAYS		?
11	PRODUCTIVITY	NO	YES	NO	?
12	TRADITIONAL TRANSMISSION	NO?	PROBABLY NOT	NO?	?
13	DUALITY OF PATTERNING	? (TRIVIAL)	NO		?

EIGHT SYSTEMS OF COMMUNICATION possess in varying degrees the 13 design-features of language. Column A refers to members of the cricket family. Column H concerns only Western music since the time of Bach. A question mark means that it is

virtue of this, AB and CD would acquire new meanings, respectively "food without danger" and "danger without food." And all three of these calls—AB, CD and AD—would now be composite rather than unitary, built out of smaller elements with their own individual meanings: A would mean "food"; B, "no danger"; C, "no food"; and D, "danger."

But this is only part of the story. The generation of a blend can have no effect unless it is understood. Human beings are so good at understanding blends that it is hard to tell a blend from a rote repetition, except in the case of slips of the tongue and some of the earliest and most tentative blends used by children. Such powers of understanding cannot be ascribed to man's prehuman ancestors. It must be supposed, therefore, that occasional blends occurred over many tens of thousands of years (perhaps, indeed, they still may occur from time to time among gibbons or the great apes), with rarely any appropriate communicative impact on hearers, before the understanding of blends became speedy enough to reinforce their production. However, once that did happen, the earlier closed system had become open and productive.

It is also possible to see how faint traces of displacement might develop in a call system even in the absence of productivity, duality and thoroughgoing traditional transmission. Suppose an early hominid, a man-ape say, caught sight of a predator without himself being seen. Suppose that for whatever reason—perhaps through fear—he sneaked silently back toward others of his band and only a bit later gave forth the danger call. This might give the whole band a better chance to escape the predator, thus bestowing at least slight survival value on whatever factor was responsible for the delay.

Something akin to communicative displacement is involved in lugging a stick or a stone around—it is like talking today about what one should do tomorrow. Of course it is not to be supposed that the first tool-carrying was purposeful, any more than that the first displaced communication was a discussion of plans. Caught in a *cul-de-sac* by a predator, however, the early hominid might strike out in terror with his stick or stone and by chance disable or drive off his enemy. In other words, the first tool-carrying had a consequence but not a purpose. Because the outcome was fortunate, it tended to reinforce whatever factor, genetic or traditional, prompted the behavior and made the outcome possible. In the end such events do lead to purposive behavior.

Although elements of displacement might arise in this fashion, on the whole it seems likely that some degree of productivity preceded any great proliferation of communicative displacement as well as any significant capacity for traditional transmission. A productive system requires the young to catch on to the ways in which whole signals are built out of smaller meaningful elements, some of which may never occur as whole signals in isolation. The young can do this only in the way that human children learn their language: by learning some utterances as whole units, in due time testing various blends based on that repertory, and finally adjusting their patterns of blending until the bulk of what they say matches what adults would say and is therefore understood. Part of this learning process is bound to take place away from the precise situations for which the responses are basically appropriate, and this means the promotion of displacement. Learning and teaching, moreover, call on any capacity for traditional transmission that the band may have. Insofar as the communicative system itself has survival value, all this bestows survival value also on the capacity

E	F	G	H
GIBBON CALLS	PARALINGUISTIC PHENOMENA	LANGUAGE	INSTRUMENTAL MUSIC
YES	YES	YES	AUDITORY, NOT VOCAL
YES	YES	YES	YES
YES, REPEATED	YES	YES	YES
YES	LARGELY YES	YES	?
YES	YES	YES	YES
YES	YES?	YES	YES
YES	YES?	YES	NO (IN GENERAL)
YES	IN PART	YES	
YES	LARGELY NO	YES	IN PART
NO	IN PART	YES, OFTEN	
NO	YES	YES	YES
?	YES	YES	YES
NO	NO	YES	

doubtful or not known if the system has the particular feature. A blank space indicates that feature cannot be determined because another feature is lacking or is indefinite.

for traditional transmission and for displacement. But these in turn increase the survival value of the communicative system. A child can be taught how to avoid certain dangers before he actually encounters them.

These developments are also necessarily related to the appearance of large and convoluted brains, which are better storage units for the conventions of a complex communicative system and for other traditionally transmitted skills and practices. Hence the adaptive value of the behavior serves to select genetically for the change in structure. A lengthened period of childhood helplessness is also a longer period of plasticity for learning. There is therefore selection for prolonged childhood and, with it, later maturity and longer life. With more for the young to learn, and with male as well as female tasks to be taught, fathers become more domesticated. The increase of displacement promotes re-

tention and foresight; a male can protect his mate and guard her jealously from other males even when he does not at the moment hunger for her.

There is excellent reason to believe that duality of patterning was the last property to be developed, because one can find little if any reason why a communicative system should have this property unless it is highly complicated. If a vocal-auditory system comes to have a larger and larger number of distinct meaningful elements, those elements inevitably come to be more and more similar to one another in sound. There is a practical limit, for any species or any machine, to the number of distinct stimuli that can be discriminated, especially when the discriminations typically have to be made in noisy conditions. Suppose that Samuel F. B. Morse, in devising his telegraph code, had proposed a signal .1 second long for "A," .2 second long for "B," and so on up to 2.6 seconds for "Z." Operators would have enormous

difficulty learning and using any such system. What Morse actually did was to incorporate the principle of duality of patterning. The telegraph operator has to learn to discriminate, in the first instance, only two lengths of pulse and about three lengths of pause. Each letter is coded into a different arrangement of these elementary meaningless units. The arrangements are easily kept apart because the few meaningless units are plainly distinguishable.

The analogy explains why it was advantageous for the forerunner of language, as it was becoming increasingly complex, to acquire duality of patterning. However it occurred, this was a major breakthrough; without it language could not possibly have achieved the efficiency and flexibility it has.

One of the basic principles of evolutionary theory holds that the initial survival value of any innovation is conservative in that it makes possible the maintenance of a largely traditional way of life in the face of changed circumstances. There was nothing in the makeup of the protohominoids that destined their descendants to become human. Some of them, indeed, did not. They made their way to ecological niches where food was plentiful and predators sufficiently avoidable, and where the development of primitive varieties of language and culture would have bestowed no advantage. They survive still, with various sorts of specialization, as the gibbons and the great apes.

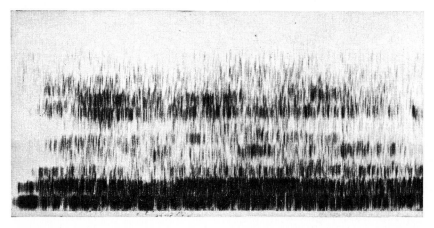

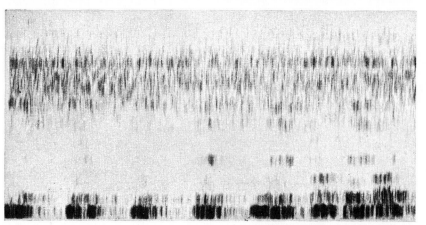

SUBHUMAN PRIMATE CALLS are represented here by sound spectrograms of the roar (*top*) and bark (*bottom*) of the howler monkey. Frequencies are shown vertically; time, horizontally. Roaring, the most prominent howler vocalization, regulates interactions and movements of groups of monkeys, and has both defensive and offensive functions. Barking has similar meanings but occurs when the monkeys are not quite so excited. Spectrograms were produced at Bell Telephone Laboratories from recordings made by Charles Southwick of the University of Southern Ohio during an expedition to Barro Colorado Island in the Canal Zone. The expedition was directed by C. R. Carpenter of Pennsylvania State University.

Man's own remote ancestors, then, must have come to live in circumstances where a slightly more flexible system of communication, the incipient carrying and shaping of tools, and a slight increase in the capacity for traditional transmission made just the difference between surviving—largely, be it noted, by the good old protohominoid way of life—and dying out. There are various possibilities. If predators become more numerous and dangerous, any nonce use of a tool as a weapon, any co-operative mode of escape or attack might restore the balance. If food became scarcer, any technique for cracking harder nuts, for foraging over a wider territory, for sharing food so gathered or storing it when it was plentiful might promote survival of the band. Only after a very long period of such small adjustments to tiny changes of living conditions could the factors involved —incipient language, incipient tool-carrying and toolmaking, incipient culture— have started leading the way to a new pattern of life, of the kind called human.

2

Dialects in the Language of the Bees

by Karl von Frisch
August 1962

*The dances that a honeybee does to direct its fellows
to a source of nectar vary from one kind of bee to
another. These variations clarify the evolution of this
remarkable system of communication*

For almost two decades my colleagues and I have been studying one of the most remarkable systems of communication that nature has evolved. This is the "language" of the bees: the dancing movements by which forager bees direct their hivemates, with great precision, to a source of food. In our earliest work we had to look for the means by which the insects communicate and, once we had found it, to learn to read the language [see "The Language of the Bees," by August Krogh; SCIENTIFIC AMERICAN Offprint 21]. Then we discovered that different varieties of the honeybee use the same basic patterns in slightly different ways; that they speak different dialects, as it were. This led us to examine the dances of other species in the hope of discovering the evolution of this marvelously complex behavior. Our investigation has thus taken us into the field of comparative linguistics.

Before beginning the story I should like to emphasize the limitations of the language metaphor. The true comparative linguist is concerned with one of the subtlest products of man's powerfully developed thought processes. The brain of a bee is the size of a grass seed and is not made for thinking. The actions of bees are mainly governed by instinct. Therefore the student of even so complicated and purposeful an activity as the communication dance must remember that he is dealing with innate patterns, impressed on the nervous system of the insects over the immense reaches of time of their phylogenetic development.

We made our initial observations on the black Austrian honeybee (*Apis mellifera carnica*). An extremely simple experiment suffices to demonstrate that these insects do communicate. If one puts a small dish of sugar water near a beehive, the dish may not be discovered

for several days. But as soon as one bee has found the dish and returned to the hive, more foragers come from the same hive. In an hour hundreds may be there.

To discover how the message is passed on we conducted a large number of experiments, marking individual bees with colored dots so that we could recognize them in the milling crowds of their fellows and building a hive with glass walls through which we could watch what was happening inside. Briefly, this is what we learned. A bee that has discovered a rich source of food near the hive performs on her return a "round dance." (Like all the other work of the colony, food-foraging is carried out by females.) She turns in circles, alternately to the left and to the right [see top illustration on next page]. This dance excites the neighboring bees; they start to troop behind the dancer and soon fly off to look for the food. They seek the kind of flower whose scent they detected on the original forager.

The richer the source of food, the more vigorous and the longer the dance. And the livelier the dance, the more strongly it arouses the other bees. If several kinds of plants are in bloom at the same time, those with the most and the sweetest nectar cause the liveliest dances. Therefore the largest number of bees fly to the blossoms where collecting is currently most rewarding. When the newly recruited helpers get home, they dance too, and so the number of foragers increases until they have drained most of the nectar from the blossoms. Then the dances slow down or stop altogether. The stream of workers now turns to other blossoms for which the dancing is livelier. The scheme provides a simple and purposeful regulation of supply and demand.

The round dance works well for flowers close to the beehive. Bees collect their

nourishment from a large circuit, however, and frequently fly several miles from the hive. To search at such distances in all directions from the hive for blossoms known only by scent would be a hopeless task. For sources farther away than about 275 feet the round dance is replaced by the "tail-wagging dance." Here again the scent of the dancer points to the specific blossoms to be sought, and the liveliness of the dance indicates the richness of the source. In addition the wagging dance transmits an exact description of the direction and distance of the goal. The amount and precision of the information far exceeds that carried by any other known communication system among animals other than man.

The bee starts the wagging dance by running a short distance in a straight line and wagging her abdomen from side to side. Then she returns in a semicircle to the starting point. Then she repeats the straight run and comes back in a semicircle on the opposite side. The cycle is repeated many times [see middle illustration on next page]. By altering the tempo of the dance the bee indicates the distance of the source. For example, an experimental feeding dish 1,000 feet away is indicated by 15 complete runs through the pattern in 30 seconds; when the dish is moved to 2,000 feet, the number drops to 11.

There is no doubt that the bees understand the message of the dance. When they fly out, they search only in the neighborhood of the indicated range, ignoring dishes set closer in or farther away. Not only that, they search only in the direction in which the original feeding dish is located.

The directional information contained in the wagging dance can be followed most easily by observing a forager's per-

ROUND DANCE, performed by moving in alternating circles to the left and to the right, is used by honeybees to indicate the presence of a nectar source near the hive.

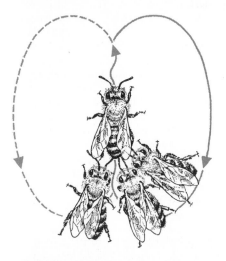

WAGGING DANCE indicates distance and direction of a nectar source farther away. Bee moves in a straight line, wagging her abdomen, then returns to her starting point.

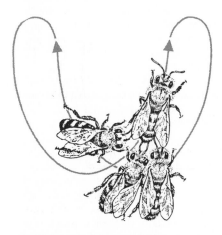

SICKLE DANCE is used by the Italian bee. She moves in a figure-eight-shaped pattern to show intermediate distance. A dancer is always followed by her hivemates.

formance when it takes place out in the open, on the small horizontal landing platform in front of the entrance to the hive. The bees dance there in hot weather, when many of them gather in front of the entrance. Under these conditions the straight portion of the dance points directly toward the goal. A variety of experiments have established that the pointing is done with respect to the sun. While flying to the feeding place, the bee observes the sun. During her dance she orients herself so that, on the straight run, she sees the sun on the same side and at the same angle. The bees trooping behind note the position of the sun during the straight run and position themselves at the same relative angle when they fly off.

The composite eye of the insect is an excellent compass for this purpose. Moreover, the bee is equipped with the second navigational requisite: a chronometer. It has a built-in time sense that enables it to compensate for the changes in the sun's position during long flights.

Usually the wagging dance is performed not on a horizontal, exposed platform but in the dark interior of the hive on the vertical surface of the honeycomb. Here the dancer uses a remarkable method of informing her mates of the correct angle with respect to the sun. She transposes from the ability to see the sun to the ability to sense gravity and thereby to recognize a vertical line. The direction to the sun is now represented by the straight upward direction along the wall. If the dancer runs straight up, this means that the feeding place is in the same direction as the sun. If the goal lies at an angle 40 degrees to the left of the sun, the wagging run points 40 degrees to the left of the vertical. The angle to the sun is represented by an equal angle with respect to the upright. The bees that follow the dancer watch her position with respect to the vertical, and when they fly off, they translate it back into orientation with respect to the light.

We have taken honeycombs from the hive and raised the young bees out of contact with older bees. Then we have brought the young bees back into the colony. They were immediately able to indicate the direction of a food source with respect to the position of the sun, to transpose directional information to the vertical and to interpret correctly the dances of the other bees. The language is genuinely innate.

When we extended our experiments to the Italian variety of honeybee (*Apis mellifera ligustica*), we found that its innate system had developed somewhat

differently. The Italian bee restricts her round dance to representing distances of only 30 feet. For sources beyond this radius she begins to point, but in a new manner that we call the sickle dance. The pattern is roughly that of a flattened figure eight bent into a semicircle [*see bottom illustration at left*]. The opening of the "sickle" faces the source of food; the vigorousness of the dance, as usual, indicates the quality of the source.

At about 120 feet the Italian bee switches to the tail-wagging dance. Even then she does not use exactly the same language as the Austrian bee does. The Italian variety dances somewhat more slowly for a given distance. We have put the two varieties together in a colony, and they work together peacefully. But as might be expected, confusion arises when they communicate. An Austrian bee aroused by the wagging dance of an Italian bee will search for the feeding place too far away.

Since they are members of the same species, the Austrian and Italian bees can interbreed. Offspring that bear the Italian bee's yellow body markings often do the sickle dance. In one experiment 16 hybrids strongly resembling their Italian parent used the sickle dance to represent intermediate distances 65 out of 66 times, whereas 15 hybrids that resembled their Austrian parent used the round dance 47 out of 49 times. On the other two occasions they did a rather dubious sickle dance: they followed the pattern but did not orient it to indicate direction.

Other strains of honeybee also exhibited variations in dialect. On the other hand, members of the same variety have proved to understand each other perfectly no matter where they come from.

Our next step was to study the language of related species. The only three known species of *Apis* in addition to our honeybee live in the Indo-Malayan region, which is thought to be the cradle of the honeybee. The Asian species are the Indian honeybee *Apis indica*, the giant bee *Apis dorsata* and the dwarf bee *Apis florea*. Under a grant from the Rockefeller Foundation my associate Martin Lindauer was able to observe them in their native habitat.

The Indian honeybee, which is so closely related to ours that it was for a long time believed to be a member of the same species, has also been domesticated for honey production. Like the European bees, it builds its hive in a dark, protected place such as the hol-

BEES ARE PAINTED with colored dots so that they can be identified during an experiment at the author's station near Munich. In this way the feeding station of a bee can be associated with its dance within the hive. The dish contains sugar water.

TWO VARIETIES OF BEE, the yellow Italian bee *Apis mellifera ligustica* and the black Austrian bee *A. mellifera carnica*, feed together. These two bees can live together in the same hive, but their dances do not have quite the same meaning. Accordingly one variety cannot accurately follow the feeding "instructions" of the other. Both of these photographs were made by Max Renner.

low of a tree. Its language is also much like that of the European bees. It employs the round dance for distances up to 10 feet, then switches directly to the tail-wagging dance. Within its dark hive the Indian bee also transposes from the visual to the gravity sense. The rhythm of the dance, however, is much slower than that of the European bees.

The giant bee also exhibits considerable similarity to its European cousins and to the Indian species in its communications. It changes from the round dance to the wagging dance at 15 feet. In its rhythm it moves at about the same rate as the Italian bee does. The

hive of the giant bee, however, is built on tree branches or other light, exposed places. The inhabitants dance on the vertical surface of the comb, converting the angle with respect to the sun correctly into an angle from the vertical. But since the comb is out in the open, the dancers can always find a spot that commands a clear view of the sky. The fact that they do this indicates that the following bees can understand the instructions better when they have direct information about the position of the sun.

In the case of the dwarf bee, Lindauer found a clearly more primitive social organization and a correspondingly less

highly developed language. The dwarf bees, which are so small that a layman would probably mistake them for winged ants, build a single comb about the size of a man's palm. It dangles from an upper branch of a small tree. When the dwarf bees return from feeding, they always alight on the upper rim of the comb, where their mates are sitting in a closely packed mass that forms a horizontal landing place for the little flyers. Here they perform their dances. They too use a round dance for distances up to 15 feet, then a wagging dance. Their rhythm is slow, like that of the Indian bee.

DIALECTS in the language of the bees are charted. The dwarf bee dances on a horizontal surface. All others dance on a vertical surface. The speed of the wagging dance carries distance instructions. The more rapidly the bee performs its wagging runs, the shorter is the distance. The figures in the squares represent the number of wagging runs in 15 seconds for each distance and kind of bee.

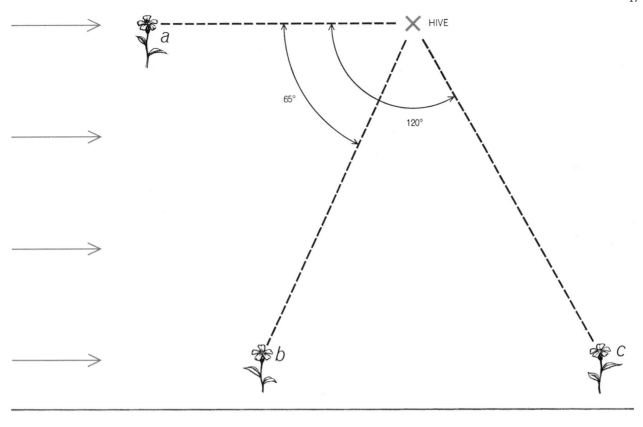

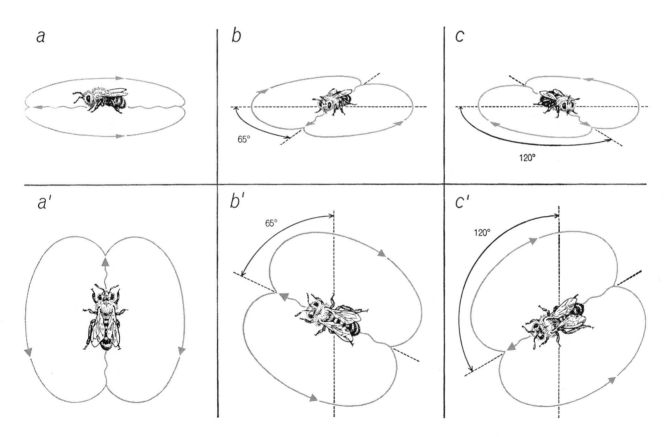

DIRECTION of a nectar source from the hive is shown by the direction in which a bee performs the straight portion of the wagging dance. The top section of the drawing shows flowers in three directions from the hive. The colored arrows represent the sun's rays. The middle section shows the dwarf bee, which dances on a horizontal surface. Her dance points directly to the goal: she orients herself to see the sun at the same angle as she saw it while flying to her food. The bottom section shows the bees that dance on a vertical surface. They transpose the visual to the gravitational sense. Movement straight up corresponds to movement toward the sun (a'). Movement at an angle to the vertical (b', c') signifies that the food lies at that same angle with respect to the sun.

The dwarf bee can dance only on a horizontal platform. Lindauer obtained striking proof of this on his field trip. When he cut off the branch to which a comb was attached and turned the comb so that the dancing platform was shifted to a vertical position, all the dancers stopped, ran up to the new top and tried to stamp out a dancing platform by running about through the mass of bees. When he left the hive in its normal position but placed an open notebook over its top, the foragers became confused and stopped dancing. In time, however, a few bees assembled on the upper surface of the notebook; then the foragers landed there and were able to perform their dances. Then, to remove every possible horizontal surface, Lindauer put a ridged, gable-shaped glass tile on top of the comb and closed the tile at both ends. In this situation the bees could not dance at all. After three days in this unnatural environment the urge to dance had become so great that a few bees tried to dance on the vertical surface. But they continued to depend on vision for their orientation and did not transpose the horizontal angle to a vertical one. Instead they looked for a dancing surface on which there was a line parallel to the direction of their flight. They tried to make a narrow horizontal path in the vertical curtain of bees, keeping their straight runs at the same angle to the sun as the angle at which they had flown when they found food. Under these circumstances only a very few bees were able to dance. Obviously the dwarf bee represents a far more primitive stage of evolution than the other species. She cannot transpose from light to gravity at all.

In trying to follow the dancing instinct farther back on the evolutionary scale, we must be satisfied with what hints we can get by observing more primitive living insects. Whereas a modern fossil rec-ord gives some of the physical development of insects, their mental past has left no trace in the petrified samples.

The use of sunlight as a means of orientation is common to many insects. It was first observed among desert ants about 50 years ago. When the ants creep out of the holes of their subterranean dwellings onto the sandy and barren desert surface, they cannot depend on landmarks for orientation because the wind constantly changes the markings of the desert sands. Yet they keep to a straight course, and when they turn around they find their way home along the same straight line. Even the changing position of the sun does not disturb them. Like the bee, the desert ant can take the shift into account and use the sun as a compass at any hour, compensating correctly for the movement of the sun in the sky.

Perhaps even more remarkable is the fact that many insects have developed an ability to transpose from sight to gravity. If a dung beetle in a dark room is placed on a horizontal surface illuminated from one side by a lamp, the beetle will creep along a straight line, maintaining the same angle to the light source for as long as it moves. If the light is turned off and the surface is tilted 90 degrees so that it is vertical, the beetle will continue to crawl along a straight line in the dark; it now maintains the same angle with respect to gravity that it earlier maintained with respect to light. This transposition is apparently an automatic process, determined by the arrangement of the nervous system. Some insects transpose less accurately, keeping the same angle but placing it sometimes to the right and sometimes to the left of the vertical without regard to the original direction with respect to the light. Some are also impartial as to up and down, so that an angle is transposed in any of four ways. Since the patterns do not transmit in-formation, their exact form makes no difference. Among the ancestors of the bees transposition behavior was probably once as meaningless as it is in the dung beetle and other insects today. In the course of evolution, however, the bee learned to make meaningful use of this central nervous mechanism in its communication system.

Both navigation by the sun and transposition, then, have evolved in a number of insects. Only the bees can use these abilities for their own orientation and for showing their mates the way to food. The straight run in the wagging dance, when performed on a horizontal surface, indicates the direction in which the bees will soon fly toward their goal. Birds do something like this; when a bird is ready to take off, it stretches its neck in the direction of its flight. Such intention movements, as they are called, sometimes influence other animals. In a flock of birds the movements can become infectious and spread until all the birds are making them. It is possible that among the honeybees the strict system of the wagging dance gradually developed out of such intention movements, performed by forager bees before they flew off toward their goal.

The most primitive communication system we have found among the bees does not contain information about distance or direction. It is used by the tiny stingless bee *Trigona iridipennis,* a distant relative of the honeybee. Lindauer observed this insect in its native Ceylon. Its colonies are less highly organized, resembling bumblebee colonies rather than those of honeybees.

When a foraging *Trigona* has found a rich source of nectar, she also communicates with her nestmates. But she does not dance. She simply runs about in great excitement on the comb, knocking against her mates, not by chance but intentionally. In this somewhat rude manner she attracts their attention to the fragrance of blossoms on her body. They fly out and search for the scent, first in the nearby surroundings, then farther away. Since they have learned neither the distance nor the direction of the goal, they make their way to the food source one by one and quite slowly.

We probably find ourselves here at the root of the language of the bees. Which way the development went in detail we do not know. But we have learned enough so that our imagination can fill in the evolutionary gaps in a general way.

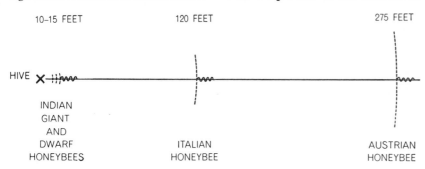

10–15 FEET	120 FEET	275 FEET

HIVE

INDIAN GIANT AND DWARF HONEYBEES | ITALIAN HONEYBEE | AUSTRIAN HONEYBEE

CHANGE FROM ROUND TO WAGGING DANCE occurs when nectar source lies beyond a certain radius of the hive. Change occurs at different distances among different bees. Because the wagging dance shows direction as well as distance, the Indian, giant and dwarf bees can give more precise information about a nearby source than the European bees can.

Mimicry in Parasitic Birds

3

by Jürgen Nicolai
October 1974

Various species of birds lay their eggs in the nest of another bird, which then incubates the eggs and feeds the young. The widow birds of Africa achieve this result by some remarkable feats of mimicry

The number of eggs a female animal produces is inversely proportional to the probability that the egg will give rise to a female that produces more eggs. All invertebrate animals and most lower vertebrates need to broadcast eggs by the hundreds and thousands in order to ensure the existence of subsequent generations. The number of eggs laid by a bird, although much smaller, also reflects the probability of reproductive success. Consider the greatest of ocean birds, the wandering albatross. It occupies breeding grounds on isolated islands of the Southern Hemisphere where it is completely undisturbed, and the female albatross lays a single egg every other year. In contrast, most species of European tits and both species of goldcrests respond to the stresses of severe winters and numerous predators by laying two yearly clutches of eggs, each numbering between eight and 12.

Any bird that is subject to severe environmental stress or predation pressure is at a reproductive disadvantage. It must incubate its eggs with the heat of its own body, and so the eggs must be kept all in one place, usually in a nest. A predator therefore needs to search out only a single target. One group of birds, the turkeylike megapods of Australasia and the Pacific, has surmounted this handicap by an ingenious stratagem. Instead of building nests they pile up mounds of plant material where they bury their eggs to be incubated by the warmth of plant decay [see "Incubator Birds," by H. J. Frith; SCIENTIFIC AMERICAN, August, 1959]. Still other bird species have discovered another solution to the problem. They deposit their eggs, one at a time, in the nest of another species; the eggs are then incubated and the hatchlings are raised by the host.

Birds that practice this kind of parasitic parenthood are found around the world. Among them are various members of the cosmopolitan family of cuckoos, some species of American cowbirds, a black-headed duck (*Heteronetta atricapilla*) in South America, all species of honey guides and certain weaverbirds in Africa. I have investigated the behavior of this last group, observing in particular the several species of a subfamily, the Viduinae, within the family of weaverbirds. The birds in this subfamily are commonly called widow birds. My work has been conducted both in the field and in our laboratory at the Max Planck Institute for Behavioral Physiology in Seewiesen.

Although a parasitic bird has overcome the disadvantage of putting all its eggs in one nest, the very nature of its solution to the problem introduces certain other difficulties. For one thing, if parasitic parenthood is to be successful, the parasite's reproductive cycle must be synchronized with the cycle of the host species. For another, it would be fatal if the host rejected either the parasite's egg or the hatchling that emerged from it. With respect to the egg a strategy of mimicry has evolved. For example, parasitic cuckoos lay eggs with markings that closely resemble those of the host's eggs. Widow-bird eggs are unmarked, as are their host's; they differ from the eggs of the host species only slightly in size and shape.

With respect to the acceptance of the hatchling the parasite strategies that have evolved are various. Several species of cowbirds punch tiny holes in the host's eggs before depositing their own, thus ensuring that no host egg ever hatches. An African honey-guide hatchling emerges from its egg armed with

formidable hooks at the tip of its beak; its host's offspring are all soon fatally wounded, leaving the parasite to consume all the food the host provides. Some cuckoo nestlings simply nudge their foster siblings out of the nest during the first few days of life; others mature so much more rapidly than their nestmates that the foster siblings' development is inhibited and they die prematurely.

In the long run, of course, strategies that result in the death of the host's young are unproductive. The parasitic parent needs to use the nests of several host pairs each year and a dwindling host population means fewer nests. The widow birds have evolved a strategy that circumvents this problem; like the egg strategy, it is imitative. Each widowbird nestling is indistinguishable from its host's nestlings in size, in color and markings, in gesture and in call. Thus the intruders can grow up among their alien nestmates with no risk of being rejected by their foster parents. Such a strategy ensures that the numbers of the host population do not diminish.

It seems surprising that the widow birds should have evolved this particular strategy. Their chosen hosts—various species of finches, the entire family Estrildidae—are noted for having mouths that are colored and marked in a complex and conspicuous manner [see illustration on page 20]. No two of the 125 species of estrildid finches have identical mouth markings. The color of the palate may be whitish, red, yellow or bluish. The palate markings may form a three-spot pattern or a five-spot pattern or may be only a fine horseshoe-shaped line; the spots themselves may be black or violet. Moreover, the fledglings' gape papillae vary in shape and color. They may be ivory white, cornflower

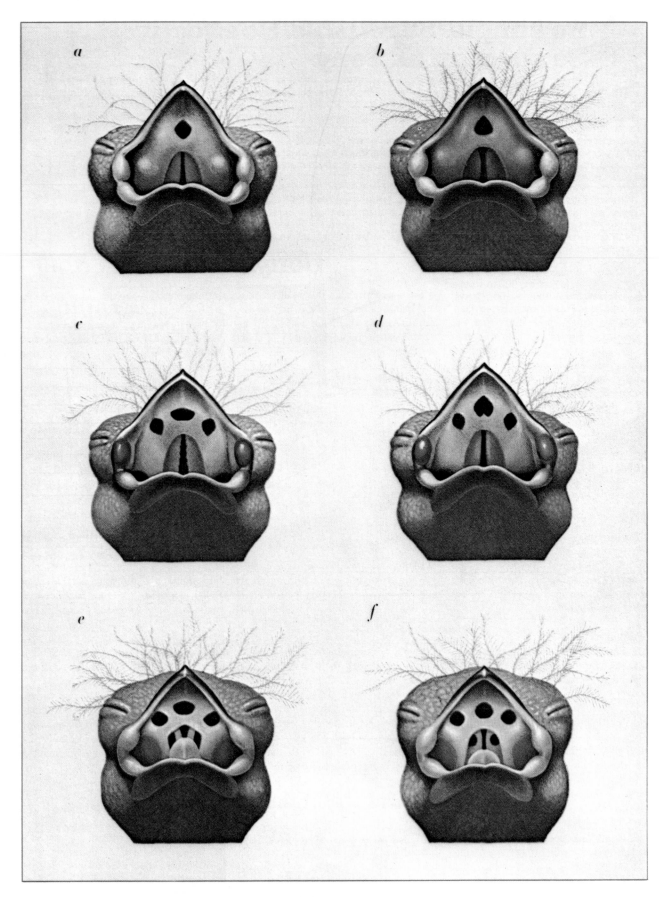

MOUTH MARKINGS of host nestlings, which stimulate the host parents' feeding response, are mimicked in detail by all the parasitic species of African widow birds. Shown here are the markings of a host-species nestling, the melba finch (*a*), and its parasitic sibling, the paradise widow bird (*b*), of a second host species, the purple grenadier (*c*), and its parasite, the straw-tailed widow bird (*d*), and of a third host-parasite pair, Jameson's fire finch (*e*) and the purple combassou (*f*). Many other mimicries of the type are known.

blue, yellow or faintly violet, and they may appear as simple thickenings or resemble small pearl-shaped warts.

In parallel with these elaborate mouth markings there has evolved among the estrildid finches a precise, genetically based "knowledge" of species-specific patterns and stimulus-receiving mechanisms that are correspondingly selective. By the simple experimental method of placing nestlings of one finch species in the nest of other species my colleagues and I have demonstrated that the parent birds will feed only the nestlings that display the appropriate species-specific markings. Even minor deviations in pattern are noted by the parent birds, and the deviants are ruthlessly weeded out by starvation.

A parasite nestling constantly interacts with its foster parents from the time of its emergence until it leaves the nest. The host birds are thus an essential part of the parasite's environment. The host sets a series of examples that instructs the parasite with respect to such matters as environmental standards and feeding habits. One instance of this process of parallel adaptation is the synchronization of the parasite's and the host's reproductive cycle.

Most species of estrildid finches breed during the rainy season. The finches' gonads begin to swell when, after months of drought, a series of showers brings the vegetation to renewed life. The timing is appropriate because the increase in the food supply that comes with the rainy season makes it easier to feed nestlings. Several finch species begin their breeding activities when the rains start; others do not begin until the middle of the rainy season or toward the end of it. A few species, such as the yellow-winged pytilia and the aurora finch of West Africa, delay their breeding until the dry season, a time when they find feeding conditions appropriate.

In each of these instances the parasitic widow birds synchronize their reproductive cycle with that of their host. One element in the cycle is that when courtship begins, the male widow bird displays a splendid and conspicuous plumage. The molt into breeding plumage occupies a period of four to six weeks. This means that the maturation of the widow bird's gonads, which initiates the molt, actually occurs sometime before the host's gonads mature.

To cite some examples, the paradise widow bird and the straw-tailed widow bird have hosts that breed during the rainy season. That requires the male

PARASITIC ADULTS, the female (a) and male (b) paradise widow bird, do not in any way mimic the appearance of the foster parents of their young, the female (c) and male (d) melba finch. The male paradise widow bird is seen in its bright breeding plumage.

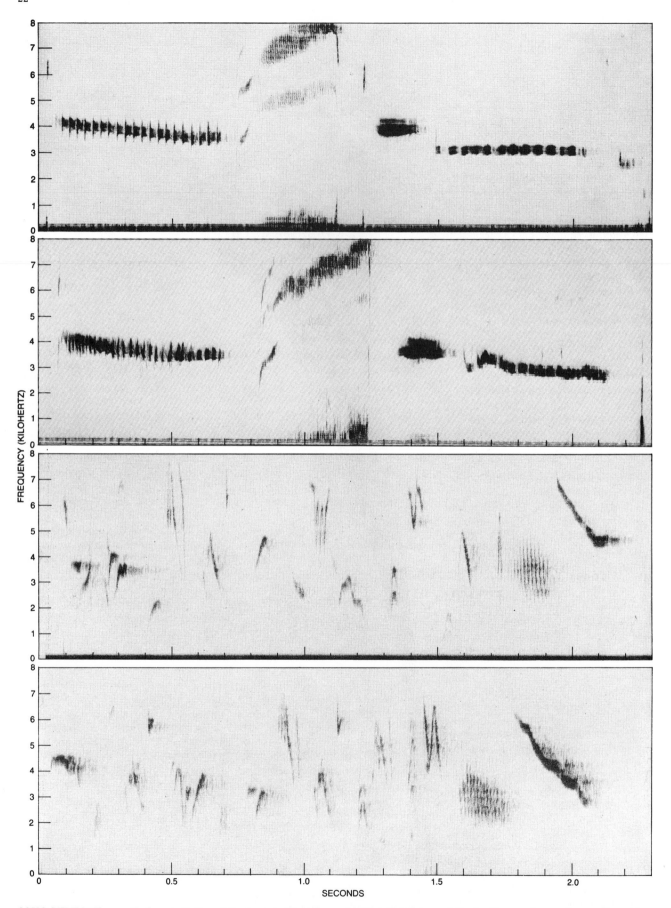

SONG MIMICRY, a meticulous imitation of the host male's call, learned by the parasite male while a juvenile, is demonstrated by these paired sonograms. The top sonogram shows the final seconds of a Damara melba finch's song; the sonogram directly below it is mimicry of this part of the finch's song by a male paradise widow bird. The third sonogram shows a two-second segment of the song of the violet-eared waxbill; the fourth is mimicry of this segment of the song by the waxbill's parasite, the shaft-tailed widow bird.

widow birds to develop their breeding plumage before the end of the dry season. Similarly, two species of widow bird, the Togo paradise widow bird and the Kongo paradise widow bird, have hosts that breed during the dry season. The male parasites' molt must therefore take place toward the end of the rainy season. Under these circumstances it is clear that the onset of the parasites' reproductive activity cannot simply be triggered by the onset of the hosts'; it is evidently set in motion by some kind of seasonal rhythm. The specific rhythms remain unidentified but one is justified in assuming that, because the rainy and dry seasons follow each other with great regularity in most of Africa, the gonads of rainy-season breeders begin to be stimulated after the passage of a certain length of dry-season time, and vice versa.

Now, in any fine-tuned system of parasitic adaptation one of the greatest potentials for disruption is accidental hybridization between species of parasites that are closely related and coexist in the same area. As far as the widow birds are concerned, any hybrid offspring would display intermediate mouth markings rather than markings that match those of their foster siblings. That in turn means they would be refused food by the host species of both parents. This hazard, with its long-term potential for the extinction of all widow birds, has been avoided by the evolution of a kind of behavior that is unknown among other parasitic birds. In brief, when the male widow bird sings, it includes in its song certain unique finch-species phrases it has learned from its foster parents.

Widow birds are polygamous. At the start of the breeding season a male stakes out a large territory that it defends against potential rivals. Throughout the breeding season the male perches on certain selected trees and bushes in the territory and sings its unique melody. If one compares the songs of various widow-bird species, either by listening or by analyzing sound spectrograms, it soon becomes apparent that the songs of all species have a few phrases in common. For example, they all include harsh chattering sounds; the motif is evidently related to the vocalizations produced by the widow birds' closest relatives, the bishop birds of the subfamily Euplectinae. Since these chatterings appear to represent an ancient genetic heritage, we call them widow-bird phrases.

The major portion of any male widow bird's song consists of quite different vocalizations. Its motifs vary from one

YOUNG PARASITES, unlike adult parasites, closely resemble their host siblings in appearance. Profiles at left show a paradise widow-bird nestling (*a*) and a melba-finch nestling (*b*) 13 days after hatching; profiles at right show a straw-tailed widow-bird nestling (*c*) and a purple-grenadier nestling (*d*) 15 days old. The young are independent after five weeks.

species to another, and each species-specific repertory perfectly imitates the motifs characteristic of the widow bird's finch host. We therefore call such motifs host phrases. They include the finch's long-distance call, its contact call, its distress and anger calls, its greeting phrases and, of course, its routine song. The parasite's mimicry of this repertory is so exact that it sounds like the finch's to the human ear and looks like it in a spectrogram [*see illustration on page 22*]. Furthermore, the host finch itself cannot distinguish between the widow bird's imitation and the song of its own species.

Let us examine in detail the song of one widow-bird species. The straw-tailed widow bird of East Africa (*Tetraenura fischeri*) ranges over the scrub savanna of that region from southern Tanzania northward into Ethiopia and Somalia. The male's breeding plumage is black and yellow and its four conspicuously elongated central tail feathers look like yellowish blades of dry grass. During the breeding season the male perches high in small trees or thornbushes and twitters its song unceasingly from early morning until sunset. The first motif in its repertory is usually the contact call of its finch host, the purple grenadier,

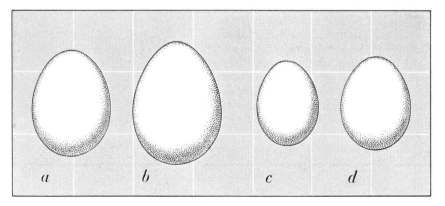

MIMICRY IN THE NEST extends to the size and shape of the egg laid by the parasite. At left is the egg of the melba finch (*a*) and of the paradise widow bird (*b*); the parasite's egg is only slightly larger and more rounded than the host's. At right is the egg of another host, the red-billed fire finch (*c*), and the egg of its parasite, the black-winged combassou (*d*). As centimeter grid shows, he host and parasite eggs are virtually identical in size and shape.

Uraeginthus ianthinogaster; this is a long trill. The mimicked phrase is repeated several times, increasing and decreasing in loudness. It is followed by other elements of the host's repertory. They include the brief "call" phrase used by the male to attract the female, the male's clacking song, a chase call, whispering nest calls and the shrill begging calls that fledglings use; in all, the mimic's repertory includes a total of eight finch motifs. Each mimicked vocalization is separated from the next by an interval, and each lasts the same length of time as the host's. The finch potpourri is interspersed with three different widow-bird phrases that, like the mimicked host melodies, occur in unpredictable sequences. The eight finch motifs give the male straw-tailed widow bird effective command of the entire vocabulary of the purple grenadier.

The same pattern of host-melody mimicry is apparent in almost all other species of widow birds. The shaft-tailed widow bird of South Africa (*Tetraenura regia*) mimics the repertory of its host, the violet-eared waxbill (*Uraeginthus granatinus*). Each of the five species of the paradise widow-bird genus (*Steganura*) copies the host melody of the particular species of the finch genus (*Pytilia*) it parasitizes. The same is true of the seven species in the genus of short-tailed black combassous (*Hypochera*) that mimic all seven species of the genus of fire finches (*Lagonosticta*). Indeed, in only two instances has it been impossible to demonstrate the presence of host phrases in a widow bird's song; these cases are the two species of the genus *Vidua,* the blue widow bird of East Africa and the pin-tailed widow bird, which is found in the sub-Saharan regions of the continent.

By determining which are the host phrases in a male widow bird's song, it is even possible to predict the identity of the host when it is not known. Such predictions have been made more than once in our laboratory after careful analysis of the songs of captive widow-bird males, and I was later able to prove their accuracy. In the field in East Africa we found the appropriate young parasites among the nestlings of exactly those species of estrildid finches that had been identified as probable hosts.

The use of host melodies in widow-bird singing serves a vital purpose: it is a barrier to hybridization. How this isolating mechanism is acquired is best shown by a review of the widow-bird life cycle. The young nestlings' first weeks of life, as they share the nest of

BREEDING PLUMAGE of parasitic widow birds develops during a four-to-six-week period. Seen here are a male straw-tailed widow bird (*a*) and its host, a purple grenadier (*b*), and below them a male purple combassou (*c*) and its host, a Jameson's fire finch (*d*). The parasite's breeding cycle must synchronize with its host's to ensure synchronous egg-laying; in order to grow breeding plumage, however, a parasite must enter its breeding cycle first.

their host siblings, are ones of constant contact with their foster parents. The parasites become independent at the age of five weeks, but even after that they continue to live for some time among their host siblings. It is only later that they form a flock with other juveniles of their own species.

During these weeks of dependence and association the young widow birds are imprinted to the host species; this imprinting is a decisive factor in their later reproductive behavior. When, at the age of seven to eight weeks, the widow-bird juveniles first engage in premature sexual behavior as all songbirds do, there arises in the parasites a quite narrow and specific interest in the activities of the host species. Whereas other songbirds not only play at building nests during this phase but also feed and court one another, the attention of the juvenile widow bird is concentrated on two aspects of its hosts' adult behavior. The focus of interest depends on the sex of the widow bird.

As the female widow bird approaches sexual maturity her interest is concentrated on the hosts' reproductive cycle. The parasite checks frequently on the progress of the host pair's nest-building. The female also synchronizes her own ovulation with that of the host female; this ensures that her own egg is ready at about the time the host female produces her second or third egg. As a consequence the young parasite will hatch at about the same time that its host siblings do and will be their equal in the competition for food.

The male widow bird's concentration is differently oriented. During the most impressionable phase of its youth its interest is focused on the vocalizations of the male foster parent. The parasite evidently disregards the songs of any other species of bird; as a result, when it reaches maturity, it is able to reproduce its host's sound patterns exactly. Although the female parasite does not sing, she becomes similarly song-imprinted, and a memory of the host's repertory remains with her for life. The imprinting becomes evident when ovulation takes place and the female's sexual drive is aroused. Once the female widow bird is in search of a mate, she "knows" that the only appropriate male partner is one who can recite the same calls and notes she heard from her foster father while she was still a nestling. Only when the courting male corresponds to this prototype will the female widow bird allow mating.

Superficially it might seem that the male's signal is merely a kind of lure, for example "I grew up among the same host species that you did!" In my view the signal contains a message with a much deeper biological meaning; it might be paraphrased as "I have inherited the same adaptive characteristics that you have and so our offspring will have the same chances of survival."

It is clear that the adult widow birds' general adaptation to their hosts' song repertory, breeding rhythms and feeding habits, along with their nestlings' perfect mimicry of foster-sibling markings, movements and calls, can only have been the result of an extended evolutionary process. As we have come to know the identity of more and more host species of estrildid finches some of the mechanisms of the process responsible for these unusual adaptations have become apparent. It seems that in effect the potential for the evolution of a new species of widow bird has arisen in the past only when a new species of host finch has evolved.

Consider the relations between hosts and parasites from a taxonomic viewpoint. Two species of the widow-bird genus *Tetraenura* are known: the straw-tailed widow birds and the shaft-tailed. The estrildid finches parasitized by these two related widow-bird species are also two species of the same genus, *Uraeginthus*. In turn five species of paradise widow birds are the parasites of five species of another finch genus, and the seven species of combassous are linked to seven species of fire finch. Even though the specific hosts of the two widow birds of the genus *Vidua* remain unknown, we are certain that they are one or another of the species in the finch genus *Estrilda*.

Such species-to-species relations can be understood only if one assumes that a long time ago the widow birds began to arise from a single viduine prototype species that had started to parasitize a single species of estrildid finches. When this ancient estrildid species began to evolve into several species, the widow birds were forced to follow suit, because only by doing so could they evolve mouth markings sufficiently like those of the evolving new species of potential hosts. Of course, each widow-bird population that failed to achieve such an adaptive process was destined to become extinct, since its mismarked offspring would starve to death in the nests of hostile hosts. In this way the evolution of the adaptively successful widow-bird species both parallels and reflects the evolution of their chosen hosts among the numerous species of estrildid finches.

4

Teaching Language to an Ape

by Ann James Premack and David Premack
October 1972

*Sarah, a young chimpanzee, has a reading and writing
vocabulary of about 130 "words." Her understanding
goes beyond the meaning of words and includes the
concepts of class and sentence structure*

Over the past 40 years several efforts have been made to teach a chimpanzee human language. In the early 1930's Winthrop and Luella Kellogg raised a female chimpanzee named Gua along with their infant son; at the age of 16 months Gua could understand about 100 words, but she never did try to speak them. In the 1940's Keith and Cathy Hayes raised a chimpanzee named Vicki in their home; she learned a large number of words and with some difficulty could mouth the words "mama," "papa" and "cup." More

recently Allen and Beatrice Gardner have taught their chimpanzee Washoe to communicate in the American Sign Language with her fingers and hands. Since 1966 in our laboratory at the University of California at Santa Barbara we have been teaching Sarah to read and write with variously shaped and colored pieces of plastic, each representing a word; Sarah has a vocabulary of about 130 terms that she uses with a reliability of between 75 and 80 percent.

Why try to teach human language to an ape? In our own case the motive was to better define the fundamental nature of language. It is often said that language is unique to the human species. Yet it is now well known that many other animals have elaborate communication systems of their own. It seems clear that language is a general system of which human language is a particular, albeit remarkably refined, form. Indeed, it is possible that certain features of human language that are considered to be uniquely human belong to the more general system, and that these features can be distinguished from those that are unique to the human information-processing regime. If, for example, an ape can be taught the rudiments of human language, it should clarify the dividing line between the general system and the human one.

There was much evidence that the chimpanzee was a good candidate for the acquisition of language before we began our project. In their natural environment chimpanzees have an extensive vocal "call system." In captivity the chimpanzee has been taught to sort pictures into classes: animate and inanimate, old and young, male and female. Moreover, the animal can classify the same item in different ways depending

SARAH, after reading the message "Sarah insert apple pail banana dish" on the magnetic board, performed the appropriate actions. To be able to make the correct interpretation that she should put the apple in the pail and the banana in the dish (not the apple, pail and banana in the dish) the chimpanzee had to understand sentence structure rather than just word order. In actual tests, most symbols were colored (*see illustration on page 29*).

on the alternatives offered. Watermelon is classified as fruit in one set of alternatives, as food in another set and as big in a third set. On the basis of these demonstrated conceptual abilities we made the assumption that the chimpanzee could be taught not only the names of specific members of a class but also the names for the classes themselves.

It is not necessary for the names to be vocal. They can just as well be based on gestures, written letters or colored stones. The important thing is to shape the language to fit the information-processing capacities of the chimpanzee. To a large extent teaching language to an animal is simply mapping out the conceptual structures the animal already possesses. By using a system of naming that suits the chimpanzee we hope to find out more about its conceptual world. Ultimately the benefit of language experiments with animals will be realized in an understanding of intelligence in terms not of scores on tests but of the underlying brain mechanisms. Only then can cognitive mechanisms for classifying stimuli, for storing and retrieving information and for problem-solving be studied in a comparative way.

The first step in teaching language is to exploit knowledge that is already present. In teaching Sarah we first mapped the simple social transaction of giving, which is something the chimpanzee does both in nature and in the laboratory. Considered in terms of cognitive and perceptual elements, the verb "give" involves a relation between two individuals and one object, that is, between the donor, the recipient and the object being transferred. In order to carry out the act of giving an animal must recognize the difference between individuals (between "Mary" and "Randy") and must perceive the difference between donors and recipients (between "Mary gives Randy" and "Randy gives Mary"). In order to be able to map out the entire transaction of giving the animal has to distinguish agents from objects, agents from one another, objects from one another and itself from others.

The trainer began the process of mapping the social transaction by placing a slice of banana between himself and Sarah. The chimpanzee, which was then about five years old, was allowed to eat the tasty morsel while the trainer looked on affectionately. After the transaction had become routine, a language element consisting of a pink plastic square was placed close to Sarah while the slice of banana was moved beyond

her reach. To obtain the fruit Sarah now had to put the plastic piece on a "language board" on the side of her cage. (The board was magnetic and the plastic square was backed with a thin piece of steel so that it would stick.) After Sarah had learned this routine the fruit was changed to an apple and she had to place a blue plastic word for apple on the board. Later several other fruits, the verb "give" and the plastic words that named each of them were introduced.

To be certain that Sarah knew the meaning of "give" it was necessary to contrast "give" with other verbs, such as "wash," "cut" and "insert." When Sarah indicated "Give apple," she was given a piece of apple. When she put "Wash apple" on the board, the apple was placed in a bowl of water and washed. In that way Sarah learned what action went with what verb.

In the first stage Sarah was required to put only one word on the board; the name of the fruit was a sufficient indicator of the social transaction. When names for different actions—verbs—were introduced, Sarah had to place two words on the board in vertical sequence. In order to be given an apple she had to write "Give apple." When recipients were named, two-word sentences were not accepted by the trainer; Sarah had to use three words. There were several trainers, and Sarah had to learn the name of each one. To facilitate the teaching of personal names, both the chimpanzees and the trainers wore their plastic-word names on a string necklace. Sarah learned the names of some of the recipients the hard way. Once she wrote "Give apple Gussie," and the trainer promptly gave the apple to another chimpanzee named Gussie. Sarah never repeated the sentence. At every stage she was required to observe the proper word sequence. "Give apple" was accepted but "Apple give" was not. When donors were to be named, Sarah had to identify all the members of the social transaction: "Mary give apple Sarah."

The interrogative was introduced with the help of the concepts "same" and "different." Sarah was given a cup and a spoon. When another cup was added, she was taught to put the two cups together. Other sets of three objects were given to her, and she had to pair the two objects that were alike. Then she was taught to place the plastic word for "same" between any two similar objects and the plastic word for "different" between unlike objects. Next what amounted to a question mark was placed

between pairs of objects. This plastic shape (which bore no resemblance to the usual kind of question mark) made the question explicit rather than implicit, as it had been in the simple matching tests. When the interrogative element was placed between a pair of cups, it meant: "What is the relation between cup A and cup B?" The choices provided Sarah were the plastic words "same" and "different." She learned to remove the interrogative particle and substitute the correct word [see top illustration on page 30]. Sarah was able to transfer what she had learned and apply the word "same" or "different" to numerous pairs of objects that had not been used in her training.

Any construction is potentially a question. From the viewpoint of structural linguistics any construction where one or more elements are deleted becomes a question. The constructions we used with Sarah were "A same A" and "A different B." Elements in these constructions were removed and the deletion was marked with the interrogative symbol; Sarah was then supplied with a choice of missing elements with which she could restore the construction to its familiar form. In principle interrogation can be taught either by removing an element from a familiar situation in the animal's world or by removing the element from a language that maps the animal's world. It is probable that one can induce questions by purposively removing key elements from a familiar situation. Suppose a chimpanzee received its daily ration of food at a specific time and place, and then one day the food was not there. A chimpanzee trained in the interrogative might inquire "Where is my food?" or, in Sarah's case, "My food is?" Sarah was never put in a situation that might induce such interrogation because for our purposes it was easier to teach Sarah to answer questions.

At first Sarah learned all her words in the context of social exchange. Later, when she had learned the concepts "name of" and "not name of," it was possible to introduce new words in a more direct way. To teach her that objects had names, the plastic word for "apple" and a real apple were placed on the table and Sarah was required to put the plastic word for "name of" between them. The same procedure was repeated for banana. After she had responded correctly several times, the symbol for "apple" and a real banana were placed on the table and Sarah had to put "not

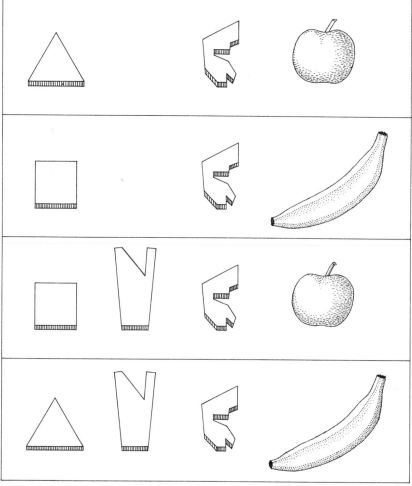

TEACHING LANGUAGE WITH LANGUAGE was the next step. Sarah was taught to put the symbol for "name of" between the word for "apple" and an apple and also between the word for "banana" and a banana. She learned the concept "not name of" in the same way. Thereafter Sarah could be taught new nouns by introducing them with "name of."

name of" between them. After she was able to perform both operations correctly new nouns could be taught quickly and explicitly. The plastic words for "raisin" and "name of" could be placed next to a real raisin and Sarah would learn the noun. Evidence of such learning came when Sarah subsequently requested "Mary give raisin Sarah" or set down "Raisin different apple."

An equally interesting linguistic leap occurred when Sarah learned the predicate adjective and could write such sentences as "Red color of apple," "Round shape of apple" and "Large size of apple." When asked for the relation between "Apple is red ? Red color of apple" and given "same" and "different" as choices, she judged the sentences to be the same. When given "Apple is red ? Apple is round," she judged the sentences to be different. The distinctions between similar and different, first learned with actual objects, was later applied by Sarah in linguistic constructions.

In English the conditional consists of the discontinuous elements "if-then," which are inconvenient and conceptually unnecessary. In symbolic logic the conditional consists of the single sign ⊃, and we taught Sarah the conditional relation with the use of a single plastic word. Before being given language training in the conditional, she was given contingency training in which she was rewarded for doing one thing but not another. For example, she was given a choice between an apple and a banana, and only when she chose the apple was she given chocolate (which she dearly loved). "If apple, then chocolate, if banana, then no chocolate" were the relations she learned; the same relations were subsequently used in sentences to teach her the name for the conditional relation.

The subject was introduced with the written construction: "Sarah take apple ? Mary give chocolate Sarah." Sarah was provided with only one plastic word: the conditional particle. She had to remove the question mark and substitute the conditional in its place to earn the apple and the chocolate. Now she was presented with: "Sarah take banana ? Mary no give chocolate Sarah." Again only the conditional symbol was provided. When Sarah replaced the question mark with the conditional symbol, she received a banana but no chocolate. After several such tests she was given a series of trials on each of the following pairs of sentences: "Sarah take apple if-then Mary give chocolate Sarah" coupled with "Sarah take banana if-then Mary no give chocolate Sarah," or "Sarah take apple if-then Mary no give chocolate Sarah" coupled with "Sarah take banana if-then Mary give chocolate Sarah."

At first Sarah made many errors, taking the wrong fruit and failing to get her beloved chocolate. After several of her strategies had failed she paid closer attention to the sentences and began choosing the fruit that gave her the chocolate. Once the conditional relation had been learned she was able to apply it to other types of sentence, for example "Mary take red if-then Sarah take apple" and "Mary take green if-then Sarah take banana." Here Sarah had to watch Mary's choice closely in order to take the correct action. With the paired sentences "Red is on green if-then Sarah take apple" and "Green is on red if-then Sarah take banana," which involved a change in the position of two colored cards, Sarah was not confused and performed well.

As a preliminary to learning the class concepts of color, shape and size Sarah was taught to identify members of the classes red and yellow, round and square and large and small. Objects that varied in most dimensions but had a particular property in common were used. Thus for teaching the word "red" a set of dissimilar, unnamed objects (a ball, a toy car, a Life Saver and so on) that had no property in common except redness were put before the chimpanzee. The only plastic word available to her was "red." After several trials on identifying red with a set of red objects and yellow with a set of yellow objects, Sarah was shifted to trials where she had to choose between "red" and "yellow" when she was shown a colored object. Finally completely new red and yellow objects were presented to her, including small cards that were identical except for their color.

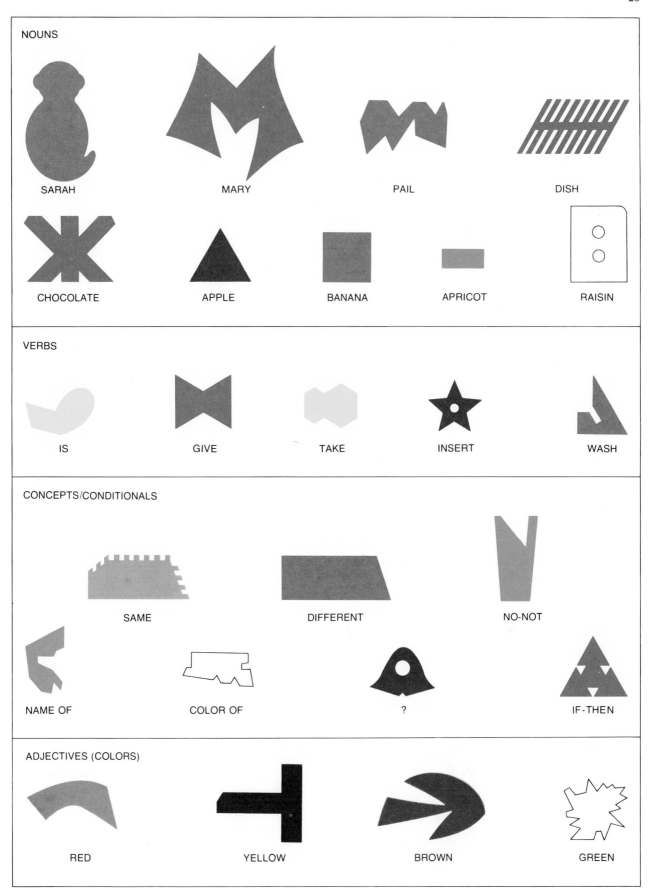

NOUNS

SARAH MARY PAIL DISH

CHOCOLATE APPLE BANANA APRICOT RAISIN

VERBS

IS GIVE TAKE INSERT WASH

CONCEPTS/CONDITIONALS

SAME DIFFERENT NO-NOT

NAME OF COLOR OF ? IF-THEN

ADJECTIVES (COLORS)

RED YELLOW BROWN GREEN

PLASTIC SYMBOLS that varied in color, shape and size were chosen as the language units to be taught to Sarah. The plastic pieces were backed with metal so that they would adhere to a magnetic board. Each plastic symbol stood for a specific word or concept. A "Chinese" convention of writing sentences vertically from top to bottom was adopted because at the beginning of her training Sarah seemed to prefer it. Sarah had to put the words in proper sequence but the orientation of the word symbols was not important.

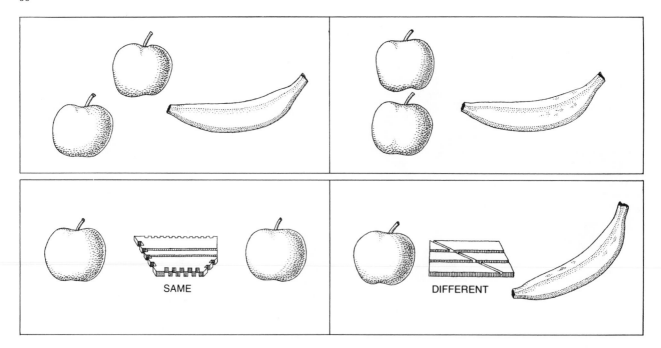

CONCEPTS "SAME" AND "DIFFERENT" were introduced into Sarah's vocabulary by teaching her to pair objects that were alike (*top illustration*). Then two identical objects, for example apples, were placed before her and she was given plastic word for "same" and induced to place word between the two objects. She was also taught to place the word for "different" between unlike objects.

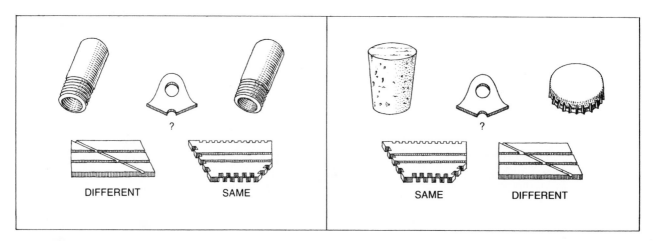

THE INTERROGATIVE was introduced with the help of the concepts "same" and "different." A plastic piece that meant "question mark" was placed between two objects and Sarah had to replace it with either the word for "same" or the word for "different."

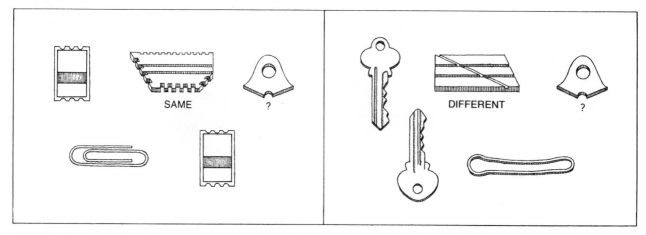

NEW VERSION OF THE INTERROGATIVE was taught by arranging an object and plastic symbols to form questions: "What is [Object A] the same as?" or "What is [Object A] different from?" Sarah had to replace question marker with the appropriate object.

Again she performed at her usual level of accuracy.

Sarah was subsequently taught the names of shapes, "round" and "square," as well as the size names "large" and "small." These words formed the basis for teaching her the names of the class concepts "color of," "shape of" and "size of." Given the interrogative "Red ? apple" or "Yellow ? banana," Sarah was required to substitute the plastic word for "color of" for the question mark. In teaching class names a good many sentences were not written on the board but were presented as hybrids. The hybrid sentences consisted of a combination of plastic words and real objects arranged in the proper sentence sequence on Sarah's worktable. Typical sentences were "Yellow ?" beside a real yellow balloon or "Red ?" beside a red wood block.

The hybrid sentences did not deter Sarah in the least. Her good performance showed that she was able to move with facility from symbols for objects to actual objects. Her behavior with hybrid constructions recalls the activity of young children, who sometimes combine spoken words with real objects they are unable to name by pointing at the objects.

Was Sarah able to think in the plastic-word language? Could she store information using the plastic words or use them to solve certain kinds of problem that she could not solve otherwise? Additional research is needed before we shall have definitive answers, but Sarah's performance suggests that the answers to both questions may be a qualified yes. To think with language requires being able to generate the meaning of words in the absence of their external representation. For Sarah to be able to match "apple" to an actual apple or "Mary" to a picture of Mary indicates that she knows the meaning of these words. It does not prove, however, that when she is given the word "apple" and no apple is present, she can think "apple," that is, mentally represent the meaning of the word to herself. The ability to achieve such mental representation is of major importance because it frees language from simple dependence on the outside world. It involves displacement: the ability to talk about things that are not actually there. That is a critical feature of language.

The hint that Sarah was able to understand words in the absence of their external referents came early in her language training. When she was given a piece of fruit and two plastic words, she was required to put the correct word for the fruit on the board before she was allowed to eat it. Surprisingly often, however, she chose the wrong word. It then dawned on us that her poor performance might be due not to errors but to her trying to express her preferences in fruit. We conducted a series of tests to determine her fruit preferences, using actual fruits in one test and only fruit names in the other. Sarah's choices between the words were much the same as her choices between the actual fruits. This result strongly suggests that she could generate the meaning of the fruit names from the plastic symbols alone.

We obtained clearer evidence at a later stage of Sarah's language training. In the same way that she could use

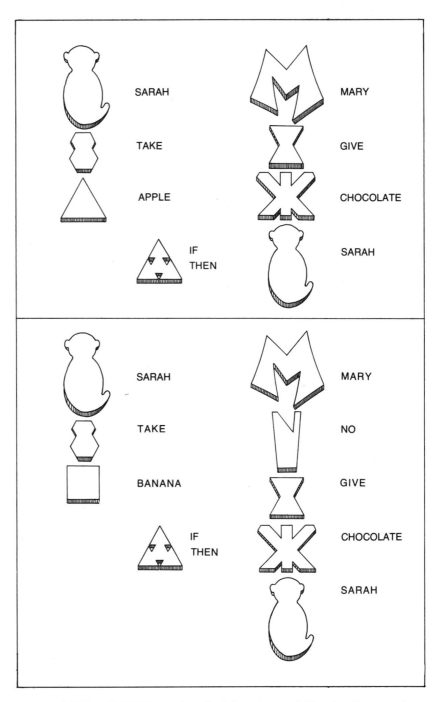

CONDITIONAL RELATION, which in English is expressed "if...then," was taught to Sarah as a single word. The plastic symbol for the conditional relation was placed between two sentences. Sarah had to pay attention to the meaning of both sentences very closely in order to make the choice that would give her a reward. Once the conditional relation was learned by means of this procedure, the chimpanzee was able to apply it to other situations.

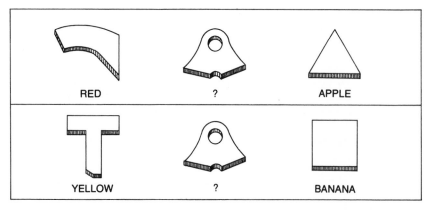

CLASS CONCEPT OF COLOR was taught with the aid of sentences such as "Red ? apple" and "Yellow ? banana." Sarah had to replace the interrogative symbol with "color of."

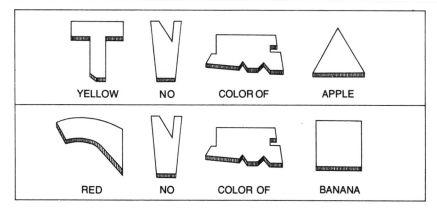

NEGATIVE CONCEPT was introduced with "no-not." When asked "Yellow ? apple" or "Red ? banana," Sarah had to replace interrogative symbol with "color of" or "not color of."

ALTERNATIVE FEATURES			
RED	GREEN	RED	RED
○	□	○	○

FEATURE ANALYSIS of an actual apple and the plastic word for "apple" was conducted. Sarah was shown an apple or the word and made to choose from alternative features: red or green, round or square, square with stem or plain square and square with stem or round. Sarah gave plastic word for "apple" same attributes she had earlier assigned to apple.

"name of" to learn new nouns, she was able to use "color of" to learn the names of new colors. For instance, the names "brown" and "green" were introduced in the sentences "Brown color of chocolate" and "Green color of grape." The only new words at this point were "brown" and "green." Later Sarah was confronted with four disks, only one of which was brown, and when she was instructed with the plastic symbols "Take brown," she took the brown disk. Since chocolate was not present at any time during the introduction of the color name "brown," the word "chocolate" in the definition must have been sufficient to have Sarah generate or picture the property brown.

What form does Sarah's supposed internal representation take? Some indication is provided by the results of a test of ability to analyze the features of an object. First Sarah was shown an actual apple and was given a series of paired comparisons that described the features of the apple, such as red v. green, round v. square and so on. She had to pick the descriptive feature that belonged to the apple. Her feature analysis of a real apple agreed nicely with our own, which is evidence of the interesting fact that a chimpanzee is capable of decomposing a complex object into features. Next the apple was removed and the blue plastic triangle that was the word for "apple" was placed before her and again she was given a paired-comparison test. She assigned the same features to the word that she had earlier assigned to the object. Her feature analysis revealed that it was not the physical properties of the word (blue and triangle) that she was describing but rather the object that was represented by the word [see bottom illustration at left].

To test Sarah's sentence comprehension she was taught to correctly follow these written instructions: "Sarah insert apple pail," "Sarah insert banana pail," "Sarah insert apple dish" and "Sarah insert banana dish." Next instructions were combined in a one-line vertical sequence ("Sarah insert apple pail Sarah insert banana dish"). The chimpanzee responded appropriately. Then the second "Sarah" and the second verb "insert" were deleted to yield the compound sentence: "Sarah insert apple pail banana dish." Sarah followed the complicated instructions at her usual level of accuracy.

The test with the compound sentence is of considerable importance, because it provides the answer to whether or not

Sarah could understand the notion of constituent structure: the hierarchical organization of a sentence. The correct interpretation of the compound sentence was "Sarah put the apple in the pail and the banana in the dish." To take the correct actions Sarah must understand that "apple" and "pail" go together but not "pail" and "banana," even though the terms appear side by side. Moreover, she must understand that the verb "insert" is at a higher level of organization and refers to both "apple" and "banana." Finally, Sarah must understand that she, as the head noun, must carry out all the actions. If Sarah were capable only of linking words in a simple chain, she would never be able to interpret the compound sentence with its deletions. The fact is that she interprets them correctly. If a child were to carry out the instructions in the same way, we would not hesitate to say that he recognizes the various levels of sentence organization: that the subject dominates the predicate and the verb in the predicate dominates the objects.

Sarah had managed to learn a code, a simple language that nevertheless included some of the characteristic features of natural language. Each step of the training program was made as simple as possible. The objective was to reduce complex notions to a series of simple and highly learnable steps. The same program that was used to teach Sarah to communicate has been successfully applied with people who have language difficulties caused by brain damage. It may also be of benefit to the autistic child.

In assessing the results of the experiment with Sarah one must be careful not to require of Sarah what one would require of a human adult. Compared with a two-year-old child, however, Sarah holds her own in language ability. In fact, language demands were made of Sarah that would never be made of a child. Man is understandably prejudiced in favor of his own species, and members of other species must perform Herculean feats before they are recognized as having similar abilities, particularly language abilities. Linguists and others who study the development of language tend to exaggerate the child's understanding of language and to be extremely skeptical of the experimentally demonstrated language abilities of the chimpanzee. It is our hope that our findings will dispel such prejudices and lead to new attempts to teach suitable languages to animals other than man.

II

LANGUAGES AND DERIVATIVE SYSTEMS

II

LANGUAGES AND DERIVATIVE SYSTEMS

INTRODUCTION

Many communities that lie on the Norwegian–Swedish border can converse with one another with little difficulty. Yet we say they speak different languages because they are divided by a political boundary. On the other hand, a person speaking Shanghainese would not be able to comprehend someone speaking Fuzhou. Yet both these "languages" are said to be dialects of Chinese, in part because they use the same written language. Furthermore, mutual intelligibility is a gradient matter that does not partition well. The community in the middle of a chain typically shares more intelligibility with its neighbors on two opposite sides than these neighbors share with each other.

For these and other reasons, the criteria commonly used in determining what is a language and what are dialects are far from clear or consistent. As a consequence, it is not possible to say exactly how many languages there are in the world today with the degree of precision, say, that a biologist can count species. An estimate that is widely accepted by linguists is between 5,000 and 10,000.

A substantial number of these languages has been described over the last century by linguists, essentially with two objectives in mind: a typological one, i.e., to determine the ways in which human languages resemble and differ from one another; and a historical one, i.e., to establish genetic relationships among them.

Typologically, much effort has gone into the search for what are called "language universals." Enough of these have been discovered in the languages of the world that encourages the metaphor that all languages are "cut from a common pattern." An example is: all languages make use of the distinction between consonants and vowels. Another one is: *almost* all languages have the subject precede the object in declarative sentences, even though the verb can be in any position.

The type of structure a language has or its degree of complexity is little influenced by the kind of society its speakers live in, except at the very superficial level of vocabulary richness. There is no evidence at this point to support the speculation that these universals are due to monogenesis, i.e., a common origin for all languages. A reasonable hypothesis, then, is that the commonality that all languages share is a consequence of the biological equipment that we all share to make language possible, i.e., the motor, perceptual, and cognitive systems upon which linguistic behavior is overlaid.

That modern languages are related to each other via ancestors that no longer exist is a historical concept that was found in linguistics quite a bit before it was argued for the speciation of organisms in biology. This principle, more than any other, was responsible for the consolidation of linguistics into a discipline in the last century. The single greatest achievement of scholarship in this area is the reconstruction of the ancestor of the far-flung family of Indo-European languages. The first article of this section, "The

Indo-European Language," by Paul Thieme, gives a perspective on this reconstruction.

Because of expansions in the colonialist period, many languages of the Indo-European family became established in parts of the world quite distant from their homelands. Foremost among these is English, which is now the native language of large populations on several continents and the primary foreign language the world over. Contrasted with many countries with much older settlement histories, the United States is rather homogeneous linguistically. However, as is shown in Hans Kurath's article, "The American Languages," there are pronounced regional differences. The variability is much greater still if we take into account differences due to social factors and those due to the numerous ethnic minorities.

In terms of sheer number of speakers, the Chinese language ranks highest in the world. The language has several rather distinctive aspects. Its system of writing is unique in that it has been used continuously for at least four millennia. The sound system holds special interest because of the lexical tones; in a sense each word is sung to its own melody. And the sparseness of its inflectional morphology is such that, time and again, Westerners are misled in thinking that there is no grammar. In the third article of this section, "The Chinese Language," by William S-Y. Wang, these distinctive aspects of the language are discussed.

In contrast to the millennia of documented history that exist for the Indo-European and Chinese languages, the Bantu language was written down only very recently and can provide little information concerning its past. Nevertheless, by carefully juxtaposing the evidence from archaeological excavations and from linguistic comparisons, much has been learned about the developments and movements of the Bantu over these 2,300 years. D. W. Phillipson's article, "The Spread of the Bantu Language," gives a lucid account of how language and pottery can combine to shed light on events of long ago.

Although the study of language change has developed along lines quite parallel to biological thinking, it is important to emphasize a fundamental difference between the two. In biology, the transmission of genetic material is virtually all *vertical*, i.e., from parents to offspring. The transmission of linguistic traits is by no means constrained this way; our linguistic behavior is significantly influenced by our peers (*horizontal*) and by speakers of other generations (*oblique*). Consequently, no language is pure in the sense that a biological species can be said to be.

Nonvertical transmission is most obvious when different populations abruptly brought into contact have to solve the problem of communicating with each other. In some cases, pidgin languages arise that are reduced in structure from the original languages. As "Pidgin Languages," by Robert A. Hall, Jr., describes, these languages have no real native speakers and typically have a restricted range of use. Once they are established to the extent that they become the native language for a new generation of speakers, they become creole languages. This type of language development is probably more prevalent than we think. Only recently have linguists begun to focus systematic attention on it.

Whereas all humans learn to speak effortlessly and naturally, indicating that there must be a significant influence from genetic facilitation, the situation is very different with writing. Many societies still do not have written languages; and in most literate societies, there are people who cannot read or write, either for social or organic reasons. Evolutionarily, writing was invented no more than a few thousand years ago, at several independent sites at different times.

Speech sounds fade rapidly. To borrow the words of T. S. Eliot:

> words move,
> music moves only in time,
> but that which is living can only die.
> Words, after speech, reach into the silence.

With the invention of writing, language at last overcame the limitations of time and space, enabling human communication to become truly cumulative. The two last articles in this section tell of some early developments in very distant parts of the world: "The Earliest Precursor of Writing," by Denise Schmandt-Besserat, and "Zapotec Writing," by Joyce Marcus.

Although the Phoenician alphabet, which emerged over 3,000 years ago, has had a decisive influence on many important languages, there are three major methods of putting speech down. In an alphabet each graph corresponds to a sound segment, i.e., a consonant or a vowel. In a syllabary, on the other hand, such as the Japanese kana, each graph corresponds to an entire syllable. The Chinese method may best be called morphosyllabic; that is, each graph gives information about both the morpheme it represents and the syllable for its pronunciation. The research that is necessary to determine the merits of each method largely remains to be done. Obviously, one important parameter that must be taken into account is the structure of the spoken language that is being written down.

SUGGESTED FURTHER READING

Books

Cavalli-Sforza, L. L., and M. W. Feldman. 1981. *Cultural Transmission and Evolution: A Quantitative Approach*. Princeton, N.J.: Princeton University Press.
Cardona, George, et al., eds. 1971. *Indo-European and Indo-Europeans*. Philadelphia: University of Pennsylvania Press.
Gelb, I. J. 1963. *A Study of Writing*. 2nd ed. Chicago: University of Chicago Press.
Greenberg, Joseph H., Charles Ferguson, and Edith A Moravcsik, eds. 1978. *Universals of Human Language*. 4 vols. Stanford: Stanford University Press.
Hymes, Dell, ed. 1971. *Pidginization and Creolization of Languages*. Cambridge, England: Cambridge University Press.
Labov, William. 1972. *Sociolinguistic Patterns*. Philadelphia: University of Pennsylvania Press.

Scientific American Articles

Chou, Hung-Hsiang. "Chinese Oracle Bones." April 1979. Offprint No. 717.
Classe, André. "The Whistled Language of La Gomera." April 1957.
Jakobson, Roman. "Verbal Communication." September 1972. Offprint No. 547.
Sundberg, Johan. "The Acoustics of the Singing Voice." March 1977. Offprint No. 356.
Whatmough, Joshua. "Natural Selection in Language." April 1952.

5

The Indo-European Language

by Paul Thieme
October 1958

The descendants of this forgotten tongue include English, Sanskrit and Greek. By comparing its "daughter languages" with one another, linguists have learned how it sounded and even where it originated

Every educated person knows that French and Spanish are "related" languages. The obvious similarity of these tongues is explained by their common descent from Latin; indeed, we could say that French and Spanish are two dialects of "modern Latin," forms of the ancestral language that have grown mutually unintelligible through long separation. Latin has simply developed somewhat differently in these two fragments of the old Western Roman Empire. Today these dialects are called Romance languages.

The other great family of European languages is of course the Germanic. It includes English, Dutch, German and the Scandinavian tongues, all descended from an ancient language—unfortunately unrecorded—called Teutonic.

Romance languages and **Teutonic,**

SANSKRIT, the classical language of India, is one of the oldest members of the Indo-European family. Its discovery by Western scholars led to the first research in historical linguistics. Shown here is an Indian religious text written in Sanskrit script in the 17th century. Sanskrit hymns, handed down orally since second millennium B.C., are better preserved than most Roman writings.

plus Greek—these were once the center of our linguistic universe. During the past 200 years, however, linguistics has been undergoing a kind of prolonged Copernican revolution. Now the familiar European tongues have been relegated to minor places in a vaster system of languages which unites Europe and Asia. Known collectively as the Indo-European languages, this superfamily is far and away the most extensive linguistic constellation in the world. It is also the most thoroughly explored: while other language families have remained largely unknown, the Indo-European family has monopolized the attention of linguists since the 18th century. The modern discipline of linguistics is itself a product of Indo-European studies. As a result of these intensive labors we have come to know a great deal about both the genealogy and the interrelationships of this rich linguistic community.

If we look at the family as a whole, several questions spring to mind. Where did these languages come from? Every family traces its descent from a common ancestor: what was our ancestral language? What did it sound like? What manner of men spoke it? How did they come to migrate over the face of the earth, spreading their tongue across the Eurasian land mass?

Linguistics can now provide definite —if incomplete—answers to some of these questions. We have reconstructed in substantial part the grammar and sound-system of the Indo-European language, as we call this ultimate forebear of the modern Indo-European family. Although much of the original vocabulary has perished, enough of it survives in later languages so that we can contrive a short dictionary. From the language, in turn, we can puzzle out some characteristics of Indo-European culture. We can even locate the Indo-European homeland.

We can never hope to reconstruct the Indo-European language in complete detail. The task would be immeasurably easier if the Indo-Europeans had only left written records. But the Indo-Europeans, unlike their Egyptian and Mesopotamian contemporaries, were illiterate. Their language was not simply forgotten, to be relearned by archaeologists of another day. It vanished without a trace, except for the many hints that we can glean and piece together from its surviving daughter languages.

The Discovery of the Language

The first clue to the existence of an Indo-European family was uncovered

INDO-EUROPEAN LANGUAGES are spoken today throughout the area shown in color on this map. The faint dotted lines are national boundaries. The broken lines in color indi-

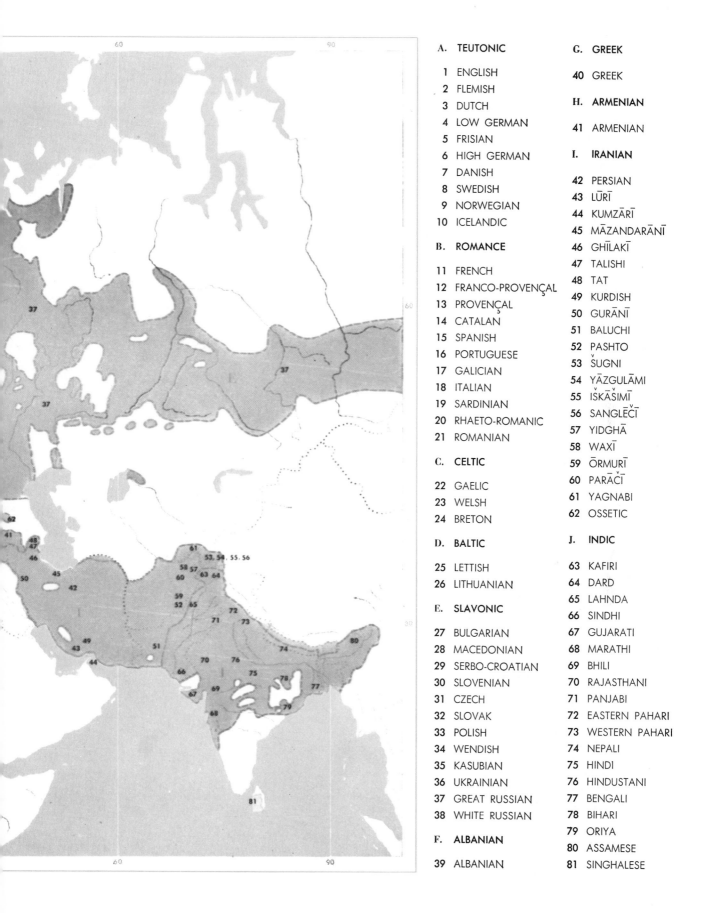

A. TEUTONIC

1 ENGLISH
2 FLEMISH
3 DUTCH
4 LOW GERMAN
5 FRISIAN
6 HIGH GERMAN
7 DANISH
8 SWEDISH
9 NORWEGIAN
10 ICELANDIC

B. ROMANCE

11 FRENCH
12 FRANCO-PROVENÇAL
13 PROVENÇAL
14 CATALAN
15 SPANISH
16 PORTUGUESE
17 GALICIAN
18 ITALIAN
19 SARDINIAN
20 RHAETO-ROMANIC
21 ROMANIAN

C. CELTIC

22 GAELIC
23 WELSH
24 BRETON

D. BALTIC

25 LETTISH
26 LITHUANIAN

E. SLAVONIC

27 BULGARIAN
28 MACEDONIAN
29 SERBO-CROATIAN
30 SLOVENIAN
31 CZECH
32 SLOVAK
33 POLISH
34 WENDISH
35 KASUBIAN
36 UKRAINIAN
37 GREAT RUSSIAN
38 WHITE RUSSIAN

F. ALBANIAN

39 ALBANIAN

G. GREEK

40 GREEK

H. ARMENIAN

41 ARMENIAN

I. IRANIAN

42 PERSIAN
43 LŪRĪ
44 KUMZĀRĪ
45 MĀZANDARĀNĪ
46 GHĪLAKĪ
47 TALISHI
48 TAT
49 KURDISH
50 GURĀNĪ
51 BALUCHI
52 PASHTO
53 ŠUGNI
54 YĀZGULĀMI
55 IŠKĀŠIMĪ
56 SANGLĒČĪ
57 YIDGHĀ
58 WAXĪ
59 ŌRMURĪ
60 PARĀČĪ
61 YAGNABI
62 OSSETIC

J. INDIC

63 KAFIRI
64 DARD
65 LAHNDA
66 SINDHI
67 GUJARATI
68 MARATHI
69 BHILI
70 RAJASTHANI
71 PANJABI
72 EASTERN PAHARI
73 WESTERN PAHARI
74 NEPALI
75 HINDI
76 HINDUSTANI
77 BENGALI
78 BIHARI
79 ORIYA
80 ASSAMESE
81 SINGHALESE

cate boundaries between the 10 groups of Indo-European languages. The language groups (*lettered A to J*) and the languages (*numbered 1 to 81*) may be identified by referring to the legend. Latin, Sanskrit and other extinct Indo-European languages are not shown.

with the opening of trade with India. In 1585, a little less than a century after Vasco da Gama first rounded the Cape of Good Hope, an Italian merchant named Filippo Sassetti made a startling discovery in India. He found that Hindu scholars were able to speak and write an ancient language, at least as venerable as Latin and Greek. Sassetti wrote a letter home about this language, which he called *Sanscruta* (Sanskrit). It bore certain resemblances, he said, to his native Italian. For example, the word for "God" (*deva*) resembled the Italian *Dio*; the word for "snake" (*sarpa*), the Italian *serpe*; the numbers "seven," "eight" and "nine" (*sapta, ashta* and *nava*), the Italian *sette, otto* and *nove*.

What did these resemblances prove? Sassetti may have imagined that Sanskrit was closely related to the "original language" spoken by Adam and Eve; perhaps that is why he chose "God" and "snake" as examples. Later it was thought that Sanskrit might be the ancestor of the European languages, including Greek and Latin. Finally it became clear that Sanskrit was simply a sister of the European tongues. The relationship received its first scientific statement in the "Indo-European hypothesis" of Sir William Jones, a jurist and orientalist in the employ of the East India Company. Addressing the Bengal Asiatic Society in 1786, Sir William pointed out that Sanskrit, in relation to Greek and Latin, "bears a stronger affinity, both in the roots of verbs and in the forms of grammar, than could possibly have been produced by accident: so strong, indeed, that no philologer could examine them all three without believing them to have sprung from some common source, which, perhaps, no longer exists; there is similar reason, though not quite so forcible, for supposing that both the Gothick and the Celtick, though blended with a very different idiom, had the same origin with the Sanskrit."

Sir William's now-famous opinion founded modern linguistics. A crucial word in the sentence quoted is "roots." Jones and his successors could not have done their work without a command of Sanskrit, then the oldest-known Indo-European language. But they also could not have done it without a knowledge of traditional Sanskrit grammar. Jones, like every linguist since, was inspired by the great Sanskrit grammarian Panini, who sometime before 500 B.C. devised a remarkably accurate and systematic technique of word analysis. Instead of grouping related forms in conjugations and declensions—as European and U. S. school-grammar does to this day—Panini's grammar analyzed the forms into their functional units: the roots, suffixes and endings.

Comparative grammar, in the strict sense, was founded by a young German named Franz Bopp. In 1816 Bopp published a book on the inflection of verbs in a group of Indo-European languages: Sanskrit, Persian, Greek, Latin and the Teutonic tongues. Essentially Bopp's book was no more than the application to a broader group of languages of Panini's technique for the analysis of Sanskrit verbs. But Bopp's motive was a historical one. By gathering cognate forms from a number of Indo-European languages he hoped to be able to infer some of the characteristics of the lost language

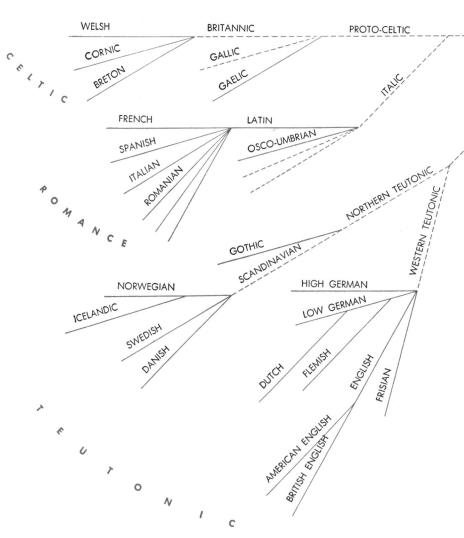

FAMILY TREE traces the descent of the modern Indo-European languages. English (*bottom of right-hand page*) stems from the Teutonic branch of Western Indo-European. Broken

—the "common source" mentioned by Jones—which was the parent of them all.

In the course of time Bopp's method has been systematically developed and refined. The "affinities" which Jones saw between certain words in related languages have come to be called "correspondences," defined by precise formulas. The "Indo-European hypothesis" has been proved beyond doubt. And many more groups of languages have been found to belong to the Indo-European family: Slavonic, Baltic, the old Italic dialects, Albanian, Armenian, Hittite and Tocharian. The "family tree" of these languages has been worked out in some detail [*see illustration on these two pages*]. It should be borne in mind, however, that when it is applied to languages a family-tree diagram is no more than a convenient graphic device. Languages do not branch off from one another at a distinct point in time; they separate gradually, by the slow accumulation of innovations. Moreover, we cannot be sure of every detail in their relationship. The affinities of the Celtic and Italic languages, or of the Baltic and Slavonic, may or may not point to a period when each of these pairs formed a

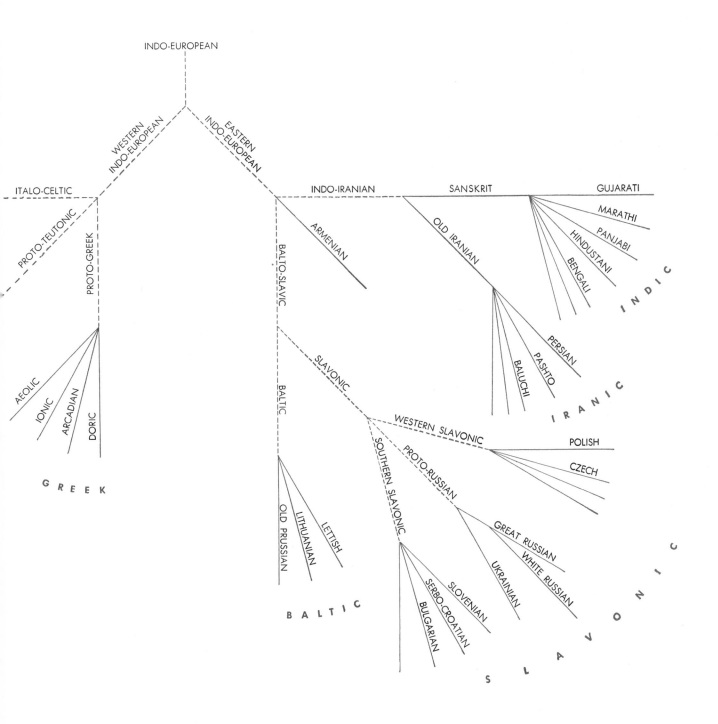

lines indicate dead languages which have left no written remains. Albanian is not shown because its lineage is not known. Tocharian and Hittite have been omitted for the same reason. Although they were spoken in Asia, they appear to belong to the Western branch.

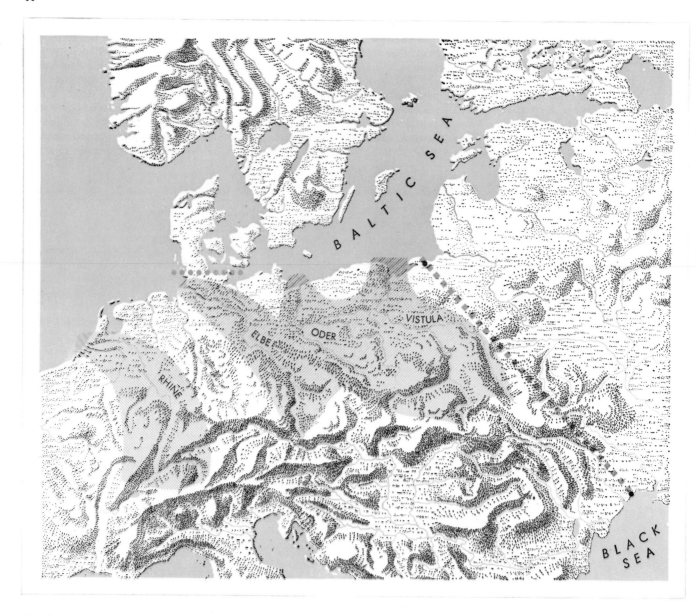

INDO-EUROPEAN HOMELAND is shown by the author to have been located within the area of this map. Since the Indo-Europeans had a word for "beech," they must have lived within the beech-bearing area of Europe; the eastern boundary of this area is indi-cated by the heavy broken line at right. Linguists have also recon-structed an Indo-European word for "turtle"; in ancient times turtles did not live north of the heavy dotted line at upper left. These two words roughly define the original Indo-European area.

common language, already distinguished from the Indo-European. Some Indo-European languages cannot be placed on the family tree because their lineage is not known. Among these are Tocharian and Hittite. These extinct languages (both rediscovered in the 20th century) were spoken in Asia but descend from the western branch of the family.

Reconstruction

Let us see how a linguist can glean information about the original Indo-European language by comparing its daughter tongues with one another. Take the following series of "correspond-ing" words: *pra* (Sanskrit), *pro* (Old Slavonic), *pro* (Greek), *pro* (Latin), *fra* (Gothic), all meaning "forward"; *pitā* (Sanskrit), *patēr* (Greek), *pater* (Latin), *fadar* (Gothic), all meaning "father." Clearly these words sprang from two words in the original Indo-European language. Now what can we say about the initial sounds the words must have had in the parent tongue? It must have been "p," as it is in the ma-jority of the languages cited. Only in Gothic does it appear as "f," and the odds are overwhelmingly in favor of its having changed from "p" to "f" in this language, rather than from "f" to "p" in all the others. Thus we know one fact about the original Indo-European lan-guage: it had an initial "p" sound. This sound remains "p" in most of the daugh-ter languages. Only in Gothic (and other Teutonic tongues) did it become "f."

Now let us take a harder example: *dasa* (Sanskrit), *deshimt* (Lithuanian), *deseti* (Old Slavonic), *deka* (Greek), *dekem* (Latin), *tehun* (Gothic), all meaning "ten"; *satam* (Sanskrit), *shim-tas* (Lithuanian), *suto* (Old Slavonic), *he-katon* (Greek), *kentum* (Latin), *hunda-* (Gothic), all meaning "hun-dred." (The spelling of some of these forms has been altered for purposes of exposition. The hyphen after the Gothic *hunda-* and certain other words in this article indicates that they are not complete words.)

Certainly the "s," "sh," "k" and "h" sounds in these words are related to one another. Which is the original? We de-cide that "k" changed into the other

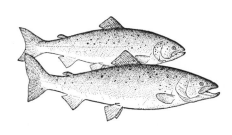

BALTIC SALMON

RHINE SALMON

LIMIT OF BEECH

NORTHERN LIMIT OF TURTLE

The area is better located by the word for "salmon"; salmon are found in rivers flowing into Baltic and North seas but not in those into Black Sea or Mediterranean.

sounds rather than *vice versa*. Phoneticians tell us that "hard" sounds like "k" often mutate into "soft" sounds like "sh." For example, the Latin word *carus* ("dear") turned into the French word *cher*; but the reverse change has not occurred.

Reconstruction would be much easier sailing but for two all-too-common events in the history of language: "convergence" and "divergence." In Sanskrit the three old Indo-European vowels "e," "o" and "a" have converged to become "a" (as in "ah"). In the Germanic languages the Indo-European vowel "e" has diverged to become "e" (as in "bet") next to certain sounds and "i" (as in "it") next to others.

Like most procedures in modern sci-

ence, linguistic reconstructions require a certain technical skill. This is emphatically not a game for amateurs. Every step is most intricate. Some people may even wonder whether there is any point to the labors of historical linguists—especially in view of the fact that the reconstructions can never be checked by immediate observation. There is no absolute certainty in the reconstruction of a lost language. The procedure is admittedly probabilistic. It can only be tested by the coherence of its results.

But the results in the reconstruction of ancestral Indo-European are heartening. By regular procedures such as those I have illustrated, we have reconstructed a sound system for Indo-European that has the simplicity and symmetry of sound systems in observable languages. We have discovered the same symmetry in our reconstructions of roots, suffixes, endings and whole words. Perhaps even more important, the Indo-European words we have reconstructed give a convincing picture of ancient Indo-European customs and geography!

The Indo-European Culture

Consider the words for "mother," "husband," "wife," "son," "daughter," "brother," "sister," "grandson," "son-in-law," "daughter-in-law," all of which we can reconstruct in Indo-European. As a group they prove that the speakers lived in families founded on marriage—which is no more than we might expect! But we obtain more specific terms too: "father-in-law," "mother-in-law," "brother-in-law," "sister-in-law." Exact correspondences in the speech usage of the oldest daughter languages which have been preserved lead to the conclusion that these expressions were used exclusively with reference to the "in-laws" of the bride, and not to those of the groom. There are no other words that would designate a husband's "father-in-law," and so on. The inference is unavoidable that the family system of the old Indo-Europeans was of a patriarchal character; that is, that the wife married into her husband's family, while the husband did not acquire an official relationship to his wife's family as he does where a matriarchal family system exists. Our positive witnesses (the accumulation of designations for the relations a woman acquires by marriage) and our negative witnesses (the complete absence of designations for the relations a man might be said to acquire by marriage) are trustworthy circumstantial evidence of this.

The Indo-Europeans had a decimal

number system that reveals traces of older counting systems. The numbers up to "four" are inflected like adjectives. They form a group by themselves, which points to an archaic method of counting by applying the thumb to the remaining four fingers in succession. Another group, evidently later arrivals in the history of Indo-European, goes up to "ten" (the Indo-European *dekmt-*). "Ten" is related to "hundred": *kmtom*, a word which came from the still earlier *dkmtom*, or "aggregate of tens." In addition to these four-finger and ten-finger counting systems there was a method of counting by twelves, presumably stemming from the application of the thumb to the twelve joints of the other four fingers. It is well known that the Teutonic languages originally distinguished a "small hundred" (100) from a "big hundred" (120). The latter is a "hundred" that results from a combination of counting by tens (the decimal system) and counting by twelves (the duodecimal system). Traces of duodecimal counting can also be found in other Indo-European languages.

Reconstruction yields an almost complete Indo-European inventory of body parts, among them some that presuppose the skilled butchering of animals. The Indo-European word for "lungs" originally meant "swimmer." We can imagine a prehistoric butcher watching the lungs float to the surface as he put the entrails of an animal into water. There is no reference in the word to the biological function of the lungs, which was presumably unknown. The heart, on the other hand, appears to have been named after the beat of the living organ.

So far as tools and weapons are concerned, we are not quite so lavishly served. We obtain single expressions for such things as "arrow," "ax," "ship," "boat," but no semantic system. This poverty is due partly to an original lack of certain concepts, and partly to the change of usage in the daughter languages. It is evident that new terms were coined as new implements were invented. We do find words for "gold" and perhaps for "silver," as well as for "ore." Unfortunately we cannot decide whether "ore" was used only with reference to copper or to both copper and bronze. It is significant that we cannot reconstruct a word for "iron," which was a later discovery. In any case we need not picture the people who spoke Indo-European as being very primitive. They possessed at least one contrivance that requires efficient tools: the wagon or cart. Two Indo-European words for "wheel" and words for "axle," "hub" and "yoke" are cumulative evidence of this.

The Indo-European Homeland

Especially interesting are the names of animals and plants, for these contain the clue to the ancient Indo-European homeland. It is evident that our reconstructed language was spoken in a territory that cannot have been large. A language as unified as the one we obtain by our reconstruction suggests a compact speech community. In prehistoric times, when communication over long distances was limited, such a community could have existed only within comparatively small boundaries.

These boundaries need not have been quite so narrow if the people who spoke Indo-European had been nomads. Nomads may cover a large territory and yet maintain the unity of their language, since their roamings repeatedly bring them in contact with others who speak their tongue. The Indo-Europeans, however, were small-scale farmers and husbandmen rather than nomads. They raised pigs, which kept them from traveling, and they had words for "barley," "stored grains," "sowing," "plowing," "grinding," "settlement" and "pasture" (*agros*), on which domesticated animals were "driven" (*ag*).

We cannot reconstruct old Indo-European words for "palm," "olive," "cypress," "vine," "laurel." On the strength of this negative evidence we can safely eliminate Asia and the Mediterranean countries as possible starting points of the Indo-European migrations. We can, however, reconstruct the following tree names: "birch," "beech," "aspen," "oak," "yew," "willow," "spruce," "alder," "ash." The evidence is not equally conclusive for each tree name; my arrangement follows the decreasing certainty. Yet in each case at least a possibility can be established, as it cannot in the case of tree names such as "cypress," "palm" and "olive."

Of the tree names the most important for our purposes is "beech." Since the beech does not grow east of a line that runs roughly from Königsberg (now Kaliningrad) on the Baltic Sea to Odessa on the northwestern shore of the Black Sea, we must conclude that the Indo-Europeans lived in Europe rather than in Asia. Scandinavia can be ruled out because we know that the beech was imported there rather late. A likely district would be the northern part of Middle Europe, say the territory between the Vistula and Elbe rivers. It is here that even now the densest accumulation

of Indo-European languages is found—languages belonging to the eastern group (Baltic and Slavonic) side by side with one of the western group (German).

That the Indo-Europeans came from this region is indicated by the animal names we can reconstruct, all of them characteristic of the region. We do not find words for "tiger," "elephant," "camel," "lion" or "leopard." We can, however, compile a bestiary that includes "wolf," "bear," "lynx," "eagle," "falcon," "owl," "crane," "thrush," "goose," "duck," "turtle," "salmon," "otter," "beaver," "fly," "hornet," "wasp," "bee" (inferred from words for "honey"), "louse" and "flea." We also find words for domesticated animals: "dog," "cattle," "sheep," "pig," "goat" and perhaps "horse." Some of these words are particularly significant. The turtle, like the beech, did not occur north of Germany in prehistoric times.

The Importance of the Salmon

It is the Indo-European word for "salmon" that most strongly supports the argument. Of all the regions where trees and animals familiar to the Indo-Europeans live, and the regions from which the Indo-Europeans could possibly have started the migrations that spread their tongue from Ireland to India, it is only along the rivers that flow into the Baltic and North seas that this particular fish could have been known. Coming from the South Atlantic, the salmon ascends these rivers in huge shoals to spawn in their upper reaches. The fish are easy to catch, and lovely to watch as they leap over obstacles in streams. Without the fat-rich food provided by the domesticated pig and the salmon, a people living in this rather cold region could hardly have grown so strong and numerous that their migration became both a necessity and a success.

The Indo-European word for "salmon" (*laks-*) survives in the original sense where the fish still occurs: Russia, the Baltic countries, Scandinavia and Germany (it is the familiar "lox" of Jewish delicatessens). In the Celtic tongues another word has replaced it; the Celts, migrating to the West, encountered the Rhine salmon, which they honored with a new name because it is even more delectable than the Baltic variety. The Italic languages, Greek and the southern Slavonic tongues, spoken where there are no salmon, soon lost the word. In some other languages it is preserved, but with altered meaning: in Ossetic, an Iranian language spoken in the Caucasus, the word means a large kind of

trout, and the Tocharian-speaking people of eastern Turkestan used it for fish in general.

Several Sanskrit words echo the importance of the salmon in Indo-European history. One, *laksha*, means "a great amount" or "100,000," in which sense it has entered Hindustani and British English with the expression "a lakh of rupees." The assumption that the Sanskrit *laksha* descends from the Indo-European *laks-* of course requires an additional hypothesis: that a word meaning "salmon" or "salmon-shoal" continued to be used in the sense of "a great amount" long after the Indo-European immigrants to India had forgotten the fish itself. There are many analogies for a development of this kind. All over the world the names of things that are notable for their quantity or density tend to designate large numbers. Thus in Iranian "beehive" is used for 10,000; in Egyptian "tadpole" (which appears in great numbers after the flood of the Nile) is used for 100,000; in Chinese "ant," for 10,000; in Semitic languages "cattle," for 100; in Sanskrit and Egyptian "lotus" (which covers lakes and swamps), for "large number." Several words in Sanskrit for "sea" also refer to large numbers. In this connection we may recall the words in *Hamlet*: ". . . to take arms against a sea of troubles, and by opposing end them."

A second Sanskrit word that I believe is a descendant of the Indo-European *laks-* is *lākshā*, which the dictionary defines as "the dark-red resinous incrustation produced on certain trees by the puncture of an insect (*Coccus lacca*) and used as a scarlet dye." This is the word from which come the English "lac" and "lacquer." *Lākshā*, in my opinion, was originally an adjective derived from the Indo-European *laks-*; meaning "of or like a salmon." A characteristic feature of the salmon is the red color of its flesh. "Salmonlike" could easily develop into "red," and this adjective could be used to designate "the red (substance)," *i.e.*, "lac."

There is even a third possible offshoot: the Sanskrit *laksha* meaning "gambling stake" or "prize." This may be derived from a word that meant "salmon-catch." The apparent boldness of this conjecture may be vindicated on two counts. First, we have another Indo-European gambling word that originally was an animal name. Exact correspondences of Greek, Latin and Sanskrit show that the Indo-Europeans knew a kind of gambling with dice, in which the most unlucky throw was called the "dog." Second, in Sanskrit the gambling stake can be designated by another word, a plural noun (*vijas*) whose primary meaning was "the leapers." The possibility that this is another old word for "salmon," which was later used in the same restricted sense as *laksha*, is rather obvious.

By a lucky accident, then, Sanskrit, spoken by people who cannot have preserved any knowledge of the salmon itself, retains traces of Indo-European words for "salmon." Taken together, these words present a singularly clear picture of the salmon's outstanding traits. It is the fish that appears in big shoals (the Sanskrit *laksha*, meaning "100,000"); that overcomes obstacles by leaping (the Sanskrit *vijas*, meaning "leapers," and later "stake"); that has red flesh (*lākshā*, meaning "lac"); that is caught as a prized food (*vijas* and *laksha*, meaning "stake" or "prize").

The Age of the Language

If we establish the home of our reconstructed language as lying between the Vistula and the Elbe, we may venture to speculate as to the time when it was spoken. According to archaeological evidence, the domesticated horse and goat did not appear there much before 3000 B.C. The other domesticated animals for which we have linguistic evidence are archaeologically demonstrable in an earlier period. Indo-European, I conjecture, was spoken on the Baltic coast of Germany late in the fourth millennium B.C. Since our oldest documents of Indo-European daughter languages (in Asia Minor and India) date from the second millennium B.C., the end of the fourth millennium would be a likely time anyhow. A thousand or 1,500 years are a time sufficiently long for the development of the changes that distinguish our oldest Sanskrit speech form from what we reconstruct as Indo-European.

Here is an old Lithuanian proverb which a Protestant minister translated into Latin in 1625 to show the similarity of Lithuanian to Latin. The proverb means "God gave the teeth; God will also give bread." In Lithuanian it reads: *Dievas dawe dantis; Dievas duos ir duonos*. The Latin version is *Deus dedit dentes; Deus dabit et panem*. Translated into an old form of Sanskrit, it would be *Devas adadāt datas; Devas dāt* (or *dadāt*) *api dhānās*. How would this same sentence sound in the reconstructed Indo-European language? A defensible guess would be: *Deivos ededōt dntns; Deivos dedōt* (or *dōt*) *dhōnās*.

The American
Languages

by Hans Kurath
January 1950

*Although most Americans speak English, U. S. speech
falls into distinct regional patterns. Some of these
have been compiled in a new Linguistic Atlas
of the Eastern states*

WE are not accustomed to think of the U. S. language as a Babel of tongues, but if one were to make the experiment of assembling individuals from a number of different localities and listening carefully to their speech, he might note some rather curious results. For example, a Rhode Islander might speak of a "dandle," a Marylander of a "cocky-horse," a coastal North Carolinian of a "hicky-horse," a western North Carolinian of a "ridy-horse," a Block Islander of a "tippity-bounce," a Cape Codder of a "tilt," a native of the lower Connecticut Valley of a "tinter," a Hudson Valley native of a "teeter-totter" and a Bostonian of a "teeterboard." All of these expressions mean the same thing—a seesaw—yet it is entirely possible that some of the nine persons would not know what the others were talking about.

American English has a surprising wealth of such localisms. The casual foreign visitor is inclined to lump them all together as "Americanisms," and to suppose, erroneously, that they are generally current throughout the U. S. More sophisticated observers are aware that New England, the South and the West show certain differences in speech, but usually they have only the vaguest notions of the actual location of these regionalisms. As a matter of fact, the expressions commonly identified as "New Englandisms" are apt to be current only east of the Connecticut River; "Southernisms" more often than not are confined to Virginia or to certain sections making up the old plantation country of the South; "Westernisms" may be common only in the Spanish Southwest or the cattle country. On the other hand there are regions with equally distinctive speech patterns that have largely escaped notice; a notable example is the broad Midland area embracing Pennsylvania and the Ohio Valley, where the vocabulary and pronunciation are as different from those of New England and the South as the latter are from each other.

Since 1931 the writer and a group of associates have been making a study, under the auspices of the American Council of Learned Societies, of local and regional speech differences in the eastern United States. We now have the data for a "Linguistic Atlas" providing a systematic record of the currency of selected words and expressions in the coastal states from Maine to Georgia and in Pennsylvania, West Virginia and eastern Ohio. As in all scientific studies, the immediate purpose was simply the collection of facts, without which a historical interpretation of American linguistic usage is impossible. In this case the results shed considerable light on U. S. migrations, settlement areas, trade areas, culture areas and other aspects of human geography and population history.

In making the survey we used the sampling method. Trained linguists went to nearly every county in these states and in each interviewed two persons—one old-fashioned and unschooled, the other a member of the middle class who had had the benefit of a grade-school or high-school education. They also interviewed one or more cultured persons in each of the larger cities. The interviewers spent from 10 to 15 hours with each individual to record his habitual usage on well over a thousand points. Most of this field work was done by Bernard Bloch, Raven I. McDavid and the late Guy S. Lowman, Jr.

All together more than 1,200 persons were interviewed, and full information was obtained, among other things, on the diffusion of some 400 local or regional expressions. A map was plotted for each expression. The boundary enclosing the area in which a given expression is current is known as an isogloss. Wherever a large number of isoglosses enclose a common area, *i.e.*, wherever the people share many folk expressions that are not current elsewhere, obviously they delimit a major speech boundary.

These studies showed that the eastern section of our country is divided into three speech areas of first importance—the North, the Midland and the South. These major areas are distinguished by certain region-wide expressions. They are split, however, into a number of subareas, each with its own local folk words and peculiarities of diction. The map at the top of the opposite page shows these major and minor boundaries. The Northern region in general includes the New England settlement area, reaching west to the Great Lakes, and the Dutch settlement in the Hudson Valley. Within it are no fewer than six distinct subdivisions: the people of northeastern, southeastern and southwestern New England, metropolitan New York, the Hudson Valley and western New York have inherited from their forebears or developed certain definite speech differences. Similarly the Midland, corresponding in general to the Pennsylvania settlement area, is segmented into several speech areas, of which one of the most distinctive is the section west and north of Philadelphia settled by the Pennsylvania Dutch. Natural geographical barriers have a great influence on population movements, and hence on language, as is demonstrated by the fact that the crest of the Alleghenies in Pennsylvania divides the eastern and western parts of the state into distinct speech areas. In the South one can find differing varieties of Southern speech in the Chesapeake Bay area, the Virginia Piedmont and the eastern sections of the Carolinas. The speech boundaries in the South tend to be sharper than in other regions, because its populations have clung more closely to the soil.

NOW there are certain key expressions that characterize each major region. You can identify a person as a Northerner if he says pail for bucket, swill for garbage, whiffletree or whippletree for the bar to which a horse is harnessed, comforter or comfortable for a heavy quilt, brook for stream. A Midlander can generally be identified by his use of the word blinds for window shades, skillet for frying pan, spouting for roof gutters. A Southerner characteristically says light-bread for wheat bread, clabber for curdled sour milk, hay shock for haycock, corn shucks for corn husks, lightwood for kindling, rock fence for stone fence, and of course "you-all." In some cases the three regions have three distinct expressions for the same thing. Thus salt pork is commonly called salt pork in the North, side meat in much of the Midland and middlin meat in much of the South. A Northerner generally calls a dragonfly a darning needle; a Midlander is likely to call it a snake feeder or snake doctor; a Southerner, a snake doctor or mosquito hawk. Corn bread is known as johnnycake in the North and corn pone in the Midland and South. To call a cow in the pasture, a Northern farmer cries "Come boss!" or "Co-boss!"; a Midlander calls "Sook!"; a Southerner calls "Co-ee!" or "Co-wench!" In New England farmers call a bull a critter, sire, toro or top cow; in the Midland they most often call it an ox, male cow or sire; in the South, a steer, male cow, beast or brute.

It is usually possible, however, to place a person much more precisely, to connect him with a particular area in his region. The areas that have been settled longest have the most distinctive speechways. Use of the word fritter for griddlecake and funnel for stovepipe spots a New Englander as a "Down-Easter." (In most of New England a funnel for pouring liquids is called a "tunnel.") The expression cleavestone peach for freestone peach, apple grunt for apple dumpling and porch for the kitchen ell place a man on Cape Cod. Dandle for seesaw and eace worm for earthworm put him on Narragansett Bay. If he calls a thunder shower a tempest and a pet lamb a cade, he is from Cape Cod or Narragansett Bay. If a New Englander says ivy for mountain laurel and angledog for earthworm, he lives in the lower Connecticut Valley. If he calls a coal hod a coal scuttle, a haystack a hay barrack and cottage cheese pot cheese, his home is in the valley of the Hudson or the Housatonic. In Maine children coast belly-bumper,

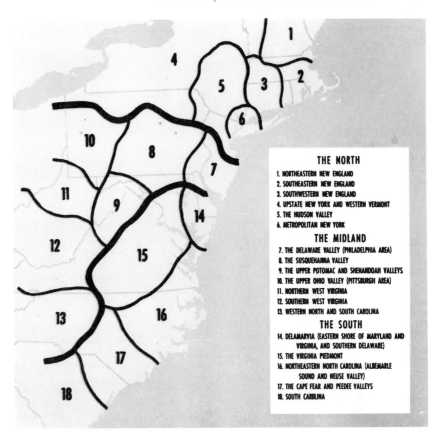

THE NORTH
1. NORTHEASTERN NEW ENGLAND
2. SOUTHEASTERN NEW ENGLAND
3. SOUTHWESTERN NEW ENGLAND
4. UPSTATE NEW YORK AND WESTERN VERMONT
5. THE HUDSON VALLEY
6. METROPOLITAN NEW YORK

THE MIDLAND
7. THE DELAWARE VALLEY (PHILADELPHIA AREA)
8. THE SUSQUEHANNA VALLEY
9. THE UPPER POTOMAC AND SHENANDOAH VALLEYS
10. THE UPPER OHIO VALLEY (PITTSBURGH AREA)
11. NORTHERN WEST VIRGINIA
12. SOUTHERN WEST VIRGINIA
13. WESTERN NORTH AND SOUTH CAROLINA

THE SOUTH
14. DELAMARVIA (EASTERN SHORE OF MARYLAND AND VIRGINIA, AND SOUTHERN DELAWARE)
15. THE VIRGINIA PIEDMONT
16. NORTHEASTERN NORTH CAROLINA (ALBEMARLE SOUND AND NEUSE VALLEY)
17. THE CAPE FEAR AND PEEDEE VALLEYS
18. SOUTH CAROLINA

LINGUISTIC MAP of the Eastern states divides them into three major areas, each distinguished by regional expressions. These are subdivided into smaller areas that are characterized by localisms of their own.

●●●● WHIFFLETREE, WHIPPLETREE
▬▬▬▬ SOOK!
▬ ▬ ▬ LIGHTWOOD

ISOGLOSSES are boundaries that define the limits of a given usage. The expression whippletree is used north of the dotted line; the cow call "Sook!" west of solid line; lightwood for kindling east of broken line.

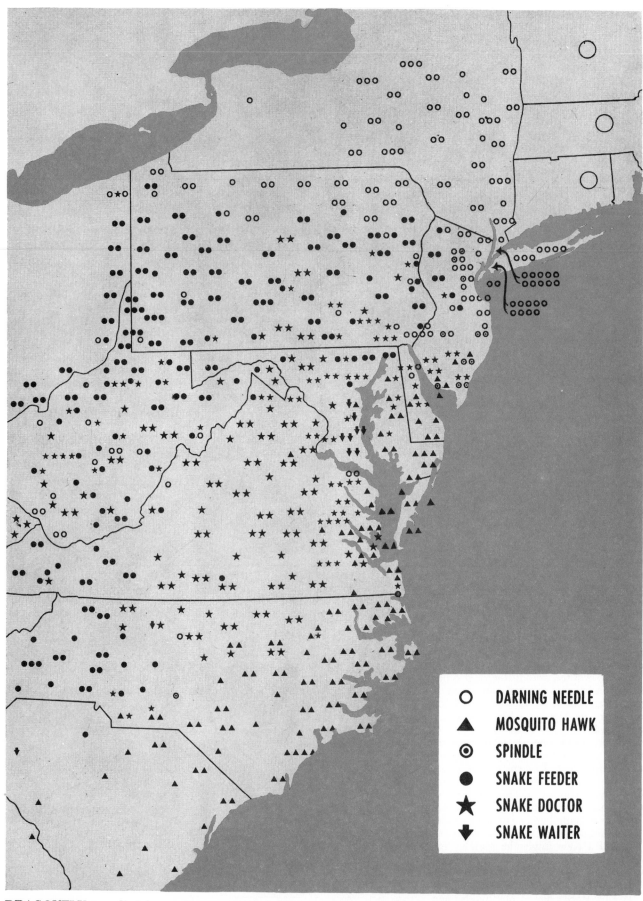

○	**DARNING NEEDLE**
▲	**MOSQUITO HAWK**
◉	**SPINDLE**
●	**SNAKE FEEDER**
★	**SNAKE DOCTOR**
↓	**SNAKE WAITER**

DRAGONFLY is called by various names in various parts of the Eastern states. Each symbol on this map represents interviews with residents of a locality. The larger symbols at the upper right indicate that darning needle is the term generally used throughout those states. Usages were recorded for many selected terms.

in the upper Connecticut Valley belly-bunt, around Massachusetts and Narragansett Bays belly-bump, on the lower Connecticut belly-gutter and in the Hudson Valley belly-wopper.

IN the South one finds even sharper local differences in speech. Around Chesapeake Bay alone there are several distinct speech areas. Thus a cowpen is called a cowpen on the Maryland Western Shore, a pound on the Eastern Shore, a cuppin in the Virginia Piedmont and a brake in the Norfolk area on the south side of the Bay. A freestone peach is named an open peach on the Eastern Shore, an openstone peach on the Western Shore, a soft peach in the Virginia Piedmont and a clearseed peach in the Norfolk area. The Carolina Shore has at least five different speech areas. In various localities of the Carolinas a storeroom is known as a lumber room, a plunder room or a trumpery room; a vest is called a wesket or a jacket; bacon is known as breakfast bacon, breakfast strips or breakfast meat; a screech owl is a scrich owl, a scrooch owl, a squinch owl or a shivering owl; the pig call is "Chook!", "Wookie!", "Vootsie!", "Goop!" or "Woopie!"

How can we account for the existence, and particularly the persistence, of so many regional and local expressions? We must first understand clearly that there are social "isoglosses" as well as geographical ones. Three levels of speech can be distinguished in the U. S.: 1) cultivated speech, which is most widespread in urban areas; 2) common speech, the language of the large middle class; 3) folk speech, which is found in rural areas. Cultivated speech tends to be national or regional in character. The homely expressions that we have been considering come mostly from the second and third levels. They are the speechways of relatively unschooled people who read little, travel little, and acquire their language largely by ear from the older generation in their immediate vicinity.

Our studies indicate that the different places of origin of the colonial settlers, geographical barriers, colonial isolation, expanding frontiers and transportation facilities, trade, social stratification, educational facilities, religious activities and political activities have all played their parts in localizing or disseminating linguistic usages. The colonists who settled the Eastern seaboard were a heterogeneous group to start with. Even among those from the British Isles a great variety of dialects, peasant and urban, were spoken: there were Yorkshiremen, Lancashiremen, Kentishmen, Hampshiremen, Ulstermen, and a small minority who spoke the dialect of the upper classes of London.

In the course of several generations in the New World each colony developed its own unique blend of provincial dialects, adding to the old-country speech a few expressions taken from the Indians and others invented as names for unfamiliar plants and animals found in their new environment. As the settlements expanded westward, the frontiersmen developed new blends of speech, dropping many of the more local expressions but retaining the more widely used regional expressions. Thus west of the Alleghenies and the Appalachians speech is less diversified than in the East and speech boundaries are less clearly defined. It is this lack of clear boundaries in the central states that is largely responsible for the fiction that a "general American" type of English exists. Actually three regional types of English are spoken in the Middle West—the Northern type in the Great Lakes Basin and upper Mississippi Valley, the Southern type in the Gulf States, and the Midland type in the valleys of the Ohio and its tributaries and along the middle course of the Mississippi.

Speech areas are not stable; they expand or shrink. The nucleus of an expanding area's growth is usually a large metropolitan center or a dominant social class whose speech is regarded as superior. In the East the cities of Boston, New York and Philadelphia have been important centers of expanding areas in speech. Boston, which has dominated eastern New England since the days of the Massachusetts Bay Colony, reached the heyday of its linguistic influence in the middle of the 19th century, when the literary and intellectual accomplishments of its writers and scholars gave it a hearing not only in New England but throughout the country. Metropolitan New York has had a striking effect upon the speechways, particularly in pronunciation, of the surrounding areas; its unique speech has supplanted New Englandisms and other local expressions on Long Island, in southwestern Connecticut, in eastern New Jersey and in the lower Hudson Valley. The linguistic influence of Philadelphia has spread westward to the Susquehanna Valley, southward almost to Baltimore and southeastward into Delaware and the Maryland Eastern Shore.

The shrinking speech areas in general are those that lack a prominent population center and fall under the influence of one or more adjoining areas of expansion. Examples of such areas are Narragansett Bay, central New England and the Virginia Tidewater, which is coming under the domination of the expanding Piedmont area. To students of language the speechways of a shrinking area provide important clues to usages of the past; those of an expanding area, to developments of the future.

What kind of development can we expect? Will our regional and local dialects eventually be smoothed out to a standard American English? There are important leveling forces at work, of course: the schools, the printed page, the radio. Our study makes it possible to trace in considerable detail the trend from local to regional to national usage of certain terms. Thus seesaw, in spite of the many local synonyms for it, is gaining more and more currency as the national term. Although the V-shaped clavicle of a fowl is still commonly called pully-bone or lucky-bone in many sections, wishbone is well along the road to ascendancy everywhere. The term andirons is superseding dog irons and firedogs; frying pan is prevailing over skillet and spider; cottage cheese is overcoming such localisms as curds, sour-milk cheese, pot cheese, Dutch cheese, clabber cheese and smearcase; shades is gaining ground over blinds and curtains.

Nevertheless, local and regional expressions are not likely to disappear entirely from our language. Many of them survive because they stand for local or regional phenomena. It is very doubtful, for example, that we shall ever have a nationally accepted term for griddlecakes made of corn meal. For one thing, they are rarely served in the Wheat Belt. It is difficult to detect any trend toward a national name for them: they are still known by a wide variety of expressions, such as johnnycakes, johnnikins, corn cakes, corn dodgers, hoe cakes, ash cakes. A similar situation exists with regard to wheat cakes. The term pancakes is generally known throughout the Eastern states, but in eastern New England they are almost always called griddlecakes, around Philadelphia hot cakes, west of Philadelphia flannel cakes and south of the Potomac battercakes or battycakes.

THE leveling forces are not quite as powerful among the folk as one might suppose. The common man hears a Babel of dialects over the radio and in the movies. He understands them, may even mimic them, but he does not acquire them. Often he is likely to regard their use in everyday speech as an affectation.

One can safely say that in some ranges of our vocabulary local and regional expressions will survive, and new ones will come into being. In the arts, the sciences and other enterprises that are organized on a national scale, the terminology tends to be nation-wide, and in our social and political life we most commonly use words that have at least regional currency. But the vocabulary of the intimate life of the home will remain rich in local and regional expressions for generations to come.

The Chinese Language

7

by William S-Y. Wang
February 1973

This melodious tongue is spoken by more people than any other. Although the Chinese system of writing is complex, the basic structure of the language is remarkably simple

To people who are familiar only with the common European languages the Chinese language is strikingly different. Yet today Chinese is spoken by more people than any other language, and Chinese literature is the world's oldest, spanning a period of 35 centuries. When we examine the structure of the Chinese language, we find that it is not conspicuously complex; indeed, in many ways it is simpler than the Western languages. But since Chinese does differ from the European languages in fundamental respects, some knowledge of its structure and historical development is indispensable to a general understanding of the nature of human language.

To the Western eye the writing system of the Chinese is altogether novel: instead of neat rows of simple alphabetic letters there are thousands of unique characters, many of which seem incredibly intricate. To the ear the language sounds rather melodious, perhaps a little like singing. When one peers below the surface, there are more surprises. The language has virtually no conjugation for its verbs and no declension for its nouns. The inevitable paradigms that Western schoolchildren have come to dread in their grammar books are totally absent

SYMBIOTIC RELATION between painting and writing in Chinese art is elegantly exemplified by a detail from "Flowering Plants and Trees" on the opposite page. The characters were written in the traditional format: in columns and from right to left. The portion of the poem that is framed by the pine branches is translated: "Jade strands hang limp in the wind. Crimson berries sparkle bright against the snow." The painting was made by Ch'en Shun in the 16th century during the Ming dynasty. It is part of the Avery Brundage Collection at the Center of Asian Art and Culture in San Francisco.

in a grammar of Chinese. For the various forms of the verb "to buy," such as "buy," "buys," "bought" and "buying," Chinese has the single form *mǎi*. (The mark over the *a* signifies that the syllable is spoken in a tone that falls and then rises. There are three other vowel marks for tones, as in *á* indicating a rising tone, *à* indicating a falling tone and *ā* indicating a level high tone.) For "book," "books," "to the books" and "of the books" the Chinese is *shū*. Most of the time it is quite clear from the context what tense or mood is intended for a verb and what number or case is intended for a noun. Hence the Chinese language does not bother much with this particular type of redundancy in its grammar. Perhaps it is this structural simplicity of the language that moved the anthropologist and linguist Edward Sapir to characterize it as "soberly logical."

The Antiquity of Chinese

Chinese is often termed a very old language. In a sense such a statement is misleading. All human languages go back to the dim uncertainty of prehistory, and at present we have no way of knowing whether or not they can all be traced back to the same root. Four thousand years ago the ancestors of the Chinese peoples spoke an early form of the Chinese language in much the same way that the ancestors of the English-speaking peoples were using an early form of the English language. Since almost nothing is known about the emergence of language in the human species, we are not in a position to say which of the world's languages evolved earlier and which later. It is rather that in the course of history some languages have been renamed more often than others (as a result of events such as migration or conquest) and the newness of the names

gives the illusion that the thing being named is new.

There is one sense, however, in which Chinese is a very old language. Sumerian is the only language we know of that has extant written materials that antedate Chinese ones. Sumerian cuneiform writing dates back some 5,000 years; the earliest Chinese writing in existence today dates back 3,500 years. But Sumerian and its derivative orthographies died out long before the beginning of the Christian Era. Chinese orthography has continued to this day, although there have been major stylistic changes.

The earliest Chinese writings are incisions on bone and tortoise shell. Most of the inscriptions are oracular, dealing with political or religious events or with the weather or warfare. Discovered toward the end of the 19th century in Chinese drugstores, where they were being sold as "dragon bones" for their medicinal value, the story of these inscriptions is a colorful chapter in the history of Chinese archaeology and philology. More than 100,000 inscribed pieces have now been found. Even though the total number of written characters on the pieces is more than a million, the number of different characters is small. The texts of the oracular inscriptions dealt with a very limited range of topics, and the same characters are repeated over and over again. Of the 2,000 to 3,000 characters on the shells and bones, about half can be read today.

Through the centuries Chinese characters have been preserved in many different mediums: metal vessels, stone drums, jade jewelry, coins, metal mirrors, bricks and tiles. The central line of development, however, has been the use of the brush on silk, bamboo, wood and ultimately on paper. A brush can produce variations in thickness whereas a stylus cannot. Such variations give the

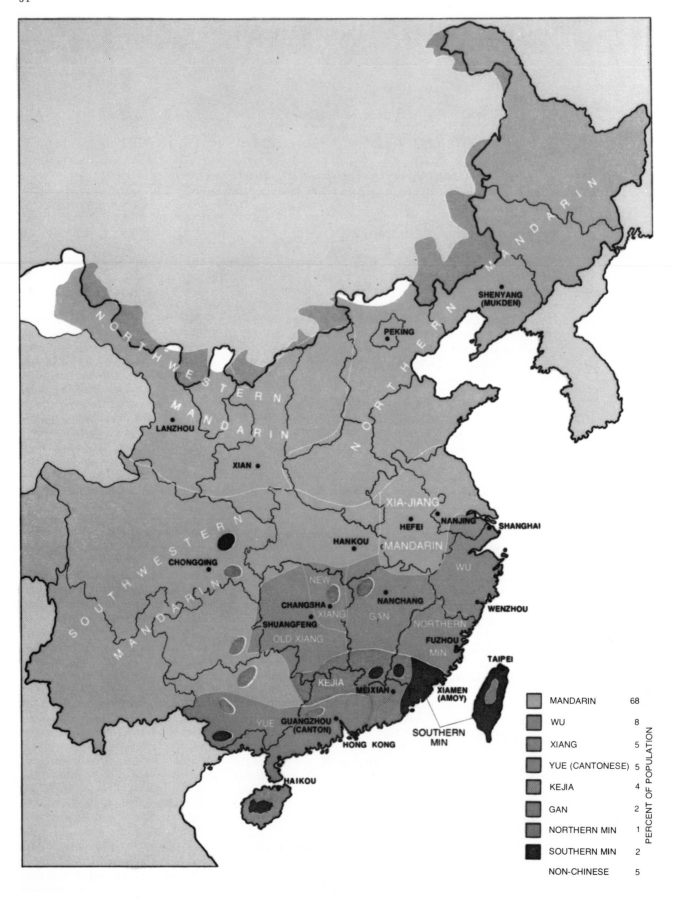

MAP OF CHINA shows the distribution of the major dialects of the Chinese language. More than two-thirds of the Chinese population speak one of the Mandarin dialects, of which the speech of Peking is the standard. It is the dialects along the southern coast, however, that have been carried to many parts of the world by Chinese emigrants. There are also several non-Chinese linguistic stocks within China. The regions to the north and west are dominated by non-Chinese languages such as Mongolian and Tibetan.

writer a much greater artistic freedom in rendering his characters.

Some of the earliest written Chinese characters were pictographic. The character for "rain" was several columns of broken lines, and the one for "horse" looked like a horse, complete with mane and four legs [see illustration on page 61]. Pictographs, however, are only a minority in the total vocabulary of Chinese. Most of the words in the language cannot be suggested by a simple picture.

Calligraphy, the elegant rendering of characters, is a highly cultivated art form that has long been prized in Chinese culture, much as painting is valued in the Western world. For the Chinese there is a close relation between painting and calligraphy. Typically a silk scroll is covered with a picture and a few lines of characters, the two carefully balanced against each other. Because of their artistic values and their long history, Chinese characters have a much greater range of variability in their size and shape than the characters of any other writing system.

The Writing System

The Chinese writing system underwent major changes in 1956, when the government of the People's Republic of China decided to simplify the characters and also to adopt a system of spelling Chinese words in Latin letters. Both measures are intended to make the reading and writing of Chinese easier to learn, a crucial step in promoting linguistic unity and raising the standard of literacy in China.

In order to understand the nature of Chinese characters and their simplification, we must first examine their internal structure. Each character is made up of two types of smaller unit called the stroke and the radical. Roughly speaking, a stroke is a line, either straight or curved, that is completed every time the pen leaves the paper. For example, the character for "sun," which is pronounced rì, looks like:

日

It is built up of four strokes [see top illustration on page 57]. Both the order and the geometric position of the strokes are important. There are approximately 20 distinct strokes in the language, so that strokes are the closest counterparts to the 26 letters of the Latin alphabet. There is no counterpart of the radicals in the orthography of other languages. The traditional set consists of 214 radicals, and these radicals are found in almost all

ORACLE-BONE INSCRIPTIONS, dating from 1300 B.C., are among the earliest-known examples of Chinese writing. They were made on ox bones and tortoise shells and were used for divination. The photograph, provided through the courtesy of Bernhard Karlgren and Jan Wirgin, shows specimens in the Museum of Far Eastern Antiquities in Stockholm.

Chinese dictionaries. A dictionary published in 1971, however, has merged some radicals, reducing the number to 189. Most radicals are also characters; for example, the "sun" radical and the character for "sun" are identical. There are thousands of characters in regular use, and the majority of them are not radicals. Each character contains only one radical, with or without a remainder.

The character for "star," pronounced *xīng*, is written:

星

There is a literary character referring to the morning sun, pronounced *lóng*, that is written:

晥

Now it can be seen that both characters contain the "sun" radical:

日

"Star" has the radical on top and a remainder, which is pronounced *shēng*, that looks like this:

生

"Morning sun" has the "sun" radical to the left; its remainder is pronounced *lóng* and is written:

龙

Almost all the recent Chinese dictionaries and reference books arrange their characters by radicals. Take for example the character for "star." To look it up one first goes to the section marked by the "sun" radical:

日

In this section all the characters that contain the "sun" radical are ordered by the number of strokes in the remainder, which is:

生

This remainder is only moderately complex, with five strokes. We would expect to find it in about the middle of the section.

A key process in the construction of characters can be illustrated with "star" and "morning sun":

星 晥

Their meanings are clearly related to the meaning of the "sun" radical. In these characters the radical is called the signific**** and the remainders are the phonetics. The phonetics indicate how the characters are to be pronounced. In "morning sun" the phonetic is *lóng*:

龙

It gives its pronunciation to the character. On the other hand, there are characters that are not pronounced like their phonetic, often for reasons of historical sound change. The phonetic in the character "star" is:

生

The phonetic is pronounced *shēng*, but the pronunciation for "star" is *xīng*.

As another example of a phonetic we can take the character for "horse." It is pronounced *mǎ* and is written:

马

When the phonetic for "horse" is combined with the signific for "woman," we have *mā*, which means "mother":

妈

When the "horse" phonetic is combined with the signific for "jade," we have *mǎ*, which means "agate":

玛

Combined with the signific for "insect," the meaning becomes "ant," and again it is pronounced *mǎ*:

蚂

When there are two "mouth" significs hovering over the "horse" phonetic, the meaning becomes "to scold," and it is pronounced *mà*:

骂

There are a large number of characters in Chinese that are constructed on the phonetic-signific plan. Thus underlying many Chinese characters there is a phonetic principle. The average Chinese can often pronounce correctly a character he has never seen before simply by making a shrewd guess at its phonetic. For example, examine the following:

铙

The signific portion means "gold." The phonetic portion is pronounced *lóng* and is written:

龙

There would be no problem in agreeing that the character should be the name of a metal or metallic compound and should be pronounced like *lóng*, even though such a character does not exist in the language.

Another fictitious character was sent to me recently by a friend as a riddle. The character has three components:

女 上 下

The first component means "woman." The second and third components also are independent characters; they are pronounced *shàng* and *xià* and respectively mean "up" and "down." We assigned the signific to the "woman" component, and the character looked like this:

婊

For the character as a whole we settled on the meaning "elevator girl." However, there is no intuitive way of pronouncing the character, since the last two components do not constitute a phonetic. The solution of pronouncing it with two syllables, *shàng-xià*, breaks a general rule of Chinese orthography, namely that for one character there is one syllable. Although reformers of the Chinese language have occasionally proposed polysyllabic characters, no such reform has ever been successful.

Chinese dictionaries and rhyme books may list tens of thousands of characters, but a knowledge of 4,000 to 7,000 characters is sufficient for, say, reading a newspaper. The form of the characters has been built up unsystematically through the centuries, and some are very intricate, requiring 30 or more strokes to write. The Chinese government's plan of simplification has gone a long way toward standardizing the form of the characters and reducing the average number of strokes per character. The net gain has been dramatic. A text written in simplified characters can contain fewer than half as many strokes as the same text written before 1956. This simplification makes the task of learning the written language considerably easier. An average of five or six strokes per character is not significantly different from the average of five or six letters per English word.

Since it is not the primary purpose of

the characters to represent sounds, the Chinese written language has been largely independent of the evolutionary changes that have taken place in the spoken language. This independence has made it possible for the written language to provide a literary continuity across thousands of years and to serve as a cohesive force binding the diverse cultures of China together.

The Evolution of the Language

The evolution of spoken Chinese, like the evolution of all other living languages, has been constant. Therefore many of the beautiful poems of the Táng dynasty of the seventh to 10th centuries no longer rhyme. If Confucius, who lived in the fifth century B.C., were to give a lecture anywhere in China today, he would not be understood. Within the large area of China dialects have evolved so far apart in their sounds that a man from Peking cannot be sure of being able to order a dinner in a Cantonese restaurant. Compared with the change in sounds, the written characters have changed little. Most of the characters Confucius used are still in books today, and many of these characters have their original meanings. The writing of Confucius is more intelligible to a modern Chinese than, say, a page of *Beowulf* is to an American. By the same token, although the Táng poems no longer rhyme, they are still enjoyed throughout China because their visual message remains the same. When the poems are read aloud by people in Peking, Shanghai or Canton, the poems sound altogether different because of the various dialects. It is rather like hearing "6 + 7 = 13" being read aloud in English, German and Norwegian. Even in Japan a Chinese with no knowledge of Japanese can manage to communicate reasonably well by writing. Chinese characters were also a significant medium of communication in Korea and in Vietnam. The independence of the characters from the spoken language has enabled them to serve as a core of culture in much of East Asia for many centuries.

A written Chinese character has a more direct connection with its meaning than a written word in English does. The sequence of letters spelling "horse" has meaning only through the mediation of the sounds they represent. The shape of the letters has no relation to the concept "horse." Little would be changed if English-speaking peoples were to take up the Cyrillic alphabet and the sounds for "horse" were represented *xopc*. To a Chi-

CHARACTER FOR "SUN" is built up with four brushstrokes: first a vertical, then a turning stroke, then the inside and finally the closure. Order and the geometric position of the strokes are important. All the components of a character should fit roughly into a square.

	OLD	SIMPLIFIED
SUN (rì)	日	日
STAR (xīng)	星	星
MORNING SUN (lóng)	曨	昽
HORSE (mǎ)	馬	马
MOTHER (mā)	媽	妈
AGATE (mǎ)	瑪	玛
ANT (mǎ)	螞	蚂
TO SCOLD (mà)	罵	骂

SIMPLIFIED CHARACTERS were introduced in 1956 by the government of the People's Republic of China. Simple characters, such as the first two, were not affected. The remaining characters, somewhat more complex, were each reduced by six strokes.

nese the character for "horse" means horse with no mediation through the sound *mǎ*. The image is so vivid that one can almost sense an abstract figure galloping across the page:

马

The other major linguistic decision made by the Chinese government was to adopt a spelling system based on the Latin alphabet. This system is called Pinyin, which literally means "spell sound." All the Chinese words spelled out in Latin letters in this article are writ-ten in Pinyin. The government has been careful to point out that Pinyin is not intended to replace the characters but rather to serve as an aid in learning pronunciation. To discontinue the use of the Chinese characters would deprive coming generations of Chinese of a rich and meaningful cultural heritage.

Standard Chinese

To discuss the Pinyin system of spelling we need to examine the sound system of what is called standard Chinese, which is based on the Peking dialect and is now being taught in all parts of China. It is a straightforward system, simpler in many ways than the easy syllables of Spanish. There is really only one aspect unfamiliar to those who speak European languages: the tones. The musical quality of the spoken Chinese language is due to the fact that almost every syllable must carry one of four basic tones. These tones are indicated by diacritical marks over the vowels. The phenomenon of tones seems to be confined to Chinese and to some of the languages of Southeast Asia that have been heavily influenced by Chinese.

One of the earliest references in the literature to tones dates back to the sixth century. When the emperor of Li-áng asked one of his scholars, Zhōu Shě, what was meant by the four tones, Zhōu responded with an elegant illustration:

天 子 圣 哲

It means "The son of heaven is divine and wise." (Chinese emperors have traditionally been regarded as sons of heaven and divine, whether or not they were wise.) The beauty of Zhōu's response lies in the fact that the first word of his phrase illustrates the first tone in the speech of that time, the second word the second tone, and so on.

Essentially every Chinese syllable has a characteristic pitch pattern (tone). Changing the tone alters the meaning just as much as changing a consonant or a vowel in English changes the meaning. In English we use a rising pitch pattern for "Jóhn?" and a falling pitch pattern for "Jòhn!" The different tones convey different attitudes, but the meaning of the word remains the same. In Chinese, however, *má* with a rising pitch pattern means "hemp" and *mà* with a falling pitch pattern means "to scold." The two meanings are no more related to each other than they would be if we were to change the vowel to get *mì*, which means "honey," or if we were to change the consonant to get *pà*, which means "to fear."

Standard Chinese has a total of four tones: rising, falling, level and dipping [*see illustration at left*]. In addition to the tone every syllable must also have a nucleus to carry the tone, usually a vowel. The tone and the nucleus are the two obligatory components of the Chinese syllable. There are also three optional components of a syllable: the initial component, which is usually a consonant; the medial component, which is a glide, and the ending, which may be either a glide or a consonant from a restricted class. There are eight possible forms a syllable can take.

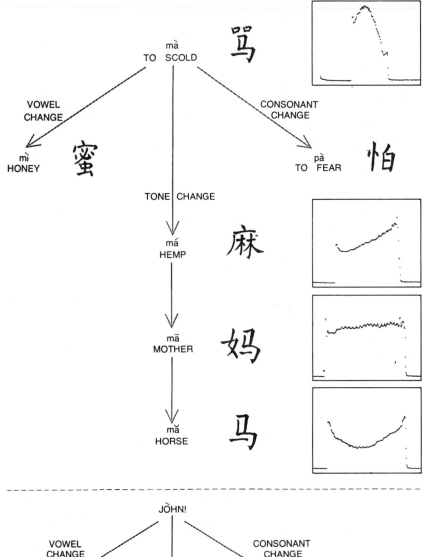

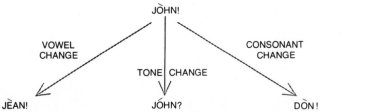

TONES are used to alter the meaning of Chinese words. Standard Chinese has only four tones: falling (as in *mà*), rising (*má*), level (*mā*) and dipping, or falling and then rising (*mǎ*). The oscillograph traces at right show the fundamental frequency of the author's voice as he spoke the words. In English, on the other hand, variation in tone is used to convey different moods; the meaning of the word being spoken does not change. In Chinese changing tone has same kind of effect on meaning of word as changing a vowel or a consonant.

	PINYIN	PHONETIC	INITIAL CONSONANT	FINAL MEDIAL, GLIDE	FINAL NUCLEUS, VOWEL	FINAL ENDING, VOWEL OR CONSONANT
FACE	liǎn	ljɛ̌n	●	●	●	●
IRON	tiě	tʰjɛ̌	●	●	●	
TO GROW	zhǎng	tʂǎŋ	●		●	●
HORSE	mǎ	mǎ	●		●	
EYE	yǎn	jɛ̌n		●	●	●
MOON	yuè	yɛ̀		●	●	
HIDDEN	yǐn	ǐn			●	●
CHAIR	yǐ	ǐ			●	

COMPONENTS OF A CHINESE SYLLABLE that are obligatory are the tone and the nucleus (usually a vowel) to carry the tone. There are three optional components in a syllable: the initial, which is usually a consonant; the medial, which is a glide, and the ending, which may be either a glide or a consonant. All together there are eight possible forms that a Chinese syllable can take.

One striking feature of Chinese words in comparison with most European words is the lack of clusters of consonants before and after the nuclear vowel. When Western words with consonant clusters are represented in Chinese, they are typically broken up so that each consonant has its own syllable. "Marx" is conventionally rendered:

马 克 思

It is pronounced mǎ-kè-sī. The first character is the one for "horse," which also happens to be a prevalent Chinese surname.

Although the Pinyin system and standard Chinese are taught in all parts of China, the languages of ethnic minorities are given full consideration. According to The Nationalities in China, a book published in Peking in 1961, there are about 30 million people belonging to minority groups. The minorities occupy about a third of the land of China, mostly in the west and northwest. Some of the groups are large: the Zhuàngs are close to eight million in number and the Uighurs about four million. The languages of some of these groups are related genetically to Chinese but belong to other linguistic families such as Altaic and Austroasiatic.

A 1956 report by the Chinese Academy of Sciences estimated that the total number of people in China who spoke one or another of the Chinese dialects was more than 500 million. Of the dialects, Mandarin has by far the most speakers: more than two-thirds of the total [see illustration on page 54]. The Western name "Mandarin" derives from the fact that the dialect was the speech of government officials, or mandarins. It corresponds to the Chinese term Guānhuà, which means "official speech." Standard Chinese is a conventionalized variety of this dialect and is known as Guóyǔ, or "national language." It also is referred to as Běifānghuà, which means "northern speech," or as Pǔtōnghuà, "common speech."

Outside China standard Chinese plays a much less important role. The dominant dialects among the 15 million Chinese in Southeast Asia are Yue and Southern Min, because it was people from the southern coastal provinces who migrated into the area. In the U.S. the Chinese are relative newcomers; they date back to 1850, when they were first drawn across the Pacific Ocean by the discovery of gold in California. Later these immigrants made up the core of the labor force that built the railroads in the American West. The ancestry of the great majority of the several hundred thousand Chinese now in the U.S. can be traced back to a small cluster of villages around Canton, all within a radius of 100 miles or so. The speech patterns of these villages are definitely of the Yue dialect group, but they differ markedly from one another. We can be sure that significant differences have arisen in the past 100 years between the speech of the American Chinese and the speech of the source villages around Canton.

Word Formation

Every language has a stock of several thousand morphemes: the bearers of the basic semantic and grammatical content. An expression such as "can openers" comprises four morphemes: "can," "open," "-er" and "-s." Some morphemes in English have more than one syllable (as in "open" and "adamant"), whereas others, such as the "-s" in "cats" and the "-t" in "slept," are single consonants. In Chinese most morphemes are exactly one syllable long. The usual division of morphemes into three major categories—noun, verb and adjective—applies to Chinese quite well. Thus in Chinese shū ("book") is a noun, mǎi ("buy") is a verb and guì ("expensive") is an adjective. These morphemes are known as contentives, in that they carry independent semantic meanings.

There is also a class of morphemes called functives. They are usually attached to contentives to modify their meaning in systematic ways and to show the relations the contentives have to one another. For example, functives attached to the contentive "prove" change its meaning: "proves," "proved," "proving," "disprove," "unproved" and "proof." Although conjugational and declensional paradigms are important in English, they are negligible in Chinese. There is, however, a sizable amount of derivational morphology in Chinese, where nouns are derived from verbs by changing the tone. Thus shǔ is a verb meaning "to count," and shù is a noun meaning "number." The verb lián means "to connect," and the noun liàn means "a chain." Mó is "to grind," and mò is "a grindstone." To derive a noun in these cases one simply changes the syllable to a falling tone. A similar example from English is deriving a noun from a verb by devoicing the final consonant: "prove"–"proof," "bathe"–"bath," "house"–"house."

The device of derivation by tone change is no longer productive in standard Chinese, but it is suspected that tonal derivation was an important process in the earlier stages of development

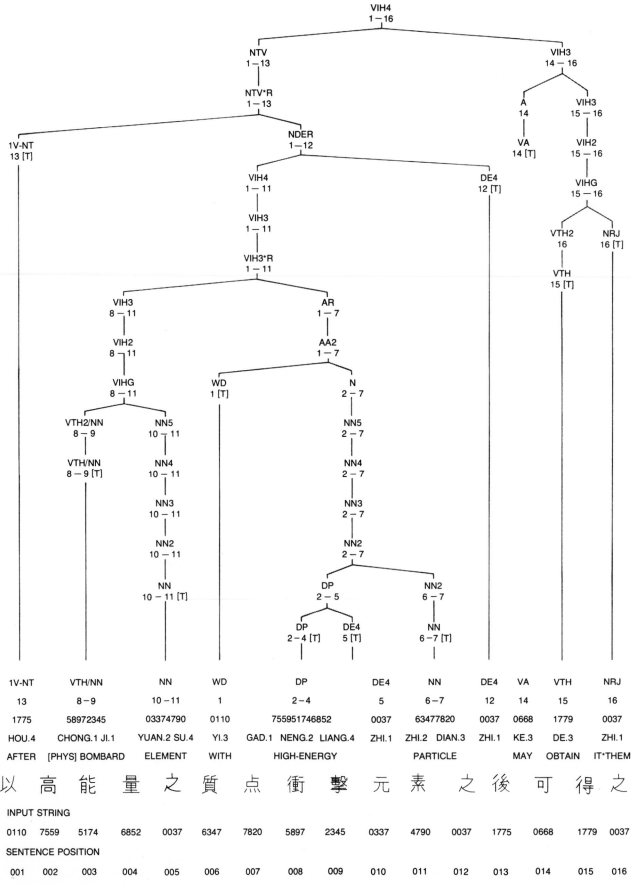

1V-NT	VTH/NN	NN	WD	DP	DE4	NN	DE4	VA	VTH	NRJ
13	8 – 9	10 – 11	1	2 – 4	5	6 – 7	12	14	15	16
1775	58972345	03374790	0110	755951746852	0037	63477820	0037	0668	1779	0037
HOU.4	CHONG.1 JI.1	YUAN.2 SU.4	YI.3	GAD.1 NENG.2 LIANG.4	ZHI.1	ZHI.2 DIAN.3	ZHI.1	KE.3	DE.3	ZHI.1
AFTER	[PHYS] BOMBARD	ELEMENT	WITH	HIGH-ENERGY		PARTICLE		MAY	OBTAIN	IT·THEM

以　高　能　量　之　質　点　衝　擊　元　素　之　後　可　得　之

INPUT STRING

| 0110 | 7559 | 5174 | 6852 | 0037 | 6347 | 7820 | 5897 | 2345 | 0337 | 4790 | 0037 | 1775 | 0668 | 1779 | 0037 |

SENTENCE POSITION

| 001 | 002 | 003 | 004 | 005 | 006 | 007 | 008 | 009 | 010 | 011 | 012 | 013 | 014 | 015 | 016 |

COMPUTER TRANSLATION of a Chinese sentence from a scientific text produces a reasonably accurate and understandable result. The string of Chinese characters is entered into the computer using a numeric code for each character. The position of each character in the sentence is also entered. The computer searches its memory for the meaning of each character and then performs syntactic analysis of the sentence. In converting the sentence into English the computer makes permutations of the word order. The sentence means: "It may be obtained after bombarding the element with high-energy particles." Research into computer analysis of Chinese is being conducted by the author and his colleagues at the phonology laboratory of the University of California at Berkeley.

of the Chinese language. In the Cantonese dialect, however, the process is still very productive. The Cantonese use tone change for forming diminutives: "candy" from "sugar," "daughter" from "female" and so on.

A common derivational device in Chinese is reduplication. Applied to nouns, it carries the meaning "every." Hence although *rén* means "person," *rénren* means "every person," *tiān* means "day" and *tiāntian* means "every day." Applied to verbs, it adds a transitory meaning to the action: *kàn* means "to look," whereas *kànkan* means "to take a look," *zǒu* means "to walk" and *zóuzou* means "to take a walk." Adverbs can be derived from adjectives by reduplication and the addition of a *de* suffix. Thus *kuài* is "quick" and *kuàikuàide* is "quickly," *lǎn* is "lazy" and *lǎnlǎnde* is "lazily."

The manner in which two-syllable adjectives reduplicate is different. Whereas a two-syllable verb, *tǎolùn* ("to discuss"), reduplicates as *tǎolùntǎolùn* ("to discuss a little"), an adjective, say *gāoxìng* ("happy"), becomes *gāogāoxìngxìngde* ("happily"). A verb reduplicates by the entire word, but the adjective reduplicates in terms of its constituent syllables.

Another device for word formation in Chinese is the conjoining of antonyms. "Buy" and "sell" combine to form "business," *mǎimài*. "Long" and "short" combine to form "length," *chángduǎn*. The derived meaning is not always straightforward. For example, *fǎn* means "turned over" and *zhèng* means "right side up." Put together, *fǎnzhèng* means "in any case."

Classifiers are a linguistic feature peculiar to Chinese and its neighboring languages. Articles, numerals and other such modifiers cannot directly precede their associated noun; there has to be an intervening classifier, which usually has negligible semantic content. In Chinese one cannot say *sān shū* ("three books") or *nèi māo* ("that cat"). One has to say *sān běn shū* ("three piece book") or *nèi zhī māo* ("that piece cat"). The terms *běn* and *zhī* here are translated as "piece" for the lack of a better counterpart in English. Such classifiers are absolutely necessary in Chinese expressions. This feature has been carried over into many pidgin and Creole languages based on Chinese, in which "three bananas" or "this man" are rendered as "three piece banana" or "this fellow man."

Sentence Formation

The basic sentence in Chinese has the order subject-verb-object, as in English. Thus the sentence *wǒmen chī jī* is word for word "We eat chicken." There is a tendency in Chinese to delete either the subject or the object. Hence *wǒmen chī* ("We eat") or *chī jī* ("Eat chicken") are both common sentences. To focus attention on the object, the Chinese speaker will move it to the beginning of the sentence. *Jī wǒmen chī*, for instance, means "We eat chicken," but it is normally used to contrast with something else we do not eat. Suppose subject deletion and moving the object to the initial position both operated on the sentence *wǒmen chī jī*. First we front the object and get *jī wǒmen chī*, and then we delete the subject and get *jī chī*. The resulting sentence would mean something like "Chicken *A* eats," and the identity of *A* normally would be clear from the context. But *jī chī* of course also means something like "The chicken eats," where *jī* is the subject of the verb. In other words, *jī chī* is an ambiguous sentence, its ambiguity arising from object fronting and subject deletion.

There is no evidence that Chinese allows either more ambiguity than English or less. In an English sentence such as "It is too hot to eat," the "it" can refer to the weather, to the food or to the animal that is doing the eating. Moreover, "hot" could mean "high in heat content" (which in Chinese is *tàng*) or it could mean "spicy" (which in Chinese is *là*).

The Chinese language as an object of study goes back as far as the beginning

	REGULAR FORMS			SCRIPT FORMS		
	TIGER	DRAGON		TIGER	DRAGON	
ANCIENT GRAPHS ABOUT 2000 B.C.						
SHELL-AND-BONE CHARACTERS jiǎgǔwén ABOUT 1400-1200 B.C.						
GREAT SEAL dàzhuàn ABOUT 1100-300 B.C.						
SMALL SEAL xiǎozhuàn 221-207 B.C.						
SCRIBE CHARACTER lìshū ABOUT 200 B.C.-A.D. 200						DOCUMENTARY SCRIPT zhāngcǎo ABOUT 200 B.C.-A.D.1700
STANDARD CHARACTERS kǎishū ABOUT A.D. 100 -PRESENT						RUNNING STYLE xíngshū ABOUT A.D. 200 -PRESENT
SIMPLIFIED CHARACTERS jiǎnzì ABOUT A.D. 100 -PRESENT						SIMPLIFIED SCRIPT CHARACTERS liánbǐ jiǎnzì ABOUT A.D.100 -PRESENT
						"MODERN" SCRIPT jìncǎo ABOUT A.D. 300 -PRESENT
						ERRATIC SCRIPT kuángcǎo ABOUT A.D. 600-1700

HISTORICAL DEVELOPMENT of pictographic characters for the two most powerful animals in Chinese mythology, the tiger and the dragon, are shown in their various stages. The earliest-known pictographic forms of the animals are at the top in red. The illustration is from *Introduction to Chinese Cursive Script*, by F. Y. Wang of Seton Hall University.

of the Christian Era. At that time the Chinese had already produced sophisticated works in dialectology and in semantic classification. The foundations for the historical study of Chinese sounds were laid during the 17th and 18th centuries by the great scholars of the Qīng dynasty, and it is on their shoulders that modern Chinese linguists stand.

The key to how a language sounded centuries ago lies in how it sounds today. The basic method is to compare the pronunciation of morphemes in contemporary dialects and to infer what their ancestral pronunciations might have been. The inference is not just a guess but is made on the basis of documentary evidence and knowledge of the general linguistic principles underlying sound change.

Given the nonphonetic nature of the Chinese writing system, it may seem an impossible task to reconstruct how the language was spoken many centuries ago. One might think that the sounds of alphabetic languages, such as Old Church Slavic or Sanskrit, would be much easier to reconstruct. Actually it is not much easier, because there is no direct way to determine how a letter was pronounced. With alphabetic languages the phonetic values must also be arrived at by inference.

Chinese has the great advantage of an abundance of ancient writings that reach back continuously in time further than the literature of any other language in the world. The fact that the form of Chinese characters is often not much influenced by changes in pronunciation is quite a convenience in helping linguists to determine which morphemes are etymologically related.

The study of Chinese dialects has been hampered in the past by an overabundance of data, which tended to make research procedures cumbersome and time-consuming. The advent of large computers has facilitated the manipulation of the data. Chin-Chuan Cheng and I, with the help of several colleagues, have developed a dialect dictionary on computer, which we call DOC. The program is in operation at the computer centers of the University of California at Berkeley and of the University of Illinois. It incorporates the pronunciation of more than 2,000 morphemes in each of 20 Chinese dialects.

Evidence is accumulating from our work with DOC that changes in language proceed in ways that are essentially parallel to biological evolution, as Charles Darwin noted in *The Descent of Man*. In both cases the mechanism of change resides in variation. When two or more variants appear, the rival forms compete for survival. For instance, in American speech the vowel in "room" varies between that of "pool" and that of "put," and the *s* in "disobey" varies between an *s* and a *z*. The major selective force, which is constant across time as well as across languages, is the ease with which the forms can be pronounced and properly perceived. This selective force determines what forms of speech will survive.

With the aid of computer programs such as DOC we have been able to run through large pools of data to locate ongoing sound changes of special interest. Some changes are just beginning, some are in midstream and some are ending. In the Cháozhōu dialect, for example, there is a change from one tone to another that has so far affected about half of the vocabulary. By having access to a large number of well-defined types of sound change, we are now in a position to study much more effectively the selective force that determines the direction of language evolution.

Another aspect of the Chinese language that has been subjected to intensive computer study is its morphology and syntax. With the collaboration of Stephen W. Chan, Benjamin K. Tsou and others, we have developed a machine dictionary with more than 70,000 entries, together with the necessary programs for translation from Chinese into English. A good measure of how well we understand the structure of a language is how well we can break it apart in a way that is suitable for translation by machine. Although we are an indefinite distance away from being able to translate a Táng poem into English without losing its exquisite sensitivity, we can do a reasonably accurate job with scientific texts [*see illustration on page 60*].

Now that relations between the People's Republic of China and Western nations are becoming more normal, interest in the Chinese language is increasing at an accelerating tempo. Considering that the Chinese language has the largest number of speakers in the world and the greatest time depth in its literature, this interest is long overdue. With the increase in interest we may look forward to deeper probings into the history and the structure of the language, and into the influence the language has had on the cultural and intellectual development of the Chinese people. These studies will surely lead to a better general understanding of the nature of human language.

8

The Spread of the Bantu Language

by D. W. Phillipson
April 1977

*Bantu is spoken by 130 million people in southern
Africa. Linguistic and archaeological evidence suggests
that the original Bantu-speakers began their migration
from a region in the north some 2,300 years ago*

The 19th-century European explorers of Africa who outfitted their expeditions at Zanzibar or the adjacent mainland were surprised and pleased by a bonus they received: their porters and escorts spoke a language that was understood through wide areas of subequatorial Africa and could understand many of the tribal dialects they encountered in the eastern half of the region. The reason was that those concerned were speaking one or another form of Bantu, a family of languages common to more than 130 million black Africans, comprising several hundred separate tribal groups, who still inhabit much of Africa south of the Equator. The Zanzibar version of the language, Ki-Swahili, is enriched with loan words from several foreign tongues; its very name comes from the Arabic word *sahil,* or "coast," so that it can be rendered as "coast dialect." The basic form of Swahili, however, is pure Bantu.

The word Bantu is an exclusively linguistic label and has no other primary implications, either of race or of culture. The family of dialects was named by a 19th-century German philologist, Wilhelm H. I. Bleek. The words *ki-ntu* and *bi-ntu* in these African dialects respectively mean "a thing" and "things"; the words *mu-ntu* and *ba-ntu,* "a man" and "men." Thus *bantu* can be construed as "people" or "the people," and this seemed to Bleek a name eminently suitable for a language held in common by so many.

Since late in the 19th century it has generally been recognized by students of linguistics that the various Bantu tongues must have come from a common ancestral language within the relatively recent past. Indeed, it has been a prime goal for students of African history to elucidate the processes responsible for this remarkably widespread linguistic distribution. Unfortunately the oral traditions of the Bantu-speakers themselves generally extend only a short distance into the past. Furthermore, no Bantu language was reduced to writing until after the time of contact with Arabs or Europeans, so that both tradition

and written records are silent on ultimate Bantu origins. To trace Bantu ancestry backward in time therefore becomes the task of archaeology and of historically oriented linguistic studies. Here I shall present the latest evidence concerning the dispersal of Bantu-speakers in Africa south of the Equator that has been developed by scholars in both disciplines.

To deal first with the archaeological evidence, from about 300 B.C. to A.D. 600 a major change took place in the greater part of Africa lying between the Equator and the Vaal River. The change was marked by the appearance of a characteristic type of pottery that clearly belongs to a single stylistic tradition even though regional variations are readily apparent. The pottery is found in association with evidence for the working of metal: iron and in some areas copper. Because this is the earliest-known evidence of metallurgy in the entire subequatorial region the cultural complex to which the artifacts belong has been named the Early Iron Age.

The often elaborate decoration and the varied forms of Early Iron Age pottery allow detailed stylistic analyses of the complex, and these analyses in turn provide a framework for studies of its subdivisions and interregional relations. Although the extreme geographical limits of the complex are still imperfectly known, more than 350 Early Iron Age sites have now been identified. Virtually all are in areas that in more recent times are known to have been inhabited by Bantu-speaking people.

In most instances the Early Iron Age population appears to have consisted of settled village dwellers who practiced an economy of mixed farming, that is, both raising crops and herding animals. In the regions to the south of central Tanzania they are the earliest followers of such a life-style to appear in the archaeological record. Indeed, the contrast between the Early Iron Age population and its predecessors is much greater in southern subequatorial Africa than it is farther to the north. There, notably in the

Rift Valley and the adjacent highlands of northern Tanzania and southern Kenya, settled communities practicing a pastoral economy and possibly cultivating cereal crops were established at least as early as 1000 B.C. To the south, however, it seems that Early Iron Age techniques of food production were introduced to a region where such practices had been virtually unknown and the indigenous population lived by hunting and gathering. Here, with the possible exception of the extreme south, pottery of the Early Iron Age is the oldest pottery known.

Many aspects of Early Iron Age culture other than pottery making and mixed farming evidently represented major innovations in most of the southern areas. The culture was introduced in full-fledged form almost everywhere, not only with respect to its various components but also as a viable socioeconomic system. Pottery that might be regarded as being in some way ancestral to Early Iron Age wares has yet to be found in any part of the region. Metallurgy too seems to have been introduced as an already efficient and fully developed technology into a region where previously even a rudimentary knowledge of metalworking did not exist. Again, the domesticated animals and several of the domesticated plants were species unknown in subequatorial Africa even in wild forms. It thus seems that the hypothesis viewing Early Iron Age culture as being alien to the region is amply supported. Evidently the culture was introduced by means of a rapid and coherent movement of people who brought with them a full-fledged culture that had undergone its formative processes elsewhere.

The scale of human migration involved in the dispersal of Early Iron Age culture in these parts of Africa is not easy to assess. Clearly the people moved in numbers sufficient to support a technology that was largely independent of the stone-tool-using technology of the peoples whose lands they were entering. Indeed, in many of these new territories the indigenous population continued to practice the traditional occupations of hunting and gathering for centuries after the arrival of the Early Iron Age settlers.

Archaeologists now recognize more than a dozen Early Iron Age regional industries, differentiated mainly on the basis of pottery styles. At least in the eastern part of subequatorial Africa these are remarkably distinct from the pottery styles that became popular in later times. Up to now the most detailed comparison of the wares of various Early Iron Age groups is one made by Robert Soper of the University of Ibadan in Nigeria. On the basis of his work and my own it is possible to discern two major ceramic subdivisions. These I have provisionally termed the eastern stream and the western stream.

Sites attributable to the eastern stream are found mainly in the coastal hinterland of East Africa, in Malawi, in southern and eastern Zambia, in most of Rhodesia and in the Transvaal, Natal and Swaziland. The western stream is represented in territories that are archaeologically less well known, but the stream is apparent in central and western Zambia and in adjacent parts of Zaïre and Angola. Although the two streams were first distinguished on the basis of pottery style, it is also evident that they are geographically distinct. Furthermore, there are significant differences between the two in terms of relative chronology and economic practices.

The earliest-known manifestation of Early Iron Age culture is found in the Great Lakes region of East Africa and is recognized by a characteristic pottery known as Urewe ware. The makers of Urewe ware were probably settled in the country around the western and south-western shores of Lake Victoria by 500 B.C. or soon thereafter. Later they spread to the eastern shore of the lake to settle in what is now southwestern Kenya. The Urewe people were certainly workers in iron; smelting furnaces of this period have been found in both Rwanda and eastern Zaïre. So far there is only indirect evidence that the Urewe people practiced agriculture. Analysis of the plant pollens in bottom sediments from Lake Victoria off southern Uganda indicates a substantial reduction in the forest cover in about the first half of the first millennium B.C. One can view this as evidence of some form of land clearing, possibly for agriculture. Those responsible for the clearing could have been Early Iron Age pioneers.

Far to the southwest of the Great Lakes, near the modern border between Angola and Zaïre on the southern fringe of the tropical forest, typical Urewe pot-

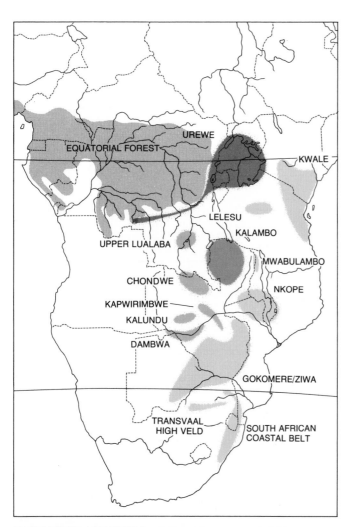

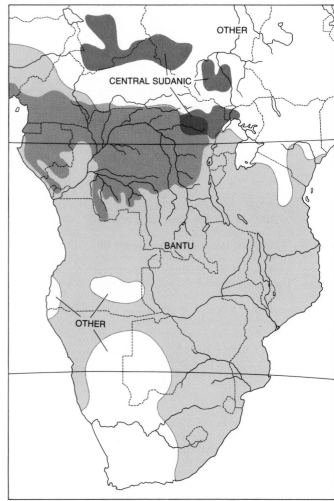

EARLY IRON AGE SITES in subequatorial Africa fall into three general classes based on pottery characteristics. The first and earliest is known as Urewe; most Urewe sites are clustered around Lake Victoria, but one western outlier, Tshikapa, is near the border between Angola and Zaïre. Sites in the class known as the eastern stream include five groups north of the Zambezi River and four to the south. Sites in the class known as the western stream include four groups; most are north of the Zambezi. Sites of the Kalambo group, near Lake Nyasa, show features of both streams.

BANTU LANGUAGES spoken by more than 130 million black Africans are distributed across Africa in a pattern strikingly similar to the distribution of Early Iron Age archaeological sites (*see map at left*). Speakers of Bantu languages are also found in the equatorial forest (*gray*) as far north as where forest gives way to savanna. There, near Lake Edward and Lake Albert, Bantu-speakers are in contact with speakers of Central Sudanic languages (*dark color*). Blanks indicate other non-Bantu areas.

tery has been found at the site of Tshika-pa. Jacques Nenquin of the State University of Ghent has been able to demonstrate that the vessels were made of local clay, rather than having been imported from the east. The significance of this extension of Urewe potmakers toward the west will become evident in what follows.

The two-stream phenomenon is most clearly recognizable in the spread of Early Iron Age culture into the south-central and southern parts of subequatorial Africa, a series of movements that began only after the initial settlement of the Great Lakes region. The eastern stream is clearly derived from the Great Lakes Urewe settlements. The western stream may either be derived from the same settlements or share a common ancestry with them. In any event the eastern stream can be shown to have reached the coastal hinterland of south-

ern Kenya, adjacent parts of Tanzania and perhaps Somalia in about the second century of the Christian Era. In the fourth century there was a rapid movement of Early Iron Age culture southward through Malawi, eastern Zambia and Rhodesia and on into the Transvaal and Swaziland. This was a further thrust of the eastern stream.

The process, which seems to have taken place with amazing speed, may have affected Rhodesia slightly later than it did Malawi and eastern Zambia. In any event a date of about A.D. 400 is indicated for the start of the Early Iron Age south of the Limpopo River, in what is now the Republic of South Africa. Not enough carbon-14 dates are yet available to establish the timing of the event with any greater precision. In the Victoria Falls region of southern Zambia, where the settling of Early Iron Age people can be shown to have stemmed

from Rhodesia, the imported culture did not reach full florescence until the sixth century.

The Early Iron Age western stream is well represented in the archaeological record only in central Zambia, west of the Luangwa River, and in an adjacent part of Rhodesia, across the Zambezi River. Related sites are also known in the province of Shaba (formerly Katanga) in Zaïre, and in a few places farther to the west, all the way to the Atlantic coast. It is known that in the coastal area pottery (not necessarily representative of the Early Iron Age complex) was in use as early as 200 B.C.

In the 11th century A.D. there was a rapid eclipse of Early Iron Age culture over almost all the eastern half of subequatorial Africa. The traditions affected included some that were typical of the western-stream settlements as well as the eastern-stream ones. The successor

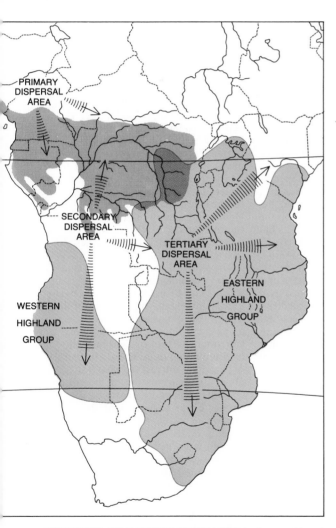

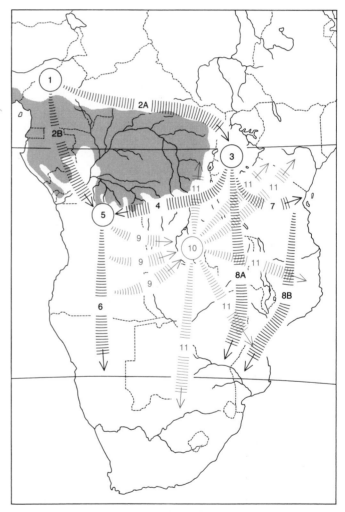

DISPERSAL OF BANTU LANGUAGES is shown schematically; the data are drawn principally from the research of Bernd Heine of the universities of Cologne and Nairobi and of David Dalby of the University of London. The homeland is near the forest margin in Cameroon; this is where modern Bantu dialects show the greatest diversity. Two further dispersals followed; the Western Highland Group of Bantu languages became established significantly earlier than the Eastern Group.

HYPOTHETICAL PROGRESSION of Bantu-speakers over some 2,000 years sees the language arising among a Neolithic people before 1000 B.C. (1). A dual movement then seems to have brought Bantu-speakers, some using iron, beyond the forest (3, 5). An east-to-west movement (4) reinforced southward expansion of languages ancestral to the Western Group (6). Early in the first millennium A.D. the eastern stream expanded to the south (7, 8). The western stream (9) gave rise to a center (10) that sent forth languages ancestral to the Eastern Group (11) in the 11th century A.D.

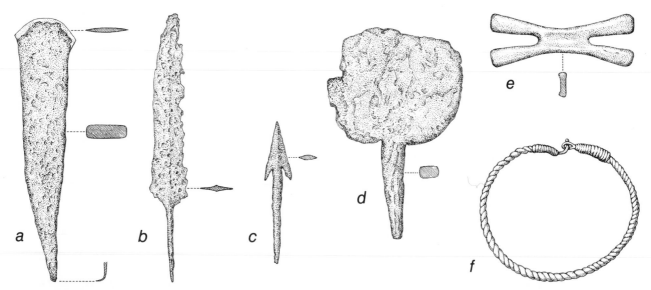

EARLY IRON AGE METALWORK found at sites in subequatorial Africa includes these characteristic artifacts. The iron axe (a) has a curved tang, and the iron spearhead (b) has a strengthening ridge on both faces. The barbed iron arrowhead (c) is tapered in cross section to provide cutting edges, and the iron hoe blade (d) has a sturdy tang. The Early Iron Age smiths were familiar with copper; the ingot of copper (e) may have been used as a form of currency, but the necklet of twisted copper wire (f) was probably only a personal ornament.

cultures, which are known collectively as later Iron Age, show considerable diversity. Nevertheless, many factors—cultural, technological and, as we shall see, linguistic—point to connections between the later Iron Age cultures and the more westerly settlements of the Early Iron Age people, particularly those in southeastern Zaïre. A significant degree of continuity between the Early Iron Age and the later Iron Age is also evident in several eastern regions, but it is by no means as marked there as it is farther to the west.

Evidence in favor of the hypothesis that the spread of Early Iron Age culture into subequatorial Africa can be correlated with the dispersal of populations speaking Bantu languages is largely circumstantial. For example, arguing backward from the present and the recent past, proponents of the hypothesis point out that the parts of Africa occupied by Bantu-speaking peoples are broadly those where evidence of Early Iron Age settlement is found. Supporting circumstantial evidence is also provided by strong indications that most of the non-Bantu-speaking inhabitants of these same areas had adopted an Iron Age culture only in part or not at all at the time of the first foreign contacts, and that some non-Bantu-speakers remain only partly acculturated to this day.

Two other items of evidence, although they too are circumstantial, are persuasive. One is the close linguistic similarity between the Bantu dialects that are now spread across an enormous range of subequatorial Africa; the similarity suggests that all the variants were probably derived from a common ancestral tongue within relatively recent times. (As we have seen, a similarly

brief history and common ancestry is attributed to Early Iron Age culture on the basis of archaeological evidence.) The other item of circumstantial evidence comes from linguistic reconstructions of proto-Bantu languages. Among the reconstructed words are a number that describe certain key elements of Early Iron Age culture.

How are such reconstructions accomplished? Where and by whom was proto-Bantu spoken? With respect to the second question most students of the problem now support, at least in its basic outlines, the view of Joseph H. Greenberg of Stanford University. Greenberg places the Bantu linguistic homeland close to the northwestern limit of the present Bantu range. Not only is this the area where the greatest diversity exists among modern Bantu dialects but also it is where a strong degree of similarity is found, both in vocabulary and in grammatical form, between the Bantu dialects and the local non-Bantu languages.

With respect to how a reconstruction is accomplished, the one that is presented below is based on the work of Bernd Heine of the universities of Cologne and Nairobi and that of David Dalby of the University of London. The complex processes involved can be summarized in a map [*see illustration at left on preceding page*]. An initial center of proto-Bantu appears to have been in the far northwest of the modern Bantu area, most probably in what is now central Cameroon. From this center dialects ancestral to those Bantu tongues found today in parts of northeastern Zaïre dispersed eastward along the northern margin of the equatorial forest.

Perhaps at roughly the same time a more direct southward expansion from

the Cameroon center brought Bantu speech along a coastal or river route to the southwestern margin of the equatorial forest near the mouth of the Congo River. From this second center Bantu dialects appear to have been introduced southward into Angola and South West Africa (Namibia). Subsequent developments apparently gave rise to a third Bantu speech center, in the area of the upper Lualaba and Kasai rivers in southeastern Zaïre. From this center Heine and Dalby derive the modern Bantu dialects of the eastern half of subequatorial Africa, all of which show strong similarities.

The study of words that have entered Bantu languages from non-Bantu sources can be used to illustrate the sequence of Bantu linguistic evolution. The most intensive current research along these lines is that being done by Christopher Ehret of the University of California at Los Angeles. His work is of particular interest for what it suggests about the transmission of the cultural traits the loan words describe. For example, Ehret suggests that the names applied to cattle and sheep by many modern Bantu-speakers were probably derived from the non-Bantu languages known collectively as Central Sudanic. These tongues are still spoken in those areas of what are now the southern Sudan, Uganda, Zaïre and the Central African Republic that lie to the northwest of Lake Albert.

To return from linguistics to archaeology, by the second millennium B.C. or even earlier a food-producing economy had become established throughout most of the Sudanic belt, the broad region that stretches across Africa between the southern fringes of the Sahara and the northern limits of the equatorial forest. Most of the cereals cultivated by Early Iron Age farmers farther to the south were species known and perhaps originally domesticated in the Sudanic belt. The animals that accompanied the Early Iron Age farmers—goats, sheep and cattle—although not originally domesticated in the region, were in all probability herded there 2,000 years before the Christian Era.

The evidence suggesting a Sudanic origin for the Early Iron Age culture is not confined to the agricultural economy. The two best-known early centers of ironworking in sub-Saharan Africa are Nok in Nigeria and Meroë in Nubia. Both are adjacent to the Sudanic belt, and the knowledge of iron metallurgy doubtless diffused rapidly through the region, although the direction of the diffusion remains to be ascertained. Still another item of evidence is found in the Sudanic pottery of the period. Although little is known about these wares, they seem to reflect the same tradition that is evident in Early Iron Age pottery. The relation is most apparent at the time, presumably in about the middle of the first millennium B.C., when knowledge of iron was spreading among the stone-tool-using farmers of the belt. Archaeologically the central part of the belt remains almost unknown, but evidence is accumulating to suggest that the populations ultimately giving rise to the Early Iron Age complex were somewhere within this general region.

Our circumstantial linguistic hypothesis linking Bantu speech with Early Iron Age culture must surmount one major obstacle. The best prehistoric evidence related to Early Iron Age culture comes almost exclusively from the territory south of the great equatorial forest, that is, the side exactly opposite the one where the culture's formative processes seem to have centered. How did the culture cross the barrier? The great forest is itself inimical to farming practices of any kind; that a farming people could make even a rapid journey through hundreds of kilometers of dense equatorial growth is inherently improbable. By what other route could the carriers of the culture have reached the subequatorial savanna?

The alternate route requires an initial movement in an easterly direction, followed by a turn to the south. Along the first part of this route we find an area east of Lake Chad where the pottery that was made in the first millennium B.C. strongly resembles Early Iron Age wares. The area is adjacent to the territory where Central Sudanic languages are spoken today. The linguistic evidence indicates that some early Bantu-speaking people acquired domestic cattle and sheep, together with the words for both animals, from speakers of Central Sudanic. Did they acquire them during the eastward stage of such a detour

around the equatorial forest? There is further evidence favoring this interpretation: around Lake Victoria, where the southward turn must have been made, we find the sites that have yielded Urewe ware.

It is appropriate at this point to emphasize the significance of the Urewe sites in the Great Lakes region. First, these Early Iron Age sites are geographically closest to the region northwest of Lake Albert that is proposed here as the homeland of the culture. Second, the carbon-14 evidence shows that Urewe pottery is the oldest of all Early Iron Age ceramics. Third, it is in the Urewe

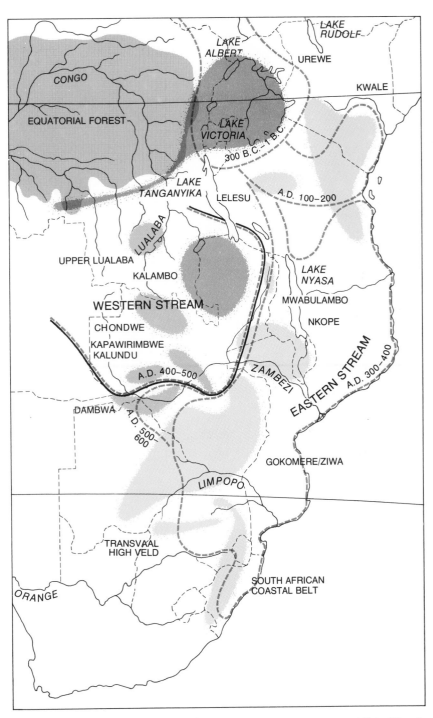

PROGRESS OF EASTERN STREAM, from initial Urewe settlements around Lake Victoria to the final Early Iron Age coastal thrust south of the Limpopo River, is divisible into two successive phases. The first is a movement southward and eastward in the second and third centuries A.D. that produced the Lelesu and Kwale groups of sites. The second and far more extensive movement was southward in the fourth and fifth centuries and produced the Mwabulambo, Nkope, Gokomere/Ziwa, Transvaal high-veld and South African coastal-belt groups. Starting in the fifth century and continuing in the sixth, an eastern movement by western-stream groups produced the Upper Lualaba, Chondwe, Kapwirimbwe and Kalundu groups, and an eastern-stream movement in the sixth and seventh centuries produced the Dambwa group.

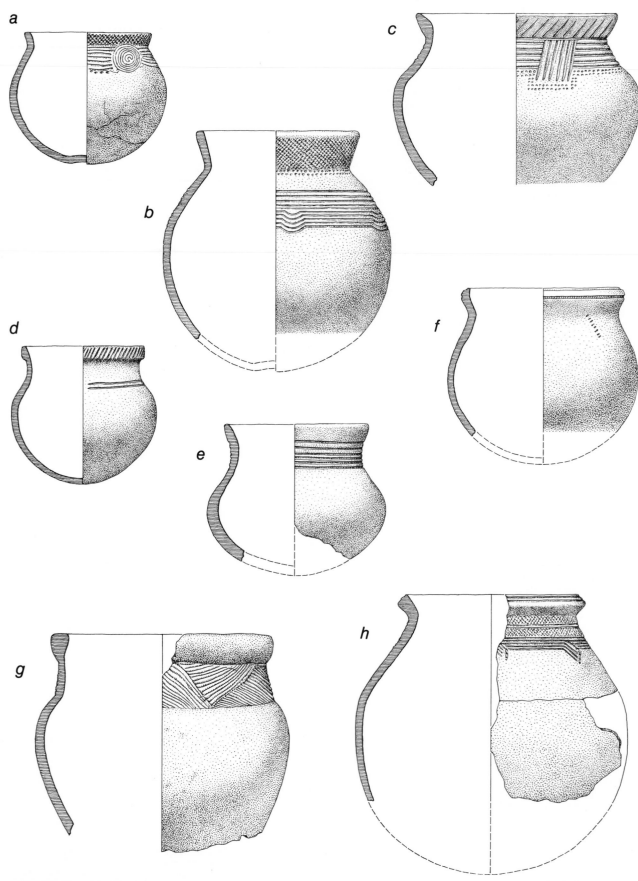

EARLY IRON AGE POTTERY from eight regions of subequatorial Africa shows strikingly similar forms, although details of decoration, lip finish and constriction of neck differ. The first example (*a*) is a pot from the western Urewe site, Tshikapa. Beside it (*b*) is a pot from one of the Lake Victoria Urewe sites. The four eastern-stream pots represent sites in the Nkope group (*c*), the Dambwa group (*d*), the Transvaal high-veld group (*e*) and the South African coastal-belt group (*f*). One western-stream example is shown (*g*); it is from a site in the Kapwirimbwe group. The largest of the eight (*h*) is from a site in the Kalambo group, whose stream relations remain uncertain.

wares that one finds preserved the greatest number of features that may be called ancestral.

Thus there is a striking similarity between the archaeological evidence that gives the Urewe sites a position early in the prehistory of the Early Iron Age culture and the linguistic evidence cited by Heine in support of an early eastward spread of the Bantu languages. I think it is a plausible further step to suggest that the language of the Urewe potters and their descendants was a Bantu dialect derived from those that spread along the northern margin of the equatorial forest to the vicinity of Lake Albert at a relatively early date. The direct modern descendants of these early dialects are Nyali and Mbuti, spoken today in a part of extreme northeastern Zaïre, where pottery is still made in an Early Iron Age style and where neighboring peoples still speak Central Sudanic languages. Both archaeology and linguistics therefore point to the area northwest of Lake Albert as the place where Early Iron Age culture underwent its formative processes. It is unfortunate that the archaeology of the region remains virtually unknown.

Some Bantu-speaking people appear to have reached the savanna south of the equatorial forest by a more westerly route leading directly south from the Cameroon homeland along or close to the Atlantic coast. It is therefore open to question whether the Early Iron Age Bantu dialect hypothesized above was spoken only by those who eventually made up the eastern stream or by all the Early Iron Age migrants. Specifically, could the people of the western stream have acquired a Bantu dialect independently? Such an independent tongue could have been derived from the southward spread of Bantu speech by a westerly route. That such was the case seems highly probable, at least in some areas. If my dating of the easterly spread of Bantu across the northern fringe of the forest barrier is even approximately correct, then at about the same time when an Early Iron Age presence is demonstrable in the southwestern savanna the carriers of the culture must have spoken western Bantu dialects. Loan words support this contention.

Loan words from Central Sudanic languages have been detected in the modern Bantu dialects spoken in areas initially colonized by migrants of the Early Iron Age western stream. Indeed, both domestic cattle and the Central Sudanic loan words related to them can be shown to have entered much of southern Africa with the western stream. Similarly, the ceramic tradition of the western stream shows strong relations with Urewe pottery. As an example, consider the Tshikapa site. The finds here may well represent an early spread of the Urewe pottery tradition (perhaps ac-

companied by a full Early Iron Age smithing-and-farming economy) to the territory in northwestern Angola where the western stream subsequently arose. There contact could have been established with those speakers of Bantu dialects who had spread southward from the Cameroon homeland.

Archaeological evidence of this early southward spread in the extreme west is found in two areas. First, pottery that resembles Early Iron Age wares is found on the island of Fernando Po in associa-

tion with a Neolithic industry characterized by finely polished stone tools that may have been hafted for use as either axes or hoes. Second, similar polished stone tools have been found in the region around the mouth of the Congo River, in association with pottery that is less ornamented than most Early Iron Age wares; the Congo sites are dated at about 200 B.C.

We do not know whether the Neolithic people of Fernando Po and the lower Congo had any domestic animals. The

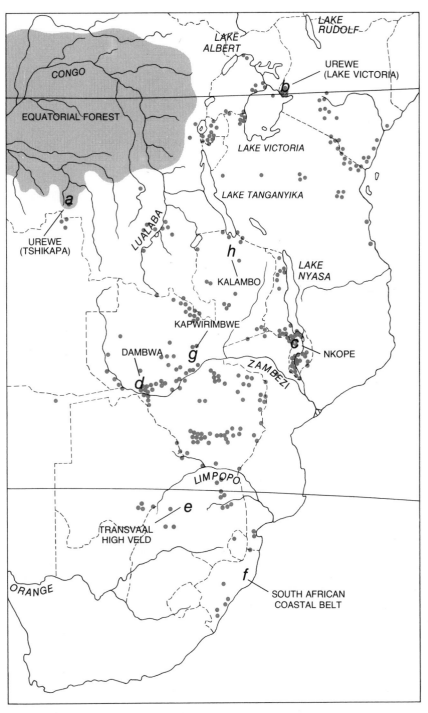

EARLY IRON AGE SITES, now numbering more than 350, are shown in relation to the modern political boundaries of subequatorial Africa. The eight groups of sites that yielded the examples of Early Iron Age pottery illustrated on the opposite page are named and located.

difficulties of moving herds through the equatorial forest suggest that the Congo people, at least, were not herdsmen. A possible exception, however, is the herding of goats. Whereas the Bantu words for cattle and sheep are probably Central Sudanic in origin, the word for goat is common to almost all Bantu languages, which suggests that goats were already a part of the agricultural economy in the Bantu homeland in Cameroon. In any event these coastal users of Neolithic tools may have practiced the variety of tropical and subtropical agriculture that concentrates on root crops such as the yam rather than on cereals. Whether or not they were Bantu-speakers pushing south from Cameroon, they were certainly a people having only a premetallurgical technology. Whether and to what extent they were farmers and herders has not yet been conclusively demonstrated.

These premetallurgical people reached the southern fringe of the equatorial forest belt along the lower reaches of the Congo. They did not, however, penetrate the opener savanna of northern Angola. Indeed, the Angolan grasslands may already have been occupied by full-fledged Early Iron Age herdsmen and grain growers who had bypassed the forest barrier by following the Great Lakes route, bringing with them a Urewe-related pottery tradition such as the one found at Tshikapa. One may envisage a meeting and fusion of the two Bantu-speaking populations: the Great Lakes group now practicing metallurgy, herding flocks and raising cereal crops, and the coast travelers still using stone tools and planting tubers. Perhaps it was this fusion that gave rise, at about the beginning of the Christian

Era, to the Bantu culture of the Kongo area in northern Angola, a culture that soon afterward spread to the more southerly highlands of Angola and South West Africa.

A final expansion of this western stream of Early Iron Age culture led migrants eastward from the highlands into west-central Zambia and southeastern Zaïre, where their presence is attested in the archaeological record beginning in about A.D. 500. It was at this point that the people of the western stream made contact with those of the eastern stream along a common boundary in central Zambia and northern Rhodesia.

In describing the progression of the western stream I have skipped the time when the people of the eastern stream were expanding rapidly southward from their initial bases in southern Kenya and northern Tanzania. Let us turn back and consider the routes the eastern stream followed in reaching the regions farther to the south. Here the archaeological evidence is more comprehensive, and one can map the general trends, notably the thrust through Malawi and eastern Zambia to Rhodesia and the Transvaal between A.D. 300 and 400, followed about 200 years later by a further spread into southwestern Zambia.

Carbon-14 dates indicate that the eastern stream was well established in Zambia and Rhodesia for a significant period before the eastward movement of the western stream established contact between the two. In its early stages the eastern stream appears to have lacked certain elements of the full-fledged Early Iron Age culture. Among these were possession of cattle and of

some sophisticated metallurgical techniques at a time when both were in the hands of the people of the western stream. The greater western-stream cultural inventory may be attributable, at least in part, to an innovative period in the Kongo area following the fusion of peoples that gave rise to the western stream.

The form of Bantu spoken by the people of the eastern stream was evidently a dialect derived from the early eastward spread of proto-Bantu from Cameroon to the Great Lakes region, enriched along the way by a number of Central Sudanic loan words relating particularly to agricultural and metallurgical technology. Dalby, Heine and others, however, have demonstrated conclusively that virtually all the modern Bantu dialects spoken in the eastern half of the Bantu linguistic area are in fact western in derivation. The distribution of these dialects, which Heine has named the Eastern Highland Group, does not coincide with the distribution of the archaeological remains identifiable with the Early Iron Age eastern stream. Instead it coincides to a remarkable degree with the archaeological distribution of later Iron Age industries.

As we have seen, these industries first appear in the archaeological record of eastern Africa during the 11th century A.D. and show connections with the region farther to the west. Indeed, the area Heine postulates as being the source of the Eastern Highland Group of dialects is almost exactly identical with the one I consider to be the homeland of many of the cultural innovations that distinguish the later Iron Age of subequatorial Africa from its predecessors. The modern distribution of the Eastern Highland languages is thus due to a second spread of Bantu speech overlying that of the Early Iron Age.

We can therefore see what a marked degree of similarity there is between the archaeological sequence of the Iron Age in subequatorial Africa and the linguistic evidence for the spread and development of the Bantu languages and their speakers. In this discussion it has been necessary to view the Iron Age Bantu-speakers alone, with little reference to the other peoples with whom they interacted. One should not, however, forget that the processes of population movement and settlement I have been describing unfolded in territory that was already occupied by a diverse population of earlier peoples, whose own distinctive life-styles were well adapted to the environment. It is not possible to take up here the substantial contributions—genetic, cultural, economic and technological—made by these earlier groups to the Iron Age peoples who eventually displaced them and who today are the major element in the population of subequatorial Africa.

DAMBWA POT, uncovered during the excavation of an Early Iron Age house at the type site, Dambwa, near Livingstone in southern Zambia, was partially buried by mud that had fallen from the house wall. Scale in foreground measures inches; beyond it at each end are the charred remains of two fallen wood poles that had supported the wall. Floor is made of puddled earth.

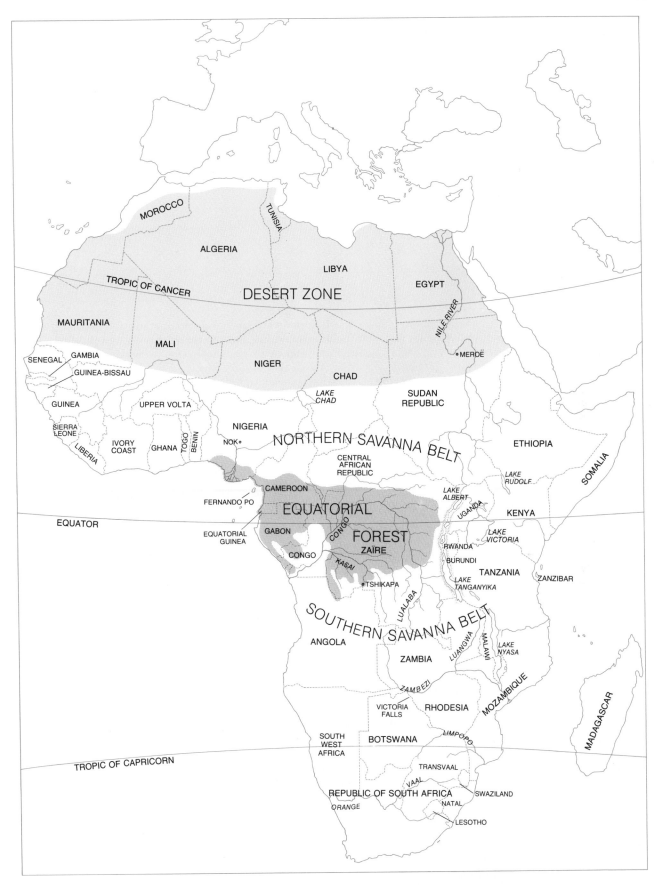

MAP content labels:
MOROCCO, TUNISIA, ALGERIA, LIBYA, EGYPT, TROPIC OF CANCER, DESERT ZONE, MAURITANIA, MALI, NIGER, CHAD, SUDAN REPUBLIC, NILE RIVER, MEROË, SENEGAL, GAMBIA, GUINEA-BISSAU, GUINEA, UPPER VOLTA, LAKE CHAD, SIERRA LEONE, LIBERIA, IVORY COAST, GHANA, TOGO, BENIN, NIGERIA, NOK, NORTHERN SAVANNA BELT, CENTRAL AFRICAN REPUBLIC, ETHIOPIA, SOMALIA, LAKE RUDOLF, CAMEROON, LAKE ALBERT, FERNANDO PO, EQUATORIAL, UGANDA, KENYA, EQUATOR, GABON, CONGO, FOREST, ZAÏRE, LAKE VICTORIA, EQUATORIAL GUINEA, CONGO, KASAI, RWANDA, BURUNDI, TSHIKAPA, LUALABA, TANZANIA, LAKE TANGANYIKA, ZANZIBAR, SOUTHERN SAVANNA BELT, ANGOLA, ZAMBIA, LUANGWA, MALAWI, LAKE NYASA, ZAMBEZI, MOZAMBIQUE, VICTORIA FALLS, RHODESIA, MADAGASCAR, SOUTH WEST AFRICA, BOTSWANA, LIMPOPO, TROPIC OF CAPRICORN, TRANSVAAL, VAAL, SWAZILAND, REPUBLIC OF SOUTH AFRICA, NATAL, ORANGE, LESOTHO

MAJOR GEOGRAPHICAL BARRIERS that inhibit north-south movement in Africa are the great desert zone along the Tropic of Cancer and the belt of equatorial forest that extends eastward almost to the shores of Lake Albert and Lake Tanganyika. Between the forest and the desert is a zone of savanna: the Sudanic belt. At its south- ern edge the equatorial forest gives way to a similar zone of savanna. The two grasslands meet in the vicinity of Lake Victoria. It was from this general region that the Early Iron Age culture of Africa began its subequatorial spread about 2,000 years ago. Political subdivisions appear on the map only where the author makes reference to them.

9

Pidgin Languages

by Robert A. Hall, Jr.
February 1959

*These humble by-products of colonialism are still useful
in contacts between peoples. Far from haphazard
grammatically, they at times evolve into national
languages called creoles*

Since the time of Columbus the course of history has largely been set by the growth of European commerce and power in the rest of the world. One much-misunderstood by-product of this historical process has been the birth, in nearly every Oriental, African and American region visited or colonized by Westerners, of a simplified form of speech, used in contacts with the native population: the so-called pidgin languages. Today, despite a certain amount of well-meant disapproval, the importance of some varieties of pidgin is increasing.

To those who speak European languages, pidgin sounds like a ludicrous mispronunciation of their own tongues; for that reason it is often castigated as a "bastard lingo" or "gibberish." Common parlance has made "pidgin" an opprobrious term for any formless speech, such as the broken-English "No tickee, no washee" attributed to Chinese laundrymen. I have even heard a professor apply the word to the language of his freshman students, simply because they wrote unimaginatively and overworked a few clichés. But investigations in Haiti, Melanesia and elsewhere have shown that real pidgin languages are far more than half-learned versions of European speech. They are languages in their own right. Their sounds and grammar have the internal consistency requisite to any stable system of communication. And whether we like them or not they are probably here to stay, for they have their own humble, but useful, function in society.

Pidgin is not the only form of mixed language. To understand the stages through which such forms of speech develop, we must make a three-way distinction between the "lingua franca," the "pidgin language" and the "creolized

language." A lingua franca is any tongue serving as a means of communication among groups that have no other language in common; for example, English in India and the Philippines. A pidgin language is a lingua franca that in the course of its adoption has become simplified and restructured. The reduced language which results from this process is

nobody's native language, but the languages of its speakers considerably influence its vocabulary and other features. Occasionally users of a pidgin language will cease to speak their native tongue and come to rely upon the pidgin entirely. In such a community children will grow up speaking pidgin as their sole language. When a pidgin is pressed into

PIDGIN AND CREOLE LANGUAGES are spoken at many points of contact between native peoples and colonial traders or rulers. Lingua Franca, the oldest known pidgin,

service as a native language, its vocabulary must greatly expand to accommodate its users' everyday needs. A reduced language, when thus re-expanded, is called a creolized language (the creole languages of Haiti and other Caribbean areas are typical).

Pidgin and creolized languages have arisen many times in history. The earliest recorded pidgin, which has given its name to the whole genus of international languages, is the original Lingua Franca, based on southern French and the Ligurian dialect of Italian and used in the Middle Ages by western Europeans ("Franks") in the eastern Mediterranean. During the epoch of colonization, as Europeans came into contact with aboriginal populations, many pidgin forms of Portuguese, Spanish, French and English became common. It is said that there was, or is, a Pidgin Portuguese in every region colonized by Portugal. Separate varieties of Pidgin English arose in North America, China, West Africa, Australia and the Pacific; in the latter region subtypes have arisen in Hawaii, New Guinea and the Solomon Islands.

Pidginized varieties of French are found in North Africa and New Caledonia.

Pidginization has occurred not only with European but also with non-European languages, as in the case of the "Chinook Jargon" based on the Chinook Indian language and spoken in fur-trading days in the U. S. Northwest. We may also cite Bazaar Malay in Southeast Asia, Swahili in Central Africa, the Pidgin Motu of Papua, Tupí-Guaraní (the so-called Lingua Gêral or "general language") in Brazil, and the Fanaga-Lò or "Kitchen Kaffir" in South Africa.

The best-known creolized languages derive from French and are spoken in Louisiana, Haiti, the Lesser Antilles, Réunion and Mauritius. English-based creole languages also exist: among them are the Gullah of the Sea Islands off South Carolina, the Taki-Taki of Dutch Guiana and the Negro English of the West Indies. Pidgin Spanish, strongly influenced by Portuguese, gave rise to the Papiamentu Creole of Curaçao and neighboring islands. The Afrikaans or "Cape Dutch" of South Africa, which is much simpler than Netherlands Dutch,

may be another creolized language, arising out of an earlier Pidgin Dutch used between settlers and natives, and adopted by white children growing up in South Africa.

People who wish to denigrate pidgin languages sometimes point out that they are not written, the implication being that any unwritten language is an unlicked bear cub, an unintelligible jargon never submitted to the necessary discipline of the schools. This reflects a basic misunderstanding of the nature of language. Most of the languages spoken by men throughout history (and before it) have never been reduced to writing, but they are no less languages. On the other hand, many modern pidgin and creole languages are quite regularly written and are even used in newspapers and education. Languages, pidgin or otherwise, are orderly by definition. Writing is no more than an external representation of most (not all) of the structure of a language.

The most orderly representation of a language is a spelling based on its pho-

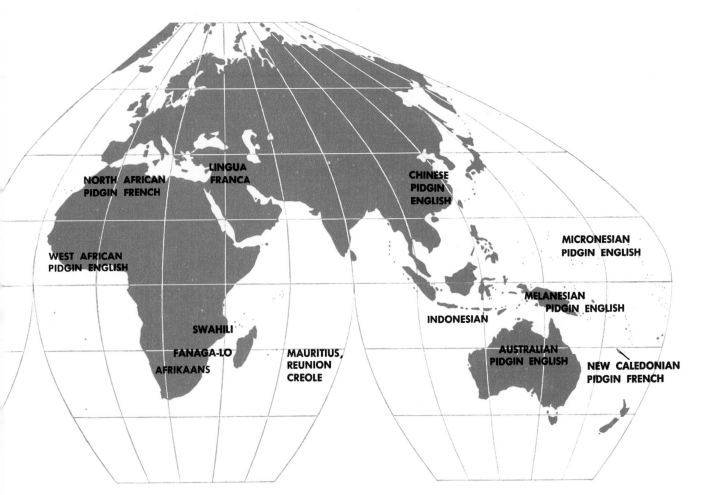

was based on French and Italian. Lingua Gêral, Chinook Jargon, Swahili, Fanaga-Lò and Indonesian have a non-European basis. Gullah and Taki-Taki stem from English, Papiamentu from Spanish and those which are here specified as creoles from French.

nemes, or functional units of sound. Nothing but confusion can result from attempts to render pidgin languages in a botched form of traditional English or French spelling. In this article I adhere strictly to phonemic spellings. For example, the Melanesian Pidgin English sentence meaning "I have three books" is "mi gat trifela buk," not "me got t'ree-fellow book." A Haitian Creole proverb meaning "He who gave the blow forgets, he who bears the scar remembers" would be "Bay-kal blié, pòté-mak sôjé," not the mock-French "Baille-calle 'blier, porter-marque songer." Readers interested in the derivation of the pidgin and creole words that I have spelled phonemically will find them in the tables beginning on this page. Phonemic spellings have been devised (mainly by missionaries) for a number of pidgin and creolized languages. This trend should be encouraged wherever possible, if only to enforce recognition of the fact that pidgin words and sounds are things in themselves and not bungled attempts to pronounce another language.

In general the phonemic systems of pidgin and creolized tongues show a certain amount of simplification. Vowel structure is often reduced to five vowels represented by "a," "e," "i," "o," "u" (pronounced as in Italian). Most French-based creoles have lost the group of French vowels pronounced with the lips rounded but with the tongue in the front of the mouth. In Haitian Creole the French word "culture" becomes "kilti" and "bleu" becomes "blé." Virtually all English-based pidgins lack the voiced and unvoiced sounds represented by "th" in English spelling: in Melanesian Pidgin "this" is "disfela" and "three" is "trifela." Similarly, the English "f" is replaced by "p," the "v" by "b" and the "sh" by "s." Thus "heavy" is "hebi" and "finish" becomes "pinis."

The pronunciation habits of a native

MELANESIAN PIDGIN	DERIVATION	SOURCE WORDS	MEANING		MELANESIAN PIDGIN	DERIVATION
ARS	ENGLISH	ARSE	BOTTOM, BASE, CAUSE, REASON, SOURCE		MAUS	ENGLISH
BAGARIMAP	ENGLISH	BUGGER 'IM UP	WRECK, RUIN		MI	ENGLISH
BALUS	GAZELLE PENINSULA LANGUAGE		PIGEON; AIRPLANE		MIFELA	ENGLISH
BILONG	ENGLISH	BELONG	OF, FOR		MONI	ENGLISH
BUK	ENGLISH	BOOK	BOOK		NADARFELA	ENGLISH
DISFELA	ENGLISH	THIS + FELLOW	THIS		OLSEM	ENGLISH
FAIT	ENGLISH	FIGHT	FIGHT		PATO	PORTUGUESE
FAITIM	ENGLISH	FIGHT + 'IM	STRIKE, BEAT, HIT		PIKININI	PORTUGUESE
FES	ENGLISH	FACE	FACE		PINIS	ENGLISH
GAMAN	ENGLISH	GAMMON	DECEIT; DECEIVE		PLANTIM	ENGLISH
GAT	ENGLISH	GOT	HAVE		PLISBOI	ENGLISH
GODAM	ENGLISH	GOD DAMN	GOLLY		RAUS	GERMAN
GRAS	ENGLISH	GRASS	ANYTHING GROWING BLADE-LIKE OUT OF A SURFACE; GRASS		REDI	ENGLISH
GUDFELA	ENGLISH	GOOD + FELLOW	GOOD		SAVE	PORTUGUESE
HAISIMAP	ENGLISH	H'IST + 'IM + UP	LIFT		SI(N)DAUN	ENGLISH
HARDWOK	ENGLISH	HARD + WORK	WORK HARD		SRANK	GERMAN
HAUS	ENGLISH	HOUSE	HOUSE; ROOM		TALATALA	POLYNESIAN
HEBI	ENGLISH	HEAVY	HEAVY		TA(M)BU	POLYNESIAN
HED	ENGLISH	HEAD	HEAD		TINKTINK	ENGLISH
I—	ENGLISH	HE	(PREDICATE-MARKER)		TOK	ENGLISH
KALABUS	ENGLISH	CALABOOSE (FROM SPANISH CALABOZO)	JAIL		TOKIM	ENGLISH
KARABAU	MALAY		WATER-BUFFALO		TRIFELA	ENGLISH
KIAU	GAZELLE PENINSULA LANGUAGE		EGG		YU	ENGLISH
KING	ENGLISH	KING	KING		YUFELA	ENGLISH
KLIR	ENGLISH	CLEAR	CLEAR		YUMI	ENGLISH
LONG	ENGLISH	ALONG	TO, AT, WITH, BY			

MELANESIAN PIDGIN ENGLISH vocabulary in this chart includes all the words of this language mentioned in the text, together with their sources and meanings. Although condemned by the United Nations as a colonial relic, Melanesian Pidgin is essential

language often carry over into a pidgin and survive, even for generations, in creoles. In the pidgin and creolized languages spoken in the Americas by the descendants of West African slaves the "r" at the end of a syllable is generally lost, as in the case of the Haitian "pòté" ("to carry," from the French "porter"). In Taki-Taki an older stratum of words has lost the "r" (*e.g.*, "gódo" for "gourd"), but newer borrowings from the English or Dutch retain the "r" (*e.g.*, "forku" for "fork"). The Cantonese Chinese merged "r" with "l," as in the Chinese Pidgin English "veli" ("very").

In Melanesian languages the con-

SOURCE WORDS	MEANING
MOUTH	MOUTH
ME	I, ME
ME + FELLOW	WE, US (NOT INCLUDING THE HEARER)
MONEY	MONEY
NOTHER + FELLOW	ANOTHER
ALL THE SAME	THUS, SO
PATO	DUCK
PEQUENINO (LITTLE)	CHILD
FINISH	ALREADY
PLANT + 'IM	BURY
POLICE + BOY	POLICE-BOY, NATIVE POLICEMAN
'RAUS (OUT!)	GET OUT
READY	READY
SABE (HE KNOWS)	KNOW
SIT DOWN	SIT, BE LOCATED
SCHRANK	CHEST OF DRAWERS
(FRIEND)	PROTESTANT
TABU	PROHIBITION; FORBIDDEN
THINK-THINK	OPINION, THOUGHT
TALK	SPEAK; SPEECH
TALK + 'IM	SPEAK TO, ADDRESS
THREE + FELLOW	THREE
YOU	YOU (SG.)
YOU + FELLOW	YOU (PL.)
YOU + ME	WE, US (INCLUDING THE HEARER)

to social unity on the multilingual island of New Guinea, and is now used in its schools.

sonants "b," "d" and "g" often begin with a nasal sound: "mb," "nd," "ng." Those who speak Melanesian carry this peculiarity over into Melanesian Pidgin, where "tabu" ("prohibition" or "forbidden") is usually "tambu," and "sidaun" ("sit" or "be located") is frequently "sindaun." Many combinations of consonants are difficult for the Melanesian, and he will insert an extra vowel into sound clusters such as "kl," "pl," "br" and "ls"; thus "klir" ("clear") often sounds like "kalír" or "kilír," and "olsem" ("so" or "thus") like "olasem." The younger generation, however, is learning to omit these interpolated vowels.

The same linguistic snobs who make sport of unwritten pidgin and creolized languages are likely to declare that these tongues have no grammar. Behind this criticism, too, lurks a misapprehension of the nature of language. Every language has a grammar, that is, a stock of linguistic forms and principles for using them. All men, no matter how primitive in other respects, speak fully structured languages. Grammar is a far older and more firmly established invention than the grammar book. One critic has asked: "How can it be said that pidgin has a grammar when it has no tenses, cases or numbers?" It is true that many forms of pidgin lack these familiar features of European grammar, but they have other devices to make up for them.

Chinese Pidgin, for instance, adds the suffix "-pisi" ("piece") to all numerals, as in "tupisi man" ("two men") and "forpisi tebal" ("four tables"). In Chinese Pidgin the suffix "-said" indicates place where, and the suffix "-taim" indicates time when. Both are added to nouns and pronouns: "hi haussaid" ("at his house"), "doksaid" ("at the dock"), "maisaid" ("where I am"), "hwattaim?" ("when?"), "distaim" ("now"). In Melanesian Pidgin there are three suffixes that serve to indicate the form and function of words. The suffix "-fela," when added to the pronouns "mi" ("I" or "me") and "yu" ("you," singular), forms the plural: "mifela" ("we" or "us"), "yufela" ("you," plural). Another suffix, also pronounced "-fela" but distinct from the foregoing, characterizes demonstratives, indefinites, numerals and one-syllable adjectives: "disfela" ("this"), "nadarfela" ("another"), "tufela" ("two"), "gudfela" ("good"). The suffix "-im" shows that a verb is transitive: "tok" means "speak," but "tokim" is "speak to" or "address"; "fait" is "fight," but "faitim" means "strike," "beat," "hit."

Some pidgin and creolized languages

employ grammatical devices that appear quite peculiar to the Western mind. In languages with West African elements, prefixes replace suffixes as indicators of grammatical relationships. Haitian Creole, for instance, has no verb tenses in our sense. Instead verbs are distinguished by a set of prefixes indicating the continuity or completion of the action performed: while "mwê châté" means "I sing," mwê ap-châté" means "I am singing" and "mwê fèk-châté" means "I have just sung."

Sometimes parts of speech, as well as the process of adding suffixes or prefixes, derive from the original native language of the speakers. Consider the pronouns of Melanesian Pidgin. Those who speak this language distinguish between "yumi" ("we" or "us," including the hearer) and "mifela" ("we" or "us," excluding the hearer). This reflects the distinction between the "inclusive" and "exclusive" first-person plural found in native Melanesian languages. Melanesian Pidgin also employs phrases formed of pronoun plus numeral, such as "mi trifela" ("the three of us") and "yu tufela" ("the two of you"). These correspond to special forms in Melanesian languages called "dual" (referring to two) or "trial" (referring to three).

Pidgins and creoles, with their simplified use of grammatical endings, rely heavily on word order to indicate the relationship between words. Simple juxtaposition serves to characterize many types of phrases; in Melanesian Pidgin, for example, a noun following another noun serves to tell some characteristic or purpose of what is referred to by the first noun: "haus moni" is "house for money," *i.e.*, "bank," and "tok gaman" is "talk characterized by deceit," *i.e.*, "falsehood." A similar combination occurs in Haitian Creole, but with the second noun indicating a possessor: "pitit rwa" means "children of a king," and "lakay mwê" means "house of me" or "my house." In Melanesian Pidgin possession is indicated by a phrase introduced by the preposition "bilong" ("of"): "pikinini bilong king" means "a king's children," and "haus bilong mi" means "my house." In Chinese Pidgin possession is shown simply by a noun or pronoun preceding the noun modified: "dat master poni" ("that master's pony") or "yu legan" ("your legs").

Those who speak Western European languages expect every full sentence to contain a predicate whose main element is a verb. But in Melanesian Pidgin and Haitian Creole (as in many other languages) the core of the predicate may

STORI BILONG TESEUS NA ARIADNE

Pidgin languages are a serviceable and, indeed, expressive mode of communication: despite their small vocabularies (and the consequent need to use circumlocutions) they can convey information, or spin a yarn, as readily as other tongues. To bring home this point, as well as to provide teaching materials for the schools of Australian New Guinea, Robert A. Hall, Jr., the author of this article, has rendered a number of familiar myths and legends into Melanesian Pidgin. This is Hall's version of the myth of Theseus and Ariadne. It tells how Minos, King of Crete, exacted from Athens a tribute of seven youths and seven maidens ("meris"), to be fed to the bull-headed Minotaur, who dwelt in the celebrated Labyrinth; how Theseus, an Athenian prince, joined the party of victims and, abetted by the Cretan princess Ariadne, slew the Minotaur, escaping the Labyrinthine maze by winding up a magic thread; and how Theseus returned with Ariadne to Athens but by failing to display the agreed-upon sign of victory (a white sail) caused his father, King Aegeus, to kill himself from grief.

I-gat wanfela ailan i-stap, nem bilong em Krit. Disfela ailan i-klostu liklik long kantri (bigples) ol i-kolim Gris. I-no klostu tru, na i-no longwe tru. Spos man i-kirap long Niu Gini, na i-laik go long Niu Briten, aitink i-longwe olsem.

Nau longtaim bifo, i-gat wanfela king i-stap long ailan Krit; nem bilong disfela king, Minos. Disfela King Minos i-no gudfela king. Em i-strongfela moa, oltaim oltaim em i-laik fait. Nau long Gris i-gat wanfela siti (taun, bigfela ples) ol i-kolim Athens. King Minos i-krosim king bilong Athens na bigfela fait i-kamap. Minos i-kisim ol man bilong fait bilong em, i-brukim bigsolwata, i-go long Athens; ol i-mekim bigfela fait, winim ol man bilong Athens. King bilong Athens (nem bilong em Aigaios) i-mas tok: "Yufela winim mi finish." Minos i-tokim em: "Spos yu no laik mi kisim siti bilong yu, bagarimapim haus, pulim meri, kukim olgeda samting, orait, yu mas mekim olsem mi tok nau. Olgeda yia yu mas selim sevenfela strongfela, yangfela man, na sevenfela naisfela yangfela meri, i-kam long Krit, baimbai mi givim ol long Minotauros, bilong em i-kaikai."

Disfela Minotauros i-wankain bulmakau man nogud, i-olsem masalai, i-gat faia i-kamaut long nos bilong em, na i-save kaikai man. Minos i-putim Minotauros i-stap long bigfela haus tumas, ol i-kolim Labirintos, i-gat plenti handat rum, plenti pasij. Spos man i-go insaid long disfela haus, em i-no kan save fashin bilong kamaut gen, na i-lus olgeda, i-go nabaut nabaut nabaut, bihain Minotauros i-lukim, i-kaikai. Disfela bigfela haus Labirintos, bifo wanfela man i-gat save, nem bilong em Dedalos, i-wokim; mi tokim yufela finish long stori bilong Dedalos na pikinini man bilong em, Ikaros.

Orait, yufela kan tinktink, ol man bilong Athens i-no laikim disfela toktok bilong King Minos. Ol i-foldaun long ni bilong em, ol i-kraiaut: "Yu marimari long mifela!" Tasol Minos i-no laik marimari. Em i-tok: "Spos yufela no mekim olsem mi tok, orait, mi kam bak gen, kisim Athens, kilim olgeda man, pulim olgeda meri, bagarimapim tru olgeda samting." Orait, nau olgeda yia ol i-bungim olgeda yangfela man meri, ol i-kisim sevenfela yangfela man (i-no gat man i-strongfela moa) na sevenfela yangfela meri (i-no gat meri i-naisfela moa), bilong selim i-go long Krit, kaikai bilong Minotauros. Ol i-sel i-go long Krit nau, long blakfela ship i-gat blakfela sel.

Nau King Aigaios, king bilong siti Athens, i-gat pikinini man, ol i-kolim Teseus. Long taim Minos i-winim ol man bilong Atenai, aitink Teseus i-gat tenfela yia. Bihain, Teseus i-kamap bigfela, i-gat wanfela ten eit yia finish, na em i-tinktink long bel bilong em: "Mi strongfela man, mi laik go kilim Minotauros." Orait, taim bilong kisim yangfela man meri i-kamap finish, na olgeda yangfela man meri bilong ples i-bung finish, Teseus nau i-kirap, i-tokim papa bilong em, King Aigaios: "Nogud yu kisim sevenfela yangfela man. Yu kisim sikisfela tasol, na mi yet, mi nambaseven." Ol i-hirim disfela toktok bilong Teseus, ol i-kirap nogud, na King Aigaios i-tok: "Kalapa! Bilong wonem yu tok olsem, Teseus! Nogud yu go long Krit, baimbai Minotauros i-kaikai yu. Yu mas stap long ples hia, na bihain, taim mi dai finish, yu king bilong Athens."

Tasol Teseus i-no chenjim tinktink bilong em, na em i-tok: "Nogat! Mi laik go long Krit, kilim disfela bulmakau nogud Minotauros, na bihain mi kam bak gen." Aigaios i-kraiaut, i-olsem longlong man,

tasol Teseus i-tok yet: "Spos mi no go, oltaim oltaim plenti gudfela yangfela man meri bilong Athens i-lus long kaikai bilong disfela bulmakau nogud. Spos mi go, baimbai mi kilim Minotauros finish, na mifela no mas selim yangfela man meri moa." Bel bilong King Aigaios i-hevi tumas, tasol em i-tokim Teseus: "Orait, yu go. Tasol spos yu winim Minotauros na yu kam bak, yu mas chenjim sel bilong ship, putim waitfela sel, baimbai mi save yu orait. Spos ship i-kam bak, i-katim blakfela sel yet, baimbai mi save yu dai finish."

Ol i-kisim sikisfela nadafela yangfela man, na sevenfela yangfela meri, na ol i-kirap nau i-go nau, brukim bigsolwata, na i-go i-go i-go i-go, bihain i-kamap long Krit. King Minos i-kisim ol, bringim ol i-kam long haus bilong em. Fashin bilong Minos i-olsem: ol i-kamap finish, Minos i-givim gudfela kaikai long ol, na long neksfela de em i-selim ol i-go long haus Labirintos, bilong Minotauros i-kaikai ol. Orait, distaim tu Minos i-rediim bigfela kaikai, na ol i-sindaun kaikai. Nau King Minos i-gat pikinini meri, nem bilong em Ariadne. Long disfela taim Ariadne aitink i-gat wanfela ten eit yia, olsem Teseus. Em i-lukim ol yangfela man meri, i-marimari long ol; na i-lukim Teseus, i-laik tru long em. Ariadne i-tinktink: "Mi laik tru long disfela yangfela man, mi no laik em i-dai. Mi laik helpim em." Bihain ol i-go slip, na Minos i-tokim ol: "Tumora mi selim yufela i-go insaid long haus Labirintos."

Long bignait, Ariadne i-go long rum Teseus i-slip long em. Teseus i-no slip yet, em i-tinktink long fashin bilong winim Minotauros. Ariadne i-kamap finish, i-tokim Teseus: "Mi laik tru long yu, na mi no laik Minotauros i-kaikai yu. Mi no laik tru long disfela fashin nogud bilong papa bilong mi. Mi laik ranwe long Krit. Mi bringim disfela tred, mi givim nau long yu. Morbeta yu fasim tred long do bilong haus Labirintos, na bihain yu katim tred i-go wantaim yu, na go go go go go, yu letim tred i-foldaun long graun, baimbai i-makim rod bilong kam bak gen. Bihain, kilim Minotauros finish, yu lukim tred i-stap we, bihainim tred, na long disfela fashin yu kan kam bak autsaid gen. Mi wetim yu klostu long do, na baimbai mi tufela i-ranwe, wantaim ol nadafela yangfela man meri."

Teseus i-tok: "Tinktink bilong yu i-nambawan tru. Mi mekim olsem yu tok." Bihain, moningtaim i-kamap finish, ol i-go long haus Labirintos. Teseus i-tokim ol wantok bilong em: "Nogud yufela go longwe insaid. Morbeta yufela wet klostu long do, na mi go insaid. Bihain, kilim Minotauros finish, mi kam bak gen, na yumi kan ranwe." Ol i-wet klostu long do, na Teseus i-go insaid long haus Labirintos.

Em i-go nabaut nabaut nabaut, tasol i-tanim tred, letim foldaun long graun, bilong em i-kan luksave rod bilong kamaut gen. Bihain Teseus i-hirim bigfela nois, na Minotauros i-ran i-kam long em. Mino-tauros i-bigfela bulmakau man, i-gat faia i-kamaut long nos bilong em; spos disfela faia i-faitim man, man i-kuk kwiktaim tumas. Teseus i-stap klostu long do bilong wanfela rum. Minotauros i-resis i-kam long Teseus, na em i-abrusim Minotauros, i-haid long do bilong disfela rum. Minotauros i-no lukim Teseus, i-fofai long em, na Teseus i-kisim bainat, i-faitim Minotauros long hafsaid klak i-stap long em, kilim Minotauros i-dai.

Kilim Minotauros finish, Teseus i-bihainim tred, i-go bak long do bilong haus Labirintos. Ol i-wetim em, na ol i-askim em: "Yu kilim Minotauros?" Teseus i-tok: "Yes, mi kilim finish." Ol i-go autsaid nau, na Ariadne i-wetim ol. Ariadne i-tok nau: "Mi tokim ol boskru finish, rediim ship na wetim yumi. Morbeta yumi go hariap nau, baimbai papa bilong mi i-save Minotauros i-dai finish, na em i-kros tru long yumi." Teseus i-tok: "Yes, yumi olgeda i-go nau. Bihain, kamap long Athens finish, baimbai yumi tufela i-marit."

Orait, ol i-hariap i-go nau, go bak long ship, na ship i-katim ol i-go long Athens. Tasol sel i-blakfela yet, na Teseus i-lusim tok bilong papa bilong em, ol i-mas chenjim sel. Ol i-no tinktink long disfela samting, na ol i-no chenjim sel. Ship i-kamap klostu long Athens nau, na King Aigaios i-lukim, i-tok: "Sel i-blakfela! Teseus i-dai finish! A, kalapa mi! A! Mi dai nau!" Ai bilong King Aigaios i-tantanim long hed bilong em, na em i-foldaun i-dai tru. Liklik taim nau, Teseus i-kamap long Athens, ol i-tokim em: "Mifela lukim blakfela sel i-stap long ship, mifela tinktink Minotauros i-kaikai yufela olgeda. Papa bilong yu tu, em i-tinktink olsem, na em i-dai nau." Teseus i-sari tumas, em i-no tinktink long putim waitfela sel. Ol i-mekim bigfela seremoni bilong man i-dai, ol i-plantim King Aigaios. Plantim finish, Teseus i-king bilong Athens nau.

Na Ariadne i-olsem wonem? Samfela stori i-tok, em i-kam bak long Athens wantaim Teseus, na Teseus i-maritim em, na bihain Ariadne i-kwin bilong Athens. Tasol samnadafela stori i-tok, Ariadne i-no go long Athens. Ol i-kamap long wanfela ailan, nem bilong em Naksos, na ol i-stap liklik taim long disfela ailan. Bihain, Teseus na ol wantok bilong em i-gowe nau, tasol Teseus i-no tinktink long Ariadne, na Ariadne i-stap nating long ailan Naksos. Bihain wanfela bigdewel, nem bilong em Bakkhos, i-bigdewel bilong wain, em i-kam maritim Ariadne. Wonem stori i-tru? Mi no save.

Em tasol, stori bilong Teseus na Ariadne.

servers are struck by the presence of words from many sources in a pidgin language; Melanesian Pidgin, for example, has borrowings from German ("raus," meaning "get out"; "srank," meaning "chest of drawers"), from native languages ("kiau," meaning "egg"; "balus," meaning "pigeon" or "airplane"), from Malay ("karabau," meaning "water buffalo"), from Polynesian ("talatala," meaning "Protestant"). It even has a few Romance words ("save," meaning "know"; "pikinini," meaning "child"; "pato," meaning "duck"). But a count of the total lexicon reveals that roughly 80 per cent of the Melanesian Pidgin vocabulary is of English origin. In English itself over 50 per cent of the words are from French, Greek, Latin and other non-English sources!

The vocabularies of pidgin languages often contain words revealing the lower-class origin of their first European speakers (Melanesian Pidgin "plantim," meaning "bury"; "kalabus," meaning "jail"), or their nautical calling (Melanesian Pidgin "haisimap," meaning "lift"; Haitian Creole "viré," meaning "turn" or "veer"). Other words seem, to fastidious Europeans, downright indecent: for example, the Melanesian Pidgin "ars," meaning "bottom"; "bagarimapim," meaning "wreck" or "ruin"; "godam," meaning "golly." In native cultures, however, European taboos are not relevant. Moreover, the meaning of the words themselves is often so greatly extended as to lose all inelegance. Thus "ars" not only means "bottom" but also "base," "cause," "reason," "source." The phrase "long ars bilong" is "because of," structurally an exact parallel to the French "à cause de."

The important feature of pidgin vocabularies is their ability to grow and their adequacy to the needs of the situations where they are used. When a pidgin becomes creolized, the vocabulary expands greatly, especially through borrowings from the language of the dominant nation in the region (e.g., Dutch in Taki-Taki and Papiamentu).

How do pidgin languages arise? Usually they spring from situations of casual contact, where a means of easy, informal communication is desired between a dominant foreign group and a subservient native population. No emphasis is laid on "correctness" or completeness. Members of the dominant group often assume that their interlocutors are childlike and must be addressed as children. Hence baby talk and similar simplifications enter into the original

formation of a pidgin. Europeans are quick to assume that the native's first, broken imitation of the foreign speech represents his optimum performance; they reply in the same broken style. When the process of language learning is arrested at this stage, and the use of the resultant simplified structure and vocabulary is institutionalized, a pidgin has been born.

Pidgin languages do not always derive from this kind of master-and-servant relationship. Indeed, they may arise between groups (of traders, for example) that have more or less equal status. But when a pidgin survives beyond the ini-

HAITIAN CREOLE	DERIVATION	SOURCE WORDS	MEANING
AP-CHÂTÉ	FRENCH	APRES (AFTER) + CHANTER (SING)	BE SINGING
BAY	FRENCH	BAILLE	GIVE
BLÉ	FRENCH	BLEU	BLUE
BLIÉ	FRENCH	OUBLIER	FORGET
BÔ	FRENCH	BON	GOOD
CHÂTÉ	FRENCH	CHANTER	SING
FÈK-CHÂTÉ	FRENCH	[NE] FAIT QUE CHANTER (ONLY SINGS)	HAVE JUST SUNG
GASÔ	FRENCH	GARÇON (BOY)	YOUNG MAN; (REGULAR) FELLOW
ISIT	FRENCH	ICI	HERE
KAL	(?)		BLOW
KILTI	FRENCH	CULTURE	CULTIVATION
KÔPLÉZÂS	FRENCH	COMPLAISANCE	COMPLAISANCE
KÔTÂPLASYÔ	FRENCH	CONTEMPLATION	CONTEMPLATION
LAKAY	(?)		HOUSE
LANWIT	FRENCH	LA NUIT (THE NIGHT)	NIGHT
LI	FRENCH	LUI (HIM)	HE, HIM; SHE, HER; IT
MAK	FRENCH	MARQUE	MARK
MWÊ	FRENCH	MOI	I, ME
NÂ	FRENCH	DANS(?)	IN
OU	FRENCH	VOUS	YOU
PA–	FRENCH	PAS	NOT
PASÉ	FRENCH	PASSER	PASS
PITIT	FRENCH	PETITE	CHILD, CHILDREN
PÔTÉ	FRENCH	PORTER	CARRY
RWA	FRENCH	ROI	KING
SÔJÉ	FRENCH	SONGER (THINK, DREAM)	REMEMBER
TÉ–	FRENCH	ÉTAIT (WAS)	(PAST TENSE MARKER)
VA–	FRENCH + WEST AFRICAN	VA (GOES) + VA– (SIGN OF FUTURE)	(FUTURE TENSE MARKER)
VIRÉ	FRENCH	VIRER (VEER)	TURN
YO	FRENCH	(DIALECTAL?)	THEY, THEM; (NOUN PLURALIZER)
ZETWAL	FRENCH	LES ÉTOILES (THE STARS)	STAR

HAITIAN CREOLE vocabulary shows the French origin of most Haitian words cited. Once a contact language between French and Negroes, it is now the native tongue of Haiti.

TAKI-TAKI	DERIVATION	SOURCE WORDS	MEANING
FÓRKU	ENGLISH	FORK	FORK
GÓ	ENGLISH	GO	GO
GÓDO	ENGLISH	GOURD	GOURD
MI	ENGLISH	ME	I, ME
SA–	ENGLISH	SHALL	(FUTURE TENSE PREFIX)
TORN	DUTCH	TORN	TOWER

TAKI-TAKI is spoken by descendants of runaway slaves in Surinam (Dutch Guiana). A creole like Haitian, it too is a native tongue based on pidgin, in this case Pidgin English.

tial stage of contact, when it persists for decades or centuries in intergroup dealings, we can assume that one group wishes to maintain social distance from the other. In the case of Chinese Pidgin English a standoffish attitude characterized both sides, for the Chinese more than matched the Europeans in their sense of national superiority. If only two language groups are involved, the side that feels it suffers loss of status because it speaks pidgin may come to insist on learning the other side's full language; this happened in China after 1900. But where those who speak many native tongues share a single pidgin, questions of status may be outweighed by an overpowering need for a means of communication. In New Guinea, with its multiplicity of tongues, Melanesian Pidgin has become a linguistic cement; without it labor relations and economic life would be impossible.

It is often assumed that a European language furnishes the pidgin vocabulary, while the "native" language supplies the pidgin grammatical structure. Chinese Pidgin English is sometimes called "Chinese spoken with English words." This notion is inexact. Close examination reveals that each form of pidgin adheres to the dominant language in grammar as well as vocabulary. The grammatical categories and types of phrase and clause in Taki-Taki, Chinese Pidgin and Melanesian Pidgin are English; those of the various creoles are North French; those of Papiamentu are Spanish. However, elements of all kinds—sounds, inflections and types of word order—can and do invade pidgin from the native tongues of the subservient group. I have already mentioned elements of Melanesian, Chinese and West African pronunciation in certain pidgins and creoles. With respect to inflection the Chinese Pidgin suffix "-pisi" is clearly

a translation of the Chinese itemizer or numeral classifier meaning "piece," and such a phrase as "Ning-Po mo far" ("beyond Ning-Po") reflects the native Chinese word order.

The creolization of a pidgin language can happen either voluntarily (as in certain modern villages in New Guinea), or involuntarily (as when Caribbean plantation owners deliberately separated slaves of the same language, in order to minimize the danger of conspiracy and revolt). In either case the children of the group speak pidgin as their first language. Thus they extend its range to meet everyday needs, either by developing its inner grammatical resources or by borrowing from outside sources, as Haitian and other creoles have done from French. Creolized languages are often subject to snobbish condemnation. This causes insecurity in their speakers, who in their anxiety commit malapropisms. For example, a Haitian Creole storyteller once said of his characters: "Yo pasé lanwit nâ-kôplézàs zétwal yo" ("they passed the night in the complaisance of the stars"); when what he meant was "kôtâplasyô" ("contemplation").

To date most creolized languages have remained on the level of despised vernaculars. Sometimes, though, a pidgin can become creolized and then, through the accidents of history, attain the status of a universally recognized national language. This is what happened in the case of Indonesian. On Java and elsewhere in the former Dutch East Indies a pidginized form of Malay, known as Bazaar Malay, was widely used as a trade language. With the help of extensive borrowings from Classical Malay, Bazaar Malay became the linguistic vehicle for the new Indonesian nationalism; as such, it was renamed "Bahasa Indonesia" ("Indonesian Language").

Now a generation of native speakers is arising, and Indonesian is developing a national standard, an official literature, and all the other appurtenances of a world language.

In recent years a new school of criticism has begun to condemn pidgin and creole languages because they often function as "status" languages, the use of which sets off a given group as socially inferior. For this reason the United Nations in 1954 called on Australia to "eradicate" pidgin from New Guinea, saying: "Melanesian Pidgin is not only not suitable as a medium of instruction, but has characteristics derived from the circumstances in which it was invented which reflect now outmoded concepts of the relationships between indigenous inhabitants and immigrant groups."

The structures of pidgin languages, although reduced in contrast to "major" languages, are nonetheless clear and consistent once they are analyzed and described in their own terms. The lowly social origin of some vocabulary items is not a justifiable reason for condemnation or ridicule; otherwise we should have to ban such English words as "moist," "petulant" or "crepitate" because they come from inelegant Latin terms. The well-meaning diatribes of anti-colonialists lose sight of the fact that, although pidgins often do serve as means of discrimination, this is not a necessary or essential part of their function. On the other hand, even if it were possible to "abolish" a language by some totalitarian fiat, a slow, costly and immensely difficult process of reeducation would be required. Once creolized, pidgin has become a native language, with full rights to consideration and respect.

To remove the stigma associated with such terms as "pidgin" or "creole," it has been suggested that these languages be re-baptized with names such as "Neo-Melanesian," "Langue Haitienne" or, for Taki-Taki, "Sranan-Tongo" ("Surinam language"). This might be a wise concession. At any rate, it is evident that no amount of puristic or anti-colonialistic condemnation will "eradicate" pidgin or creolized languages. We should be duly respectful of the role of pidgin as a source of social cohesion in multilingual regions. Quite possibly some current forms of pidgin are future national languages in embryo. In all likelihood new pidgins will continue to arise when the situation calls for them, and will either die out when the need is gone, or acquire longer life through the creative process of creolization.

10

The Earliest Precursor of Writing

by Denise Schmandt-Besserat
June 1978

Long before the Sumerians invented writing, accounts in western Asia were kept with clay tokens of various distinctive shapes. It appears that the tokens gave rise to the Sumerian ideographs

What led to writing? The art itself is a good example of what students of the past call independent invention, since systems of writing have evolved in isolation at different times in different parts of the world. For example, one system—the Chinese ideogram—can be traced to its origin in archaic signs engraved on the scapular bones of sheep or the shells of turtles in the second millennium B.C. as a means of asking questions of heaven. Roughly 1,000 years later an entirely independent system of writing arose halfway around the world in Mesoamerica. It combined a simple system of numerical notation with complex hieroglyphs and was principally used to indicate the dates of various events according to an elaborate calendrical system.

Both Chinese and Maya writing were relatively late inventions. Some one system of writing must have been the earliest, and it is from such an initial point that we may begin the search for the antecedents of the art. The credit for being the first to write texts is usually given to the Sumerians of Mesopotamia. By the last century of the fourth millennium B.C. the officials of such Sumerian city-states as Uruk had developed a system of recording numerals, pictographs and ideographs on specially prepared clay surfaces. (A pictograph is a more or less realistic portrayal of the object it is supposed to represent; an ideograph is an abstract sign.)

At Uruk a team of German archaeologists directed by Julius Jordan turned up many examples of these archaic records in 1929 and 1930. The texts, about 1,000 of them, were first analyzed by Adam Falkenstein and his students. Today additional discoveries have in-creased the total number of Uruk and Uruk-style texts to about 4,000, and Falkenstein's pioneer efforts are being continued mainly by Hans J. Nissen of the Free University of Berlin and his associate Margaret W. Green.

Although the clay blanks used by the Uruk scribes are universally referred to as tablets, a word with the connotation of flatness, they are actually convex. Individual characters were inscribed in the clay by means of a stylus made of wood, bone or ivory, with one end blunt and the other pointed. The characters were basically of two kinds. Numerical signs were impressed into the clay; all other signs, pictographs and ideographs alike, were incised with the pointed end of the stylus. The repertory of characters used by the Uruk scribes was large; it is estimated at no fewer than 1,500 separate signs.

Hypotheses about the origin of writing generally postulate an evolution from the concrete to the abstract: an initial pictographic stage that in the course of time and perhaps because of the carelessness of scribes becomes increasingly schematic. The Uruk tablets contradict this line of thought. Most of the 1,500 signs (Falkenstein compiled 950 of them) are totally abstract ideographs; the few pictographs represent such wild animals as the wolf and the fox or items of advanced technology such as the chariot and the sledge. Indeed, the Uruk texts remain largely undeciphered and an enigma to epigraphers. The few ideographic signs that have been identified are those that can be traced back stage by stage from a known cuneiform character of later times to an archaic Sumerian prototype. From the fragmentary textual contents that such identities allow it appears that the scribes of Uruk mainly recorded such matters as business transactions and land sales. Some of the terms that appear most frequently are those for bread, beer, sheep, cattle and clothing.

After Jordan's discovery at Uruk other archaeologists found similar texts elsewhere in Mesopotamia. More were found in Iran: at Susa, at Chogha Mish and as far off as Godin Tepe, some 350 kilometers north of Uruk. In recent years tablets in the Uruk style have been unearthed in Syria at Habuba Kabira and Jebel Aruda, nearly 800 kilometers to the northwest. At Uruk the tablets had been found in a temple complex; most of the others came to light in the ruins of private houses, where the presence of seals and the seal-marked clay stoppers for jars indicate some kind of mercantile activity.

The fact that the Uruk texts contradict the hypothesis that the earliest form of writing would be pictographic has inclined many epigraphers to the view that the tablets, even though they bear the earliest-known writing, must represent a stage in the evolution of the art that is already advanced. The pictographic hypothesis has been revived anew. The fact that no writing of this kind has yet appeared at sites of the fourth millennium B.C. and even earlier is explained away by postulating that the writing of earlier millenniums was recorded exclusively on perishable mediums that vanished long ago, such as parchment, papyrus or wood.

I have an alternative proposal. Research into the first uses of clay in the Near East over the past several years suggests that several characteristics of the Uruk material provide important clues to what kinds of visible symbols actually preceded the archaic Sumerian texts. These clues include the choice of clay as a material for documents, the convex profile of the Uruk tablets and the appearance of the characters recorded on them.

Nuzi, a city site of the second mil-

CLAY TOKENS FROM SUSA, a city site in Iran, are seen in the composite photograph on the opposite page. The tokens, in the collection of the Musée du Louvre, are about 5,000 years old. The five tokens in the top row represent some of the commonest shapes: a sphere, a half-sphere, a disk, a cone and a tetrahedron. The more elaborate tokens in the next row have been marked with incisions or impressions. Unperforated and perforated versions of similar tokens appear in the third and fourth rows. Tokens in the bottom two rows vary in shape and marking; some can be equated with early Sumerian ideographs (*see illustration on pages 86 and 87*).

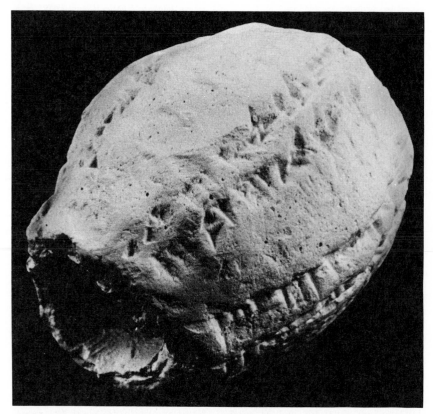

EGG-SHAPED HOLLOW TABLET was found in the palace ruins at Nuzi, a Mesopotamian city site of the second millennium B.C. The cuneiform inscription on its surface lists 48 animals. On being opened the tablet was found to contain 48 counters. The counters were lost before an accurate description had been prepared, but Nuzi texts suggest their use for reckoning.

SPHERICAL BULLA, an envelope of clay with tokens enclosed, was excavated from levels of the third millennium B.C. at Tepe Yahya, a site in south-central Iran halfway between the Indus Valley and lower Mesopotamia. Three tokens (*right*) were enclosed: a cone and two spheres.

lennium B.C. in Iraq, was excavated by the American School of Oriental Research in Baghdad between 1927 and 1931. Nearly 30 years later, reviewing an analysis of the Nuzi palace archives, A. Leo Oppenheim of the Oriental Institute of the University of Chicago reported the existence of a recording system that made use of "counters," or tokens. According to the Nuzi texts, such tokens were used for accounting purposes; they were spoken of as being "deposited," "transferred" and "removed."

Oppenheim visualized a kind of dual bookkeeping system in the Nuzi texts; in addition to the scribes' elaborate cuneiform records the palace administration had parallel tangible accounts. For example, one token of a particular kind might represent each of the animals in the palace herds. When new animals were born in the spring, the appropriate number of new tokens would be added; when animals were slaughtered, the appropriate number of tokens would be withdrawn. The tokens were probably also moved from one shelf to another when animals were moved from one herder or pasture to another, when sheep were shorn and so forth.

The discovery of a hollow egg-shaped tablet in the palace ruins supported Oppenheim's hypothesis. The inscription on the face of the tablet turned out to be a list of 48 animals. The hollow tablet rattled, and when one end of it was carefully opened, 48 tokens were found inside. Presumably the combination of a written list and countable tokens represented a transfer of animals from one palace service to another. Unfortunately we have no accurate description of the tokens; they were subsequently lost.

The Nuzi archives are dated to about 1500 B.C. The great Elamite site, Susa, has levels that are more than 1,500 years older. The digging at Susa, undertaken by French investigators, began in the 1880's and continues to this day. Six years after Oppenheim's 1958 report Pierre Amiet of the Musée du Louvre was able to confirm the existence of a similar accounting system at Susa. The token containers at Susa, unlike the container from Nuzi, were hollow clay spheres. Amiet called them "bullae"; so far about 70 of them have been found. The tokens they contain are clay modeled in a variety of geometric forms, including spheres, disks, cylinders, cones and tetrahedrons.

Amiet's finding was one of great significance; not only did it demonstrate that bullae and tokens were in existence at least a millennium and a half before they appeared at Nuzi but also it showed that they were as old or older than the earliest written records at Uruk. Indeed, it later became clear that the tokens, at least, were very much older.

In 1969 I began a research project

BULLA FROM SUSA shows two rows of surface impressions that match in number and shape the tokens it contained (*foreground*): one large cone, three small cones (*bottom row*) and three disks (*top row*). Tablets with incised representations of tokens probably evolved next.

with the objective of discovering when and in what ways clay first came to be used in the Near East. The making of pottery is of course the most familiar use of clay, but before the appearance of pottery man was making clay beads, modeling clay figurines, molding bricks out of clay and using clay for mortar. As a start on my project I visited museums in the U.S., in Europe and in various Near Eastern cities that had collections of clay artifacts dating back to the seventh, eighth and ninth millenniums B.C. This interval of time, beginning around 11,000 years ago and ending a little more than 8,000 years ago, saw the firm establishment of the first farming settlements in western Asia.

In the museum collections, along with the beads, bricks and figurines I had expected to find, I encountered what was to me an unforeseen category of objects: small clay artifacts of various forms. As I later came to realize, the forms were like those Amiet had found inside his Susa bullae: spheres, disks, cones, tetrahedrons, ovoids, triangles (or crescents), biconoids (double cones joined at the base), rectangles and other odd shapes difficult to describe. Could these artifacts, some of them 5,000 years older than the tokens from Susa, also have served as tokens?

I began to compile my own master catalogue of these oddities, listing each token that was known to have come from a specific site. In summary, I found that whereas all of them were small, measuring on the average from one centimeter to two centimeters in their greatest dimension, many were of two distinct sizes. For example, there were small cones about a centimeter high and large cones three to four centimeters high. There were also thin disks, only three millimeters thick, and thick ones, as much as two centimeters thick. Other variations were evident. For example, in addition to whole spheres I found quarter-, half- and three-quarter spheres. Some of the tokens had additional features. Many were incised with deep lines; some had small clay pellets or coils on them and others bore shallow circular punch marks.

The tokens had all been modeled by hand. Either a small lump of clay had been rolled between the palms of the hands or the lump had been pinched between the fingertips. The clay was of a fine texture but showed no sign of special preparation (such as the addition of tempering substances, a practice in pottery making that enhances hardness after firing). All the tokens had, however, been fired to ensure their durability. Most of them varied in color from buff to red, but some had become gray and even blackish.

I found that the tokens were present in virtually all museum collections of artifacts from the Neolithic period in western Asia. An extreme example of abundance is provided by the early village site of Jarmo in Iraq, first occupied some 8,500 years ago. Jarmo has yielded a total of 1,153 spheres, 206 disks and 106 cones. Reports generally indicate that the excavators found the tokens scattered over the floors of houses located in various parts of a site. If the tokens had once been kept in containers, such as baskets or pouches, these had disintegrated long ago. Nevertheless, there is evidence suggesting that the tokens were segregated from other artifacts and even implying what their function was. The reports indicate that many were found in clusters numbering 15 or more and that the clusters were located in storage areas within the houses.

As I reviewed the museum collections and the related site reports I became increasingly puzzled by the apparent omnipresence of the tokens. They had been found in sites from as far west as Beldibi in what is now southwestern Turkey to as far east as Chanhu Daro in what is now Pakistan. Tokens had even been unearthed at an eighth-millennium-B.C. site on the Nile near Khartoum.

At the same time I found that some site reports failed to take note of the tokens that had been collected, or men-

84

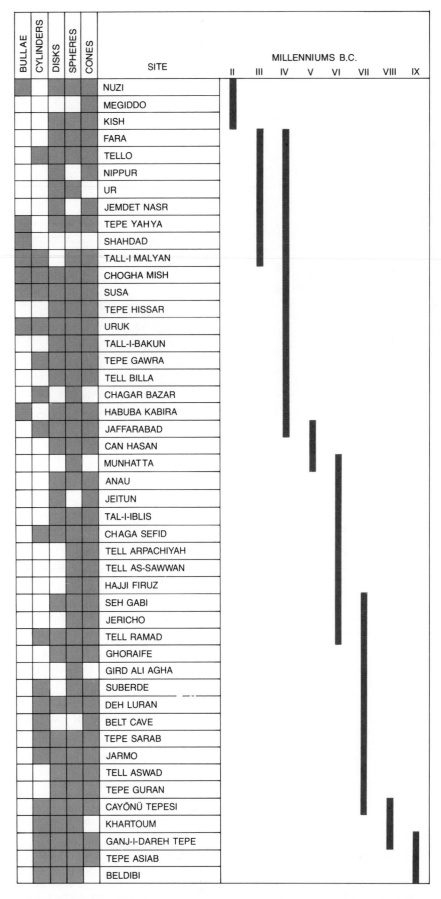

SITES WHERE TOKENS APPEAR represent a span of time from the ninth millennium B.C. to the second. As many as 20 variations on four basic token shapes are present at the earliest sites. Clay envelopes as containers for tokens do not appear before the fourth millennium B.C.

tioned them only casually. When the tokens were noted, the heading might read "objects of uncertain purpose," "children's playthings," "game pieces" or "amulets." As an example, the tokens from Tello in Iraq were interpreted by their discoverer, Henri de Genouillac, as amulets that expressed the residents' desire for "personal identification." Another example appears in Carleton S. Coon's report on Belt Cave in Iran: "From levels 11 and 12 come five mysterious...clay objects, looking like nothing in the world but suppositories. What they were used for is anyone's guess."

The realization that the tokens were all artifacts of the same kind was also hampered because, when they were listed at all in the site reports, they usually appeared under not one heading but several headings depending on their shape. For example, cones have been described as schematic female figurines, as phallic symbols, as gaming pieces and as nails, and spheres were mostly interpreted as marbles or as sling missiles.

Having studied at the École du Louvre, I was familiar with the work of Amiet. Nevertheless, I had compiled a catalogue of hundreds of tokens before I at last realized how much like Amiet's tokens from Susa these far earlier clay artifacts were. At first it seemed impossible that the two groups could be related; a minimum of 5,000 years separated the tokens of Neolithic times from those of Bronze Age Susa. As I extended my investigations to include later clay artifacts, dating from the seventh millennium B.C. to the fourth millennium and later, I found to my surprise that similar clay tokens had been found in substantial numbers at sites representative of the entire time span. Evidently a system of accounting that made use of tokens was widely used not only at Nuzi and Susa but throughout western Asia from as long ago as the ninth millennium B.C. to as recently as the second millennium.

The system appears to have been much the same as many other early, and even not so early, methods of account keeping. Classical scholars are familiar with the Roman system of making "calculations" with pebbles (*calculi* in Latin). Up to the end of the 18th century the British treasury still worked with counters to calculate taxes. For that matter, the shepherds of Iraq to this day use pebbles to account for the animals in their flocks, and the abacus is still the standard calculator in the markets of Asia. The archaic token system of western Asia was if anything only somewhat more complex than its later counterparts.

Considered overall, the system had some 15 major classes of tokens, further divided into some 200 subclasses on the basis of size, marking or fractional vari-

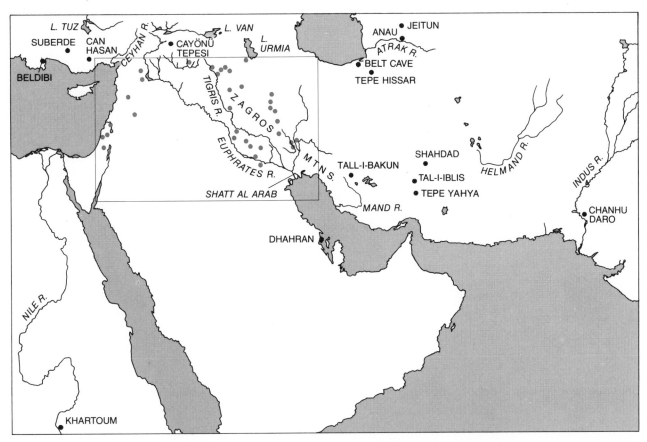

GEOGRAPHICAL DISTRIBUTION of tokens extends from as far north as the Caspian border of Iran to as far south as Khartoum and from Asia Minor eastward to the Indus Valley. Sites identified only by dots (*color*) within a rectangle here are named in the map below.

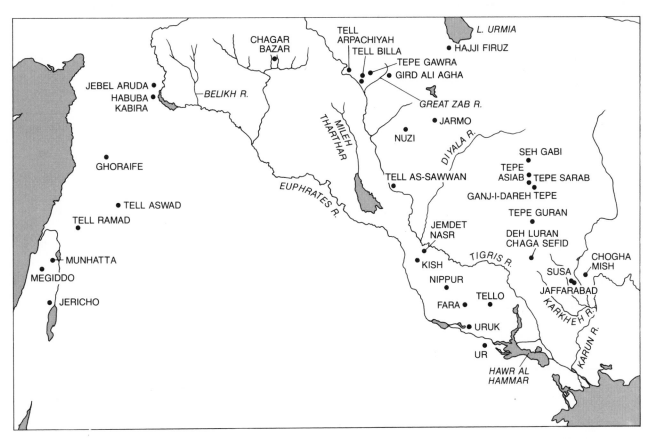

CLUSTERING OF SITES in the drainage of the upper and lower Tigris and the lower Euphrates and in the Zagros region of Iran is more a reflection of the availability of study collections than a measure of the actual extent and frequency of token use in the area.

ation, as in the case of the quarter-, half- and three-quarter spheres. Evidently each particular shape had a meaning of its own; a few appear to represent numerical values and others specific objects, commodities in particular.

It is not necessary to theorize about some of these meanings; a number of ideographs on the Uruk tablets almost exactly reproduce in two dimensions many of the tokens. For example, Uruk arbitrary signs for numerals, such as a small cone-shaped impression for the number one, a circular impression for the number 10 and a larger cone-shaped impression for the number 60 are

matched by tokens: small cones, spheres and large cones. Further examples of ideographs that match tokens include, under the general heading of commodities, the Uruk symbol for sheep (a circle enclosing a cross), matched by disk-shaped tokens incised with a cross, and the Uruk symbol for a garment (a circle enclosing four parallel lines), matched by disk-shaped tokens incised with four parallel lines. Still other examples are ideographs for metal and oil and more clearly pictographic symbols for cattle, dogs and what are evidently vessels; each tablet sign can be matched with a similarly shaped and marked token. In

addition, the forms of many still unread Sumerian ideographs appear to match other tokens.

Why did such a repertory of three-dimensional symbols come into existence? It cannot simply be a coincidence that the first tokens appear early in the Neolithic period, a time of profound change in human society. It was then that an earlier subsistence pattern, based on hunting and gathering, was transformed by the impact of plant and animal domestication and the development of a farming way of life. The new agricultural economy, although it un-

TOKEN TYPE I		II		III		IV		V		VI	
SPHERE		DISK		CONE		TETRAHEDRON		BICONOID		OVOID	
TOKENS	SUMERIAN PICTOGRAPHS	TOKENS	SUMERIAN PICTOGRAPHS	TOKENS	SUMERIAN PICTOGRAPHS	TOKENS	SUMERIAN PICTOGRAPHS	TOKENS	SUMERIAN PICTOGRAPHS	TOKENS	SUMERIAN PICTOGRAPHS
NUMERAL 10		SEAT		NUMERAL 1				GOOD, SWEET		NAIL	
NUMERAL 10		GARMENT, CLOTH		NUMERAL 60				LEGAL DECISION, TRIAL, PEACE		OIL	
NUMERAL 10		GARMENT, CLOTH		NUMERAL 600				HEART, WOMB		ANIMAL (UNIDENTIFIED)	
NUMERAL 100 OR 3,600		WOOL		BREAD		GARMENT, CLOTH		BRACELET, RING			
NUMERAL 36,000		SHEEP		PERFUME				PLACE, COUNTRY			
		EWE									

FIFTY-TWO TOKENS, representative of 12 major categories of token types, have been matched here with incised characters that appear in the earliest Sumerian inscriptions. Most of the inscriptions cannot be read. Here, if the meaning of the symbol is known, the

doubtedly increased the production of food, would have been accompanied by new problems.

Perhaps the most crucial would have been food storage. Some portion of each annual yield had to be allocated for the farm family's own subsistence and some portion had to be set aside as seed for the next year's crop. Still another portion could have been reserved for barter with those who were ready to provide exotic products and raw materials in exchange for foodstuffs. It seems possible that the need to keep track of such allocations and transactions was enough to stimulate development of a recording system.

The earliest tokens now known are those from two sites in the Zagros region of Iran: Tepe Asiab and Ganj-i-Dareh Tepe. The people of both communities seem to have tended flocks and were possibly experimenting with crops around 8500 B.C., although at the same time they continued to hunt game and gather wild plants. The clay tokens they made were quite sophisticated in form. There were four basic types of token: spheres, disks, cones and cylinders. In addition there were tetrahedrons, ovoids, triangles, rectangles, bent coils and schematic animal forms. Subtypes included half-spheres and cones,

spheres and disks with incisions and with punch marks. The set totaled 20 individual symbols.

The Neolithic period and the succeeding Chalcolithic period, or Copper Age, in western Asia lasted about 5,000 years. Over this substantial span one finds surprisingly few changes in the tokens, a fact that may indicate how well suited to the needs of an early agricultural economy this recording system was. In about 6500 B.C., 2,000 years after the rise of the first Zagros farming communities, another Iranian village, Tepe Sarab, began to flourish. The token inventory from excavations at Tepe

VII CYLINDER		IX TRIANGLE		XI RECTANGLE		XIII VESSEL		XIV ANIMAL		XV MISCELLANEOUS	
TOKENS	SUMERIAN PICTOGRAPHS	TOKENS	SUMERIAN PICTOGRAPHS	TOKENS	SUMERIAN PICTOGRAPHS	TOKENS	SUMERIAN PICTOGRAPHS	TOKENS	SUMERIAN PICTOGRAPHS	TOKENS	SUMERIAN PICTOGRAPHS
WOOD						TYPE OF VESSEL		DOG		BED	
		STONE VESSEL		GRANARY		SHEEP'S MILK VESSEL		COW			
		METAL				TYPE OF VESSEL		LION			
		HILL				TYPE OF VESSEL					
				MAT, RUG							

equivalent word in English appears. The Sumerian numerical symbols equated with the various spherical and conical tokens are actual impressions in the surface of the tablet. In two instances (sphere) incised lines are added; in a third (cone) a circular punch mark is added.

Sarab shows no increase in the number of main types and an increase in subtypes from 20 only to 28, among them a four-sided pyramid and a stylized ox skull that is probably representative of cattle.

Perhaps it was during the Chalcolithic period that the agricultural surpluses of individual community members came to be pooled by means of taxes in kind, with the supervision of the surplus put into the hands of public officials such as temple attendants. If that is the case, the need to keep track of individual contributions evidently failed to bring any significant modification in the recording system. The tokens unearthed at four sites that flourished between 5500 and 4500 B.C.—Tell Arpachiyah and Tell as-Sawwan in Iraq and Chaga Sefid and Jaffarabad in Iran—reflect no more than minor developments. A new type of token, the biconoid, appears, and among some of the subtypes painted black lines and dots have taken the place of incisions and punch marks.

Early in the Bronze Age, between 3500 and 3100 B.C., there were significant changes in the recording system. This period saw an economic advance quite as remarkable in its own way as the rise of the farming economy that laid the foundation for it. The new development was the emergence of cities. Surveys of ancient sites in western Asia indicate a drastic increase in the population of Iraq and Iran; urban centers with many inhabitants begin to appear close to the earlier village settlements.

Craft specialization and the beginnings of mass production appear at this time. The bronze smithies and their products gave the age its name, but craftsmen other than smiths also arose, concentrated in various areas. The invention of the potter's wheel allowed the development of a pottery industry, and the output of various mass-production kilns came to be distributed over great distances. A similar trend is apparent in the manufacture of stone vessels, and the development of an expanded trade network is indicated by the appearance in Iraq of such exotic materials as lapis lazuli.

The development of an urban economy, rooted in trade, must have multiplied the demands on the traditional recording system. Not only production but also inventories, shipments and wage payments had to be noted, and merchants needed to preserve records of their transactions. By the last century of the fourth millennium B.C. the pressure of complex business accountancy on the token system becomes apparent both in the symbols and in how the tokens were used.

To consider the symbols first, six sites of the late fourth millennium B.C. in Iraq (Uruk, Tello and Fara), in Iran (Susa and Chogha Mish) and in Syria (Habuba Kabira) have yielded tokens representative of the full range of early shapes. In addition, some new shapes appear, among them parabolas, rhomboids and replicas of vessels. Even more significant than the appearance of new shapes, however, is the great proliferation of subtypes indicated by a variety of incised markings on the tokens. It is also now that a few of the tokens begin to have appliqué markings: added pellets or coils of clay.

The six sites have yielded a total of 660 tokens dating to about 3100 B.C. Of this number 363, or 55 percent, are marked with incisions. Most of the incisions are deep grooves made with the pointed end of a stylus; the grooves are placed conspicuously and with a clear concern for symmetry. On rounded tokens such as spheres, cones, ovoids and cylinders the incisions usually run around the equator and are thus visible from any aspect. On flat tokens such as disks, triangles and rectangles the incisions appear only on one face.

Most of the incisions present a pattern of parallel lines, although incised crosses and crisscross patterns are also found. The number of parallel lines would not seem to be random: there can be as many as 10 incisions, and the frequency of one-stroke, two-stroke, three-stroke and five-stroke patterns is conspicuous. It is noteworthy that with the exception of two-stroke patterns odd-numbered patterns are the most frequent.

Although incised patterns are by far the most abundant, 26 of the tokens (some 4 percent of the total) show circular impressions apparently made by punching the clay with the blunt end of a stylus. Some of the punched tokens bear a single impression. Others show a cluster of six punches, arranged either in a single row or in two rows with three impressions each.

As for changes in how the tokens were used, it is significant that 198 of them, or 30 percent of the total, are perforated. The perforated tokens run the gamut of types and include subtypes of the unmarked, incised and punched variety. In effect this means that tokens of any type or subtype were available in both unperforated and perforated forms. The perforations are so small that only a thin string could have passed through them. Of the explanations that come to mind one is that all 15 types of tokens and their 250 subtypes are nothing more than individual amulets that the early Bronze Age urban folk of western Asia wore on strings around their neck or wrist. I reject this explanation on two grounds. First, none of the perforated tokens that I have examined shows any evidence of being used as an amulet, such as wear polish or erosion around

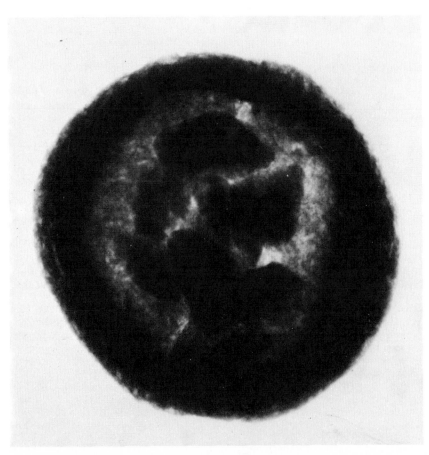

X RAY OF UNOPENED BULLA reveals tokens, some apparently cones and others ovoids. Age of the bulla is unknown; it was an isolated surface find near Dhahran in Saudi Arabia.

the string hole. Second, it seems preposterous that such a complex repertory of forms, so widespread in geographical distribution and manufactured with such remarkable uniformity, should have served as personal adornment in 30 percent of the cases and for some other purpose in the remaining 70 percent.

I prefer the hypothesis that some tokens representative of a specific transaction were strung together as a record. It seems at least plausible that the complexity of record keeping in an urban economy might have given rise to duplicate tokens suitable for stringing.

The stringing of tokens, if that is what the perforated tokens imply, would be only one change in how these symbolic bits of clay were used at the end of the fourth millennium B.C. A much more significant change is the first appearance at this time of clay bullae, or envelopes, such as those Amiet found as containers of tokens at Susa. The existence of a bulla is clear-cut direct evidence of the user's desire to segregate the tokens representing one or another transaction. The envelope could easily be made by pressing the fingers into a lump of clay about the size of a tennis ball, creating a cavity large enough to hold several tokens; the envelope could then be sealed with a patch of clay.

There is no doubt in my mind that such bullae were invented to provide the parties to a transaction with the kind of smooth clay surface that according to Sumerian custom could be marked by the personal seals of the individuals concerned as a validation of the event. The fact that most of the 350 bullae so far discovered bear the impressions of two different seals lends support to my conviction. Amiet has suggested that the Susa bullae may have served as bills of lading. In this view a rural producer of, say, textiles would consign a shipment of goods to an urban middleman, sending along with the shipment a bulla that contained a number of tokens descriptive of the kind and quantity of merchandise shipped. By breaking the bulla the recipient of the shipment could verify the makeup of the shipment; moreover, the need to deliver an intact bulla would inhibit the carrier from tampering with the merchandise in transit. This sealed transfer of tokens between trade partners represents an entirely new way of using the ancient recording system.

The innovation had one serious drawback. The seals impressed on the smooth exterior of the bulla served to validate each transmission, but if the seal impressions were to be preserved, the bulla had to remain intact. How, then, could one determine what tokens were enclosed and how many? A solution to the problem was soon found. The surface of the bulla was marked so that in addition to the validating seal impressions, it bore images of all the enclosed tokens.

TABLETS FROM URUK show the convex shape that may reflect their evolution from hollow bullae. Impressions represent numerals. Tablets are in the Pergamon Museum in Berlin.

The most striking example of this stratagem is a bulla that proved to contain six grooved ovoid tokens. Each of the six tokens had been pressed into the surface of the bulla before being stored inside it; they fit the surface imprints exactly. This means of recording the contents of a bulla on its exterior was not, however, universally practiced. On most bullae the impression was made with a thumb or a stylus; a circular impression stood for a sphere or a disk, a semicircular or triangular impression stood for a cone, and so forth.

The bulla markings were clearly not invented to take the place of the token system of record keeping. Nevertheless, that is what happened. One can visualize the process. At first the innovation flourished because of its convenience; anyone could "read" what tokens a bulla contained and how many without destroying the envelope and its seal impressions. What then happened was virtually inevitable, and the substitution of two-dimensional portrayals of the tokens for the tokens themselves would seem to have been the crucial link between the archaic recording system and writing. The hollow bullae with their enclosed tokens would have been replaced by inscribed solid clay objects: tablets. The strings, baskets and shelf loads of tokens in the archives would have given way to representative signs inscribed on tablets, that is, to written records.

The convex profile of the early Uruk tablets may well be a morphological feature inherited from the spherical bullae. Much the same may be true of the

selection as a writing surface of a material as unsuitable as clay, a soft and easily smeared medium that must be dried or baked if it is to be preserved. There can be little doubt about the relation between the shapes and markings of the tokens and the supposed arbitrary forms of many Uruk ideographs. No fewer than 33 clear-cut identities exist between the ideographs and two-dimensional representations of tokens and more than twice that many are possible.

To summarize, the earliest examples of writing in Mesopotamia may not, as many have assumed, be the result of pure invention. Instead they appear to be a novel application late in the fourth millennium B.C. of a recording system that was indigenous to western Asia from early Neolithic times onward. In this view the appearance of writing in Mesopotamia represents a logical step in the evolution of a system of record keeping that originated some 11,000 years ago.

On this hypothesis the fact that the system was used without significant modification until late in the fourth millennium B.C. seems attributable to the comparatively simple record-keeping requirements of the preceding 5,000 years. With the rise of cities and the development of large-scale trade the system was pushed onto a new track. Images of the tokens soon supplanted the tokens themselves, and the evolution of symbolic objects into ideographs led to the rapid adoption of writing all across western Asia.

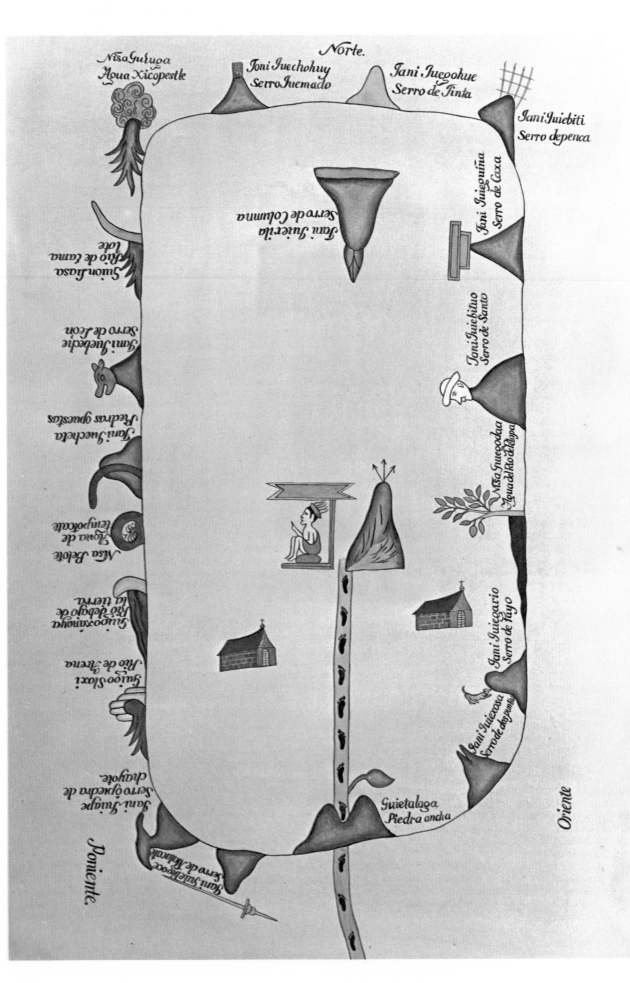

Norte.

Nisa Guruga
Agua Xicopestle

Ioni Iuechohuy
Serro Iuemado

Iani Iuegohue
Serro de Tinta

Iani Iuiebiti
Serro depenca

Iani Iueguiña
Serro de Caxa

Iani Iuietila
Serro de Columna

Iani Iuiebiliio
Serro de Santo

Suonfiasa
Rio de Iuana Iate

Iani Iuebchie
Serro de Leon

Nisa Iuegodaa
Agua del Rio de Telapa

Iani Iuebcta
Piedras opuestas

Nisa Belote
Agua de Tempocticle

Guiooxiaqua
Rio debajo de
la tierra.

Iani Iuiegario
Serro de Iayo

Guigo Sloxi
Rio de Iierra

Iani Iuiexasa
Serro de dos puntas

Iani Iuiape
Serro ópedra de
chiapote.

Guietalaga
Piedra ancha

Iani Iuebluoc
Serro de Iulurla

Poniente.

Oriente

11

Zapotec Writing

by Joyce Marcus
February 1980

*Among the high cultures of Mexico before the Spanish
conquest was the Zapotec. Its hieroglyphs, mostly
carved from 500 B.C. to A.D. 700, record the rise and
decline of the Zapotec state*

Among the pre-Columbian cultures of the New World the civilizations of Mesoamerica—the region from Mexico south to Guatemala and Honduras—were unique in their possession of a true form of writing: a series of hieroglyphs arranged in vertical columns and in many instances combined with numerals. The glyphs were at least indirectly related to a spoken language. Although there were many regional variations, the four major systems were those of the Maya of southern Mexico, Belize, Guatemala and Honduras, of the Aztec of central Mexico and of the Mixtec and Zapotec of southwestern Mexico.

Of the four the Zapotec system was the oldest. It appeared perhaps as early as 600 B.C. in the Valley of Oaxaca, some 550 kilometers south of Mexico City. The Zapotec system is also the least studied of the four, so that an understanding of its evolutionary relation to the later writings of the Maya, the Aztec and the Mixtec is still lacking. Early Zapotec writing is found primarily in the form of inscriptions on stone monuments and paintings on the walls of tombs in the Valley of Oaxaca. If the inscriptions could be deciphered, they might be combined with existing archaeological information to fill in part of the otherwise unrecorded history of the Zapotec people.

With this possibility in mind I have been working since 1972 to record the more than 500 stone inscriptions that have been found in the Valley of Oaxaca and to put them in context. My research has built on the pioneering work of two

Mexican archaeologists, Alfonso Caso and Ignacio Bernal, and has been integrated with the recent work of two of my colleagues in the U.S.: Richard E. Blanton of Purdue University, who has carried out an analysis of the ancient Zapotec capital, Monte Albán, as an urban area, and Kent V. Flannery of the University of Michigan, who is studying the sequence of settlements in the Valley of Oaxaca that preceded the founding of Monte Albán.

Several previous studies of Zapotec writing have sought to interpret the inscriptions not in their own right but in terms of the better-known writings of the Aztec, the Mixtec and the Maya. This is unfortunate. Although some conventions are shared by the four systems, the languages the systems record belong to three different families: Zapotec and Mixtec belong to the Otomanguean family, Aztec to the Utoaztecan and Maya to the Macro-Mayan. To assign either Maya, Aztec or Mixtec names to Zapotec glyphs does little to advance understanding. Indeed, in some instances it serves to blur the interesting and significant differences among the four writing systems.

For my interpretive framework I have selected the extensive documents bearing on the Zapotec people that were compiled by their Spanish conquerors late in the 16th century. These include descriptions of the Zapotec calendar, the Zapotec political organization and religion and the grammar and vocabulary of the Zapotec language. Zapotec scribes, at the request of the Spaniards,

also wrote down genealogies and prepared regional maps. Here I shall attempt to trace the evolution of Zapotec writing and simultaneously to reconstruct Zapotec political history. In doing so I shall combine information from the historical documents with what is known of the shared conventions of the four Mesoamerican writing systems and with the archaeological evidence from Oaxaca, in particular the inscribed monuments.

In the 16th century Zapotec society was divided into two classes that did not intermarry. The upper stratum consisted of the hereditary rulers (*coqui*) and their families, along with minor nobles (*xoana*). The lower stratum consisted of commoners and slaves. Great emphasis was put on the order of birth of noble children: rulers were frequently recruited from the elder offspring and priests from the younger. Military campaigns were fought by noble officers commanding commoner soldiers. Nobles frequently formed political alliances by marrying into the elite families of other communities; commoners usually married within their village. Royal ancestors were venerated and were thought to have considerable supernatural power over the affairs of their descendants.

The Zapotec of the 16th century kept two calendars, one secular and the other ritual. The secular calendar of 365 days (*yza*) was divided into 18 "moons" of 20 days and one period of five days. The ritual calendar of 260 days (*pije* or *piye*) was divided into four units of 65 days called "lightnings" (*cocijo*) or "great spirits" (*pitào*). Each 65-day period was further divided into five periods (*cocii*) of 13 days (*chij*).

Each day in the ritual calendar was designated by one of 20 day-name glyphs combined with a number between 1 and 13. The combination of day-name glyphs and numbers gave rise to the 260 days of the sacred cycle. Each day had its own ritual significance, and Zapotec rulers and nobles were named for the day on which they were born. Typical of the noble names that appear on Zapotec stone monuments are "1 Tiger," "8 Deer," "5 Flower" and "11 Monkey."

The Zapotec people also used toponyms, glyphic "place signs" for important places or landmarks, mountains in particular. Several examples appear in an important pictorial document, the Lienzo de Guevea, that shows the lands belonging to the Zapotec town of Santiago de Guevea in 1540. Running around the edges of the picture are place signs accompanied by labels in Spanish (and in Zapotec, written in the Spanish alphabet) indicating the town borders; examples are "Hill of the Puma," "River of the Tadpole" and "Hill of the Spindle Whorl." Elsewhere in the picture is a genealogical list that presents the Zapotec rulers at Zaachila and on the Isthmus of Tehuantepec dating from the last century before the Spanish conquest.

Sixteenth-century documents such as this one provide a reasonable framework for efforts to interpret the ancient inscribed monuments of the Valley of Oaxaca. For example, many of the inscriptions evidently deal with the feats of ancient Zapotec rulers: their conquests, the sacrifice of their captives, their royal line of descent, their marriages and the names of their important dependencies and tributary districts. The names of many of the rulers are taken from the 260-day calendar, and their territories are defined by toponyms, usually the names of mountains.

Of the carved stone monuments in the Valley of Oaxaca the earliest may have been erected as long ago as 1000 B.C. The first monuments that include glyphs, however, do not appear until the interval between 600 and 200 B.C. This was a time of important political change. During what is known to archaeologists as the Rosario phase (700 to 500 B.C.) a number of regional and presumably competitive chiefdoms flourished in the valley. Each of these political units included one relatively large village with civic or ceremonial structures and smaller hamlets that lacked such public buildings.

In about 500 B.C. many of these valley chiefdoms disappeared or were greatly reduced, and a new kind of community was founded. The new community was on top of Monte Albán, a height near the center of the valley that rises some 400 meters above the valley floor. Blanton's study shows that the community, by far the largest in the valley, was initially divided into at least three separate residential areas. The arrangement suggests that the new stronghold may have been founded by previously competing groups that had come together in some kind of Zapotec confederacy.

During the initial phase of settlement, Monte Albán Period I (500 to 200 B.C.), the occupants of the mountaintop erected three kilometers of defensive walls. Most of this building was done late in the period. At the same time the settlers carved more than 300 stone monuments, the largest number known at any site in Mesoamerica. In none of the subsequent periods at Monte Albán were a fourth as many monuments erected. The Period I monuments, in keeping

MAIN PLAZA at Monte Albán dominates the most central of the five hills where the city stood; it measures 150 by 300 meters. Seen in **the foreground is Structure J, erected during Monte Albán Period II. More than 40 inscribed "conquest slabs" were displayed on its walls.**

with the settlement's defensive walls, mainly portrayed military themes.

Of the shared conventions in Mesoamerican iconography some of the most widespread are those that depict captives. Prisoners are displayed in humiliation; they are stripped naked and bound, and their posture is awkward and distorted. Their captors, in contrast, are dressed in elegant regalia and are posed in rigid dignity. If a prisoner has been sacrificed, he is shown with his eyes closed and his mouth open, and in many instances with flowery scrolls, presumably representing blood, issuing from his wounds. To give one example, the Maya built many open galleries where prisoners were depicted in this way; the carvings were set into staircases so that the victors could figuratively "tread on the bodies" of the conquered when they were approaching the building at the head of the stairs, usually a temple. The Aztec built displays that served a similar purpose: the *tzompantli,* a rack or wall consisting of the skulls of enemy dead.

The earliest-known Zapotec carving representative of this convention was found some 15 kilometers north of Monte Albán at San José Mogote, a large civic and ceremonial center belonging to the Rosario phase. Known as monument No. 3, it depicts a sprawled naked human figure. Between the figure's legs an ornate dot (indicating the numeral 1) is accompanied by the Zapotec glyph *xoo,* meaning "earthquake" or "motion." The inscription is the oldest evidence known for the existence of the Zapotec 260-day calendar. It may record the name of the individual. Because San José Mogote appears to have been virtually abandoned at the end of the Rosario phase, presumably as part of the founding of Monte Albán, monument No. 3 was probably made sometime between 700 and 500 B.C.

The setting of Monte Albán is five interconnected hills, and the settlement covers an area of 6.5 square kilometers. A central hilltop is occupied by the Main Plaza, measuring 150 by 300 meters. Its principal structures are the North Platform, which held the royal residence and the temples of the Zapotec nobility, the South Platform, which held other temples, a large ball court along the east side of the plaza and a series of peripheral palaces and temples. Mound X, a temple site, lies northeast of the Main Plaza. Building L, a structure important to this discussion, stands in the southwest corner of the plaza. These various structures were built and rebuilt at different times. For example, Building L was erected during Period I, when the population of Monte Albán was at least 10,000. The two platforms and the ball court were built during subsequent periods.

As one of the first public buildings

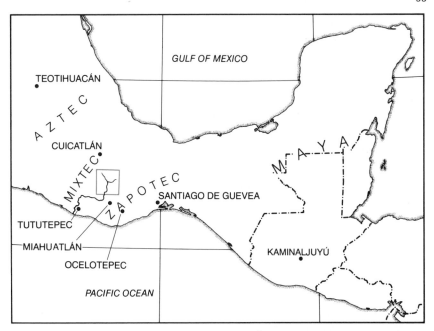

FOUR MAJOR SYSTEMS of hieroglyphic writing in the pre-Columbian New World were those of the Maya in eastern Mexico, Guatemala, Belize, Honduras and parts of El Salvador, of the Aztec of central Mexico and of the Mixtec and the Zapotec of southwestern Mexico. The influence of the Mexican city of Teotihuacán extended at least as far as Kaminaljuyú in Guatemala. The Valley of Oaxaca, inside rectangle, is shown in detail in the illustration below.

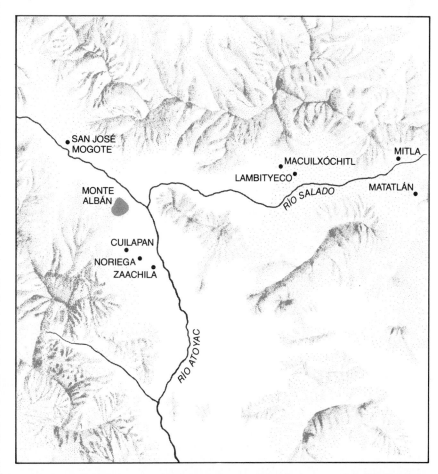

VALLEY OF OAXACA, centered on the confluence of the Río Atoyac and the Río Salado in the Sierra Madre del Sur, was the cradle of Zapotec civilization. From soon after 500 B.C. until A.D. 700 Monte Albán (*color*) was the capital of the then united valley. Before and after that period separate valley settlements were independent. The rulers of these districts in later times, mindful of their royal heritage, frequently entered into alliances by means of intermarriage.

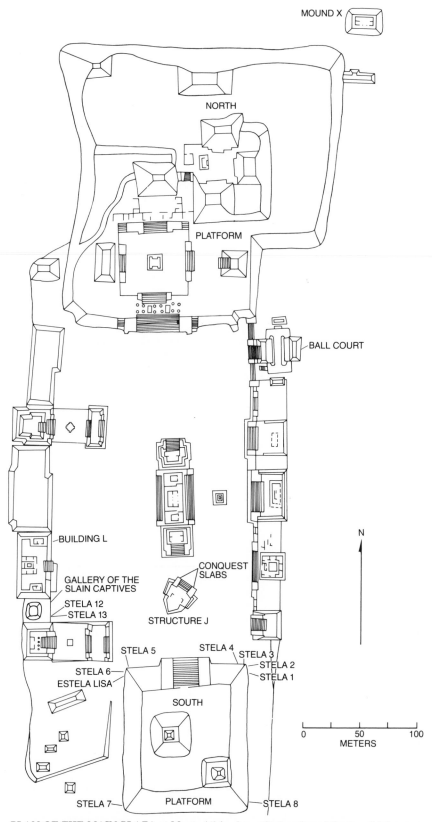

MOUND X

NORTH

PLATFORM

BALL COURT

BUILDING L

GALLERY OF THE
SLAIN CAPTIVES

STELA 12
STELA 13

CONQUEST
SLABS

STRUCTURE J

N

STELA 5   STELA 4
                   STELA 3
                   STELA 2
STELA 6   STELA 1
ESTELA LISA

SOUTH

0   50   100
        METERS

STELA 7   PLATFORM   STELA 8

PLAN OF THE MAIN PLAZA at Monte Albán shows the location of the two chief monument displays: the gallery of the slain captives along the east face of Building L and the 40-odd conquest slabs of Structure J. Of the stelae also located on the plan, No. 12 and No. 13 near the gallery of the captives carry the earliest Zapotec "text." Four of the nine stelae at the corners of the South Platform (*clockwise No. 1, No. 8, No. 7 and the* **estela lisa**) **describe a visit by personages from Teotihuacán. Such a contact is also indicated on a monument found at Mound X. The stelae are shown where they were first found and not where they now stand. Building L was built during Monte Albán Period I (500 to 200 B.C.) and Structure J during Period II (200 B.C. to A.D. 100). The north and south platforms were built during Period III (A.D. 100–600).**

erected by the founders of Monte Albán, Building L lay partially destroyed and buried under layers of later Zapotec construction until 1931, when its massive remains were first uncovered by archaeologists working at the site. The building was cleared between 1931 and 1936; photographs and drawings made at the time, along with the surviving parts of the structure, all indicate that the east face of Building L originally featured a great gallery of stone figures arranged in four rows and probably numbering in the hundreds. Each of the figures was a grotesquely sprawled naked human body with closed eyes. Some of the figures had blood scrolls issuing from one or more wounds.

In the lowest of the four rows each figure was upright and faced to the right. In the second row the figures were arrayed horizontally. In the third row the figures were again upright but faced to the left. In the top row they were again horizontal. The figures in the lowest row, those closest to observers, were the most elaborately carved. Many were adorned with necklaces, earplugs and complex hair arrangements; name glyphs are also common. The figures in the top row, those farthest away, were the least ornate.

For almost a century these Monte Albán figures have been the subject of almost every conceivable interpretation. Some of them, displaced from Building L, were among the first sculptures found at the site. Scholars have called them "dancers," "swimmers," "ecstatic priests" and even "medical anomalies." Indeed, Building L is still often called Los Danzantes, "the dancers." In 1962 Michael D. Coe of Yale University, who is familiar with the iconography of prisoner depictions throughout Mesoamerica, identified the Building L "dancers" as slain or ritually sacrificed captives. His interpretation might have been reached earlier if Building L had remained intact. Long before the Spanish conquest, however, the structure had been partially destroyed, and the inhabitants of Monte Albán had later used more than 100 of the figures as masonry for buildings in the plaza and elsewhere.

Attempts have been made to put the figures in chronological order on the basis of carving style, increasing degree of elaboration and so on. In my opinion the available archaeological evidence suggests that all the figures were carved at about the same time and were originally positioned as I have described them, with the more elaborate figures featured in the lower rows. The display, as it originally appeared, must have been one of the most impressive works of military propaganda in all Mesoamerica.

The figures were not necessarily the only elements in the display. At the south end of the gallery at Building L are two carved stones. Known as Stela

No. 12 and Stela No. 13, they bear one of the oldest glyph texts known at Monte Albán. Although the exact relation of the stelae to the gallery has never been worked out, some of the photographs made in the 1930's show the stones fitted so close together that they almost certainly once formed a single two-column inscription.

In the inscription both calendric and noncalendric glyphs appear. Of the calendric glyphs some seem to be day signs and others are possibly month signs. An example of a possible month-sign glyph is the last one in the second column [*see illustration on page 98*]. This glyph appears on monuments elsewhere at Monte Albán in association with numbers higher than 13. (In the 260-day calendar no day sign can be associated with a number higher than 13, but month signs in the secular calendar can be associated with numbers as high as 19.) One of the calendric glyphs is a year sign; within the surrounding raised area appears what is known as a year bearer.

The noncalendric glyphs on the two stelae are sandwiched between the calendric glyphs. The third glyphs from the top seem to be the subjects of phrases or clauses. The second glyphs from the top evidently represent parts of hands. These glyphs are known as hand compounds. In the Maya and Aztec writing systems such representations of hands are parts of verbs; the Zapotec hand compounds at Monte Albán may be verbs of action.

Blanton's urban analysis has shown that during Period II at Monte Albán (200 B.C to A.D. 100) the population of the settlement grew to approximately 20,000. The settlers remained sheltered behind the three-kilometer wall, which stood as high as four meters along the gentler northern and western slopes of the site. During this period the Zapotec state also expanded its political, economic and military influence beyond the limits of the Valley of Oaxaca, reaching out into territories that had formerly been autonomous.

One of the major public buildings erected in the plaza during Period II was Structure J, notable for its arrowhead-shaped ground plan. Set into the walls of Structure J were more than 40 carved stone slabs. Caso has suggested that each of these "conquest slabs" represents a location subjugated by the rulers of Monte Albán in the period of expansion. All the slab carvings include the following elements: (1) a "hill" or "place" glyph, signifying "the hill of" or "the place of," (2) a glyph (or combination of glyphs) above the hill or place glyph, evidently representing the name of the hill or place, and (3) below the hill or place glyph an upside-down human head, the headdress of which varies from slab to slab.

Caso took these heads to represent the slain rulers of the subjugated areas and suggested that the various headdresses were regionally distinctive, thereby reinforcing the sense of the locational glyphs that appeared above them. A few of the slabs also bear glyphic texts. In their most complete form they include year signs, month signs and day signs along with noncalendric glyphs that are perhaps related to the time when a certain place was subjugated.

I consider Caso's interpretation of the conquest slabs to be essentially correct. This opinion is reinforced by the resemblance between the locational glyphs and the Zapotec descriptions of places that appear in later documents such as the Lienzo de Guevea. On this analogy it could be suggested that the 40 slabs rep-

SACRIFICED PRISONER appears on monument No. 3 from San José Mogote, a site north of Monte Albán. The monument was probably made between 700 and 500 B.C. The closed eye, the open mouth and the "scrolls" of blood emerging from the chest signify that the prisoner is dead. Between his legs appear (*color*) an ornate dot (representing the numeral 1) and a Zapotec glyph meaning "earthquake." The dual inscription may record the name of the prisoner.

resent 40 landmarks: for example, "Hill of the Rabbit," "Hill of the Bird" and "Hill of the Chili Plant." Such landmarks could have described the limits of Monte Albán territory in Period II. It is even possible that the original location of the slabs on the walls of Structure J reflected the sequence of these landmarks along the Zapotec frontier. This, however, can never be proved; many of the slabs had fallen out of place before Caso studied them.

It would obviously be useful to learn the location of the landmarks, even though it is unlikely that as many as a third of them could ever be precisely located. I have suggested, however, that a few of them might be traced by comparing them with the listing in a historical document, the Codex Mendoza. This codex is a 16th-century Aztec work listing 35 locales in Oaxaca that were paying tribute to Aztec overlords at the time. It depicts many locales by means of hill glyphs and I suspected that these glyphs might simply be Aztec versions of Zapotec place-names.

Since I made this suggestion I have found four codex place glyphs that closely resemble certain conquest-slab glyphs. The names of the four places, all of them within 140 kilometers of Oaxaca City, are Miahuapan (modern Miahuatlán), an Aztec name meaning "Place in the Water of the Maize Tassels"; Cuicatlán, Aztec for "Place of Song"; Tototepec (modern Tututepec), Aztec for "Hill of the Bird," and Ocelotepec, Aztec for "Hill of the Jaguar." The conquest-slab glyphs and the codex glyphs that are in close accord with these place-names respectively show maize tassels in an irrigation canal, a human head with a feathered speech scroll emerging from its mouth, a bird on the top of a hill and a jaguar on the top of a hill [see illustration on page 99].

Such a correlation between a 16th-century Aztec codex and Zapotec glyphs of Period II implies some 1,500 years of place-name continuity. Hence my suggestion is no more than a hypothesis, subject to proof or disproof by future analysis. Recently, however, work by Charles Spencer of the University of Michigan and Elsa M. Redmond of Yale University in the vicinity of Cuicatlán, the "Place of Song," has provided a degree of confirmation. It appears that in this originally autonomous region control passed into Zapotec hands at about the end of Period I or the beginning of Period II. At one outlying Cuicatlán settlement the conquerors erected an edifice of skulls of the *tzompantli* type. Farther to the north they fortified a mountaintop, closing off the main route from Oaxaca to the neighboring Valley of Tehuacán. Spencer and Redmond find that pottery of Monte Albán Period II extends no farther than this mountain fort. Only pottery of Tehuacán style appears beyond it.

Similar archaeological tests of my hypothesis remain to be done at the other three towns. This should not be impossible. Tututepec and Miahuatlán in particular include the remains of substantial Monte Albán II settlements. It would also be heartening to discover the identity of still other conquest-slab place glyphs.

During Period III at Monte Albán (A.D. 100 to 600) the settlement grew to cover more than six square kilometers; Blanton estimates that the population reached some 30,000. The five centuries of Period III are divided into two subphases (IIIa and IIIb), and the settlement reached its maximum size during the second subphase. Throughout the period, however, Zapotec territorial expansion seems to have slowed, perhaps because Monte Albán was now competing economically with an even larger metropolis.

That metropolis was Teotihuacán, 500 kilometers to the north in the basin of Mexico. During the same 500-year interval Monte Albán's northern competitor had expanded to cover 25 square kilometers; René Millon of the University of Rochester estimates that its population was then more than 100,000. Although the region tributary to Teotihuacán is still not well defined, it must have been many times larger than that of Monte Albán, and its zone of influence must have been larger still. For example, there is evidence of Teotihuacán influence at the Maya site of Kaminaljuyú, 900 kilometers to the south in Guatemala. Clara Millon of the University of Rochester has suggested that one particular kind of head ornamentation at Teotihuacán, the "tassel headdress," is associated with the representation of certain personages who evidently traveled to distant parts of Mesoamerica, perhaps in some kind of ambassadorial capacity. Support for this suggestion is found at the Guatemala site in portrayals of the tassel headdress on painted pottery.

The Millons find evidence of a special

GALLERY OF THE CAPTIVES at Building L in the Main Plaza of Monte Albán had this appearance when it was discovered under later levels of construction in 1931. The alternating courses of vertical and horizontal representations of sacrificed prisoners may once have in-relationship between Teotihuacán and Monte Albán. For example, a Zapotec colony apparently existed for a century (from about A.D. 200 to 300) on the western outskirts of Teotihuacán. The Zapotec enclave extended over more than a hectare (2.5 acres); its remains include residences, graves, funerary urns and other pottery of the Monte Albán style. The stone doorjamb of one tomb is inscribed with a Zapotec glyph.

No corresponding Teotihuacán colony has been found by Blanton at Monte Albán. Some stone monuments of subphase IIIa, however, give evidence of relations between these two great cities of Mesoamerica. Perhaps the most impressive single structure built at Monte Albán during phase IIIa is the South Platform of the Main Plaza. It is a truncated pyramid 15 meters high and more than 100 meters on a side at the base. A num-

ber of stone monuments stood at the four corners of the pyramid.

Eight of the monuments echo the militaristic themes of Period I and Period II. Six show captives, evidently prisoners of superior status, with their arms tied behind their back. Below each captive is a hill glyph, presumably indicating his place of origin. The figures on the other two monuments contrast vividly with the six captives; they are elegantly

cluded more than 300 figures. More than 100 of the carved stones were removed to be reused as masonry elsewhere in Monte Albán.

When the display was first erected, it must have been one of the most impressive works of military propaganda anywhere in Mesoamerica.

costumed and armed with lances. They presumably represent Zapotec leaders.

When these monuments were discovered early in this century, along with a ninth stela that bore no figure and was therefore called the *estela lisa* (plain stela), they did not appear to bear any inscriptions other than the human figures and hill glyphs. Later work on the South Platform in the 1950's revealed, however, that four of the monuments were also inscribed on their edges and elsewhere. The four were stelae No. 1 (northeast corner), No. 7 (southwest corner), No. 8 (southeast corner) and the *estela lisa* (northwest corner). In the course of investigating these inscriptions Jorge Acosta of the Mexican National Institute of Anthropology and History found that stone offering boxes had been placed at three of the platform's four corners. The boxes contained seashells, jade and pottery of the Monte Albán IIIa style.

The edge inscriptions of the four monuments all present much the same information. Eight named individuals in two groups of four are depicted in all. They are shown leaving a place where temples are decorated in the style of one district of Teotihuacán: Tetitla. All the travelers are wearing the kind of tassel headdress identified by Clara Millon as being possibly ambassadorial. The eight are then seen arriving at a place named "Hill of 1 Jaguar," where they are greeted by an official wearing a typical Zapotec headdress. In view of the physical association between the stelae and the offering boxes, it is not unlikely that the visit of the eight travelers coincided with the dedication of the South Platform. "Hill of 1 Jaguar" could be the name of all or part of Monte Albán.

Although each of the inscriptions presents the same information, the inscriptions vary in detail. For example, Stela No. 7 shows four of the travelers, accompanied by their name glyphs. On Stela No. 8 the same four travelers are presented in a different manner. Each is represented by a tassel headdress, an incense burner of the Teotihuacán style and then a calendric name and a nickname. Three of the calendric names can be read as follows: "5 Turquoise," "12 Skull" and "7 [?] *N*." (The question mark indicates that the identification of the number is not certain, and the letter *N* is Caso's designation for this still undeciphered Zapotec glyph.)

The other four travelers are named on the underside of the *estela lisa*. These names are easier to read: "13 Knot," "9 Monkey," "1 Owl" and "Treble Scroll." (The last designation is a common iconographic symbol at Teotihuacán.) The four travelers are seen being greeted by a Zapotec ruler whose name is given as "8 [followed by an undeciphered glyph]" and whose residence is given as "Hill of 1 Jaguar." Inscriptions on the upper and lower edges of Stela No. 1 make reference to the same four travelers in abbreviated form; the travelers' footprints are also shown leading away from a temple of the Tetitla style.

As the Millons have pointed out, no depiction of a Teotihuacán personage on a Zapotec monument shows him in military garb or bearing weapons. For example, the tassel-headdress figures on the South Platform monuments are dressed in ceremonial costumes and are carrying pouches of copal, the incense burned in Mesoamerican ritual. One may conclude that whereas the relations between Monte Albán and some of its other neighbors were often hostile the visit of the Teotihuacán personages to "Hill of 1 Jaguar" constituted peaceful foreign relations.

Further information on relations between Monte Albán and Teotihuacán came to light in 1936, when a carved slab of polished travertine was discovered on Mound X, to the northeast of the Main Plaza. Two figures are depicted on this slab, known as the Lápida de Bazán. One figure, on the left, is dressed in Teotihuacán style and holds a pouch of copal in one hand. The other is costumed as a jaguar in the style of the lords of Monte Albán. Caso, who was the first to recognize the figure on the left as a

TWO-COLUMN TEXT, almost certainly once a single inscription, is one of the earliest inscriptions known at Monte Albán. It is untranslated, but many of the glyphs can be interpreted (*see plan at right*). A-1 is a calendric glyph, specifically the year sign "4 Serpent." A-2 is noncalendric; a hand with the thumb prominent, it may be a verb. The meaning of A-3 is not known. A-4 is calendric; its reading is "8 Water," and it may be a day sign. B-1 is calendric; its reading appears to be "10 Jaguar." It may be a month sign or a calendric name. B-2, a hand grasping an object, is noncalendric; like A-2, it may be a verb. B-3, a profile head with a finger below it, may be a personal name. Part of the reading of B-4, a calendric glyph, is "4"; the other part is undeciphered. Its use on other monuments shows it is a month sign.

Teotihuacán personage, read his calendric name as "8 Turquoise." The name of the jaguar lord is "3 Turquoise."

Accompanying each figure is a column of glyphs. Neither "text" contains any calendric signs, and so it seems plausible that the inscriptions are essentially narrative ones and that they are probably historical and political in character. Teotihuacán is alluded to twice: by the depiction of a tassel headdress (column A, glyph 6, or A-6) and by the depiction of a foot wearing a Teotihuacán-style sandal (B-4). Travel is indicated by footprints (A-7 and B-6) and flowery speech by scrolls issuing from a head (A-5) and from a "jaguar nose" (B-7). An incense burner of Zapotec style is shown (A-8), as is a hand holding a single bean (A-4). According to 16th-century accounts, beans were used by Zapotec diviners to help decide important issues. Here the depiction of a single bean may indicate that after beans had been removed from a pile by twos, fours and so forth in the manner prescribed in the 16th century, this remaining "odd number" decided whatever was at issue. The inscriptions also include a number of hand-gesture glyphs, the kind I have suggested were possibly verbs of action. Finally, the series of glyphs A-5 through A-7 might be read: "Representative from Teotihuacán came to confer."

Pending a complete decipherment of the Lápida de Bazán I regard it tentatively as being a record of an agreement between representatives of the two cities. In my interpretation the representatives traveled, met, spoke, consulted diviners and burned incense. This last action would have established the binding quality of their agreement by putting it in a sacred context. It was probably through diplomatic encounters such as this one that Monte Albán and its far larger neighbor Teotihuacán maintained a healthy social distance, regulated their tributary boundaries and preserved their special relationship.

In about A.D. 600 the great metropolis of Teotihuacán was virtually abandoned. Many of its temples and major buildings were burned. In theory this crisis might have given the rulers of Monte Albán a favorable opportunity to expand the Zapotec realm. For reasons unknown, however, at about this same time Monte Albán also began to decline. Although the Zapotec capital was never burned and never entirely abandoned, public construction around the Main Plaza came to an end with the close of Period III in about A.D. 700.

From a peak of some 30,000 in subphase IIIb the population of Monte Albán shrank rapidly during the succeeding periods: Period IV (A.D. 700 to 1000) and Period V (1000 to 1520). By the year 1300 only 4,000 to 8,000 inhabitants still remained. What had hap-

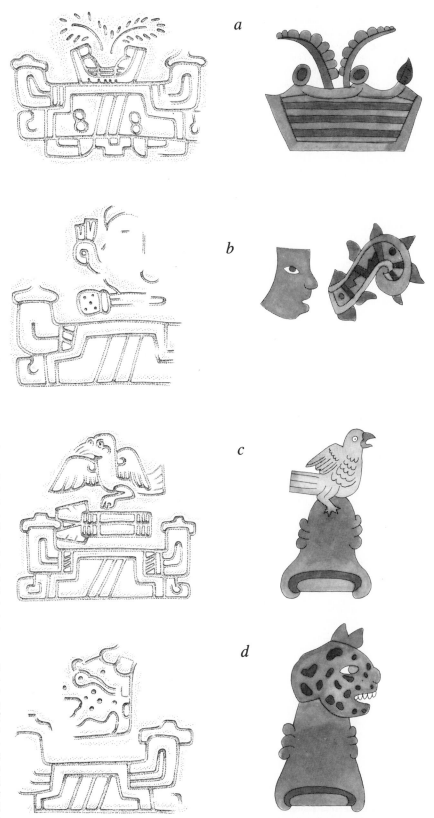

FOUR TOPONYMS, glyphs descriptive of geographical locations, appear at the left; they are selected from the more than 40 such glyphs carved on the conquest slabs of Structure J at Monte Albán. At the right are four matching toponyms from a painted Aztec document that lists locales in Oaxaca that were paying tribute to the Aztec in the 16th century. The Aztec names associated with the toponyms are (*a*) Miahuapan, "Place in the Water of the Maize Tassels," (*b*) Cuicatlán, "Place of Song," (*c*) Tototepec, "Hill of the Bird," and (*d*) Ocelotepec, "Hill of the Jaguar." The resemblance between the Aztec toponyms and Zapotec glyphs suggests that the Aztec overlords may simply have translated long-standing Zapotec place-names. The four locales, all within 140 kilometers of Oaxaca City, are now known by their Aztec names.

pened? Blanton has suggested that one motive for maintaining a large population during Period III was to provide a deterrent to possible Teotihuacán expansion into the Oaxaca region. If that was the case, the collapse of Teotihuacán would have removed a major incentive for maintaining an urban center at

Monte Albán. In any event the confederacy centered on Monte Albán for more than 1,000 years began to dissolve as the urban population drifted away to various competing civic and ceremonial centers on the floor of the valley. Not until the arrival of the Spaniards in 1529 was the Valley of Oaxaca again united.

Many of the competing centers (Cuilapan, Zaachila, Macuilxóchitl, Mitla, Matatlán, Lambityeco and others) had already existed as villages when Monte Albán was first founded. Some had begun to grow again toward the end of subphase IIIb, as if anticipating the decline of the mountain city. During Peri-

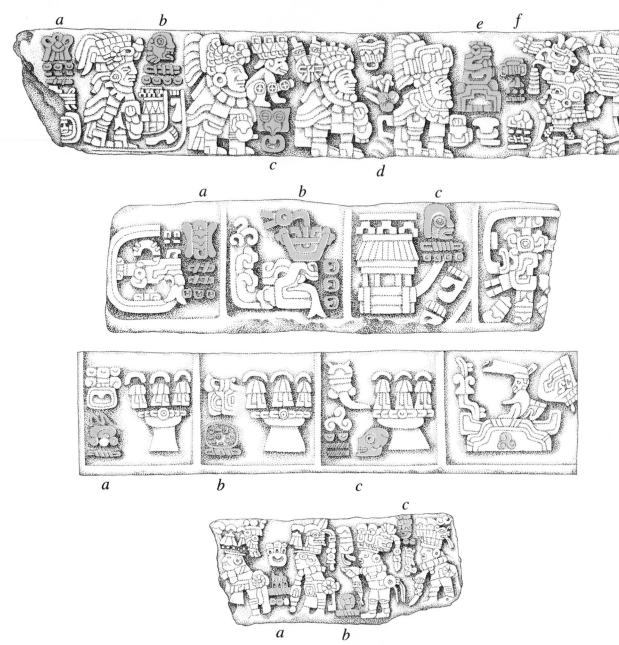

"VISITOR" INSCRIPTIONS appear on four monuments at the corners of the South Platform in the Main Plaza of Monte Albán. The inscriptions convey the same information in different ways: Eight personages have come from Teotihuacán on a peaceful visit. The top inscription appears on a monument known as the *estela lisa*. Four of the personages appear, all facing to the right. Their names, marked in color from left to right, are (*a*) "13 Knot," (*b*) "9 Monkey," (*c*) "1 Owl" and (*d*) "Treble Scroll." Directly before "Treble Scroll" appears the toponym "Hill of 1 Jaguar" (*e*). Facing the four personages is a Zapotec ruler in full regalia; his name (*f*) is given as "8 [unknown]." The second inscription appears on Stela No. 1. The visitors are not seen but are identified by name; the names are (*a*) "13 Knot," (*b*) "3 [Caso's glyph *C*]" and (*c*) "9 Monkey." A fourth name probably appeared at the far right, but that part of the carving is missing. Associated with

"9 Monkey" is a reference to Teotihuacán in the form of a temple facade characteristic of one city district and a reference to travel (*lower right*) in the form of ascending footprints. The third inscription appears on Stela No. 8. The names but not the figures of the visitors seen in the fourth inscription appear in the same order, left to right (*color*). To the right of each name is an incense burner with a "tassel headdress" on top. The inscription includes the toponym known as a hill sign. Within it is the treble-scroll sign prominent in Teotihuacán iconography (*see* d *in top inscription*); the toponym may therefore refer to the city. The fourth inscription is on Stela No. 7; four visitors appear, all facing to the left. Three are named: (*a*) "7 [?] [Caso's glyph *N*]," (*b*) "5 [Caso's glyph *D*]" and (*c*) "12 Skull." All four are wearing the tassel headdress that identifies them as Teotihuacán envoys; the three whose hands are shown carry pouches of copal.

od IV all these valley centers expanded rapidly; this was perhaps in part the result of simple internal growth, but the expansion must also have come partly from the absorption of immigrants from Monte Albán. Many of the valley centers were still important politically, economically and religiously when the Spaniards set down the first extended descriptions of the Zapotec people in the period from A.D. 1579 to 1581.

As Period III ended and Period IV began at Monte Albán one innovation was the appearance of a new kind of stone monument I call a genealogical register. Unlike the large stone monuments of the preceding periods, which were obviously meant to be viewed from some distance, the genealogical registers are small and can only be read close up. Many that I have measured are only from 50 to 60 centimeters high and from 30 to 40 centimeters wide. Instead of being set up in public buildings these small stones appear to have been installed in the residences of the Zapotec elite or (as at Cuilapan and Lambityeco) placed in their tombs. The inscriptions on the registers do not echo the militaristic themes of the earlier periods at Monte Albán; they record the births, ancestry and marriages of the Zapotec rulers and nobles of the time.

Particularly common on the registers are depictions of royal marriages. After the decline of Monte Albán such unions were one of the chief means by which the Zapotecs established political alliances between important communities. The royal husband and wife are usually shown facing each other, seated on woven mats or poised above hill glyphs; in some instances their calendric names are included. The couple may be shown burning incense or sharing a cup of chocolate or pulque. Above them appears a glyphic element Caso has named the "Jaws of the Sky," along with other iconographic elements indicative of royal descent.

On the more elaborate genealogical registers one can trace a record of events affecting the royal personage. For example, the register may begin with the marriage of the subject's parents, then continue with the subject's own birth and perhaps conclude with the subject's marriage. The events are displayed in panel form, one above the other. I believe they are meant to be read from the bottom, where the older events are depicted, to the top, where the most recent events appear. Moreover, they should be read alternately from left to right and from right to left in the reading system known as boustrophedon (from the Greek meaning "as the plow ox turns").

Both the order of reading of these registers and their content are highly significant. First, it may seem surprising that a reading system known in Europe in classical Greek times should have been in-

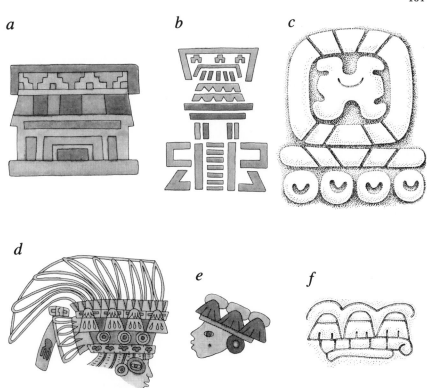

RELATIONS BETWEEN MONTE ALBÁN AND TEOTIHUACÁN are reflected in the art of both cities. The mural painting of a Teotihuacán temple facade in the Tetitla district (*a*) is elaborated in a Teotihuacán pot decoration (*b*). A Tetitla-style temple facade appears on Stela No. 1 at Monte Albán (*see illustration on opposite page*). The Zapotec calendric glyph "9 Earthquake" (*c*) appears on the jamb of a tomb entrance in the Zapotec enclave at Teotihuacán; the same element appears on monument No. 3 at San José Mogote. Mural paintings at Teotihuacán (*d*) provide the details of the tassel headdress associated with important travelers from Teotihuacán. These personages evidently impressed the Maya of Guatemala, to judge from a simplified representation of the headdress (*e*) on a bowl from the site of Kaminaljuyú. The same Teotihuacán-style headdress appears on such monuments at Monte Albán as Stela No. 8 (*see illustration on opposite page*) and the Lápida de Bazán (*f and illustration on next page*).

vented independently in the pre-Columbian New World for the display of genealogical information. The fact is that there is a New World precedent for the system among the Mixtec, who were close neighbors of the Zapotec. Living immediately to the north and west, the Mixtec in the 15th and 16th centuries painted genealogical and other records on screen-folded deer hide, and these codices are meant to be read in boustrophedon style. The origins of this Mixtec painted-record tradition remain obscure, but the possibility that Zapotec genealogical registers, carved on stone between A.D. 700 and 900, were meant to be read in alternate directions suggests that the concept is an ancient one in the New World.

It will be instructive to examine a Zapotec genealogical register in detail. I have selected as an example one that is now preserved in the National Museum of Anthropology in Mexico City. It is said to have come from Zaachila, a valley-floor site that rose to prominence as Monte Albán declined, and it appears to record two generations of a royal family. In its upper panel is a typical wedding

scene. A man is seated on a woven mat and a woman is kneeling; each is holding a pottery vessel. The woman's calendric name is "3 Serpent" and the man's is "6 Earthquake." (The serpent glyph is Caso's glyph *M*; the earthquake glyph is his glyph *L*.) Above the couple are the "Jaws of the Sky," flanked by stylized conch shells. Descending from the "Jaws of the Sky" is a personage, perhaps ancestral or perhaps mythical, holding in one hand a strand of beads.

In the lower panel an older couple are seen, seated on hill signs. In my order of reading they are presumably ancestral to either the husband or the wife in the upper panel. The woman's name is "11 Monkey." (The monkey glyph is Caso's glyph *O*.) The man's name, depending on whether or not the two dots behind his back are included with the dot and bar on his knee, is either "6 Flower" or "8 Flower." (The flower glyph is Caso's glyph *D*.)

One striking feature of this register is a series of 13 day signs and numerical coefficients that begins at the top right and runs down the right side of the small stone. They are all calendric glyphs taken from the 260-day ritual calendar, but

they are in an order that makes no calendric sense. Are they perhaps a list of personal names? Supporting such an interpretation is the fact that the series includes the names of the couple shown in the upper panel, "3 Serpent" and "6 Earthquake." I suggest that the vertical series records the names of the ancestors of the husband or of the wife (or of both) in the upper panel.

The vertical series is accompanied at

LÁPIDA DE BAZÁN, a slab of polished travertine, was unearthed in 1936 at Mound X, to the northeast of the Main Plaza at Monte Albán. The figure at the left, "8 Turquoise" (*colored glyphs*), is evidently a visitor from Teotihuacán. The figure at the right, "3 Turquoise," dressed as a jaguar lord, is presumably the ruler, or some high official, of Monte Albán. The two columns of glyphs (A *and* B *on plan at top left*) include no calendric glyphs; it thus seems plausible that their intention is narrative. Teotihuacán is alluded to twice: by a tassel headdress (*A-6*) and by a Teotihuacán-style sandal (*B-4*). Travel is indicated by footprints (*A-7, B-6*) and flowery speech by two scrolls (*A-5, B-7*). Ritual is suggested by an incense burner (*A-8*), divination by a hand holding a single bean (*A-4*). Hand glyphs (*B-1, B-2*) may be verbs. The monument may well commemorate a time when representatives of the two powers met to ratify an agreement.

the bottom of the register by two shorter columns of glyphs that are not fully interpretable. One column includes the image of an open right hand, which again may represent a verb of action. The other column must record a date; it includes the calendric expression "8 [followed by Caso's glyph N]," above which is a glyph Caso has identified as a year sign. The date may be when the couple in the upper panel were married.

A second example is a famous genealogical register found in a tomb at Noriega, not far from Zaachila. Its inscription occupies three panels. The top and middle panels seem to trace the life of a young noble from birth to later childhood. The bottom panel again bears the "Jaws of the Sky," appearing above a hill sign that is flanked by two reptilian heads. In what may be an ancestral or mythical scene a man named "10 Vessel [?]" and a woman named "9 Serpent" appear on each side of the "Jaws of the Sky."

The middle panel is evidently meant to be read from left to right. Proceeding in that order, one sees at the left a woman, "2 Water," giving birth to a child, "2 Vessel [?]." At the center is a large male figure with a distinctive headdress; he is presenting something to the child. At the right the child, now old enough to sit up, faces a male figure, perhaps its father. If one now reverses the reading order and starts at the right side of the top panel, one again sees the child's mother. She holds a staff similar to the ones, known as "manikin scepters," that appear on contemporaneous Maya monuments. At the center the child, now still older, reappears; its head band is being adjusted by an unidentified adult. At the left appears the man, again possibly the child's father, who was seen before at the right of the middle panel.

Dominating the top panel is another Zapotec iconographic element: a "flying turtle." It bears the name "5 Skull." The turtle's head is similar in appearance to the other reptilian heads in the bottom panel. Historical documents suggest that the Zapotec sometimes visualized the "sacred clouds" from which their rulers were descended as having the appearance of flying turtles. Thus both of the iconographic elements of the Noriega register, the "Jaws of the Sky" and the "flying turtle," are consistent with the concept of a genealogical record.

This review of the later Zapotec inscriptions brings my discussion to the point where an overall summary is possible. First, I believe it is clear that all Zapotec inscriptions, early or late, are associated with Zapotec political history. Can evolutionary trends be identified? I believe progress is evident from an early phase, when the "message" of an inscription was conveyed very simply in a mainly pictorial way, to a later

GENEALOGICAL REGISTER from Zaachila, in the Valley of Oaxaca, portrays two generations in a royal family after the decline of Monte Albán. A long inscription occupies three of the four sides of this small monument. The royal couple in the lower panel are "11 Monkey" (*upper colored glyphs*) and "6 [perhaps 8] Flower" (*lower glyphs*) depending on whether the two numeral dots behind the man's back are added to his name glyphs. The upper panel evidently records the marriage of a royal couple. Emerging from the "Jaws of the Sky" (*top*) is a figure (*colored outline*) holding a string of beads. The couple's names (*color*) are "3 Serpent" (*left*) and "6 Earthquake" (*right*). The names also appear in the inscription (*color at top right*).

phase, when more complex glyphic displays served to elaborate the pictorial message.

For example, it was in Period I that the largest number of monuments at Monte Albán, the 300-odd "dancers," were created. The overall impact of this display must have been powerful, but the individual monuments conveyed relatively little information. Far fewer monuments are known from Period II, but some of these 50 or so works carry double rows of glyphs, and the individual monuments convey much more infor-

mation than any "dancer" monument does. Indeed, many Zapotec glyphs make their first appearance in Period II. Finally, the first subphase of Period III is almost monument-poor: only 15 or so monuments were raised at Monte Albán. The number and variety of the glyphs on these few monuments, however, represent a further substantial increase in the amount of information conveyed.

To recapitulate, early in Zapotec history the common themes of the monuments were scenes of captives and lists of conquered places. This is the kind of propaganda one associates with an emerging state that is fighting to take control over previously autonomous regions and wants to discourage resistance. Once Monte Albán had become a major urban center, the capital of what was unquestionably the most powerful state in the highlands of southern Mexico, its monuments begin to deal with diplomacy. The Lápida de Bazán and the four stelae at the corners of the South Platform reflect peaceful Zapotec dealings with Teotihuacán. With the decline of Monte Albán after Period III and the rise of smaller competitive centers in the Valley of Oaxaca, one of the major concerns of the new Zapotec elite became the affirmation of their royal status.

As far as monumental inscriptions are concerned, that affirmation was achieved by means of the genealogical registers: displays that recorded the ruler's marriage and ancestry and in some instances were even placed in the antechamber of the royal tomb, where the record could be consulted by future generations. Even after the Spanish conquest, as the Lienzo de Guevea demonstrates, the Zapotec people were still greatly concerned with the ancestry of their rulers and with the named landmarks that defined their territory.

REGISTER FROM NORIEGA, another Valley of Oaxaca site, includes in its bottom panel the "Jaws of the Sky" (colored outline) and two reptilian heads (color). In the middle panel, reading from left to right, a woman, "2 Water" (upper colored glyphs), gives birth to a child, "2 Vessel" (lower glyphs). A male with a headdress is at the center; at the right the child is now old enough to sit up. It faces a male figure, possibly its father. In the top panel, reading from right to left, the child's mother appears again; she holds a "manikin scepter." At the center the child appears again, still older; an unidentified adult adjusts the child's headband. The child faces a man at the far left, again possibly its father (the headdresses are alike). At top center is seen a "flying turtle" (colored outline): its head resembles the reptilian heads in the bottom panel. It bears the name "5 Skull" (colored glyphs). The image of the turtle, like the "Jaws of the Sky," reinforced the genealogical context of the inscription: the royal descent of a newborn heir.

We are still a long way from being able to "read" Zapotec writing in the way that Egyptian and even Maya hieroglyphs can be read. Major topics for further study are the lists of places mentioned as important landmarks, the "hand gestures" that may represent verbs of action, the noncalendric glyphs, which appear to be related to political and ritual information, the correlation between the Zapotec and the European calendars, the correspondences between Zapotec writing and the Zapotec spoken language and finally the evolutionary relation between the Zapotec system of writing and the systems of the Mixtec, the Aztec and the Maya. Only when progress has been made in these topics will it be possible to appreciate fully the contribution of this remarkable people to pre-Columbian literacy. And it is a contribution that must be understood in its own terms and not simply in terms of later and better-known systems.

III

LANGUAGE AS BIOLOGICAL AND SOCIAL BEHAVIOR

LANGUAGE AS BIOLOGICAL AND SOCIAL BEHAVIOR III

INTRODUCTION

Research on how language is served by the brain confronts a supreme intellectual challenge that poses a double dilemma in epistemology: What are the limits in a quest in which brain is studying brain and language is probing language? Nonetheless, as this section documents, some progress has been made toward understanding the intricate relations between brain and language and toward simulation of linguistic behavior by computer.

Recognition of the role of the brain came quite late in various world cultures. The Aristotelians attributed the seat of the soul and the center of all sensations to the heart. This view has left its traces in many phrases of our language, so we speak of a kind heart, a cold heart, and so on. In English, courage is stoutheartedness; but in Chinese, it is attributed to the size of the gallbladder, and in Arabic, it is the liver that holds love.

A good deal of what we know about language and the brain came in the last century or so. When the impairment of a linguistic function is highly correlated with damage to a particular region of the brain, the possibility arises that the function is served by that region. Research on such correlations was difficult because the brain could not be directly accessed for in-depth examination while the patient was exhibiting the dysfunction. However, with the advent of new techniques such as electroencephalography, blood-flow studies, and especially the recent methods of computerized axial tomography, new horizons are opening up.

In Norman Geschwind's work, we find some of the most lucid statements on how language is organized in the brain and how such organization may have evolved in the cortex. The evidence is abundant that not all brain tissues are equally involved in every mental behavior. In the article reprinted here, however, "Specializations of the Human Brain," Geschwind suggests that there exist brain tissues which are exclusively specialized for language—a hypothesis that is being intensively examined at present.

The next four articles each provided an additional vantage point. An adequate theory of the psychobiology of language must eventually knit together all these observations into an integrated fabric. In "The Acquisition of Language," Breyne Arlene Moskowitz discusses some aspects of how the first language is acquired. This must rank among the highest intellectual achievements in a person's life, with a necessary assist, of course, from the genes.

While speech comes naturally, reading and writing are independent skills that require concentrated effort. For a variety of reasons, some biological and some social, many people never acquire one or both of these skills adequately and are severely handicapped in a society where much power lies with the written word. Peter Dunn-Rankin's article, "The Visual Characteristics of Words," provides a discussion on how the word is perceived.

In many parts of the world, people typically use two or more languages in their day-to-day activities. One might be the language of the region, for example, and the other the language officially sponsored by the government. In a pluralistic city like San Francisco, the language of the neighborhood may be Spanish, Chinese, Japanese, Russian, Tagalog, or a wealth of others. The question naturally follows: How does the brain accommodate a second language, or a third? Paul A. Kolers' article, "Bilingualism and Information Processing," deals with a component of this question from an experimental viewpoint.

Cultures value differently the ability to speak well. "Fluent," "eloquent," "articulate," "glib," and "tongue-tied," are some of the adjectives used in this society, where often enough it is the fast talker who wins the political office or the business contract. To Confucius, however, a superior person was someone of few words. Indeed, there are communities in various parts of the world in which social visits involve long periods of shared silence—a situation that would produce discomfort and embarrassment in our culture.

"Slips of the Tongue," by Victoria A. Fromkin, deals with one dimension of the ability to speak well, or rather the inverse of it: making speech errors. By analyzing the nature of these errors with the tools of a linguist, she suggests some interesting hypotheses on language organization in the brain.

This section concludes with two articles on the application of computer methods to language: "The Synthesis of Speech," by James L. Flanagan," and "Speech Recognition by Computer," by Steven E. Levinson and Mark Y. Liberman. There has always been work here in a variety of areas, including machine translation, text comprehension, and information retrieval. The two papers included here represent areas that show clearer signs of success, perhaps because they tie in more readily to the powerful methods of electronics and signal processing that have developed rapidly in recent years.

With the explosive growth of microcomputers recently, speech synthesis and language processing are becoming increasingly available to secondary schools and to private homes. Such developments are found to broaden the base of interest in, and deepen our knowledge of, the nature of human communication.

SUGGESTED FURTHER READING

Books

Albert, Martin L., and Loraine K. Obler. 1978. *The Bilingual Brain*. New York: Academic Press.

Brown, Roger. 1973. *A First Language*. Cambridge: Harvard University Press.

Lenneberg, Eric H. and Elizabeth, eds. 1975. *Foundations of Language Development*. 2 vols. New York: Academic Press.

Miller, George A., and Philip N. Johnson-Laird. 1976. *Language and Perception*. Cambridge: Harvard University Press.

Reed, Carroll E., ed. 1971. *The Learning of Language*. New York: Appleton-Century-Crofts.

Tzeng, Ovid, and Harry Singer, eds. 1981. *The Perception of Print: Reading Research in Experimental Psychology*. Hillsdale, N.J.: Lawrence Erlbaum Associates.

Scientific American Articles

Broadbent, Donald E. "Attention and the Perception of Speech." April 1962. Offprint No. 467.

Chapanis, Alphonse. "Interactive Human Communication." March 1975.

Geschwind, Norman. "Language and the Brain." April 1972. Offprint No. 1246.

Irwin, Orvis C. "Infant Speech." September 1949. Offprint No. 417.

Kimura, Doreen. "The Asymmetry of the Human Brain." March 1973. Offprint No. 554.

Kolers, Paul A. "Experiments in Reading." July 72. Offprint No. 545.

Krauss, Robert M., and Sam Glucksberg. "Social and Nonsocial Speech." February 1977. Offprint No. 576.

Luria, A. R. "The Functional Organization of the Brain." March 1970. Offprint No. 526.

Ostwald, Peter F., and Philip Peltzman. "The Cry of the Human Infant." March 1974. Offprint No. 558.

Yngve, Victor H. "Computer Programs for Translation." June 1962.

12

Specializations of the Human Brain

by Norman Geschwind
September 1979

Certain higher faculties, such as language, depend on specialized regions in the human brain. On a larger scale the two cerebral hemispheres are specialized for different kinds of mental activity

The nervous systems of all animals have a number of basic functions in common, most notably the control of movement and the analysis of sensation. What distinguishes the human brain is the variety of more specialized activities it is capable of learning. The preeminent example is language: no one is born knowing a language, but virtually everyone learns to speak and to understand the spoken word, and people of all cultures can be taught to write and to read. Music is also universal in man: people with no formal training are able to recognize and to reproduce dozens of melodies. Similarly, almost everyone can draw simple figures, and the ability to make accurate renderings is not rare.

At least some of these higher functions of the human brain are governed by dedicated networks of neurons. It has been known for more than 100 years, for example, that at least two delimited regions of the cerebral cortex are essential to linguistic competence; they seem to be organized explicitly for the processing of verbal information. Certain structures on the inner surface of the underside of the temporal lobe, including the hippocampus, are apparently necessary for the long-term retention of memories. In some cases the functional specialization of a neural system seems to be quite narrowly defined: hence one area on both sides of the human cerebral cortex is concerned primarily with the recognition of faces. It is likely that other mental activities are also associated with particular neural networks. Musical and artistic abilities, for example, appear to depend on specialized systems in the brain, although the circuitry has not yet been worked out.

Another distinctive characteristic of the human brain is the allocation of functions to the two cerebral hemispheres. That the human brain is not fully symmetrical in its functioning could be guessed from at least one observation of daily experience: most of the human population favors the right hand, which is controlled by the left side of the brain. Linguistic abilities also reside mainly on the left side. For these reasons the left cerebral hemisphere was once said to be the dominant one and the right side of the brain was thought to be subservient. In recent years this concept has been revised as it has become apparent that each hemisphere has its own specialized talents. Those for which the right cortex is dominant include some features of aptitudes for music and for the recognition of complex visual patterns. The right hemisphere is also the more important one for the expression and recognition of emotion. In the past few years these functional asymmetries have been matched with anatomical ones, and a start has been made on exploring their prevalence in species other than man.

In man as in other mammalian species large areas of the cerebral cortex are given over to comparatively elementary sensory and motor functions. An arch that extends roughly from ear to ear across the roof of the brain is the primary motor cortex, which exercises voluntary control over the muscles. Parallel to this arch and just behind it is the primary somatic sensory area, where signals are received from the skin, the bones, the joints and the muscles. Almost every region of the body is represented by a corresponding region in both the primary motor cortex and the somatic sensory cortex. At the back of the brain, and particularly on the inner surface of the occipital lobes, is the primary visual cortex. The primary auditory areas are in the temporal lobes; olfaction is focused in a region on the underside of the frontal lobes.

The primary motor and sensory areas are specialized in the sense that each one is dedicated to a specified function, but the functions themselves are of general utility, and the areas are called on in a great variety of activities. Moreover, homologous areas are found in all species that have a well-developed cerebral cortex. My main concern in this article is with certain regions of the cortex that govern a narrower range of behavior. Some of these highly specialized areas may be common to many species but others may be uniquely human.

A series of experiments dealing with learning in monkeys illustrates how fine the functional distinction can be between two networks of neurons. A monkey can be taught to choose consistently one object or pattern from a pair. The task is made somewhat more difficult if the objects are presented and then withdrawn and the monkey is allowed to indicate its choice only after a delay during which the objects are hidden behind a screen. It has been found that performance on this test is impaired markedly if a small region of the frontal lobes is destroyed on both sides of the brain. Difficulty can also be introduced into the experiment by making the patterns complex but allowing a choice to be made while the patterns are still in sight. Damage to a quite different area of the cortex reduces ability to carry out this task, but it has no effect on the delay test.

These experiments also illustrate one of the principal means for acquiring information about the functions of the brain. When a particular site is damaged by disease or injury, a well-defined deficiency in behavior sometimes ensues. In many cases one may conclude that some aspects of the behavior affected are normally dependent on the part of the brain that has been destroyed. In man the commonest cause of brain damage is cerebral thrombosis, or stroke, the occlusion of arteries in the brain, which results in the death of the tissues the blocked arteries supply. By 1920 the study of patients who had sustained such damage had led to the identification of several functional regions of the brain, including the language areas.

The study of the effects of damage to the brain is still an important method of investigating brain function, but other techniques have since been developed. One of the most important was brought to a high level of development by the German neurosurgeon Otfrid Foerster and by Wilder Penfield of the Montreal Neurological Institute. They studied the responses in the conscious patient un-

REPRODUCED BY LEFT HAND (RIGHT HEMISPHERE)   MODEL PATTERN   REPRODUCED BY RIGHT HAND (LEFT HEMISPHERE)

CAPABILITIES OF THE TWO HEMISPHERES of the human cerebral cortex were tested in a subject whose hemispheres had been surgically isolated from each other. The surgical procedure consisted in cutting the two main bundles of nerve fibers that connect the hemispheres: the corpus callosum and the anterior commissure. In the test each of the patterns in the middle column was presented to the subject, who was asked to reproduce it by assembling colored blocks. The assembly was carried out either with the right hand alone (which communicates mainly with the left hemisphere) or with the left hand alone (which is controlled primarily by the right hemisphere). Errors were equally frequent with either hand, but the kinds of error typical of each hand were quite different. The results suggest that each side of the brain may bring a separate set of skills to bear on such a task, a finding consistent with other evidence that the hemispheres are specialized for different functions. What is equally apparent, however, is that neither hemisphere alone is competent in the analysis of such patterns; the two hemispheres must cooperate. The test was conducted by Edith Kaplan of the Boston Veterans Administration Hospital.

dergoing brain surgery that follow electrical stimulation of various sites in the brain. In this way they were able to map the regions responsible for a number of functions. Apart from the importance of this technique for the study of the brain, it is of clinical benefit since it enables the surgeon to avoid areas where damage might be crippling.

Surgical procedures developed for the control of severe epilepsy have also contributed much information. One method of treating persistent epileptic seizures (adopted only when other therapies have failed) is to remove the region of the cortex from which the seizures arise. The functional deficits that sometimes result from this procedure have been studied in detail by Brenda Milner of the Montreal Neurological Institute.

The specializations of the hemispheres can be studied in people who have sustained damage to the commissures that connect the two sides of the brain, the most important of these being the corpus callosum. In the first such cases, studied at the end of the 19th century by Jules Déjerine in France and by Hugo Liepmann in Germany, the damage had been caused by strokes. More recently isolation of the hemispheres by surgical sectioning of the commissures

has been employed for the relief of epilepsy. Studies of such "split brain" patients by Roger W. Sperry of the California Institute of Technology and by Michael S. Gazzaniga of the Cornell University Medical College have provided increasingly detailed knowledge of the functions of the separated hemispheres. Doreen Kimura, who is now at the University of Western Ontario, pioneered in the development of a technique, called dichotic listening, that provides information about hemispheric specialization in the intact human brain.

The specialized regions of the brain that have been investigated in the greatest detail are those involved in language. In the 1860's the French investigator Paul Broca pointed out that damage to a particular region of the cortex consistently gives rise to an aphasia, or speech disorder. The region is on the side of the frontal lobes, and it is now called the anterior language area, or simply Broca's area. Broca went on to make a second major discovery. He showed that whereas damage to this area on the left side of the brain leads to aphasia, similar damage to the corresponding area on the right side leaves the faculty of speech intact. This finding

has since been amply confirmed: well over 95 percent of the aphasias caused by brain damage result from damage to the left hemisphere.

Broca's area is adjacent to the face area of the motor cortex, which controls the muscles of the face, the tongue, the jaw and the throat. When Broca's area is destroyed by a stroke, there is almost always severe damage to the face area in the left hemisphere as well, and so it might be thought that the disruption of speech is caused by partial paralysis of the muscles required for articulation. That some other explanation is required is easily demonstrated. First, damage to the corresponding area on the right side of the brain does not cause aphasia, although a similar weakness of the facial muscles results. Furthermore, in Broca's aphasia it is known that the muscles that function poorly in speech operate normally in other tasks. The evidence is quite simple: the patient with Broca's aphasia can speak only with great difficulty, but he can sing with ease and often with elegance. The speech of a patient with Broca's aphasia also has features, such as faulty grammar, that cannot be explained by a muscular failure.

Another kind of aphasia was identified in 1874 by the German investiga-

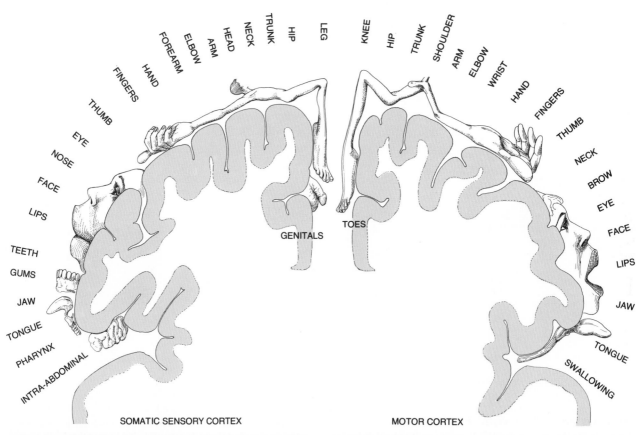

SOMATIC SENSORY AND MOTOR REGIONS of the cerebral cortex are specialized in the sense that every site in these regions can be associated with some part of the body. In other words, most of the body can be mapped onto the cortex, yielding two distorted homunculi. The distortions come about because the area of the cortex dedicated to a part of the body is proportional not to that part's actual size but to the precision with which it must be controlled. In man the motor and somatic sensory regions given over to the face and to the hands are greatly exaggerated. Only half of each cortical region is shown: the left somatic sensory area (which receives sensations primarily from the right side of the body) and the right motor cortex (which exercises control over movement in the left half of the body).

tor Carl Wernicke. It is associated with damage to another site in the cortex, also in the left hemisphere, but in the temporal lobe rather than the frontal lobe. This region, which is now called Wernicke's area, lies between the primary auditory cortex and a structure called the angular gyrus, which probably mediates between visual and auditory centers of the brain. It has since been learned that Wernicke's area and Broca's area are connected by a bundle of nerve fibers, the arcuate fasciculus.

A lesion in either Broca's area or Wernicke's area leads to a disruption of speech, but the nature of the two disorders is quite different. In Broca's aphasia speech is labored and slow and articulation is impaired. The response to a question will often make sense, but it generally cannot be expressed as a fully formed or grammatical sentence. There is particular difficulty with the inflection of verbs, with pronouns and connective words and with complex grammatical constructions. As a result the speech has a telegraphic style. For example, a patient asked about a dental appointment said, hesitantly and indistinctly: "Yes... Monday... Dad and Dick... Wednesday nine o'clock... 10 o'clock... doctors... and... teeth." The same kinds of errors are made in writing.

In Wernicke's aphasia speech is phonetically and even grammatically normal, but it is semantically deviant. Words are often strung together with considerable facility and with the proper inflections, so that the utterance has the recognizable structure of a sentence. The words chosen, however, are often inappropriate, and they sometimes include nonsensical syllables or words. Even when the individual words are correct, the utterance as a whole may express its meaning in a remarkably roundabout way. A patient who was asked to describe a picture that showed two boys stealing cookies behind a woman's back reported: "Mother is away here working her work to get her better, but when she's looking the two boys looking the other part. She's working another time."

From an analysis of these defects Wernicke formulated a model of language production in the brain. Much new information has been added in the past 100 years, but the general principles Wernicke elaborated still seem valid. In this model the underlying structure of an utterance arises in Wernicke's area. It is then transferred through the arcuate fasciculus to Broca's area, where it evokes a detailed and coordinated program for vocalization. The program is passed on to the adjacent face area of the motor cortex, which activates the appropriate muscles of the mouth, the lips, the tongue, the larynx and so on.

Wernicke's area not only has a part

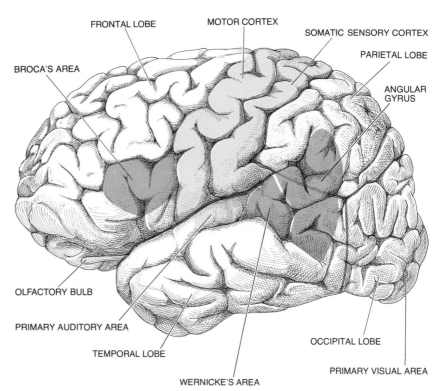

FRONTAL LOBE   MOTOR CORTEX   SOMATIC SENSORY CORTEX   PARIETAL LOBE   ANGULAR GYRUS   BROCA'S AREA   OLFACTORY BULB   PRIMARY AUDITORY AREA   TEMPORAL LOBE   WERNICKE'S AREA   OCCIPITAL LOBE   PRIMARY VISUAL AREA

MAP OF THE HUMAN CORTEX shows regions whose functional specializations have been identified. Much of the cortex is given over to comparatively elementary functions: the generation of movement and the primary analysis of sensations. These areas, which include the motor and somatic sensory regions and the primary visual, auditory and olfactory areas, are present in all species that have a well-developed cortex and are called on in the course of many activities. Several other regions (*dark color*) are more narrowly specialized. Broca's area and Wernicke's area are involved in the production and comprehension of language. The angular gyrus is thought to mediate between visual and auditory forms of information. These functional specializations have been detected only on the left side of the brain; the corresponding areas of the right hemisphere do not have the same linguistic competence. The right hemisphere, which is not shown, has its own specialized abilities, including the analysis of some aspects of music and of complex visual patterns. The anatomical regions associated with these faculties, however, are not as well defined as the language areas. Even in the left hemisphere the assignment of functions to sites in the cortex is only approximate; some areas may have functions in addition to those indicated, and some functions may be carried out in more than one place.

in speaking but also has a major role in the comprehension of the spoken word and in reading and writing. When a word is heard, the sound is initially received in the primary auditory cortex, but the signal must pass through the adjacent Wernicke's area if it is to be understood as a verbal message. When a word is read, the visual pattern (from the primary visual cortex) is transmitted to the angular gyrus, which applies a transformation that elicits the auditory form of the word in Wernicke's area. Writing a word in response to an oral instruction requires information to be passed along the same pathways in the opposite direction: from the auditory cortex to Wernicke's area to the angular gyrus.

This model explains many of the symptoms that characterize the aphasias. A lesion in Broca's area disturbs the production of speech but has a much smaller effect on comprehension. Damage to Wernicke's area, on the other hand, disrupts all aspects of the use of language. The effects of certain rarer le-

sions are also in accord with the model. For example, destruction of the arcuate fasciculus, disconnecting Wernicke's area from Broca's area, leaves speech fluent and well articulated but semantically aberrant; Broca's area is operating but it is not receiving information from Wernicke's area. Because the latter center is also functional, however, comprehension of spoken and written words is almost normal. Writing is disrupted in all aphasias where speech is abnormal, but the neural circuits employed in writing are not known in detail.

Lesions in the angular gyrus have the effect of disconnecting the systems involved in auditory language and written language. Patients with injuries in certain areas of the angular gyrus may speak and understand speech normally, but they have difficulty with written language. The comprehension of a written word seems to require that the auditory form of the word be evoked in Wernicke's area. Damage to the angular gyrus seems to interrupt communication between the visual cortex and Wernicke's area, so that comprehension of written language is impaired.

Although the partitioning of linguistic functions among several sites in the cortex is now supported by much evidence, the rigidity of these assignments should not be overemphasized. The pessimistic view that damage to tissue in these areas inevitably leads to a permanent linguistic impairment is unwarranted. Actually a considerable degree of recovery is often observed. The neural tissue destroyed by an arterial thrombosis cannot be regenerated, but it seems the functions of the damaged areas can often be assumed, at least in part, by other regions. In some cases the recovery probably reflects the existence of an alternative store of learning on the opposite side of the brain, which remains dormant until the dominant side is injured. In other cases the function is taken over by neurons in areas adjacent to or surrounding the damaged site. Patrick D. Wall of University College London has shown that there is a fringe of such dormant but potentially active cells adjacent to the somatic sensory cortex, and it seems likely that similar fringe regions exist throughout the brain. Jay P. Mohr, who is now at the University of Southern Alabama, and his co-workers have shown that the prospects for recovery from Broca's aphasia are quite good provided the region destroyed is not too large. One interpretation of these findings suggests that regions bordering on Broca's area share its specialization in latent form.

Although the detailed mechanism of recovery is not known, it has been established that some groups of patients are more likely than others to regain their linguistic competence. Children, particularly children younger than eight, often make an excellent recovery. Left-handed people also make better progress than right-handers. Even among right-handers those who have left-handed parents, siblings or children are more likely to recover than those with no family history of left-handedness. The relation between handedness and recovery from damage to the language areas suggests that cerebral dominance for handedness and dominance for language are not totally independent.

A disorder of the brain that is startling because its effects are so narrowly circumscribed is prosopagnosia; it is a failure to recognize faces. In the normal individual the ability to identify people from their faces is itself quite remarkable. At a glance one can name a person from facial features alone, even though the features may change substantially over the years or may be presented in a highly distorted form, as in a caricature. In a patient with prosopagnosia this talent for association is abolished.

What is most remarkable about the disorder is its specificity. In general it is accompanied by few other neurological symptoms except for the loss of some part of the visual field, sometimes on both sides and sometimes only in the left half of space. Most mental tasks, in-

cluding those that require the processing of visual information, are done without particular difficulty; for example, the patient can usually read and correctly name seen objects. What he cannot do is look at a person or at a photograph of a face and name the person. He may even fail to recognize his wife or his children. It is not the identity of familiar people that has been lost to him, however, but only the connection between the face and the identity. When a familiar person speaks, the patient knows the voice and can say the name immediately. The perception of facial features is also unimpaired, since the patient can often describe a face in detail and can usually match a photograph made from the front with a profile of the same person. The deficiency seems to be confined to forming associations between faces and identities.

The lesions that cause prosopagnosia are as stereotyped as the disorder itself. Damage is found on the underside of both occipital lobes, extending forward to the inner surface of the temporal lobes. The implication is that some neural network within this region is specialized for the rapid and reliable recognition of human faces. It may seem that a disproportionate share of the brain's resources is being devoted to a rather limited task. It should be kept in mind, however, that the recognition of people as individuals is a valuable talent in a highly social animal, and there has probably been strong selectional pressure to improve its efficiency.

Similar capacities probably exist in other social species. Gary W. Van Hoesen, formerly in my department at the Harvard Medical School and now at the University of Iowa College of Medicine, has begun to investigate the neurological basis of face recognition in the rhesus monkey. So far he has demonstrated that the monkeys can readily discriminate between other monkeys on the basis of facial photographs. The neural structures called into play by this task have not, however, been identified.

Until recently little was known about the physiological basis of memory, one of the most important functions of the human brain. Through the study of some highly specific disorders, however, it has been possible to identify areas or structures in the brain that are involved in certain memory processes. For example, the examination of different forms of anterograde amnesia—an inability to learn new information—has revealed the role of the temporal lobes in memory. In particular, the striking disability of a patient whom Milner has studied for more than 25 years demonstrates the importance in memory of structures on the inner surface of the temporal lobes, such as the hippocampus.

In 1953 the patient had submitted to a radical surgical procedure in which

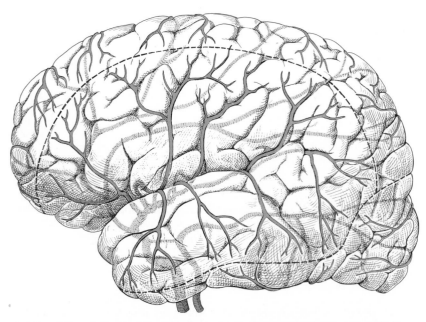

VASCULAR SYSTEM OF THE BRAIN has had an important part in the mapping of functional regions in the cerebral cortex. The normal functions of an area can often be inferred from the disturbance or impairment of behavior that results when the area is damaged. The commonest cause of such damage is the occlusion of an artery supplying the cortex, which leads to the death of the tissue nourished by that artery. Broca's area and Wernicke's area were identified in this way about 100 years ago, when patients with distinctive aphasias, or speech defects, were found by postmortem examination to have damage in those areas of the left hemisphere.

much of the hippocampus and several associated structures in both temporal lobes were destroyed. After the operation the skills and knowledge the patient had acquired up to that time remained largely intact, and he was and still is able to attend normally to ongoing events. In fact, he seems to be able to register limited amounts of new information in the usual manner. Within a short time, however, most of the newly learned information ceases to be available to him.

Milner has interviewed and tested the patient at intervals since the operation, and she has found that his severe anterograde amnesia has changed very little during that time. He has also exhibited an extensive although patchy retrograde amnesia (about the years before the operation), but that has improved appreciably. In the absence of distraction he can retain, say, a three-digit number for many minutes by means of verbal rehearsal or with the aid of an elaborate mnemonic device. Once his attention has been momentarily diverted, however, he cannot remember the number or the mnemonic device to which he devoted so much effort. He cannot even remember the task itself. Living from moment to moment, he has not been able to learn his address or to remember where the objects he uses every day are kept in his home. He fails to recognize people who have visited him regularly for many years.

The bilateral surgery that resulted in this memory impairment is, for obvious reasons, no longer done, but similar lesions on the inner surface of the temporal lobes have occasionally resulted from operations on one side of the brain in a patient with unsuspected damage to the opposite lobe. Comparable memory deficits result, and so the role of the inner surface of the temporal lobes in memory function is now widely accepted. Moreover, the fact that these patients generally retain their faculties of perception supports the distinction made by many workers between a short-term memory process and a long-term process by which more stable storage of information is achieved. It is clearly the second process that is impaired in the patients described above, but the nature of the impairment is a matter of controversy. Some think the problem is a failure of consolidation, that is, transferring information from short-term to long-term storage. Others hold that the information is transferred and stored but cannot be retrieved. The ultimate resolution of these conflicting theories will require a clearer specification of the neural circuitry of memory.

At a glance the brain appears to have perfect bilateral symmetry, like most other organs of the body. It might therefore be expected that the two halves of the brain would also be functionally equivalent, just as the two kid-

SPEAKING A HEARD WORD

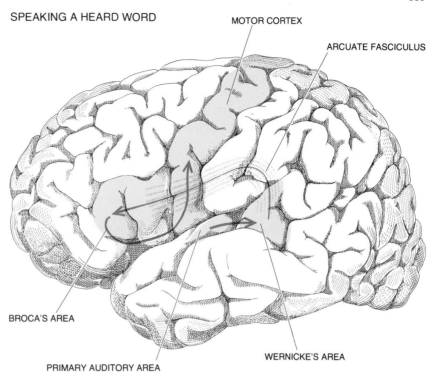

SPEAKING A WRITTEN WORD

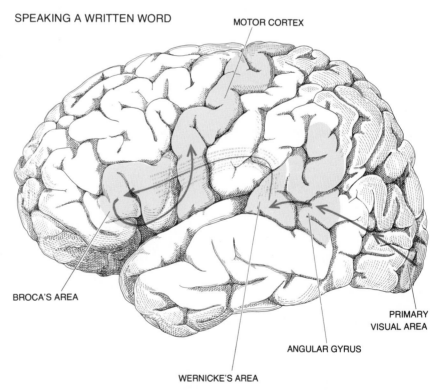

LINGUISTIC COMPETENCE requires the cooperation of several areas of the cortex. When a word is heard (*upper diagram*), the sensation from the ears is received by the primary auditory cortex, but the word cannot be understood until the signal has been processed in Wernicke's area nearby. If the word is to be spoken, some representation of it is thought to be transmitted from Wernicke's area to Broca's area, through a bundle of nerve fibers called the arcuate fasciculus. In Broca's area the word evokes a detailed program for articulation, which is supplied to the face area of the motor cortex. The motor cortex in turn drives the muscles of the lips, the tongue, the larynx and so on. When a written word is read (*lower diagram*), the sensation is first registered by the primary visual cortex. It is then thought to be relayed to the angular gyrus, which associates the visual form of the word with the corresponding auditory pattern in Wernicke's area. Speaking the word then draws on the same systems of neurons as before.

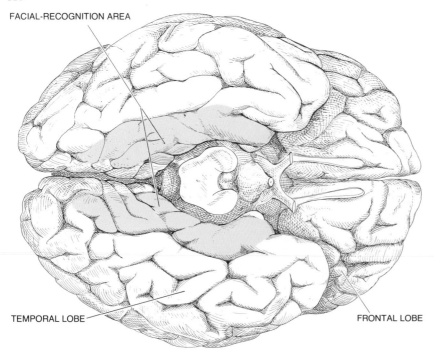

FACIAL-RECOGNITION AREA

TEMPORAL LOBE

FRONTAL LOBE

RECOGNITION OF FACES is a faculty that seems to be governed by regions on the underside of the temporal and occipital lobes on both sides of the cortex, which is seen here from below. A lesion that destroys this area impairs the ability to identify a person by facial features but has almost no other effects. There is often some loss of vision, but the patient can read, can name objects on sight and can even match a full-face portrait with a profile of the same person. People can also be recognized by their voices. The only ability that is lost is the ability to recognize people by their faces, and that loss can be so severe that close relatives are not recognized.

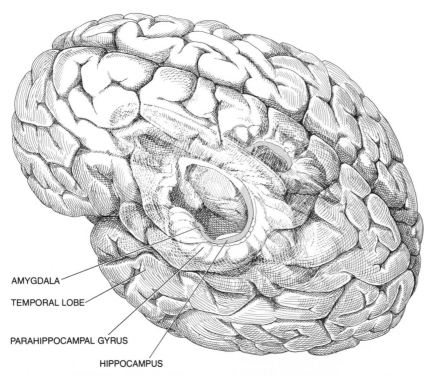

AMYGDALA

TEMPORAL LOBE

PARAHIPPOCAMPAL GYRUS

HIPPOCAMPUS

CERTAIN MEMORY PROCESSES appear to be associated with structures on the inner surface of the temporal lobes, such as the hippocampus (color). Bilateral lesions of these areas have been shown to cause a severe and lasting memory disorder characterized by the inability to learn new information. Patients with lesions of this type appear to have undiminished powers of perception, but they are largely incapable of incorporating new information into their long-term store. Acute lesions in this region of a single temporal lobe sometimes result in similar but less persistent memory disorders that reflect the contrasting specializations of the hemispheres: the type of information that cannot be learned varies according to the side the lesion is on.

neys or the two lungs are. Actually many of the more specialized functions are found in only one hemisphere or the other. Even the apparent anatomical symmetry turns out to be illusory.

In the primary motor and sensory areas of the cortex the assignment of duties to the two hemispheres follows a simple pattern: each side of the brain is concerned mainly with the opposite side of the body. Most of the nerve fibers in the pathways that radiate from the motor and somatic sensory areas cross to the opposite side of the nervous system at some point in their course. Hence the muscles of the right hand and foot are controlled primarily by the left motor cortex, and sensory impulses from the right side go mainly to the left somatic sensory cortex. Each ear has connections to the auditory cortex on both sides of the brain, but the connections to the contralateral side are stronger. The distribution of signals from the eyes is somewhat more complicated. The optic nerves are arranged so that images from the right half of space in both eyes are projected onto the left visual cortex; the left visual field from both eyes goes to the right hemisphere. As a result of this pattern of contralateral connections the sensory and motor functions of the two hemispheres are kept separate, but they are largely symmetrical. Each half of the brain is concerned with half of the body and half of the visual field.

The distribution of the more specialized functions is quite different, and it is profoundly asymmetrical. I have indicated above that linguistic ability is dependent primarily on the left hemisphere. There is reason to believe the right side of the brain is more important for the perception of melodies, one item of evidence being the ease with which aphasic patients with left-hemisphere damage can sing. The perception and analysis of nonverbal visual patterns, such as perspective drawings, is largely a function of the right hemisphere, although the left hemisphere also makes a distinctive contribution to such tasks. These asymmetries are also reflected in partial memory defects that can result from lesions in a single temporal lobe. A left temporal lobectomy can impair the ability to retain verbal material but can leave intact the ability to remember spatial locations, faces, melodies and abstract visual patterns.

In everyday life this lateralization of function can seldom be detected because information is readily passed between the hemispheres through several commissures, including the corpus callosum. Even when the interconnections are severed, the full effects of cerebral dominance can be observed only in laboratory situations, where it is possible to ensure that sensory information reaches only one hemisphere at a time and that a motor response comes from only one hemisphere. Under these conditions a

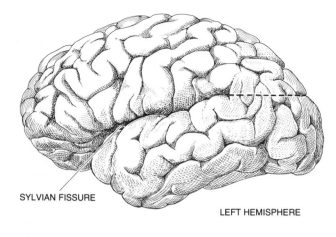

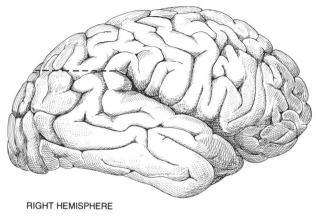

SYLVIAN FISSURE

LEFT HEMISPHERE

RIGHT HEMISPHERE

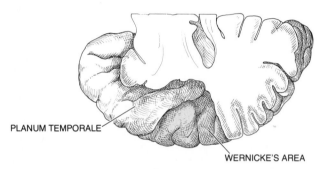

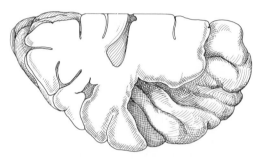

PLANUM TEMPORALE

WERNICKE'S AREA

ANATOMICAL ASYMMETRY of the cortex has been detected in the human brain and may be related to the distinctive functional specializations of the two hemispheres. One asymmetry is readily observed in the intact brain: the sylvian fissure, which defines the upper margin of the temporal lobe, rises more steeply on the right side of the brain. A more striking asymmetry is found on the planum tem-

porale, which forms the upper surface of the temporal lobe, and which can be seen only when the sylvian fissure is opened. The posterior part of the planum temporale is usually much larger on the left side. The enlarged region is part of Wernicke's area, suggesting that the asymmetry may be related to the linguistic dominance of the left hemisphere. The distribution of the asymmetries varies with handedness.

remarkable pattern of behavior is observed. If an object is placed in a patient's left hand or if it is presented only to his left visual field, he cannot say its name. The failure is not one of recognition, since the patient is able to match related objects, but the perception received only in the right hemisphere cannot be associated with a name that is known only to the left hemisphere.

The specialization of the isolated hemispheres should not be overstated, however. The right half of the brain does have some rudimentary linguistic ability. Moreover, there are doubtless many tasks where the two hemispheres ordinarily act in concert. In one test administered after surgical isolation of the hemispheres the patient is asked to reproduce a simple pattern by assembling colored blocks. In some cases errors are frequent whether the task is completed with the left hand or the right, but they are characteristically different kinds of errors. It appears that neither hemisphere alone is competent in this task and that the two must cooperate.

One of the most surprising recent findings is that different emotional reactions follow damage to the right and left sides of the brain. Lesions in most areas on the left side are accompanied

by the feelings of loss that might be expected as a result of any serious injury. The patient is disturbed by his disability and often is depressed. Damage in much of the right hemisphere sometimes leaves the patient unconcerned with his condition. Guido Gainotti of the Catholic University of Rome has made a detailed compilation of these differences in emotional response.

Emotion and "state of mind" are often associated with the structures of the limbic system, at the core of the brain, but in recent years it has been recognized that the cerebral cortex, particularly the right hemisphere of the cortex, also makes an important contribution. Lesions in the right hemisphere not only give rise to inappropriate emotional responses to the patient's own condition but also impair his recognition of emotion in others. A patient with damage on the left side may not be able to comprehend a statement, but in many cases he can still recognize the emotional tone with which it is spoken. A patient with a disorder of the right hemisphere usually understands the meaning of what is said, but he often fails to recognize that it is spoken in an angry or a humorous way.

Although cerebral dominance has been known in the human brain for more than a century, comparable asym-

metries in other species have been recognized only in the past few years. A pioneer in this endeavor is Fernando Nottebohm of Rockefeller University, who has studied the neural basis of singing in songbirds. In most of the species he has studied so far, but not in all of them, the left side of the brain is more important for singing. Examples of dominance in mammals other than man have also been described, although in much less detail. Under certain conditions damage to the right side of the brain in rats alters emotional behavior, as Victor H. Denenberg of the University of Connecticut has shown. Dominance of the left cerebral cortex for some auditory tasks has been discovered in one species of monkey by James H. Dewson III, who is now at Stanford University. Michael Petersen and other investigators at the University of Michigan and at Rockefeller University have shown that the left hemisphere is dominant in the recognition of species-specific cries in Japanese macaques, which employ an unusual variety of such signals. So far, however, no definitive example of functional asymmetry has been described in the brains of the great apes, the closest relations of man.

For many years it was the prevailing view of neurologists that the func-

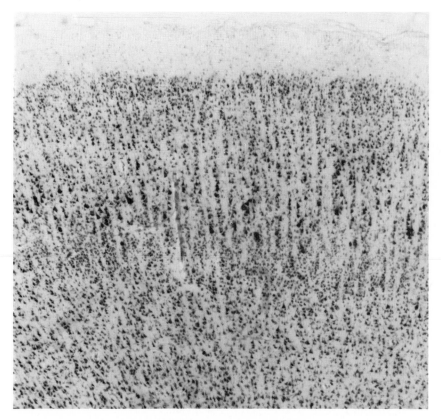

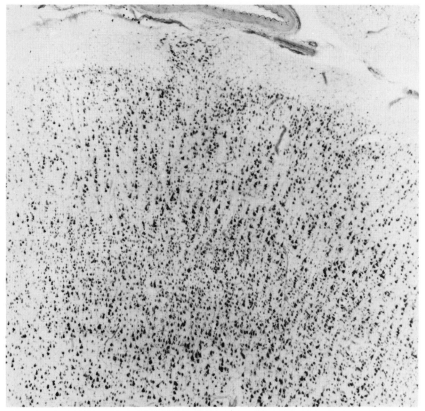

ABNORMAL CELLULAR ARCHITECTURE has been found in a language area of a patient with a developmental reading disorder. The top photomicrograph is a section of the normal cortex from the posterior portion of the planum temporale, the region that makes up part of Wernicke's area. Several layers can be perceived and the cells have a characteristic columnar organization. The bottom photograph is a section from the same region in a patient with dyslexia. One peculiarity is the presence of nerve-cell bodies in the most superficial layer (*near top of photograph*), where they are normally absent. Moreover, throughout the tissue the arrangement of cells is disrupted. The abnormality was found by Albert M. Galaburda of the Harvard Medical School and Thomas Kemper of the Boston University School of Medicine.

tional asymmetries of the brain could not be correlated with anatomical asymmetries. If there were any significant differences between the hemispheres, it was assumed, they would have been noted long ago by surgeons or pathologists. About 10 years ago my colleague Walter Levitsky and I decided to look into this matter again, following some earlier observations by the German neurologist Richard Arwed Pfeifer. We examined 100 human brains, paying particular attention to a region called the planum temporale, which lies on the upper surface of the temporal lobe and is hidden within the sylvian fissure that runs along each side of the brain. Our study was concerned only with gross anatomy, and we employed no instruments more elaborate than a camera and a ruler; nevertheless, we found unequivocal evidence of asymmetry. In general the length and orientation of the sylvian fissures is different on opposite sides of the head. What is more significant, the posterior area of the planum temporale, which forms part of Wernicke's area, is generally larger on the left side. The differences are not subtle and can easily be seen with the unaided eye.

Juhn A. Wada of the University of British Columbia subsequently showed that the asymmetry of the planum temporale can be detected in the human fetus. It therefore appears that the enlargement of the left planum cannot be a response to the development of linguistic competence in childhood. On the contrary, the superior linguistic talent of the left hemisphere may result from the anatomical bias.

More recently my colleague Albert M. Galaburda has discovered that the enlargement of the left planum can be explained in terms of the cellular organization of the tissue. On the planum is a region with a distinctive cellular architecture, designated *Tpt*. Galaburda found that the extent of the *Tpt* region is considerably greater in the left hemisphere; in the first brain he examined it was more than seven times as large on the left side as it was on the right.

Galaburda and Thomas Kemper of the Boston University School of Medicine also examined the brain of an accident victim who had suffered from persistent dyslexia. He found that the *Tpt* areas in the two hemispheres were of approximately equal size. Furthermore, the cellular structure of the *Tpt* area on the left side was abnormal. The neurons in the normal cortex are arranged in a sequence of layers, each of which has a distinctive population of cells. In the brain of the dyslexic the strata were disrupted, one conspicuous anomaly being the presence of cell bodies of neurons in the most superficial layer of the cortex, where they are normally absent. Islands of cortical tissue were also found in the white matter of the brain, where they do not belong. Although no firm conclusion can be drawn from a single case, it does seem striking that a structural abnormality would be found in the language area of a patient who was known to have a linguistic disability.

A new line of research on brain asymmetry has lately been opened by my colleague Marjorie J. LeMay. She has devised several methods for detecting anatomical asymmetry in the living person. One of these methods is cerebral arteriography, in which a substance opaque to X rays is injected into the bloodstream and the distribution of the substance is monitored as it flows through the cranial arteries. Arteriography is often employed in the diagnosis of brain tumors and other brain diseases, and the arteriograms LeMay examined had been made for diagnostic purposes. One of the cranial arteries (the middle cerebral artery) follows the groove of the sylvian fissure, and LeMay showed that the position of the artery in the arteriogram reveals the length and orientation of the fissure. She found that in most people the middle cerebral artery on the right side of the head is inclined more steeply and ultimately ascends higher than the corresponding artery on the left side.

LeMay has also detected brain asymmetries by computed axial tomography, the process whereby an image of the skull in cross section is reconstructed from a set of X-ray projections. In these images a peculiar, skewed departure from bilateral symmetry is observed. In right-handed people the right frontal lobe is usually wider than the left, but the left parietal and occipital lobes are wider than the right. The inner surface of the skull itself bulges at the right front and the left rear to accommodate the protuberances.

LeMay has even reported finding asymmetries in cranial endocasts made from the fossil skulls of Neanderthal man and other hominids. A ridge on the inner surface of the skull corresponds to the sylvian fissure; where the ridge is preserved well enough to make an impression in an endocast LeMay finds the same pattern of asymmetry that is observed in modern man, suggesting that hemispheric dominance had already emerged at least 30,000 years ago. LeMay and I have shown that asymmetries of the sylvian fissures exist in the great apes but not in monkeys. (Grace H. Yeni-Komshian and Dennis A. Benson of the Johns Hopkins University School of Medicine have reported similar findings.) If a functional correlative to this anatomical bias can be discovered, an animal model of cerebral dominance in the anthropoid apes would become available.

One of the most commonplace manifestations of cerebral dominance is also one of the most puzzling: the phenomenon of handedness. Many animals exhibit a form of handedness; for example, if a monkey is made to carry out a task with only one hand, it will consistently use the same one. In any large population of monkeys, however, left- and right-handed individuals are equally common. In the human population no more than 9 percent are left-handed. This considerable bias toward right-handedness may represent a unique specialization of the human brain.

The genetics and heritability of handedness is a controversial topic. In mice Robert V. Collins of the Jackson Laboratory in Bar Harbor, Me., has shown that continued inbreeding of right-handed animals does not increase the prevalence of right-handedness in their offspring. The pattern in man is quite different. Marian Annett of the Lanchester Polytechnic in England has proposed a theory in which one allele of a gene pair favors the development of right-handedness, but there is no complementary allele for left-handedness. In the ab-

sence of the right-favoring allele handedness is randomly determined.

Studies undertaken by LeMay and her co-workers have revealed that the distribution of brain asymmetries in left-handed people is different from that in right-handers. In right-handed individuals, and hence in most of the population, the right sylvian fissure is higher than the left in 67 percent of the brains examined. The left fissure is higher in 8 percent and the two fissures rise to approximately equal height in 25 percent. In the left-handed population a substantial majority (71 percent) have approximate symmetry of the sylvian fissures. Among the remainder the right fissure is still more likely to be the higher (21 percent v. 7 percent). The asymmetries observed by tomography also have a different distribution in right-handers and left-handers. Again in the left-handed segment of the population the asymmetries tend to be less pronounced. These findings are in qualitative agreement with the theory proposed by Annett.

If functions as narrowly defined as facial recognition are accorded specific neural networks in the brain, it seems likely that many other functions are represented in a similar way. For example, one of the major goals of child rearing is to teach a set of highly differentiated responses to emotional stimuli, such as anger and fear. The child must also be taught the appropriate responses to stimuli from its internal milieu, such as hunger or fullness of the bladder or bowel. Most children learn these patterns of behavior just as they learn a language, suggesting that here too special-purpose processors may be present. As yet little is known about such neural systems. Indeed, even as the mapping of specialized regions continues, the next major task must be confronted: that of describing their internal operation.

The Acquisition of Language

by Breyne Arlene Moskowitz
November 1978

*How do children learn to speak? It seems they do so
in a highly methodical way: they break the language
down into its simplest parts and develop the rules they
need to put the parts together*

An adult who finds herself in a group of people speaking an unfamiliar foreign language may feel quite uncomfortable. The strange language sounds like gibberish: mysterious strings of sound, rising and falling in unpredictable patterns. Each person speaking the language knows when to speak, how to construct the strings and how to interpret other people's strings, but the individual who does not know anything about the language cannot pick out separate words or sounds, let alone discern meanings. She may feel overwhelmed, ignorant and even childlike. It is possible that she is returning to a vague memory from her very early childhood, because the experience of an adult listening to a foreign language comes close to duplicating the experience of an infant listening to the "foreign" language spoken by everyone around her. Like the adult, the child is confronted with the task of learning a language about which she knows nothing.

The task of acquiring language is one for which the adult has lost most of her aptitude but one the child will perform with remarkable skill. Within a short span of time and with almost no direct instruction the child will analyze the language completely. In fact, although many subtle refinements are added between the ages of five and 10, most children have completed the greater part of the basic language-acquisition process by the age of five. By that time a child will have dissected the language into its minimal separable units of sound and meaning; she will have discovered the rules for recombining sounds into words, the meanings of individual words and the rules for recombining words into meaningful sentences, and she will have internalized the intricate patterns of taking turns in dialogue. All in all she will have established herself linguistically as a full-fledged member of a social community, informed about the most subtle details of her native language as it is spoken in a wide variety of situations.

The speed with which children accomplish the complex process of language acquisition is particularly impressive. Ten linguists working full time for 10 years to analyze the structure of the English language could not program a computer with the ability for language acquired by an average child in the first 10 or even five years of life. In spite of the scale of the task and even in spite of adverse conditions—emotional instability, physical disability and so on—children learn to speak. How do they go about it? By what process does a child learn language?

What Is Language?

In order to understand how language is learned it is necessary to understand what language is. The issue is confused by two factors. First, language is learned in early childhood, and adults have few memories of the intense effort that went into the learning process, just as they do not remember the process of learning to walk. Second, adults do have conscious memories of being taught the few grammatical rules that are prescribed as "correct" usage, or the norms of "standard" language. It is difficult for adults to dissociate their memories of school lessons from those of true language learning, but the rules learned in school are only the conventions of an educated society. They are arbitrary finishing touches of embroidery on a thick fabric of language that each child weaves for herself before arriving in the English teacher's classroom. The fabric is grammar: the set of rules that describe how to structure language.

The grammar of language includes rules of phonology, which describe how to put sounds together to form words; rules of syntax, which describe how to put words together to form sentences; rules of semantics, which describe how to interpret the meaning of words and sentences, and rules of pragmatics, which describe how to participate in a conversation, how to sequence sentences and how to anticipate the information needed by an interlocutor. The

internal grammar each adult has constructed is identical with that of every other adult in all but a few superficial details. Therefore each adult can create or understand an infinite number of sentences she has never heard before. She knows what is acceptable as a word or a sentence and what is not acceptable, and her judgments on these issues concur with those of other adults. For example, speakers of English generally agree that the sentence "Ideas green sleep colorless furiously" is ungrammatical and that the sentence "Colorless green ideas sleep furiously" is grammatical but makes no sense semantically. There is similar agreement on the grammatical relations represented by word order. For example, it is clear that the sentences "John hit Mary" and "Mary hit John" have different meanings although they consist of the same words, and that the sentence "Flying planes can be dangerous" has two possible meanings. At the level of individual words all adult speakers can agree that "brick" is an English word, that "blick" is not an English word but could be one (that is, there is an accidental gap in the adult lexicon, or internal vocabulary) and that "bnick" is not an English word and could not be one.

How children go about learning the grammar that makes communication possible has always fascinated adults, particularly parents, psychologists and investigators of language. Until recently diary keeping was the primary method of study in this area. For example, in 1877 Charles Darwin published an account of his son's development that includes notes on language learning. Unfortunately most of the diarists used inconsistent or incomplete notations to record what they heard (or what they thought they heard), and most of the diaries were only partial listings of emerging types of sentences with inadequate information on developing word meanings. Although the very best of them, such as W. F. Leopold's classic *Speech Development of a Bilingual Child*, continue to be a rich resource for contemporary investigators, advances in audio and video recording equipment have made modern diaries generally much more valuable. In the 1960's, however, new discoveries inspired linguists and psychologists to approach the study of language acquisition in a new, systematic way, oriented less toward long-term diary keeping and more toward a search for the patterns in a child's speech at any given time.

An event that revolutionized linguistics was the publication in 1957 of Noam Chomsky's *Syntactic Structures.* Chomsky's investigation of the structure of grammars revealed that language systems were far deeper and more complex than had been suspected. And of course if linguistics was more complicated, then language learning had to be more complicated. In the 21 years since the publication of *Syntactic Structures* the disciplines of linguistics and child language have come of age. The study of the acquisition of language has benefited not only from the increasingly sophisticated understanding of linguistics but also from the improved understanding of cognitive development as it is related to language. The improvements in recording technology have made experimentation in this area more reliable and more detailed, so that investigators framing new and deeper questions are able to accurately capture both rare occurrences and developing structures.

The picture that is emerging from the more sophisticated investigations reveals the child as an active language learner, continually analyzing what she hears and proceeding in a methodical, predictable way to put together the jigsaw puzzle of language. Different children learn language in similar ways. It is

not known how many processes are involved in language learning, but the few that have been observed appear repeatedly, from child to child and from language to language. All the examples I shall discuss here concern children who are learning English, but identical processes have been observed in children learning French, Russian, Finnish, Chinese, Zulu and many other languages.

Children learn the systems of grammar—phonology, syntax, semantics, lexicon and pragmatics—by breaking each system down into its smallest combinable parts and then developing rules for combining the parts. In the first two years of life a child spends much time working on one part of the task, disassembling the language to find the separate sounds that can be put together to form words and the separate words that can be put together to form sentences. After the age of two the basic process continues to be refined, and many more sounds and words are produced. The other part of language acquisition—developing rules for combining the basic elements of language—is carried out in a very methodical way: the most general rules are hypothesized first, and as time passes they are successively narrowed down by the addition of more precise rules applying to a more restricted set of sentences. The procedure is the same in any area of language learning, whether the child is acquiring syntax or phonology or semantics. For example, at the earliest stage of acquiring negatives a child does not have at her command the same range of negative structures that an adult does. She has constructed only a single very general rule: Attach "no" to the beginning of any sentence constructed by the other rules of grammar.

At this stage all negative sentences will be formed according to that rule.

Throughout the acquisition process a child continually revises and refines the rules of her internal grammar, learning increasingly detailed subrules until she achieves a set of rules that enables her to create the full array of complex, adult sentences. The process of refinement continues at least until the age of 10 and probably considerably longer for most children. By the time a child is six or seven, however, the changes in her grammar may be so subtle and sophisticated that they go unnoticed. In general children approach language learning economically, devoting their energy to broad issues before dealing with specific ones. They cope with clear-cut questions first and sort out the details later, and they may adopt any one of a variety of methods for circumventing details of a language system they have not yet dealt with.

Prerequisites for Language

Although some children verbalize much more than others and some increase the length of their utterances much faster than others, all children overgeneralize a single rule before learning to apply it more narrowly and before constructing other less widely applicable rules, and all children speak in one-word sentences before they speak in two-word sentences. The similarities in language learning for different children and different languages are so great that many linguists have believed at one time or another that the human brain is preprogrammed for language learning. Some linguists continue to believe language is innate and only the surface details of the particular language spoken in a child's environment need to be learned. The speed with which children learn language gives this view much appeal. As more parallels between language and other areas of cognition are revealed, however, there is greater reason to believe any language specialization that exists in the child is only one aspect of more general cognitive abilities of the brain.

Whatever the built-in properties the brain brings to the task of language learning may be, it is now known that a child who hears no language learns no language, and that a child learns only the language spoken in her environment. Most infants coo and babble during the first six months of life, but congenitally deaf children have been observed to cease babbling after six months, whereas normal infants continue to babble. A child does not learn language, however, simply by hearing it spoken. A boy with normal hearing but with deaf parents who communicated by the American Sign Language was exposed to television every day so that he would learn English. Because the child

(1)	BOY	CAT	MAN	HOUSE	FOOT FEET
(2)			MEN		
(3)	BOYS	CATS	MANS	HOUSE	FOOTS FEETS
(4)	BOYSəZ	CATSəZ CATəZ	MANSəZ MENəZ	HOUSəZ	FOOTSəZ FEETSəZ
(5)	BOYS	CATS	MANS	HOUSES	FEETS
(6)	BOYS	CATS	MEN	HOUSES	FEET

SORTING OUT OF COMPETING PRONUNCIATIONS that results in the correct plural forms of nouns takes place in the six stages shown in this illustration. Children usually learn the singular forms of nouns first (*1*), although in some cases an irregular plural form such as "feet" may be learned as a singular or as a free variant of a singular. Other irregular plurals may appear for a brief period (*2*), but soon they are replaced by plurals made according to the most general rule possible: To make a noun plural add the sound "s" or "z" to it (*3*). Words such as "house" or "rose," which already end in an "s"- or "z"-like sound, are usually left in their singular forms at this stage. When words of this type do not have irregular plural forms, adults make them plural by adding an "əz" sound. (The vowel "ə" is pronounced like the unstressed word "a.") Some children demonstrate their mastery of this usage by tacking "əz" endings indiscriminately onto nouns (*4*). That stage is brief and use of the ending is quickly narrowed down (*5*). At this point only irregular plurals remain to be learned, and since no new rulemaking is needed, children may go on to harder problems and leave final stage (*6*) for later.

was asthmatic and was confined to his home he interacted only with people at home, where his family and all their visitors communicated in sign language. By the age of three he was fluent in sign language but neither understood nor spoke English. It appears that in order to learn a language a child must also be able to interact with real people in that language. A television set does not suffice as the sole medium for language learning because, even though it can ask questions, it cannot respond to a child's answers. A child, then, can develop language only if there is language in her environment and if she can employ that language to communicate with other people in her immediate environment.

Caretaker Speech

In constructing a grammar children have only a limited amount of information available to them, namely the language they hear spoken around them. (Until about the age of three a child models her language on that of her parents; afterward the language of her peer group tends to become more important.) There is no question, however, that the language environments children inhabit are restructured, usually unintentionally, by the adults who take care of them. Recent studies show that there are several ways caretakers systematically modify the child's environment, making the task of language acquisition simpler.

	WALK	PLAY	NEED	COME	GO
(1)	WALK	PLAY	NEED	COME	GO
(2)				CAME	WENT
(3)	WALKED	PLAYED	NEED	COMED	GOED
(4)	WALKEDəD	PLAYEDəD	NEEDəD	CAMEDəD COMEDəD	GOED WENTəD
(5)	WALKED	PLAYED	NEEDED	COMED	GOED
(6)	WALKED	PLAYED	NEEDED	CAME	WENT

DEVELOPMENT OF PAST-TENSE FORMS OF VERBS also takes place in six stages. After the present-tense forms are learned (1) irregular past-tense forms may appear briefly (2). The first and most general rule that is postulated is: To put a verb into the past tense add a "t" or "d" sound (3). In adult speech verbs such as "want" or "need," which already end in a "t" or "d" sound, are put into the past tense by adding "əd" sound. Many children go through brief stage in which they add "əd" endings to any existing verb forms (4). Once the use of "əd" ending has been narrowed down (5), only irregular past-tense forms remain to be learned (6).

Caretaker speech is a distinct speech register that differs from others in its simplified vocabulary, the systematic phonological simplification of some words, higher pitch, exaggerated intonation, short, simple sentences and a high proportion of questions (among mothers) or imperatives (among fathers). Speech with the first two characteristics is formally designated Baby Talk. Baby Talk is a subsystem of caretaker speech that has been studied over a wide range of languages and cultures. Its characteristics appear to be universal: in languages as diverse as English, Arabic, Comanche and Gilyak (a Paleo-Siberian language) there are simplified vocabulary items for terms relating to food, toys, animals and body functions. Some words are phonologically simplified, frequently by the duplication of syllables, as in "wawa" for "water" and "choochoo" for "train," or by the reduction of consonant clusters, as in "tummy" for "stomach" and "scambled eggs" for "scrambled eggs." (Many types of phonological simplification seem to mimic the phonological structure of an infant's own early vocabulary.)

Perhaps the most pervasive characteristic of caretaker speech is its syntactic simplification. While a child is still babbling, adults may address long, complex sentences to her, but as soon as she begins to utter meaningful, identifiable words they almost invariably speak to her in very simple sentences. Over the next few years of the child's language development the speech addressed to her by her caretakers may well be describable by a grammar only six months in advance of her own.

The functions of the various language modifications in caretaker speech are not equally apparent. It is possible that higher pitch and exaggerated intonation serve to alert a child to pay attention to what she is hearing. As for Baby Talk, there is no reason to believe the use of phonologically simplified words in any way affects a child's learning of pronunciation. Baby Talk may have only a psychological function, marking speech as being affectionate. On the other hand, syntactic simplification has a clear function. Consider the speech adults address to other adults; it is full of false starts and long, rambling, highly complex sentences. It is not surprising that elaborate theories of innate language ability arose during the years when linguists examined the speech adults addressed to adults and assumed that the speech addressed to children was similar. Indeed, it is hard to imagine how a child could derive the rules of language from such input. The wide study of caretaker speech conducted over the past eight years has shown that children do not face this problem. Rather it appears they construct their initial grammars on the basis of the short, simple, grammatical sentences that are addressed to them in the first year or two they speak.

Correcting Language

Caretakers simplify children's language-analysis task in other ways. For example, adults talk with other adults about complex ideas, but they talk with children about the here and now, minimizing discussion of feelings, displaced events and so on. Adults accept children's syntactic and phonological "errors," which are a normal part of the acquisition process. It is important to understand that when children make such errors, they are not producing flawed or incomplete replicas of adult sentences; they are producing sentences that are correct and grammatical with respect to their own current internalized grammar. Indeed, children's errors are essential data for students of child language because it is the consistent departures from the adult model that indicate the nature of a child's current hypotheses about the grammar of language. There are a number of memorized, unanalyzed sentences in any child's output of language. If a child says, "Nobody likes me," there is no way of knowing whether she has memorized the sentence intact or has figured out the rules for constructing the sentence. On the other hand, a sentence such as "Nobody don't like me" is clearly not a memorized form but one that reflects an intermediate stage of a developing grammar.

Since each child's utterances at a particular stage are from her own point of view grammatically correct, it is not surprising that children are fairly impervious to the correction of their language by adults, indeed to any attempts to teach them language. Consider the boy who lamented to his mother, "Nobody don't like me." His mother seized the opportunity to correct him, replying, "Nobody likes me." The child repeated his original version and the mother her modified one a total of eight times until in desperation the mother said, "Now listen carefully! Nobody likes me." Finally her son got the idea and dutifully replied, "Oh! Nobody don't likes me." As the example demonstrates, children do not always understand exactly what it is the adult is correcting. The information the adult is trying to impart may be at odds with the information in the child's head, namely the rules the child is postulating for producing language. The surface correction of a sentence does not give the child a clue about how to revise the rule that produced the sentence.

It seems to be virtually impossible to speed up the language-learning process. Experiments conducted by Russian investigators show that it is extremely difficult to teach children a detail of language more than a few days before they would learn it themselves. Adults sometimes do, of course, attempt to teach children rules of language, expecting them to learn by imitation, but Courtney B. Cazden of Harvard University found that children benefit less from frequent adult correction of their errors than from true conversational interaction. Indeed, correcting errors can interrupt that interaction, which is, after all, the function of language. (One way children may try to secure such interaction is by asking "Why?" Children go through a stage of asking a question repeatedly. It serves to keep the conversation going, which may be the child's real aim. For example, a two-and-a-half-year-old named Stanford asked "Why?" and was given the nonsense answer: "Because the moon is made of green cheese." Although the response was not at all germane to the conversation, Stanford was happy with it and again asked "Why?" Many silly answers later the adult had tired of the conversation but Stanford had not. He was clearly not seeking information. What he needed was to practice the form of social conversation before dealing with its function. Asking "Why?" served that purpose well.)

In point of fact adults rarely correct children's ungrammatical sentences. For example, one mother, on hearing "Tommy fall my truck down," turned to Tommy with "Did you fall Stevie's truck down?" Since imitation seems to have little role in the language-acquisition process, however, it is probably just as well that most adults are either too charmed by children's errors or too busy to correct them.

Practice does appear to have an important function in the child's language-learning process. Many children have been observed purposefully practicing language when they are alone, for example in a crib or a playpen. Ruth H. Weir of Stanford University hid a tape recorder in her son's bedroom and recorded his talk after he was put to bed. She found that he played with words and phrases, stringing together sequences of similar sounds and of variations on a phrase or on the use of a word: "What color...what color blanket...what color mop...what color glass...what color TV...red ant...fire...like lipstick ...blanket...now the blue blanket... what color TV...what color horse... then what color table...then what color fire...here yellow spoon." Children who do not have much opportunity to be alone may use dialogue in a similar fashion. When Weir tried to record the bedtime monologues of her second child, whose room adjoined that of the first, she obtained through-the-wall conversations instead.

The One-Word Stage

The first stage of child language is one in which the maximum sentence length is one word; it is followed by a stage in which the maximum sentence length is two words. Early in the one-word stage there are only a few words in a child's vocabulary, but as months go by her lexicon expands with increasing rapidity. The early words are primarily concrete nouns and verbs; more abstract words such as adjectives are acquired later. By the time the child is uttering two-word sentences with some regularity, her lexicon may include hundreds of words.

When a child can say only one word at a time and knows only five words in all, choosing which one to say may not be a complex task. But how does she decide which word to say when she knows 100 words or more? Patricia M. Greenfield of the University of California at Los Angeles and Joshua H. Smith of Stanford have suggested that an important criterion is informativeness, that is, the child selects a word reflecting what is new in a particular situation. Greenfield and Smith also found that a newly acquired word is first used for naming and only later for asking for something.

Superficially the one-word stage

CHILDREN'S AVERAGE VOCABULARY SIZE increases rapidly between the ages of one and a half and six and a half. The number of children tested in each sample age group is shown in color. Data are based on work done by Madorah E. Smith of University of Hawaii.

seems easy to understand: a child says one word at a time, and so each word is a complete sentence with its own sentence intonation. Ten years ago a child in the one-word stage was thought to be learning word meanings but not syntax. Recently, however, students of child language have seen less of a distinction between the one-word stage as a period of word learning and the subsequent period, beginning with the two-word stage, as one of syntax acquisition. It now seems clear that the infant is engaged in an enormous amount of syntactic analysis in the one-word stage, and indeed that her syntactic abilities are reflected in her utterances and in her accurate perception of multiword sentences addressed to her.

Ronald Scollon of the University of Hawaii and Lois Bloom of Columbia University have pointed out independently that important patterns in word choice in the one-word stage can be found by examining larger segments of children's speech. Scollon observed that a 19-month-old named Brenda was able to use a vertical construction (a series of one-word sentences) to express what an adult might say with a horizontal construction (a multiword sentence). Brenda's pronunciation, which is represented phonetically below, was imperfect and Scollon did not understand her words at the time. Later, when he transcribed the tape of their conversation, he heard the sound of a passing car immediately preceding the conversation and was able to identify Brenda's words as follows:

Brenda: "Car [pronounced 'ka']. Car. Car. Car."
Scollon: "What?"
Brenda: "Go. Go."
Scollon: [Undecipherable.]
Brenda: "Bus [pronounced 'baish']. Bus. Bus. Bus. Bus. Bus. Bus. Bus."
Scollon: "What? Oh, bicycle? Is that what you said?"
Brenda: "Not ['na']."
Scollon: "No?"
Brenda: "Not."
Scollon: "No. I got it wrong."

Brenda was not yet able to combine two words syntactically to express "Hearing that car reminds me that we went on the bus yesterday. No, not on a bicycle." She could express that concept, however, by combining words sequentially. Thus the one-word stage is not just a time for learning the meaning of words. In that period a child is developing hypotheses about putting words together in sentences, and she is already putting sentences together in meaningful groups. The next step will be to put two words together to form a single sentence.

The Two-Word Stage

The two-word stage is a time for experimenting with many binary semantic-syntactic relations such as possessor-

possessed ("Mommy sock"), actor-action ("Cat sleeping") and action-object ("Drink soup"). When two-word sentences first began to appear in Brenda's speech, they were primarily of the following forms: subject noun and verb (as in "Monster go"), verb and object (as in "Read it") and verb or noun and location (as in "Bring home" and "Tree down"). She also continued to use vertical constructions in the two-word stage, providing herself with a means of expressing ideas that were still too advanced for her syntax. Therefore once again a description of Brenda's isolated sentences does not show her full abilities at this point in her linguistic development. Consider a later conversation Scollon had with Brenda:

Brenda: "Tape corder. Use it. Use it."
Scollon: "Use it for what?"
Brenda: "Talk. Corder talk. Brenda talk."

Brenda's use of vertical constructions to express concepts she is still unable to encode syntactically is just one example of a strategy employed by children in all areas of cognitive development. As Jean Piaget of the University of Geneva and Dan I. Slobin of the University of California at Berkeley put it, new forms are used for old functions and new functions are expressed by old forms. Long before Brenda acquired the complex syntactic form "Use the tape recorder to record me talking" she was able to use her old forms—two-word sentences and vertical construction—to express the new function. Later, when that function was old, she would develop new forms to express it. The controlled dovetailing of form and function can be observed in all areas of language acquisition. For example, before children acquire the past tense they may employ adverbs of time such as "yesterday" with present-tense verbs to express past time, saying "I do it yesterday" before "I dood it."

Bloom has provided a rare view of an intermediate stage between the one-word and the two-word stages in which the two-word construction—a new form—served only an old function. For several weeks Bloom's daughter Alison uttered two-word sentences all of which included the word "wida." Bloom tried hard to find the meaning of "wida" before realizing that it had no meaning. It was, she concluded, simply a placeholder. This case is the clearest ever reported of a new form preceding new functions. The two-word stage is an important time for practicing functions that will later have expanded forms and practicing forms that will later expand their functions.

Telegraphic Speech

There is no three-word stage in child language. For a few years after the end of the two-word stage children do produce rather short sentences, but the al-

STAGE 1	No . . . wipe finger.
	No a boy bed.
	No singing song.
	No the sun shining.
	No money.
	No sit there.
	No play that.
	No fall!
	Not . . . fit.
	Not a teddy bear.
	More . . . no.
	Wear mitten no.
STAGE 2	I can't catch you.
	I can't see you.
	We can't talk.
	You can't dance.
	I don't want it.
	I don't like him.
	I don't know his name.
	No pinch me.
	Book say no.
	Touch the snow no.
	This a radiator no.
	No square . . . is clown.
	Don't bite me yet.
	Don't leave me.
	Don't wake me up . . . again.
	He not little, he big.
	That no fish school.
	That no Mommy.
	There no squirrels.
	He no bite you.
	I no want envelope.
	I no taste them.
STAGE 3	We can't make another broom.
	I don't want cover on it.
	I gave him some so he won't cry.
	No, I don't have a book.
	I am not a doctor.
	It's not cold.
	Don't put the two wings on.
	I didn't did it.
	You didn't caught me.
	I not hurt him.
	Ask me if I not made mistake.
	Because I don't want somebody to wake me up.
	I didn't see something.
	I isn't . . . I not sad.
	This not ice cream.
	This no good.
	I not crying.
	That not turning.
	He not taking the walls down.

THREE STAGES in the acquisition of negative sentences were studied by Ursula Bellugi of the Salk Institute for Biological Studies and Edward S. Klima of the University of California at San Diego. They observed that in the first stage almost all negative sentences appear to be formulated according to the rule: Attach "no" or "not" to the beginning of a sentence to make it negative. In the second stage additional rules are postulated that allow the formation of sentences in which "no," "not," "can't" and "don't" appear after the subject and before the verb. In the third stage several issues remain to be worked out, in particular the agreement of pronouns in negative sentences (*dark color*), the inclusion of the forms of the verb "to be" (*gray*) and the correct use of the auxiliary "do" (*white*). In adult speech the auxiliary "do" often carries tense and other functional markings such as the negative; children in third stage may replace it by "not" or use it redundantly to mark tense that is already marked on the main verb.

most inviolable length constraints that characterized the first two stages have disappeared. The absence of a three-word stage has not been satisfactorily explained as yet; the answer may have to do with the fact that many basic semantic relations are binary and few are ternary. In any case a great deal is known about the sequential development in the language of the period following the two-word stage. Roger Brown of Harvard has named that language telegraphic speech. (It should be noted that there is no specific age at which a child enters any of these stages of language acquisition and further that there is no particular correlation between intelligence and speed of acquisition.)

Early telegraphic speech is characterized by short, simple sentences made up primarily of content words: words that are rich in semantic content, usually nouns and verbs. The speech is called telegraphic because the sentences lack function "words": tense endings on verbs and plural endings on nouns, prepositions, conjunctions, articles and so on. As the telegraphic-speech stage progresses, function words are gradually added to sentences. This process has possibly been studied more thoroughly than any other in language acquisition, and a fairly predictable order in the addition of function words has been observed. The same principles that govern the order of acquisition of function words in English have been shown to operate in many other languages, including some, such as Finnish and Russian, that express the same grammatical relations with particularly rich systems of noun and verb suffixes.

In English many grammatical relations are represented by a fixed word order. For example, in the sentence "The dog followed Jamie to school" it is clear it is the dog that did the following. Normal word order in English requires that the subject come before the verb, and so people who speak English recognize "the dog" as the subject of the sentence. In other languages a noun may be marked as a subject not by its position with respect to the other words in the sentence but by a noun suffix, so that in adult sentences word order may be quite flexible. Until children begin to acquire suffixes and other function words, however, they employ fixed word order to express grammatical relations no matter how flexible adult word order may be. In English the strong propensity to follow word order rigidly shows up in children's interpretations of passive sentences such as "Jamie was followed by the dog." At an early age children may interpret some passive sentences correctly, but by age three they begin to ignore the function words such as "was" and "by" in passive sentences and adopt the fixed word-order interpretation. In other words, since "Jamie" appears before the verb, Jamie is assumed to be the actor, or the noun doing the following.

Function Words

In spite of its grammatical dependence on word order, the English language makes use of enough function words to illustrate the basic principles that determine the order in which such words are acquired. The progressive tense ending "-ing," as in "He going," is acquired first, long before the present-tense third-person singular ending "-s," as in "He goes." The "-s" itself is acquired long before the past tense endings, as in "He goed." Once again the child proves to be a sensible linguist, learning first the tense that exhibits the least variation in form. The "-ing" ending is pronounced only one way, regard-

CHILD'S LEXICAL ITEM	FIRST REFERENTS	OTHER REFERENTS IN ORDER OF OCCURRENCE	GENERAL AREA OF SEMANTIC EXTENSION
MOOI	MOON	CAKE ROUND MARKS ON WINDOWS WRITING ON WINDOWS AND IN BOOKS ROUND SHAPES IN BOOKS TOOLING ON LEATHER BOOK COVERS ROUND POSTMARKS LETTER "O"	SHAPE
BOW-WOW	DOG	FUR PIECE WITH GLASS EYES FATHER'S CUFFLINKS PEARL BUTTONS ON DRESS BATH THERMOMETER	SHAPE
KOTIBAIZ	BARS OF COT	LARGE TOY ABACUS TOAST RACK WITH PARALLEL BARS PICTURE OF BUILDING WITH COLUMNS	SHAPE
BÉBÉ	REFLECTION OF CHILD (SELF) IN MIRROR	PHOTOGRAPH OF SELF ALL PHOTOGRAPHS ALL PICTURES ALL BOOKS WITH PICTURES ALL BOOKS	SHAPE
VOV-VOV	DOG	KITTENS HENS ALL ANIMALS AT A ZOO PICTURE OF PIGS DANCING	SHAPE
ASS	GOAT WITH ROUGH HIDE ON WHEELS	THINGS THAT MOVE: ANIMALS, SISTER, WAGON... ALL MOVING THINGS ALL THINGS WITH A ROUGH SURFACE	MOVEMENT TEXTURE
TUTU	TRAIN	ENGINE MOVING TRAIN JOURNEY	MOVEMENT
FLY	FLY	SPECKS OF DIRT DUST ALL SMALL INSECTS CHILD'S OWN TOES CRUMBS OF BREAD A TOAD	SIZE
QUACK	DUCK ON WATER	ALL BIRDS AND INSECTS ALL COINS (AFTER SEEING AN EAGLE ON THE FACE OF A COIN)	SIZE
KOKO	COCKEREL'S CROWING	TUNES PLAYED ON A VIOLIN TUNES PLAYED ON A PIANO TUNES PLAYED ON AN ACCORDION TUNES PLAYED ON A PHONOGRAPH ALL MUSIC MERRY-GO-ROUND	SOUND
DANY	SOUND OF A BELL	CLOCK TELEPHONE DOORBELLS	SOUND

CHILDREN OVERGENERALIZE WORD MEANINGS, using words they acquire early in place of words they have not yet acquired. Eve V. Clark of Stanford University has observed that when a word first appears in a child's lexicon, it refers to a specific object but the child quickly extends semantic domain of word, using it to refer to many other things. Eventually meaning of the word is narrowed down until it coincides with adult usage. Clark found that children most frequently base the semantic extension of a word on shape of its first referent.

less of the pronunciation of the verb to which it is attached. The verb endings "-s" and "-ed," however, vary in their pronunciation: compare "cuts (s)," "cuddles (z)," "crushes (əz)," "walked (t)," "played (d)" and "halted (əd)." (The vowel "ə," called "shwa," is pronounced like the unstressed word "a.") Furthermore, present progressive ("-ing") forms are used with greater frequency than any other tense in the speech children hear. Finally, no verb has an irregular "-ing" form, but some verbs do have irregular third-person present-tense singular forms and many have irregular past-tense forms. (The same pattern of learning earliest those forms that exhibit the least variation shows up much more dramatically in languages such as Finnish and Russian, where the paradigms of inflection are much richer.)

The past tense is acquired after the progressive and present tenses, because the relative time it represents is conceptually more difficult. The future tense ("will" and a verb) is formed regularly in English and is as predictable as the progressive tense, but it is a much more abstract concept than the past tense. Therefore it is acquired much later. In the same way the prepositions "in" and "on" appear earlier than any others, at about the same time as "-ing," but prepositions such as "behind" and "in front of," whose correct usage depends on the speaker's frame of reference, are acquired much later.

It is particularly interesting to note that there are three English morphemes that are pronounced identically but are acquired at different times. They are the plural "-s," the possessive "-s" and the third-person singular tense ending "-s," and they are acquired in the order of

listing. Roman Jakobson of Harvard has suggested that the explanation of this phenomenon has to do with the complexity of the different relations the morphemes signal: the singular-plural distinction is at the word level, the possessive relates two nouns at the phrase level and the tense ending relates a noun and a verb at the clause level.

The forms of the verb "to be"—"is," "are" and so on—are among the last of the function words to be acquired, particularly in their present-tense forms. Past- and future-tense forms of "to be" carry tense information, of course, but present-tense forms are essentially meaningless, and omitting them is a very sensible strategy for a child who must maximize the information content of a sentence and place priorities on linguistic structures still to be tackled.

Plurals

When there are competing pronunciations available, as in the case of the plural and past tenses, the process of sorting them out also follows a predictable pattern. Consider the acquisition of the English plural, in which six distinct stages can be observed. In English, as in many other (but not all) languages, nouns have both singular and plural forms. Children usually use the singular forms first, both in situations where the singular form would be appropriate and in situations where the plural form would be appropriate. In instances where the plural form is irregular in the adult model, however, a child may not recognize it as such and may use it in place of the singular or as a free variant of the singular. Thus in the first stage of acquisition, before either the concept of a plu-

ral or the linguistic devices for expressing a plural are acquired, a child may say "two cat" or point to "one feet."

When plurals begin to appear regularly, the child forms them according to the most general rule of English plural formation. At this point it is the child's overgeneralization of the rule, resulting in words such as "mans," "foots" or "feets," that shows she has hypothesized the rule: Add the sound /s/ or /z/ to the end of a word to make it plural. (The slashes indicate pronounced sounds, which are not to be confused with the letters used in spelling.)

For many children the overgeneralized forms of the irregular nouns are actually the earliest /s/ and /z/ plurals to appear, preceding "boys," "cats" and other regular forms by hours or days. The period of overgeneralization is considered to be the third stage in the acquisition of plurals because for many children there is an intermediate second stage in which irregular plurals such as "men" actually do appear. Concerned parents may regard the change from the second-stage "men" to the third-stage "mans" as a regression, but in reality it demonstrates progress from an individual memorized item to the application of a general rule.

In the third stage the small number of words that already end in a sound resembling /s/ or /z/, such as "house," "rose" and "bush," are used without any plural ending. Adults normally make such words plural by adding the suffix /əz/. Children usually relegate this detail to the remainder pile, to be dealt with at a later time. When they return to the problem, there is often a short fourth stage of perhaps a day, in which the child delightedly demonstrates her

(1) Laura (2:2):	(4) Andrew (2:0):	(7) Jamie (6:0):
Her want some more. Her want some more candy.	Put that on. Andrew put that on.	Jamie: Why are you doing that? Mother: What? Jamie: Why are you writing what I say down? Mother: What? Jamie: Why are you writing down what I say?
(2) Laura (2:2):	(5) Andrew (2:1):	(8) Jamie (6:3):
Where my tiger? Where my tiger book?	All wet. This shoe all wet.	Jamie: Who do you think is the importantest kid in the world except me? Mother: What did you say, Jamie? Jamie: Who do you think is the specialest kid in the world not counting me?
		(9) Jamie (6:6):
		Jamie: Who are you versing? Adult: What? Jamie: I wanted to know who he was playing against.
(3) Laura (2:2):	(6) Benjy (2:3):	(10) Jamie (6:10):
Let's dooz this. Let's do this. Let's do this puzzle.	Broke it. Broke it. Broke it I did.	Jamie: I figured something you might like out. Mother: What did you say? Jamie: I figured out something you might like.

CHILDREN CORRECT THEIR SPEECH in ways that reflect the improvements they are currently making on their internal grammar. For example, Laura (*1–3*) is increasing the length of her sentences, encoding more information by embellishing a noun phrase. Andrew (*4, 5*) and Benjy (*6*) appear to be adding subjects to familiar verb-phrase sentences. Jamie (*7–10*) seems to be working on much more subtle refinements such as the placement of verb particles, for example the "down" of "writing down." (Each child's age at time of correction is given in years and months.) Corrections shown here were recorded by Judy S. Reilly of University of California at Los Angeles.

solution by tacking /əz/ endings indiscriminately onto nouns no matter what sound they end in and no matter how many other plural markings they may already have. A child may wake up one morning and throw herself into this stage with all the zeal of a kitten playing with its first ball of string.

Within a few days the novelty wears off and the child enters a less flamboyant fifth stage, in which only irregular plurals still deviate from the model forms. The rapid progression through the fourth stage does not mean that she suddenly focused her attention on the problem of /əz/ plurals. It is more likely that she had the problem at the back of her mind throughout the third stage. She was probably silently formulating hypotheses about the occurrence of /əz/ and testing them against the plurals she was hearing. Finding the right rule required discovering the phonological specification of the class of nouns that take /əz/ plurals.

Arriving at the sixth and final stage in the acquisition of plurals does not require the formulation of any new rules. All that is needed is the simple memorizing of irregular forms. Being rational, the child relegates such minor details to the lowest-priority remainder pile and turns her attention to more interesting linguistic questions. Hence a five-year-old may still not have entered the last stage. In fact, a child in the penultimate stage may not be at all receptive to being taught irregular plurals. For example, a child named Erica pointed to a picture of some "mouses," and her mother corrected her by saying "mice." Erica and her mother each repeated their own version two more times, and then Erica resolved the standoff by turning to a picture of "ducks." She avoided the picture of the mice for several days. Two years later, of course, Erica was perfectly able to say "mice."

Negative Sentences

One of the pioneering language-acquisition studies of the 1960's was undertaken at Harvard by a research group headed by Brown. The group studied the development in the language of three children over a period of several years. Two members of the group, Ursula Bellugi and Edward S. Klima, looked specifically at the changes in the children's negative sentences over the course of the project. They found that negative structures, like other subsystems of the syntactic component of grammar, are acquired in an orderly, rule-governed way.

When the project began, the forms of negative sentences the children employed were quite simple. It appeared that they had incorporated the following rule into their grammar: To make a sentence negative attach "no" or "not" to the beginning of it. On rare occasions,

possibly when a child had forgotten to anticipate the negative, "no" could be attached to the end of a sentence, but negative words could not appear inside a sentence.

In the next stage the children continued to follow this rule, but they had also hypothesized and incorporated into their grammars more complex rules that allowed them to generate sentences in which the negatives "no," "not," "can't" and "don't" appeared after the subject and before the verb. These rules constituted quite an advance over attaching a negative word externally to a sentence. Furthermore, some of the primitive imperative sentences constructed at this stage began with "don't" rather than "no." On the other hand, "can't" never appeared at the beginning of a sentence, and neither "can" nor "do" appeared as an auxiliary, as they do in adult speech: "I can do it." These facts suggest that at this point "can't" and "don't" were unanalyzed negative forms rather than contractions of "cannot" and "do not," but that although "can't" and "don't" each seemed to be interchangeable with "no," they were no longer interchangeable with each other.

In the third stage of acquiring negatives many more details of the negative system had appeared in the children's speech. The main feature of the system that still remained to be worked out was the use of pronouns in negative sentences. At this stage the children said "I didn't see something" and "I don't want somebody to wake me up." The pronouns "somebody" and "something" were later replaced with "nobody" and "nothing" and ultimately with the properly concorded forms "anybody" and "anything."

Many features of telegraphic speech were still evident in the third stage. The form "is" of the verb "to be" was frequently omitted, as in "This no good." In adult speech the auxiliary "do" often functions as a dummy verb to carry tense and other markings; for example, in "I didn't see it," "do" carries the tense and the negative. In the children's speech at this stage "do" appeared occasionally, but the children had not yet figured out its entire function. Therefore in some sentences the auxiliary "do" was omitted and the negative "not" appeared alone, as in "I not hurt him." In other sentences, such as "I didn't did it," the negative auxiliary form of "do" appears to be correct but is actually an unanalyzed, memorized item; at this stage the tense is regularly marked on the main verb, which in this example happens also to be "do."

Many children acquire negatives in the same way that the children in the Harvard study did, but subsequent investigations have shown that there is more than one way to learn a language. Carol B. Lord of U.C.L.A. identified a quite different strategy employed by a

two-year-old named Jennifer. From 24 to 28 months Jennifer used "no" only as a single-word utterance. In order to produce a negative sentence she simply spoke an ordinary sentence with a higher pitch. For example, "I want put it on" spoken with a high pitch meant "I don't want to put it on." Lord noticed that many of the negative sentences adults addressed to Jennifer were spoken with an elevated pitch. Children tend to pay more attention to the beginning and ending of sentences, and in adult speech negative words usually appear in the middle of sentences. With good reason, then, Jennifer seemed to have hypothesized that one makes a sentence negative by uttering it with a higher pitch. Other children have been found to follow the same strategy. There are clearly variations in the hypotheses children make in the process of constructing grammar.

Semantics

Up to this point I have mainly discussed the acquisition of syntactic rules, in part because in the years following the publication of Chomsky's *Syntactic Structures* child-language research in this area flourished. Syntactic rules, which govern the ordering of words in a sentence, are not all a child needs to know about language, however, and after the first flush of excitement over Chomsky's work investigators began to ask questions about other areas of language acquisition. Consider the development of the rules of semantics, which govern the way words are interpreted. Eve V. Clark of Stanford reexamined old diary studies and noticed that the development in the meaning of words during the first several months of the one-word stage seemed to follow a basic pattern.

The first time children in the studies used a word, Clark noted, it seemed to be as a proper noun, as the name of a specific object. Almost immediately, however, the children generalized the word based on some feature of the original object and used it to refer to many other objects. For example, a child named Hildegard first used "tick-tock" as the name for her father's watch, but she quickly broadened the meaning of the word, first to include all clocks, then all watches, then a gas meter, then a fire-hose wound on a spool and then a bathroom scale with a round dial. Her generalizations appear to be based on her observation of common features of shape: roundness, dials and so on. In general the children in the diary studies overextended meanings based on similarities of movement, texture, size and, most frequently, shape.

As the children progressed, the meanings of words were narrowed down until eventually they more or less coincided with the meanings accepted by adult speakers of the language. The narrow-

CHILDREN'S SPEECH IS STUDIED to determine what grammatical rules, which describe how language is structured, they have developed. The author, shown here recording the language output of two young children, works with children in their homes so that their speech is as unconstrained as possible. The search for the regularities in children's language has revealed that in any area of language acquisition they follow the same basic procedure: hypothesizing rules, trying them out and then modifying them. Children formulate the most general rules first and apply them across the board; narrower rules are added later, with exceptions and highly irregular forms. Examples discussed in article concern children learning English, but same process has been observed in children learning other languages.

ing-down process has not been studied intensively, but it seems likely that the process has no fixed end point. Rather it appears that the meanings of words continue to expand and contract through adulthood, long after other types of language acquisition have ceased.

One of the problems encountered in trying to understand the acquisition of semantics is that it is often difficult to determine the precise meaning a child has constructed for a word. Some interesting observations have been made, however, concerning the development of the meanings of the pairs of words that function as opposites in adult language. Margaret Donaldson and George Balfour of the University of Edinburgh asked children from three to five years old which one of two cardboard trees had "more" apples on it. They asked other children of the same age which tree had "less" apples. (Each child was interviewed individually.) Almost all the children in both groups responded by pointing to the tree with more apples on it. Moreover, the children who had been asked to point to the tree with "less" apples showed no hesitation in choosing the tree with more apples. They did not act as though they did not know the meaning of "less"; rather they acted as if they did know the meaning and "less" meant "more."

Subsequent studies have revealed similar systematic error making in the acquisition of other pairs of opposites such as "same" and "different," "big" and "little," "wide" and "narrow" and "tall" and "short." In every case the pattern of learning is the same: one word of the pair is learned first and its meaning is overextended to apply to the other word in the pair. The first word learned is always the unmarked word of the pair, that is, the word adults use when they do not want to indicate either one of the opposites. (For example, in the case of "wide" and "narrow," "wide" is the unmarked word: asking "How wide is the road?" does not suggest that the road is wide, but asking "How narrow is the road?" does suggest that the road is narrow.)

Clark observed a more intricate pattern of error production in the acquisition of the words "before" and "after." Consider the four different types of sentence represented by (1) "He jumped the gate before he patted the dog," (2) "Before he patted the dog he jumped the gate," (3) "He patted the dog after he jumped the gate" and (4) "After he jumped the gate he patted the dog." Clark found that the way the children she observed interpreted sentences such as these could be divided into four stages.

In the first stage the children disregarded the words "before" and "after" in all four of these sentence types and assumed that the event of the first clause took place before the event of the second clause. With this order-of-mention strategy the first and fourth sentence types were interpreted correctly but the second and third sentence types were not. In the second stage sentences using "before" were interpreted correctly but an order-of-mention strategy was still adopted for sentences that used "after." Hence sentences of the fourth type were interpreted correctly but sentences of the third type were not. In the next stage both the third and the fourth sentence types were interpreted incorrectly, suggesting that the children had adopted the strategy that "after" actually meant "before." Finally, in the fourth stage both "before" and "after" were interpreted appropriately.

It appears, then, that in learning the meaning of a pair of words such as "more" and "less" or "before" and "after" children acquire first the part of the meaning that is common to both words and only later the part of the meaning that distinguishes the two. Linguists have not yet developed satisfactory ways of separating the components of meaning that make up a single word, but it seems clear that when such components can be identified, it will be established that, for example, "more" and "less" have a large number of components in common and differ only in a single component specifying the pole of the dimension. Beyond the studies of opposites there has been little investigation of the period of semantic acquisition that follows the early period of rampant overgeneralization. How children past the early stage learn the meanings of other kinds of words is still not well understood.

Phonology

Just as children overgeneralize word meanings and sentence structures, so do they overgeneralize sounds, using sounds they have learned in place of sounds they have not yet acquired. Just as a child may use the word "not" correctly in one sentence but instead of another negative word in a second sentence, so may she correctly contrast /p/ and /b/ at the beginnings of words but employ /p/ at the ends of words, regardless of whether the adult models end with /p/ or /b/. Children also acquire the details of the phonological system in very regular ways. The ways in which they acquire individual sounds, however, are highly idiosyncratic, and so for many years the patterns eluded diarists, who tended to look only at the order in which sounds were acquired. Jakobson made a major advance in this area by suggesting that it was not individual sounds children acquire in an orderly way but the distinctive features of sound, that is, the minimal differences, or contrasts, between sounds. In other words, when a child begins to contrast /p/ and /b/, she also begins to contrast all the other pairs of sounds that, like /p/ and /b/, differ only in the absence or presence of vocal-cord vibration. In English these pairs include /t/ and /d/, and /k/ and the hard /g/. It is the acquisition of this contrast and not of the six individual sounds that is predictable. Jakobson's extensive examination of the diary data for a wide variety of languages supported his theory. Almost all current work in phonological theory rests on the theory of distinctive features that grew out of his work.

My own recent work suggests that phonological units even more basic than the distinctive features play an important part in the early acquisition process. At an early stage, when there are relatively few words in a child's repertory, unanalyzed syllables appear to be the basic unit of the sound system. By designating these syllables as unanalyzed I mean that the child is not able to separate them into their component consonants and vowels. Only later in the acquisition process does such division into smaller units become possible. The gradual discovery of successively smaller units that can form the basis of the phonological system is an important part of the process.

At an even earlier stage, before a child has uttered any words, she is accomplishing a great deal of linguistic learning, working with a unit of phonological organization even more primitive than the syllable. That unit can be defined in terms of pitch contours. By the late babbling period children already control the intonation, or pitch modulation, contours of the language they are learning. At that stage the child sounds as if she is uttering reasonably long sentences, and adult listeners may have the impression they are not quite catching the child's words. There are no words to catch, only random strings of babbled sounds with recognizable, correctly produced question or statement intonation contours. The sounds may accidentally be similar to some of those found in adult English. These sentence-length utterances are called sentence units, and in the phonological system of the child at this stage they are comparable to the consonant-and-vowel segments, syllables and distinctive features that appear in the phonological systems of later stages. The syllables and segments that appear when the period of word learning begins are in no way related to the vast repertory of babbling sounds. Only the intonation contours are carried over from the babbling stage into the later period.

No matter what language environment a child grows up in, the intonation contours characteristic of adult speech in that environment are the linguistic information learned earliest. Some recent studies suggest that it is possible to identify the language environment of a child from her babbling intonation during the second year of life. Other studies suggest that children can be distinguished at an even earlier age on the basis of whether or not their language environment is a tone language, that is, a language in which words spoken with different pitches are identifiable as different words, even though they may have the same sequence of consonants and vowels. To put it another way, "ma" spoken with a high pitch and "ma" spoken with a low pitch can be as different to someone speaking a tone language as "ma" and "pa" are to someone speaking English. (Many African and Asian languages are tone languages.) Tones are learned very early, and entire tone systems are mastered long before other areas of phonology. The extremely early acquisition of pitch patterns may help to explain the difficulty adults have in learning the intonation of a second language.

Phonetics

There is one significant way in which the acquisition of phonology differs from the acquisition of other language systems. As a child is acquiring the phonological system she must also learn the phonetic realization of the system: the actual details of physiological and acoustic phonetics, which call for the coordination of a complex set of muscle movements. Some children complete the process of learning how to pronounce things earlier than others, but differences of this kind are usually not related to the learning of the phonological system. Brown had what has become a classic conversation with a child who referred to a "fis." Brown repeated "fis," and the child indignantly corrected him, saying "fis." After several such exchanges Brown tried "fish," and the child, finally satisfied, replied, "Yes, fis." It is clear that although the child was still not able to pronounce the distinction between the sounds "s" and "sh," he knew such a systematic phonological distinction existed. Such phonetic muddying of the phonological waters complicates the study of this area of acquisition. Since the child's knowledge of the phonological system may not show up in her speech, it is not easy to determine what a child knows about the system without engaging in complex experimentation and creative hypothesizing.

Children whose phonological system produces only simple words such as "mama" and "papa" actually have a greater phonetic repertory than their utterances suggest. Evidence of that repertory is found in the late babbling stage, when children are working with sentence units and are making a large array of sounds. They do not lose their phonetic ability overnight, but they must constrain it systematically. Going on to the next-higher stage of language learning, the phonological system, is more important to the child than the details of facile pronunciation. Much later, after the phonological system has been acquired, the details of pronunciation receive more attention.

In the period following the babbling period the persisting phonetic facility gets less and less exercise. The vast majority of a child's utterances fail to reflect her real ability to pronounce things accurately; they do, however, reflect her growing ability to pronounce things systematically. (For a child who grows up learning only one language the movements of the muscles of the vocal tract ultimately become so overpracticed that it is difficult to learn new pronunciations during adulthood. On the other hand, people who learn at least two languages in early childhood appear to retain a greater flexibility of the vocal musculature and are more likely to learn to speak an additional language in their adult years without the "accent" of their native language.)

In learning to pronounce, then, a child must acquire a sound system that includes the divergent systems of phonology and phonetics. The acquisition of phonology differs from that of phonetics in requiring the creation of a representation of language in the mind of the child. This representation is necessary because of the abstract nature of the units of phonological structure. From only the acoustic signal of adult language the child must derive successively more abstract phonological units: first intonations, then syllables, then distinctive features and finally consonant-and-vowel segments. There are, for example, few clear segment boundaries in the acoustic signal the child receives, and so the consonant-and-vowel units could hardly be derived if the child had no internal representation of language.

At the same time that a child is building a phonological representation of language she is learning to manipulate all the phonetic variations of language, learning to produce each one precisely and automatically. The dual process of phonetics and phonology acquisition is one of the most difficult in all of language learning. Indeed, although a great deal of syntactic and semantic acquisition has yet to take place, it is usually at the completion of the process of learning to pronounce that adults consider a child to be a full-fledged language speaker and stop using any form of caretaker speech.

Abnormal Language Development

There seems to be little question that the human brain is best suited to language learning before puberty. Foreign languages are certainly learned most easily at that time. Furthermore, it has been observed that people who learn more than one language in childhood have an easier time learning additional languages in later years. It seems to be extremely important for a child to exercise the language-learning faculty. Children who are not exposed to any learnable language during the crucial years, for example children who are deaf before they can speak, generally grow up with the handicap of having little or no language. The handicap is unnecessary: deaf children of deaf parents who communicate by means of the American Sign Language do not grow up without language. They live in an environment where they can make full use of their language-learning abilities, and they are reasonably fluent in sign language by age three, right on the developmental schedule. Deaf children who grow up communicating by means of sign language have a much easier time learning English as a second language than deaf children in oral-speech programs learning English as a first language.

The study of child language acquisition has made important contributions to the study of abnormal speech development. Some investigators of child language have looked at children whose language development is abnormal in the hope of finding the conditions that are necessary and sufficient for normal development; others have looked at the development of language in normal children in the hope of helping children whose language development is abnormal. It now appears that many of the severe language abnormalities found in children can in some way be traced to interruptions of the normal acquisition process. The improved understanding of the normal process is being exploited to create treatment programs for children with such problems. In the past therapeutic methods for children with language problems have emphasized the memorizing of language routines, but methods now being developed would allow a child to work with her own language-learning abilities. For example, the American Sign Language has been taught successfully to several autistic children. Many of these nonverbal and antisocial children have learned in this way to communicate with therapists, in some cases becoming more socially responsive. (Why sign language should be so successful with some autistic children is unclear; it may have to do with the fact that a sign lasts longer than an auditory signal.)

There are still many questions to be answered in the various areas I have discussed, but in general a great deal of progress has been made in understanding child language over the past 20 years. The study of the acquisition of language has come of age. It is now a genuinely interdisciplinary field where psychologists, neurosurgeons and linguists work together to penetrate the mechanisms of perception and cognition as well as the mechanisms of language.

The Visual Characteristics of Words

by Peter Dunn-Rankin
January 1978

What are the visual cues that good readers use to recognize letters and words? Tests seeking such insights may provide a basis for instruction in more effective reading strategies

Over the past 10 years or so I have conducted a series of experiments aimed at exploring an aspect of the general question of how people learn to read. My particular interest has focused on the visual characteristics of words, a subject that seemed at first to be narrowly defined and comparatively simple. In effect the purpose of this investigation has been to seek an answer to the specific question: What is it that a person sees when he looks at a letter or a word?

From the beginning my experiments have been based on the assumption that words are complex graphic stimuli containing a variety of potential cues that can be utilized in letter and word recognition. The difficulty many children have in learning the order and direction of letters within words indicates that the ability to recognize letters and words is not determined solely by innate visual capacity. For example, many children have not yet learned to distinguish between words containing different arrangements of the same letters. The words "saw" and "was" are often confused in an error known as a reversal. Some letters, particularly in a lowercase English type font, can be rotated or inverted to achieve similarity. Thus p can be obtained by inverting b. Words containing these letters, such as "pig" and "big," are sometimes puzzling to beginning readers. Many letters, of course, are already similar without rotation or inversion. For instance, letters such as h and n, or e and c, may be perceived incorrectly, and words such as "hot" and "not," or "cat" and "eat," may therefore be confused.

Most children are left on their own when it comes to learning how to recognize letters and words. Although some external agent—a parent or a teacher—usually reinforces the correct response, the particular features a child uses in remembering a given letter or word appear to be largely a matter of trial and error. Accordingly different children develop different strategies for recognizing graphic stimuli, and some strategies are clearly more effective than others.

It is easy to think of cases of inefficient visual processing. For example, suppose I am teaching a young child the lowercase letters. The letter b is printed on a white card. In the upper right-hand corner of the card a black smudge is all that remains of a spider that somehow lost its way into the stack of cards. I hold the card up and say: "This is a b. Can you say the letter b?" Assuming I get an affirmative reply, I might then say "Good" and go on to repeat the process with other letters. Why, however, does the child remember that this particular graphic symbol has the name b and not h or d? If he remembers from the mark of the dead spider, the strategy cannot be termed efficient for future use, because few other b's are likely to have this particular visual cue associated with them.

If good readers consistently notice certain attributes of letters or words and poor readers look elsewhere, the possibility arises of making instruction in the visual strategy of reading more effective. Before methods of teaching effective cues can be entertained, however, it is necessary to isolate the most significant visual features of letters and words. Unfortunately the strategies good readers use in making visual discriminations remain elusive, because they are formulated intuitively. Cues and rules are normally not verbalized, because most of them are not clearly understood as such by readers.

The basic visual features of the lowercase letters have been analyzed in many ways. Most investigators, however, consider such letters as being made up of five simple components. These features can be remembered by the mnemonic word "loves," which graphically represents a vertical line (l), a closed circular curve (o), an angular intersection (v), a horizontal line with a curve (e) and a cyclical curve (s). Almost all the English lowercase letters can be constructed by varying the direction of the basic modules represented by these five letters. Here simplicity can be a disadvantage for children who have not yet learned to distinguish directions, since the English lowercase letters present many rotational similarities. For instance, the four letters p, b, d and q are rotationally similar, as are n and u, f and t, m and w, and s, z and a.

In most studies of letter discrimination one of the letters in the test set is the same as the target letter. Such trials are called absolute discrimination tasks because the subject either matches the letter or does not. In experiments of this type the number of errors is normally very small. Hence it is possible to establish only a few gross categories of discriminability, based on an average rate of error of, say, zero percent and 5 percent.

In a study that I conducted in 1968 all 210 possible pairs of 21 English lowercase alphabet letters were tested by comparing their relative similarity to each target letter. By analyzing the cumulative choices made by 315 second- and third-grade children over all possible pairings, sets of linear scale values could be assigned to the lowercase letters in terms of their relative similarity to every other letter in the test alphabet [*see illustration on page 139*]. The letters not included in this study, because of their comparative infrequency in English, were j, q, v, x and z. Each of the 21 scaled letters was plotted in a frame of reference running from zero to 100. Zero indicates no error in choosing the letter most like the target letter, and 100 indicates no error in choosing the letter most unlike the target letter. The scales are organized by similar letter groups.

The scales in this study have been

adopted in many other experiments on visual perception. They provide a basis for letter selection in discrimination-learning tasks and data for the construction of tests to diagnose the visual-discrimination ability of children learning to read. In addition they are useful for studies of word errors resulting from letter confusion.

Starting with the five basic letter modules, a hierarchical learning process can be visualized in which "modules of form" (curve, angle, vertical line and so on) are used as the feature cues for letter

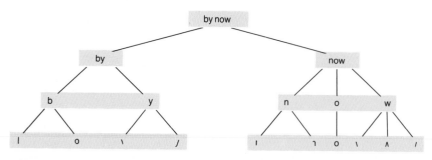

HIERARCHICAL ANALYSIS, in this case of the phrase "by now," views reading as a progressive feature-recognition process in which a few basic "modules of form" (curves, angles, vertical lines and so on) serve as the cues for the recognition of letters, which in turn serve as the cues for recognizing syllables and words, which in turn serve as cues for recognizing phrases.

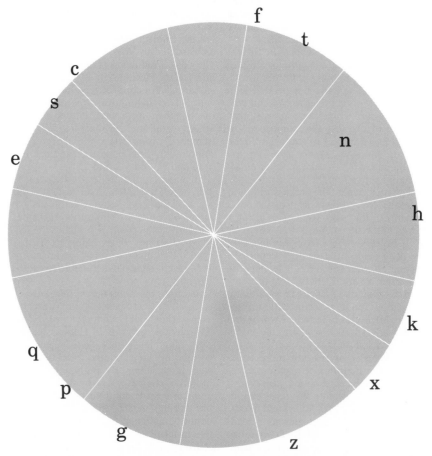

LETTER WHEEL represents the results of a multidimensional letter-discrimination analysis in which a record was made of the reaction time of 45 children and adults to a set of 13 letters paired in all possible ways. In this experiment the two paired letters were first hidden by a shutter. When they were exposed, a clock was started. As soon as the subject being tested pressed a switch indicating that the letters were "different" the clock stopped. The length of time it took for the subject to respond was then used as a measure of letter similarity. The results suggest that the important visual features of letters are perceived not as being immutable but rather as melding into each other in a continuous way. In this circular representation extremely unlike letters tend to be opposite each other. The letter n is not on the circumference of the wheel because it shares certain characteristics with e, s and c; its left vertical component and its striking similarity to h, however, place it closer to the letters with vertically ascending components.

recognition. In this case letters are the cues for the recognition of syllables and words, and syllables and words are in turn the basic features necessary for recognizing phrases. According to this model, the recognition of the phrase "by now" can be thought of as being developed in such a way that at any one level of integration no more than 3 ± 2 units of a lower level can be combined [*see top illustration at left*]. Phrases rarely contain more than 3 ± 2 words; words rarely contain more than 3 ± 2 syllables; syllables rarely contain more than 3 ± 2 letters, and letters rarely contain more than 3 ± 2 letter features.

This model of the hierarchy of visual features is incomplete because it lacks a representation of how the primary features are integrated into larger units. Several workers have suggested that the processing of the visual features of letters and words is serial, or sequential, but recent research suggests that familiar stimuli are perceived and processed in a parallel, or integrated, fashion.

Evidence for the latter hypothesis is found in an analysis of the reaction times of individual subjects to a complete set of letters paired in all possible ways. The length of time it takes for someone to respond to such stimuli appears to be closely related to reading level, particularly for mature readers. Important findings have resulted from the analysis of the reaction times of 45 children and adults who responded to the question of whether two letters were the same or different. In this experiment two letters, placed side by side on a card, are hidden by a shutter. When they are exposed, a clock starts. As soon as the subject presses a switch indicating that the letters are "different," the clock stops. The length of time it takes the subject to respond is recorded in hundredths of a second. The reaction time then serves as a measure of letter similarity. A matrix of these similarities is analyzed with the aid of a technique called individual-differences scaling [*see bottom illustration at left*].

The 13 letters selected for this study (f, t, n, h, k, x, z, g, p, q, e, s and c) were chosen because they could be combined in various ways to form pairs containing similar letter features. More letters were not included because the increase in paired comparisons makes the task too tiring for young children. The multidimensional scaling analysis takes the form of a circular pattern of letters much like a color wheel. This representation suggests that the dimensions of letters are not immutable but integrative; in other words, one letter melds into the next in a continuous way. A general division can be suggested for the 13 letters (in terms of angle v. curve or ascender v. descender). The letter k is opposite e, and t is opposite g, for example. At any point on the wheel, however, both factors must be considered.

The letter wheel indicates that a parallel processing approach to the perception of familiar letters is preferable to a serial model. Most of the 13 letters contain two or more of the basic constituents, and an analogy between primary-color combinations and letter-feature combinations is strongly suggested. Just as orange is seen as a unique color even though it is a combination of red and yellow, so are the letters of the letter wheel seen as integrated units that are combinations of basic features. In this model x combines with l to produce k, and l combines with n to produce h, yet h and k are perceived as wholes.

Further reinforcement for an integrative perception of familiar units comes from the fact that the two basic dimensions indicated (curve v. angle, ascender v. descender) are in general relied on equally by all subjects. A unique by-product of the newer scaling methods is that individual weights can be determined for each subject on each dimension found. When I plotted the positions of the 45 subjects with respect to the use they made of these two dimensions, it was clear that none of the subjects, young or old, good reader or poor, chose one feature exclusively. Some subjects, however, recognized the combination of the two basic features more readily than others. These subjects were also the most mature readers in the sample. Such a result might be an artifact of consistency of response or might reflect the importance of these dimensions to perception in reading, or both.

Immature and mature readers can also be distinguished in terms of their reliance on letter frequency for recognition. Where adults will distinguish between a and z because one is curved and the other is angular, very young children make the distinction because a is familiar and z is unfamiliar, confirming the idea that frequent exposure to stimuli such as letters provides a level of satiation necessary for automatic response. It follows that the identification of simple stimuli such as letters should not serve as a variable in tests aimed at identifying good and poor readers beyond the second or third grade. More complicated stimuli (such as words), however, do provide pattern-discrimination tasks at a level that is complex enough for determining good and poor readers in all elementary grades.

I first tested my developmental hypothesis for the visual discrimination of words with a device called the word-preference inventory. In this experiment I would show the child a target word such as "sore" and present two pseudowords similar to "sore" but containing specific kinds of errors. For the target word "sore" I might present "ssore" (in which the extra s is called an addition)

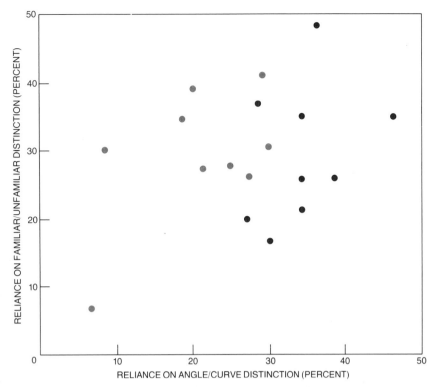

IMMATURE AND MATURE READERS can be distinguished in terms of their reliance on letter frequency for recognition. As this two-dimensional graph shows, adults (*black dots*) tend to distinguish the letters a and z because one is curved and the other is angular, whereas very young children (*colored dots*) make the distinction because a is familiar and z is unfamiliar.

and "core" (in which c is a misperception of s). Mature readers usually choose "ssore" as more like the target, whereas younger readers choose "core" as more like it. When adults and kindergarten children were asked which pseudoword, "hoat" or "qoat," looked more like the target word "boat," 85 percent of the adults preferred "hoat," whereas 80 percent of the children chose "qoat." (In these pseudowords h is defined as a misperception of b in the target word, whereas q is a rotation of b.)

The distribution of choices in this test for children in elementary school suggests that an adult view of word similarity only begins to be approximated by the time a child reaches the third grade and that even in the sixth grade there are differences in pseudoword choice between adults and children. Somewhere between the second and fourth grades it appears that most students change their strategy of reading: they start guessing what the words are from the context and start using phonetic cues to help them guess. For a lower socioeconomic group the change might be observed between the third and fifth grades. Approximately 10 percent of the children tested in the fourth and fifth grades revealed immature and probably ineffective visual strategies. These children were also found to be below-average readers.

The Swedish psychologist Benny Brodda, in the course of testing whether or not prospective trade names in Sweden are similar to existing ones, has found that the letter order of the two words being compared is the most important factor in word similarity. He uses letter order as the primary basis for his test of whether or not two words are similar. I have also used letter order in test items in my word-preference inventory. Some poor readers will consistently choose words that are not in order, that is, words that represent reversals or permutations of the original target word, whereas good readers choose other errors instead.

In order to assess the phonetic bias of the word-preference inventory, the 51-item test was also administered to 240 native Japanese children in the fourth and fifth grades. When the responses of the Japanese children were compared with those of the American children, the basic factors of letter order and word unity were found in both cultures. A phonetic bias was not found. The distinction between rotation and misperception, a factor noticed in the American population, was not made by the Japanese children. An explanation for this difference is that the traditional Japanese script has no characters that can be made equivalent by rotation. The Japanese have been modernizing their type fonts, however, and in at least one of the new fonts some of the characters are rotationally equivalent. This ty-

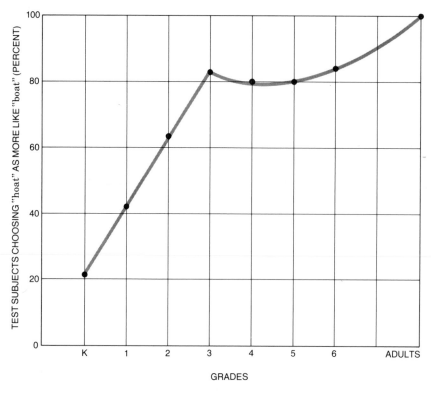

DIFFERENT READING STRATEGIES employed by children and adults are reflected in this graph, which shows the distribution of responses to a question in one of the author's tests, called the word-preference inventory. Both the children and the adults were asked which pseudoword, "hoat" or "qoat," looked more like the target word "boat." At one extreme 80 percent of the kindergarten children tested chose "qoat" (in which q is a rotation of b), whereas 85 percent of the adults preferred "hoat" (in which h is a misperception of b). The adult view of word similarity only begins to be approximated by the time a child reaches the third grade. At about that stage most children appear to change their reading strategy: they begin to guess what the words are from the context. For below-average readers the change is observed somewhat later.

pographical simplification may create some directional reading difficulty for Japanese children where there has been none.

A different kind of study of word similarity involves taking approximately 100 words from a newspaper article and having people group words they think look most alike. Analyses of this kind indicate that there are four basic features adults rely on in determining whether words are visually similar. The first factor is whether or not the beginning letter or letters are the same. The second factor is similarity in word length. The third factor is similar word endings such as "-ing," "-ed," "-ly" and "-igh." The fourth factor is similar internal letters or letter combinations. The combinations could include letters with ascending components (such as l, d and t) or those with descending ones (such as g and y). Letter combinations, either adjacent or separated in the word, are important visual cues used in word recognition. The beginning letter, however, is the dominant visual characteristic of a word. Its importance is also confirmed by other studies.

Word length has been questioned as an effective feature in word perception and recognition because of its high correlation with infrequency of usage: long words are less familiar. In a recent study, however, I was able to confirm the importance of word length as a visual feature utilized in estimating word similarity. I conducted an individual-differences scaling of 10 words that begin with the same letter, using measurements both of reaction times and of percent overlap to determine similarity, and the results were almost identical. The dominance of word length was apparent from this study.

Since there are many words that begin with the same letter and many words of the same length, initial letter and length cannot be independently useful as cues to word recognition. I therefore made a survey to determine the frequency with which both features are found in elementary-school textbooks. The results showed that fewer than 1 percent of the possible pairs of different words have both features in common, suggesting that their combination can be an important visual characteristic in word perception. One has only to take any newspaper article and count the number of word pairs having the same length and also beginning with the same letter to realize that the total is less than 1 percent of the possible pairs.

Some of my experiments have involved the use of afterimages: visual images that persist after the stimulus has ceased. I first noticed the usefulness of the afterimage as a representation of the visual focal point during a camping trip in 1969. A gas lamp was hung in the tent where I was reading, and I was drawn to stare at it for some reason, perhaps because it was not working well. When I looked back at the page, I saw the afterimage of the bright gas mantle clearly superposed on the printed material at each visual fixation point. I immediately began dotting the fixation points as I read.

Four years later, during a sabbatical at the University of Stockholm, I began to study this phenomenon systematically and to use it in the search for effective cues to letter and word identification. (I was unaware that Hermann von Helmholtz had used a similar technique almost a century earlier.) At that time I discovered by accident that the apparent size of the image is a function of the distance at which it is projected. By creating afterimages from small light sources at a distance of two or three meters the apparent afterimage can be made quite small when one looks at a surface held a short distance away. The image can, in fact, be made small enough to be accurately pinpointed within a line set in a common textbook type font.

In experiments exploiting the afterimage phenomenon the subject is asked to fixate on a screened 40-watt lamp projected from a dark, unlighted background through a hole one centimeter in diameter located at a distance of approximately three meters. The subject gazes at the source for about a minute and a half, or until the light appears to "swim" or "shimmer" and a gray afterimage appears whenever the subject switches his gaze to a white sheet of paper. As an aid in locating the afterimage the subject is asked to close his eyes for a moment. A bright dot or flash of light is invariably reported by subjects at the same position as the afterimage. The stimuli are usually typed letters or drawn black figures on nonreflective white cards or paper.

The projected afterimage varies among individuals but is commonly described as consisting of two types, one following the other. First, a dark gray spot a millimeter or two in diameter is seen superposed on a white or light gray background. Wherever the subject looks the center of the gray dot is taken as the focal point. This gray image lasts for

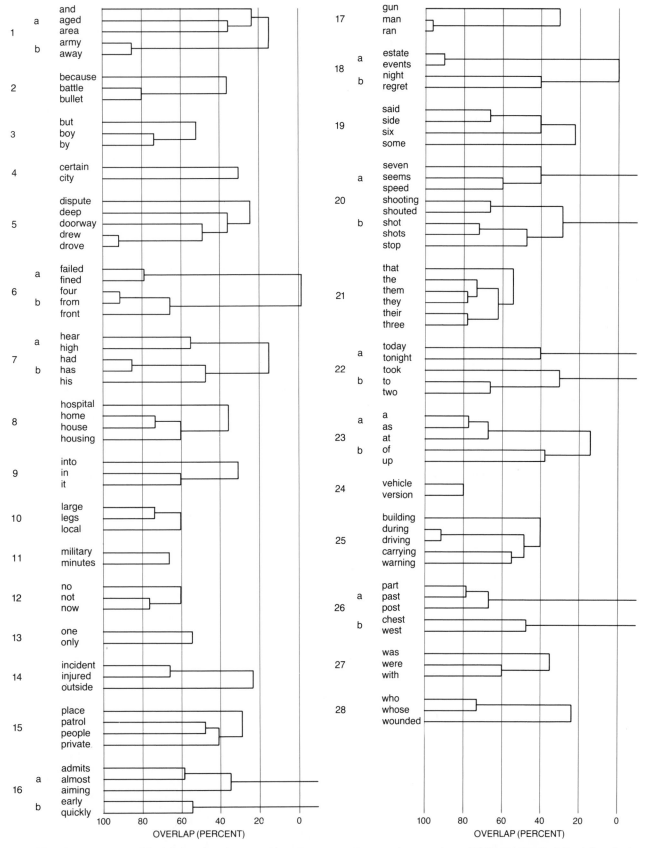

CLUSTERING of visually similar words results from a different kind of study, in which the test subjects were given a newspaper article containing approximately 100 words and were asked to group together words they thought looked most alike. Such findings, organized into hierarchical tables such as this one, indicate that there are four ba-

sic features adults perceive as being important in determining whether words are visually similar: similar beginning letters, similar word length, similar word endings and similar internal letters or letter combinations. Of these four factors similar beginning letters appear to be the most important, a finding that is confirmed by other studies.

about 30 seconds and is followed by a pink or red circular image of approximately the same size, which persists for as long as three minutes. Several positions of the afterimage are easily remembered by the subject as he looks at the test image.

Preliminary studies of this kind indicate that as words increase in length the subjects' focal point moves progressively to the right of the initial letter. The Dutch psychologist Herman Bouma has shown that subjects can see farther to the right of a fixation point than they can to the left. It seemed reasonable to Bouma that in an English word such as "today" the ideal focal point should be located slightly to the left of center, say over the o, since this would be an efficient place for viewing the entire word. As it turns out, among mature readers this point is indeed the place where the word is most frequently fixated.

On returning from Stockholm to my laboratory at the University of Hawaii I continued my experiments on afterimages. One such study involved three different groups of words. Each group began with similar spellings but varied in length. The words were randomized and were typed in elite type on white paper. After inducing afterimages of the words five graduate students in educational psychology at the university marked their focal points for each word on two separate occasions. The results for all the focal points on these occasions were consolidated for the words that had similar beginnings [see illustration on this page]. When the median focal points were connected by straight lines with the words arranged in a triangular fashion, the results showed that the focal point is fairly central. The variation of the position, however, increases markedly with longer words, suggesting a greater choice of stimuli that are effective to look at and also indicating that longer words may cause some subjects to adjust their focal point to the left as a strategy for clearly seeing the initial letter. In almost all cases one focal point suffices for each word. The focal points are also characteristically found on the upper borders of the lowercase letters.

This study and others indicate that for stimuli such as words and short phrases the afterimage can be an accurate approximation of the focal point. The results show that the focal point does not fall haphazardly on the stimulus and that it is not evenly distributed. This finding suggests a mechanism for subconscious visual preprocessing. It may be that the preprocessing, although it is an innate capacity of human beings, is susceptible to development by frequent exposure to such symbolic stimuli as letters and words. In the mature reader the preprocessing usually results in efficient placement of the focal point. In the studies reported here almost all the focal points were observed on the upper contours of the stimuli centered around (and in a sense attracted by) unique letters, usually internally placed vowels or consonants with ascending letter features. All focal-point studies suggest a peripheral unconscious control of focalization in which the focal points of mature readers are such that vision is efficiently utilized.

It is unwarranted to assume that the recognition of visual features is solely responsible for reading skill. For material in which the context is familiar, glances may be cursory and mostly confirmatory. The following sentence, for example, is printed backward: ".rat eht saw tac ehT"

Read through the sentence once from right to left. Careful reading reveals the nonsensical statement "The cat was the tar." Most subjects, however, read "The cat saw the rat" or "The cat was the rat." Here habit and context are so strong that they misinform. Where words or their context are unfamiliar the processing of smaller units of stimuli becomes more apparent, and the letters of an extremely unfamiliar word may even be studied individually.

To cite another example, read the following sentence and count all the f's: "The first fine fishing day of the year we finally flew to Alaska for five days of

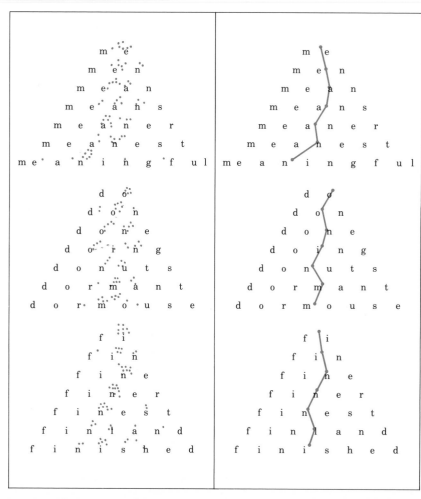

FOCAL POINTS of test subjects looking at words can be accurately estimated by first generating a strong point afterimage in each subject and then having the subject mark the position of the afterimage when different words are presented as stimuli. In this demonstration of the afterimage technique the colored dots over the words at left represent all the focal points recorded for five different subjects on two separate occasions when the subjects were presented with three sets of words that had similar beginnings but varying lengths. The words have been arbitrarily arranged in a triangular fashion in the illustration and the spacing between the letters has been exaggerated. The colored zigzag lines superposed on the word triangles at right connect the median focal points recorded for each set of words. The results show that the focal points tend to be located fairly centrally in each case, usually on the upper borders of the lowercase letters. The variance in the position of the focal points increases with longer words, although in almost all cases one focal point suffices for each word. There is a slight tendency on the part of some subjects to adjust the focal point to the left with longer words, perhaps as a strategy for clearly seeing the initial letter. Subjects were graduate students in pyschology.

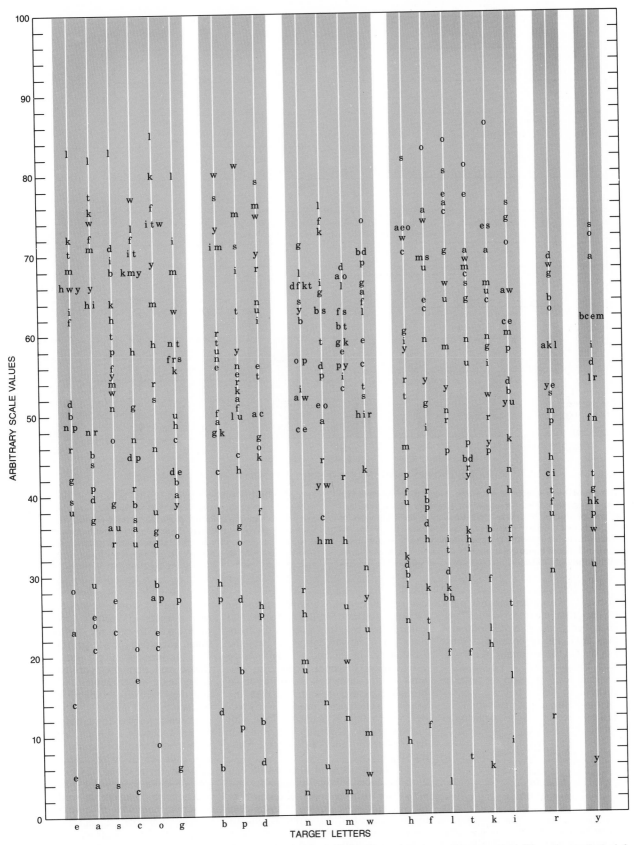

LETTER-SIMILARITY SCALES were constructed by the author on the basis of a letter-discrimination test in which 21 lowercase letters were matched in pairs to determine their relative similarity to one another. The cumulative choices made by 315 second- and third-grade children over all 210 possible pairings were then analyzed, and sets of linear scale values were assigned to the letters in terms of their relative similarity to each target letter. (The comparatively infrequent letters not included in the study were j, q, v, x and z.) In the arbitrary frame of reference in which the letters are plotted here zero indicates no error in choosing a letter most like the target letter, and 100 indicates no error in choosing the letter most unlike target letter. The scales are organized by similar letter groups (*colored bands*).

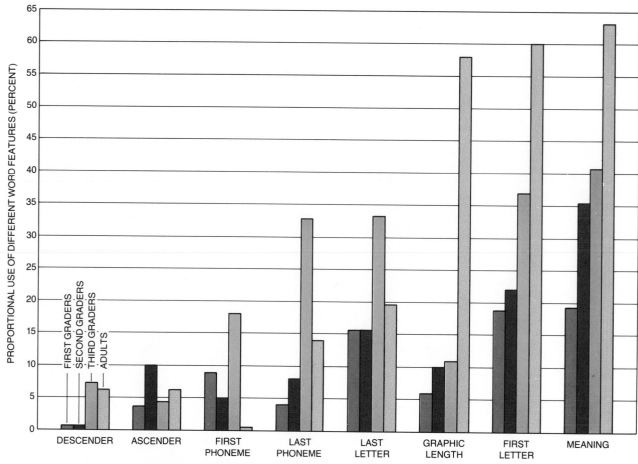

ANALYSIS of the proportional use made of eight different word features in the preferred word-recognition strategies of children and adults was conducted by Selvin Chin-Chance of the University of Hawaii. The eight objective measures of word similarity, identified at the bottom, included semantic features, phonetic features and meaning along with visual features for a set of 24 carefully chosen words. In addition the eight objective measures of word similarity were cor-related with each subject's own subjective estimate of word similari-ty. The results of this experiment showed that whereas phonetic cues are popular among children, particularly third-graders, they are not used extensively by adults, perhaps because "sounding out the word" is too slow a process for an efficient recognition strategy. Instead ma-ture readers tend to place greater emphasis on meaning, first letters and graphic length in establishing the similarity between word pairs.

real fishing." Most people count eight f's, the ones that begin the words. They fail to notice that the word "of" also contains an f. Partly because one ex-pects to see f at the beginning of a word, but also because "of" is phonetically pronounced "ov," the specific letter is not noticed.

Something similar happens when one is asked to read the following phrase in this form:

Paris
in the
the spring.

The familiar content and a guessing strategy make one overlook the sec-ond "the" in "the spring." In such experi-ences meaning dominates the visual sys-tem. When one is asked to read the fol-lowing two sentences, "Loveisnowhere," "Theytoldhimtobeatthefrontdoor," one

can read either "Love is now here" or "Love is nowhere" in the first case, and either "They told him to be at the front door" or "They told him to beat the front door" in the second. To a large extent one's personal experience dic-tates which statement is the more proba-ble one. Context, sound and meaning are used as nonvisual cues to word rec-ognition by skillful readers. Along with visual cues they constitute a complex of features employed in an effective read-ing strategy.

In a recent doctoral dissertation one of my students, Selvin Chin-Chance, an-alyzed semantic features, phonetic fea-tures and meaning along with visual fea-tures for a set of 24 carefully chosen words. A separate quantitative measure of similarity between each of the 276 pairs of the 24 words was determined for eight different word features: as-cenders, descenders, first phoneme, last phoneme, last letter, graphic length, first letter and meaning. After breaking

down the 24 words into two separate lists subjects at various grade levels were asked to rate the similarity be-tween each pair of words. The words were embedded in phrases, and the phrase and then the word were read aloud by the experimenter. At the same time they were also available to the sub-ject in a printed text.

For each word pair a correlation was obtained between the eight objective measures of similarity and the subject's own estimate of word similarity. For each subject a set of 524 correlations over 68 word pairs was available. The questions to be answered were: Which objective measures of similarity most agreed with the subject's estimate? Could a subject's personal strategy for estimating word similarity be deter-mined objectively?

The results show that in general the word-similarity strategies adopted by adults rely primarily on meaning, first letter and graphic length. The developmental processes involved in word perception therefore appear to be similar to those found in my other studies. The most important aspect of these results, however, is that they demonstrate that phonetic cues were not extensively used by the mature reader, perhaps because such processing is too slow; it may be that "sounding out the word" is too time-consuming and unnecessary. Phonetic cues, on the other hand, are frequently used by third-grade children. Although many elementary-school children lack consistent strategies for estimating word similarity, children whose responses reveal a consistent strategy also score highest on tests of reading comprehension.

It is reasonable to assume that reading begins with the perception of graphic stimuli. Although some visual material appears to be unnoticed or irrelevant, it may be wrong to assume that familiar material goes unseen or unattended. For example, the Australian psychologist John Ross has shown that the visual system of a mature person can process depth information in less than .0002 second [see "The Resources of Binocular Perception," by John Ross; SCIENTIFIC AMERICAN, March, 1976]. This processing is at least 100 times faster than the average time it takes a person to shift from one visual focal point to another. Processing at this rate is therefore essentially subliminal, or unconscious. It is possible that familiar material is processed at a similar level by some kind of automatic process.

The automatic-preprocessing model of reading states that as the subject's exposure to any given stimulus increases, there is a point at which the stimulus can be preprocessed prior to a conscious awareness. Although some stimuli may be quite complex for the immature subject, they can be at the automatic level for the experienced reader. Thus fewer and fewer focal points are needed as the reading material becomes increasingly familiar. Familiarity can be attained by frequency of meaningful exposure to the actual visual stimulus or by the familiar content and semantic order in which it is embedded; in other words, common phrases could be automatically preprocessed by means of context cues or phonetic structure as well as by visual familiarity. This model indicates that for the young or inexperienced subject most graphic stimuli are complex and must be handled in feature units that are processed through conscious awareness. What is complex for the inexperienced reader may be at the preprocessing level for the more mature reader. Since such processing is learned, concentrating on such useful word features as beginning letter and word length should help in attaining the automatic level of word recognition and reading.

15 Bilingualism and Information Processing

by Paul A. Kolers
March 1968

A person who can speak two languages has clearly mastered two sets of symbols. Experiments that cause the two sets to interact provide important clues to how the mind works

Is the human mind too complex to be a profitable object of study? Many investigators have felt that it is, and yet one approach to it has always seemed promising. One of the principal activities of the human mind is the manipulation of symbols; might not an investigation of the way people use symbols yield some insights into the workings of the mind?

If so, a person who can speak two languages with reasonable fluency is of particular interest, because he works with two distinct sets of symbols. By presenting a bilingual subject with information in one language and then testing him in the other, the investigator should be able to learn much about the mental operations involved in the acquisition, storage and retrieval of the information. This has been the objective of experiments my colleagues and I have conducted with bilingual subjects in the Research Laboratory of Electronics at the Massachusetts Institute of Technology and in the Center for Cognitive Studies at Harvard University.

At the outset a qualification is in order. The experiments were concerned only with words, whereas the mind also receives and manipulates information in many other forms. One can remember the appearance of an object, the tonal quality of a musical instrument, the texture of a surface or the smell of a flower without being able to describe them precisely in words. The reader can remind himself of this fact by trying to find words for the smell of a rose. Nonetheless, much of a human being's thinking is expressed in words; they are clearly his principal means of receiving, storing, manipulating and transmitting information. The question of how words are involved in these processes is now the subject of intensive inquiry.

Let me proceed to our own work with an anecdote. Once when I was visiting Belgrade I set out with a colleague to buy a certain kind of decorated shoe—a part of the national costume of Yugoslavia—that had caught his eye. We tried several shops, where, with a combination of German, French, guidebook Serbian and gestures, he tried to get what he wanted. Finally we found a shop that had the shoes, but not in the right size.

As we started to leave, two other men came into the store speaking Italian. My friend listened and then said in Spanish, "They don't have that size; I just asked." One of the newcomers said, "Why do you speak Spanish to us? We're speaking Italian." "I know," said my friend in Spanish, "but I don't speak Italian. Can't you understand me? I understand you." "Well then," said the other man in French, "it is not so good. How is your French?" My friend answered in French, "I don't understand why you don't understand Spanish when you know Italian. My French is poor. Do you speak German?" "But yes, all right, let us speak German. Where do you come from?" My friend replied in German, "The United States. And where are you from?" The reply—in English—was "We're from New York," and everyone laughed. The entire exchange, involving the use of five languages, lasted for less than a minute.

I tell this story not only because it illustrates a number of aspects of the skilled use of languages but also because it was in thinking about the implications of the episode that I became interested in bilingualism. One point the story makes about the skilled user of two or more languages is that he can switch readily from one language to another. A second point is that the changeover is usually total: the people in the episode did not speak a mixture of Italian, Spanish, French, German and English; they spoke one or another exclusively.

Let us consider what such switching entails. In some languages, such as English and French, the meaning of a sentence is strongly dependent on the sequence of the words. The point is well made by the contrast between "The dog bit the man" and "The man bit the dog." The individual words are identical; the meanings are not. In other languages, such as German and Latin, meaning is less dependent on word order because the subjects and objects of sentences are indicated by case endings and the declension of articles. The difference in German between "Der Hund biss den Mann" and "Den Mann biss der Hund" is more one of emphasis than of meaning. Even though the order of words is different, both sentences translate as "The dog bit the man," although the second sentence might be taken to indicate a particular man.

There are of course many rules that characterize the use of a language. The body of rules is the grammar of the language; the individual words are its lexicon. The two men speaking in the Belgrade store did at least three things when they switched languages. They selected words from five different lexicons. They used words in different order, that is, they used different grammatical rules to generate meaningful sequences of words. They also made sounds in different ways, that is, they used a German accent for German, a French accent for French and so on. Moreover, although they were performing a complicated psychological task in switching among linguistic codes, they did not really have to think about the process.

One of our experiments was aimed at assessing the psychological cost of such code-switching. We were interested not only in the mental processes of a bilingual person when he hears or reads either of his languages but also in what is involved when he speaks or writes either of them. Our approach made use of passages of connected discourse, some of which violated normal grammatical rules. In one session bilingual subjects read such passages silently and then were tested for comprehension of what they had read. In a second session they read the passages aloud.

Four abbreviated passages are shown in the illustration on the next page. Two of them are wholly unilingual—one in English and one in French. The other two are mixed; both are made up of some English words and some French ones, but in the first the word order is English and in the second it is French. All four passages convey the same message.

Before testing our subjects we had established how much time other subjects needed to read unilingual passages of the same length as the experimental passages and get a score of 75 percent correct on a comprehension test. Our experimental subjects were then asked to read the various unilingual and mixed passages in exactly that length of time. One might think that in order to under-

stand a mixed passage a subject would have to translate all the words into one language or to switch between linguistic codes in some other way. If so, one might expect that the subjects would be so busy translating and switching that they would have less time to consider the meaning of the passage. Hence they would get a lower score on a comprehension test of a mixed passage than on one of a unilingual passage.

Our findings, however, were that the subjects had almost identical scores on comprehension tests following the silent reading of unilingual and mixed passages. I concluded that a skilled reader of two languages can—in reading silently—comprehend a passage readily no matter to what extent words from either language are mixed in the passage. He apparently does not have to do any switching between linguistic codes when the passages are read. (We have not yet done the experiment to test if the same ease of comprehension is evident when a bilingual person listens to a message in which words from his two languages are mixed.)

The results were markedly different when we had our subjects read various passages aloud instead of silently. They needed more time to read the mixed passages than to read the unilingual ones. Evidently reading aloud entailed some kind of code-switching between lan-

guages; the reader could not move as smoothly through "his horse, followed de deux bassets" as he could through "his horse, followed by two hounds."

We had constructed the passages in such a way that the unilingual ones contained an average of 110 words of English or French. The mixed passages contained 55 words from each language. We therefore were in a position to measure the amount of time required for code-switching by seeing how long it took a subject to read one passage in English and one in French and then subtracting the average of those times from the amount of time it took to read a mixed passage. Dividing the difference by the number of linguistic transitions in a mixed passage—the number of times a switch occurred between English and French—we determined that the average amount of time required for each switch in code was a third of a second. That is, it took a subject a third of a second longer, on the average, to read something like "his horse, followed de deux bassets" than to read "his horse, followed by two hounds."

Doubtless some of the difference is attributable to mechanical effects: the subject must physically adjust his vocal apparatus in switching from the sounds of one language to the sounds of another. We are not sure how much of the difference is due to such adjustments, but

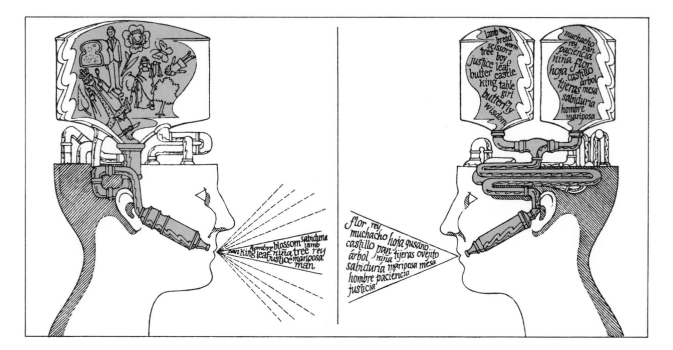

TWO HYPOTHESES about the way a bilingual person handles information are represented by two arrangements of tanks. One hypothesis (left) is that all his information is stored centrally, or in one tank, and that he has access to it equally with both languages, which are represented by the various taps. The other (right) is that his information is stored in linguistically associated ways, or in separate tanks. Experiments by the author indicated that the actual situation of a bilingual person combines parts of both hypotheses.

His horse, followed by two hounds, made the earth re-sound under its even tread. Drops of ice stuck to his cloak. A strong wind was blowing. One side of the horizon lighted up, and in the whiteness of the early morning light, he saw rabbits hopping at the edge of their burrows.

Son cheval, suivi de deux bassets, en marchant d'un pas égal faisait résonner la terre. Des gouttes de verglas se collaient à son manteau. Une brise violente soufflait. Un côté de l'horizon s'éclaircit; et, dans la blancheur du crépuscule, il aperçut des lapins sautillant au bord de leurs terriers.

His horse, followed de deux bassets, faisait la terre ré-sonner under its even tread. Des gouttes de verglas stuck to his manteau. Une violente brise was blowing. One side de l'horizon lighted up, and dans la blancheur of the early morning light, il aperçut rabbits hopping at the bord de leurs terriers.

Son cheval, suivi by two hounds, en marchant d'un pas égal, made resound the earth. Drops of ice se collaient à son cloak. A wind strong soufflait. Un côté of the horizon s'éclaircit; et, in the whiteness du crépuscule, he saw des lapins sautillant au edge of their burrows.

SIMILAR PASSAGES of connected discourse were used in experiments with bilingual persons. The passages present the same message in four ways: unilingually in English and French and bilingually in mixed form, one favoring English word order and the other French. Subjects reading mixed passages silently lost no time switching between languages, whereas in reading aloud they took longer with mixed passages than with unilingual ones.

from control experiments involving code-switching in English alone we have concluded that a significant portion of the code-switching interval is occupied by a mental operation. The operation can be described as a "call time," meaning the amount of time the mind needs to organize a set of procedures for handling a piece of information. The length of call time probably varies from person to person. It may vary also with the procedure being called. In reading a science textbook, for example, one sees words, pictures, formulas and other kinds of symbol and uses different procedures for each of them. The length of time required to call the appropriate procedures may also differ.

The experiments with mixed passages involved the important matter of context. Clearly the fact that each of the passages had a context—a thematic continuity—made it easier for the subjects to comprehend the passages. In some instances context is created by the system of symbols itself, as when a writer uses words to tell the reader what topic he is discussing. Other systems of symbols are different. Computer programmers and engineers, for example, cannot usually understand each other's programs or circuit drawings until they are told separately what the program or the drawing is designed to do—what its context is. (How subtle one's dependence on context can be is illustrated by a recent newspaper story that described the bewilderment of a foreign visitor to New York when he saw a sign saying, "BUS STOP. NO STANDING." Lacking the context that would be familiar to any New Yorker driving a car, he at first took the sign to mean that he was supposed to sit down while waiting for the bus.)

Words and other symbols, however, are not always embedded in a context. I wanted to investigate how the mind dealt with words that were isolated from context. To that end I undertook two other experiments. Before I describe them I need to supply some context.

Many bilingual people say that they think differently and respond with different emotions to the same experience in their two languages. For example, reading a poem or a play in French and reading its translation in English are said to create markedly different feelings and impressions. It is difficult to assess these introspective statements, if only because emotive texts are notoriously difficult to translate well. As Robert Frost once remarked, when a poem is translated, the poetry is often lost.

Nonetheless, if one accepts the premise that such statements reflect a genuine mental experience, one wonders about its nature. In particular we wondered whether the difference in impression arises from the difficulty of translating words accurately or from some overall property of languages and the contexts in which they are used. To put the question another way, we wondered how verbal symbols are stored in the mind.

Perhaps a metaphor will help to clarify the issue. Regard the mind as a storage tank and languages as taps. Is all the information that words represent stored in some central tank in the mind, so that if a person is bilingual he has access to the same information even though he is using two different taps? If so, one could expect a variety of taps: some could be large and some small; some could release the contents of the tank as a spray and some as a stream. That is, the taps might be regarded as the rules of grammar that affect the translation of information in the mind into sentences. The information being tapped would always be the same, but its appearance and form would differ (according to the grammar being used) in such characteristics as word order, tense agreement and the like.

Another possibility is that the information in the mind of a bilingual person depends fundamentally on the language that was used to put it there. To continue the metaphor, such a person would have two tanks in his mind, each with its own tap. The tanks would reflect a situation in which the rules for using a language are indelibly stamped on the information stored, so that the bilingual person has access to different information when he uses the different taps.

The first of the two alternatives can be described as common storage of information. The second entails separate storage [see illustration on page 143]. The alternatives define two extreme ways of characterizing the issue. If common storage were the case, the differences in reading a poem in two languages would be due entirely to the difficulty of translation. If separate storage were the case, the difference would be due to other kinds of experience. The fact is, as I shall show with a description of the experiments, that neither extreme alternative correctly describes the mental storage of information. A third arrangement that combines features of the other two seems to be required.

The method I chose for examining the extreme alternatives was a word-association test in which the subject is required to say the first word that comes to mind in response to a stimulus word. For example, a large percentage of English-speaking adults respond to "table" with "chair" and to "black" with "white." My subjects were students whose native languages were German, Spanish or Thai but who were also fluent in English. In my tests the subjects responded in their native language to a list of words in that language; they responded in English to the same list in

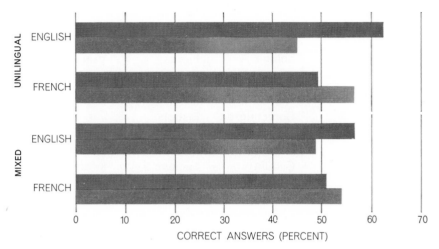

WRITTEN TESTS of comprehension of unilingual and mixed passages produced these results for Americans (*black*) and Europeans (*color*). The scores are roughly equivalent for all conditions, although the subjects did somewhat better with texts favoring their native syntax.

BILINGUAL SIGNS, a common sight in Quebec, are indicative of a situation in which use of two languages is an ordinary matter. Quebec often uses pictorial signs as an alternative.

	ENGLISH	GERMAN	SPANISH	THAI
EVOCATIVE	man	Mann	hombre	poo chai
	table	Tisch	mesa	dto
	bread	Brot	pan	ka-nom bpung
	boy	Junge	muchacho	dek poo chai
	blossom	Blüte	flor	dauk mai barn
	girl	Mädchen	niña	dek poo ying
	butter	Butter	mantequilla	nur-ie
	scissors	Schere	tijeras	gkan gkrai
ABSTRACTIONS	freedom	Freiheit	libertad	say-ree parp
	justice	Gerechtigkeit	justicia	yoo-dti tum
	law	Gesetz	ley	gkot mai
	honor	Ehre	honor	gkee-at-dti
	patience	Geduld	paciencia	kwam ot-ton
	wisdom	Weisheit	sabiduría	kwam raub roo
	duty	Pflicht	el deber	nah tee
	civilization	Zivilisation	civilización	ah-ra-ya tum
THINGS	lamb	Lamm	ovejita	look gkaa
	thorn	Dorn	espina	nam
	butterfly	Schmetterling	mariposa	pee sur-ah
	worm	Wurm	gusano	naun
	smoke	Rauch	humo	kwan
	castle	Schloss	castillo	bprah-sart
	tree	Baum	árbol	dton mai
	Norway	Norwegen	Noruega	nor-way
FEELINGS	pain	Schmerz	dolor	chjep bpoo-at
	hate	Hass	odio	kwam gklee-at
	jealousy	Eifersucht	celos	heung
	fear	Furcht	miedo	kwam gklau
	love	Liebe	amor	kwam ruk
	guilt	Schuld	culpa	kwam pit
	sadness	Traurigkeit	tristeza	kwam sow
	pity	Mitleid	piedad	song sarn

LEXICON OF WORDS used in word-association tests of the kind shown in the upper illustration on the opposite page was in four categories. The first contains words that evoke similar responses when used as stimulus words; for example, most people hearing "man" will respond "woman." Other categories are self-explanatory. Thai words are presented here in transliteration, whereas subjects familiar with the language saw them in Thai alphabet.

English, and they responded in one language to stimulus words presented in the other. A typical selection of words is shown in all four languages in the illustration above.

Consider the German words *Haus* (house) and *Tisch* (table). Suppose a person fluent in German and English who was taking the German-German association test responded to *Tisch* with *Haus*. Would he respond to *table* with *house*

or with some other word, such as *chair?* And how would he respond when the stimulus was in one language and he was asked to react in the other?

If the hypothesis of a common store of information were correct, one would expect a large percentage of responses to be similar in all the tests, since the concepts with which the subject was dealing would be essentially the same regardless of the language he was speak-

ing. On the other hand, if information were stored according to language, one would expect the percentage of such direct translations to be low; for example, the subject might respond to *Tisch* with *Haus* in the German-German test and to *table* with *chair* in the English-English test.

Our finding was that about a fifth of the responses were the same in a bilingual subject's two languages. That is too large a percentage to warrant the belief that the meanings of words were stored completely in linguistically separate tanks. On the other hand, the large number of responses (about a quarter of the total) confined to one language or another enabled us to reject the idea that the meanings existed in a single tank for which the languages were merely taps. The bilingual person does not have a single store of meanings in his mind that he taps with his two languages. What it comes down to is that access to the information one has in one's mind is in some cases restricted to the language by which—or, more broadly, the context in which—it was encoded.

What are these cases? An indication is provided by the different responses we received to different categories of words. Some of the words we used referred to concrete objects; examples are *lamb, thorn, tree*. Other words were more abstract: *freedom, justice, wisdom, materialism*. Still other words—*hate, jealousy, love, guilt*—referred to feelings.

Our results revealed that words referring to concrete, manipulable objects were more likely to elicit similar responses in the bilingual person's two languages than abstract words. The abstract words in turn elicited a larger number of similar responses than the words referring to feelings. To put the matter another way, *love* and *Liebe* or *democracy* and *Demokratie* do not mean the same thing to someone familiar with English and German, even though they are dictionary translations of one another. He has different contexts and different expectations for each of the two words in the pairs. In contrast, words that refer to objects that people in various countries manipulate in similar ways—objects such as pencils, books and desks—have very similar meanings in the two languages. The idea that there are operational definitions of terms, as many philosophers of science put it, seems to have some psychological reality as one basis of meaning.

Our work showed that some information can be stored in such a way that it is readily accessible in either of two languages. Other information is, in terms of its accessibility, closely bound to the language by which it was stored in the mind. In another set of experiments we explored the way in which words are stored and retrieved. The question was: Are words perceived and then stored in the memory as individual items or does the process take place in terms of their meanings?

Our experiment was based on a phenomenon first studied in detail by Nancy C. Waugh, a former colleague of mine who is now at the Harvard Medical School. She found that if a subject was presented with a unilingual list of words, some of which were repeated, his ability to recall a given word was directly proportional to the number of times it had been repeated. If a subject is shown, say, 120 words one at a time for about a second each, and if a few of the words are repeated on the list, he is twice as likely to recall a word presented four times as one presented twice.

My colleagues and I wondered what the result would be if a list were presented with some words appearing in two languages. Taking as an example the English word *fold* and its French translation *pli*, would a bilingual subject seeing each of them two or three times in a long list of words presented singly recall *fold* and *pli* according to the frequency with which each appeared or would his recall reflect the frequency of occurrence of the common meaning of the two words? An English-French list typical of the ones we used appears in the top illustration on the next page; the reader must remember that the subject saw the words one at a time and not in a complete array as in the illustration. Among the words that translate each other are *fold* and *pli* and *ten* and *dix;* among the words that are not translated are *herd* and *fonds* (funds).

The results showed that the percentage of recall increased linearly with the frequency of occurrence of meaning [*see bottom illustration on next page*]. Presenting *fold* twice and *pli* twice produces the same effect on the recall of either word as presenting either one four times. Since *fold* and *pli* neither look alike nor sound alike, it cannot be the words themselves that interact in perception and memory. Our subjects did not see and store the words individually as visual or phonetic objects; they stored them in terms of their meaning.

The implication is clear that the subjects were able to code and store verbal items in some form other than the language in which the items appeared. A further implication is that information repeated in different languages (different symbol systems) is as well retained as information repeated in a single language. The amount of information that can be retained, however, is not increased by using different symbol systems for storing it, but access to the information is increased.

To put the point more concretely, suppose one wanted to give a student two lessons in geography. If the student knew two languages, he would retain as much geography from one lesson in each language as from two lessons in one of them. Moreover, he would be able to talk about geography readily in both languages. On the other hand, teaching him geography in one language and also teaching him a second language would not necessarily enable him to express his knowledge of geography in the second language without some kind of additional instruction. The information one has and the mechanisms or rules used to acquire it are clearly separate aspects of memory.

I have so far described two aspects of the use of verbal symbol systems: the mental switching that characterizes the successful use of different languages and one of the ways language limits access to information stored in the memory. A third aspect involves the set of rules a

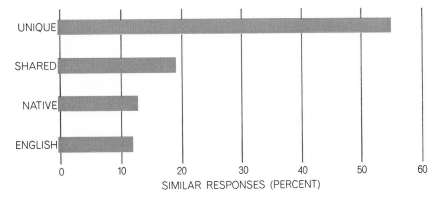

INTRALINGUAL

ENGLISH	ENGLISH
table	dish
boy	girl
king	queen
house	window

SPANISH	SPANISH
mesa	silla
muchacho	hombre
rey	reina
casa	madre

INTERLINGUAL

ENGLISH	SPANISH
table	silla
boy	niña
king	reina
house	blanco

SPANISH	ENGLISH
mesa	chair
muchacho	trousers
rey	queen
casa	mother

TYPICAL RESPONSES in a word-association test were given by a subject whose native language was Spanish. He was asked to respond in Spanish to Spanish stimulus words, in English to the same words in English and in each language to stimulus words in the other.

SUMMARY OF RESPONSES to interlingual word-association tests shows that more than half of the responses were unique, that is, not shared between languages. For example, in the upper illustration on this page the response *blanco* to *house* in the English-Spanish test differed from the response *window* to *house* in the English-English test. In contrast, *silla* was the response to both *table* and *mesa* and would be scored as a "native" response; answers of *reina* and *queen* to *king* are translations and are scored as "shared" responses.

ten	nerve	riz	tique
herd	truffe	isthme	preux
fold	paste	dix	fouet
soul	ice	glace	game
spout	gust	riz	clash
fonds	soul	âme	deux
jeu	truffe	fonds	game
tain	dix	crook	leaf
deux	preux	pli	bulk
pli	seing	bonne	golf
stub	ten	pli	bonne
bonne	nerf	spout	rampe
herd	rampe	golf	seing
âme	maid	two	gust
fold	maid	whip	clash
tain	jig	pâte	two
fold	truffe	psaume	whip
pli	gust	maid	âme
gust	preux	leaf	maid
bulk	cook	bonne	rampe
fouet	preux	clash	soul
fold	bulk	leaf	tain
riz	ice	glace	deux
riz	jeu	leaf	golf
two	juge	whip	fouet

STORAGE OF WORDS was tested with lists in which a subject saw, one at a time, words in both his languages. Some were repeated in the same language, others in both languages by means of translations; for example, *ten* and *dix* translate each other. Recall is improved by repetition. The question was whether recall of translated words would reflect the frequency with which their common meaning appeared or only the frequency with which the words themselves appeared. The results showed that words are stored in terms of their meanings.

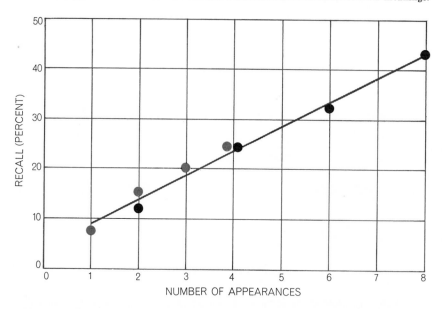

PERCENT OF RECALL was essentially the same for words repeated in one language (*colored circles*) and for words repeated as translations (*black circles*). Since most of the translations, such as *snow* and *neige*, do not resemble one another, the results show that the concept is the decisive factor in recall and that two languages increase access to concepts.

person learns for employing a language. In some of our experiments we found that such rules affect his linguistic performance in subtle ways.

Earlier I described how our bilingual subjects switched between their languages. Such switching is not always perfect, particularly in the daily use of language. Linguists use the word calque, which is the French word for "imitation," to describe the interference of one linguistic system with another. Examples of calques appear in the semi-Germanic sentences "Throw the baby out the window a bottle" and "Throw mama from the train a kiss." I have heard Hebrew-speaking people (Israeli students in the U.S.) inadvertently say "spoontea" for "teaspoon" and "cuptea" for "teacup." (In Hebrew the adjective always follows the noun.) Once I heard such a student say "washdisher" for "dishwasher." The last example is of particular linguistic interest because the Hebrew for "dishwasher" translates literally as "washerdish"; the speaker, however, combined the Hebrew word order with the English sequence of syllables.

In sum, speakers of a language develop linguistic habits, or characteristic ways of ordering words. One effect of these habits was revealed when our bilingual subjects were asked to read aloud linguistically mixed passages of the kind described at the beginning of this article [see illustration, page 144]. The rule we had used for constructing the passages gave rise to many cases in which the normal word order of English or French was violated. Two examples in the illustration are "made resound the earth" and "une violente brise."

Subjects reading the passages aloud sometimes said "made the earth resound" and "une brise violente." Thus they showed that their experience with the normal syntactic forms affected their way of speaking words presented visually. In effect, the students were producing calques, but in a direction opposite to the normal one. Usually a calque distorts a verbal expression by applying a syntactic form of one language to words in another. In our experiment the subjects' ingrained skills in using the rules of English and French induced them to rectify word sequences that had been distorted deliberately.

The various experiments I have described embody some significant implications for both education and the study of the mind. Education entails the acquisition of information and the use of mental skills. Languages, as I have shown, can train one's mind in the way it orders and uses information. The phenomenon of bilingualism enables us to give people information or teach people a skill in one language and find out if the information or the skill can be expressed in another language. In this way we can separate for study the mental processes used in acquiring or manipulating information from the information itself.

One example of the difference between mental skills and information is found in mathematics. Nearly all our bilingual subjects remarked during interviews that they did mathematical operations in the language in which they were taught the operations. They could always tell us the results of their operations in either language, and they could even describe what operations they had performed and how they had performed them, but the operations could be performed in only one way. Indeed, a bilingual colleague once told me that, having moved from France to the U.S. at the age of 12, he does his arithmetic in French and his calculus in English.

The point to be made is that mental activities and information learned in one context are not necessarily available for use in another. They often have to be learned anew in the second context, although perhaps with less time and effort. The fact is, however, that relatively little is known about how the activities of the mind affect one another. The study of bilingualism, being a study of the interaction of symbol systems and the way they affect one's acquisition and use of information, promises to provide valuable information on these questions.

IMPORTANCE OF CONTEXT in understanding a language is indicated by a foreign visitor's reaction to a sign such as this one in New York. Not being an American motorist, he thought the sign meant that he should sit on the curb while he waited for a bus.

Slips of the Tongue

by Victoria A. Fromkin
December 1973

They are a good deal more than amusing (or embarrassing) errors of speech. The collection and analysis of such errors provides important clues to how speech is organized in the nervous system

The Reverend William A. Spooner, dean and warden of New College, Oxford, is famous in the English-speaking world as the man who had a special talent for slips of the tongue in which two sounds of an intended utterance are transposed. Although it is not certain that he actually made slips of this type, many "spoonerisms" are legendary. "Work is the curse of the drinking classes," he is alleged to have said when he meant "Drink is the curse of the working classes." Among other well-known spoonerisms are (in an address to a rural audience) "Noble tons of soil" and (in chiding a student) "You have hissed all my mystery lectures. I saw you fight a liar in the back quad; in fact, you have tasted the whole worm." Perhaps the most endearing of these slips is "the queer old dean" for "the dear old queen."

Speech errors have been used in literature by such writers as Rabelais, Shakespeare, Schiller and George Meredith. Nearly 300 years before the transposition speech error became known as a spoonerism, Henry Peacham quotes in *The Compleat Gentleman* a man who said "Sir, I must goe dye a beggar" instead of "I must goe buy a dagger." In recent years humorous bloopers made by radio and television announcers have been published in books and even preserved on records. The general awareness of the regularity of the occurrence of speech errors is shown in a column by Herb Caen in the *San Francisco Chronicle* of March 7, 1972: "The Tuck-Fortner Report [newscasts] is off Channel 2, much to the relief of those who worry about spoonerisms. Oddly enough, it was Mike Tuck who committed the only near miss in the history of the program, introducing Banker Fortney Stark as 'Fartney Stork.'"

In *The Psychopathology of Everyday Life* Sigmund Freud attempted to show that "[such] disturbances of speech may be the result of complicated psychical influences, of elements outside the same word, sentence or sequence of spoken words." In discussing the unconscious forces that he postulated as the cause of speech errors, Freud speculated "whether the mechanisms of this [speech] disturbance cannot also suggest the probable laws of the formation of speech."

Karl Spencer Lashley, a pioneer in neurophysiology, regarded speech as the "window through which the physiologist can view the cerebral life." He regarded speech errors as evidence that behavior can only be accounted for by positing "a series of hierarchies of organization: the order of vocal movements in pronouncing the word, the order of words in the sentence, the order of sentences in the paragraph." Disordering of these hierarchical units, he said, may occur at any stage, which would account for the diversity of observed speech errors.

In spite of the universality of various types of speech error, it was not until the 19th century that scholars began to pay serious attention to such utterances as evidence for psychological and linguistic theories. Hermann Paul, a German philologist, was probably the first linguist to suggest that an examination of speech errors might provide important clues to one cause of language change. Other linguists have been interested in slips of the tongue as a means of finding out what it is we learn and store in our minds when we learn a language.

A person's knowledge of a language cannot be equated solely with the words and sentences he utters and understands. If all the utterances of a person, or a number of persons, were recorded for an hour, a day, a week, a month, a year or even a lifetime, the corpus of these utterances would not in itself constitute the language he speaks. No one book can contain a complete human language. It is highly unlikely that this English sentence will have been printed before: "The Watergate scandal was caused by green-skinned, three-headed, cloven-footed Martians dressed in pink tights who penetrated the top-secret files of the Pentagon." Whether or not it is true, the preceding sentence is a grammatical English sentence that can be understood by any person with a knowledge of the language, yet it could not have been included in an English-language book before I had written it.

What makes it possible for a person to produce and understand novel sentences? If we are to understand the nature of language, we must be able to explain this ability. It cannot be accounted for simply by listing all possible sentences; in principle the number of sentences is infinite. For any sentence of length n one can produce a sentence of length $n + 1$. For example: "This is the house that Jack built. This is the malt that lay in the house that Jack built. It is questionable that this is the malt that lay in the house that Jack built. I know that it is questionable that this is the malt that lay in the house that Jack built."

Given the finite storage capacity of the brain, one cannot store all possible sentences of a language. We can of course store the words of a language because they are finite in number. In no language, however, are sentences formed by putting words together at random. "Built Jack that house the is this" is not an English sentence. Furthermore, although the number of words in a language is finite, the speakers of a language have the ability to create and adopt new words, for example Brillo and Kleenex. But just as there are rules for well-formed sentences, so there are rules for well-formed words; "Glooper" could be an acceptable word for a new product, but "nga" would never be used in English even though it is a perfectly good word in the Twi language of the Ashanti in western Africa.

Knowledge of a language must therefore include rules for the formation of words and sentences. In order to account for a speaker's ability to form a potentially infinite set of sentences and for his linguistic judgments concerning the well-formedness of words and sentences, linguistic theorists posit that what is learned in language acquisition is a grammar that includes a finite set of basic elements and a finite set of rules for their combination, including a recursive element to allow the formation of sentences of unlimited length [see illustration on next page]. Furthermore, there must be a hierarchy of such ele-

ments: discrete elements of sound (phonemes) combine in restricted ways to form syllables, which combine to form meaningful units (morphemes or words), which are combined to form phrases, which are combined into sentences [see top illustration on page 154].

All attempts to describe language and to account for our linguistic abilities assume the discreteness of each of these linguistic units. Yet the sounds we produce and the sounds we hear when we are talking are continuous signals, and examination of the physical properties of these acoustic signals does not reveal individual discrete sounds, words or phrases [see bottom illustration on page 154]. It has been impossible, however, to account for our linguistic abilities without positing a grammar consisting of discrete units and rules. This has al-

ways been intuitively accepted, as is indicated by the ancient Hindu myth in which the god Indra is said to have broken speech down into its distinct elements, thereby creating language. The classical Greeks also recognized the difference between the continuous nature of speech and the discrete nature of language. The messenger of the gods, Hermes, is also the god of speech because he was always on the move. In Plato's *Cratylus* dialogue (the oldest extant philosophical essay dealing exclusively with language) one of Hermes' namesakes, Hermogenes, asks Socrates if language can be analyzed by taking it apart. Socrates answers that doing so is the only way one can proceed.

The reality of the discrete elements of language and their rules of combination cannot be found by looking into the brains of speakers. It is here that systematic errors of speech can yield useful evidence.

Looked at from the viewpoint of linguistic behavior or performance, speech can be considered a communication system in which the concept to be conveyed must undergo a number of transformations. The message is generated in the brain of the speaker, encoded into the linguistic form of the language being spoken and transformed into neural signals that are sent to the muscles of the vocal tract, which transform the message into articulatory configurations. The acoustic signal must then be decoded by the listener to recover the original message. Thus the input signal that presumably starts as a string of individual discrete sounds organized into phrases and words ends up as a semicontinuous signal that the receiver must change back into the original string of discrete units. The grammar that represents our knowledge of the language allows us to encode and decode an utterance.

Difficulties are encountered in attempts to model the actual behavior of a speaker because the only phenomena in this communication system that can be examined are the semicontinuous muscular movements of the vocal tract, the dynamic articulatory configurations and the acoustic signals. As in other communication systems, however, noise in any of the stages or connecting channels involved in speech can distort the original message. Most errors of speech would seem to be the result of noise or interference at the stage of linguistic encoding. Such errors can tell us something about a process that is not otherwise observable, and about the abstract grammar that underlies linguistic behavior.

Over the past five years I have re-

WILLIAM A. SPOONER was famous for his reputed lapses of speech, in which he would transpose two or more sounds, for example "blushing crow" for "crushing blow." Such speech errors are now called spoonerisms. This caricature of Spooner is by Sir Leslie Ward, whose work appeared in *Vanity Fair* under the pseudonym of Spy. Spooner was born in 1844 and died in 1930. A clergyman, he served as dean and warden of New College, Oxford.

corded more than 6,000 spontaneous errors of speech. In order to prevent the inclusion of errors of perception each item has been attested to by at least one other person. The deviant utterances that I give as examples hereafter are taken from this corpus.

According to all linguists who have analyzed spontaneous speech errors, the errors are nonrandom and predictable. Although one cannot predict when an error will occur or what the particular error will be, one can predict the kinds of error that will occur. Such predictions are based on our knowledge of the mental grammar utilized by speakers when they produce utterances. For example, many errors involve the abstract, discrete elements of sound we call phonemes. Although we cannot find these elements either in the moving articulators or in the acoustic signal, the fact that we learn to read and write with alphabetic symbols shows that they exist. In addition, if these discrete units were not real units used in speaking, we could not explain speech errors in which such segments must be involved. Substitution of one segment for another occurs: a later phoneme may be anticipated ("taddle tennis" instead of "paddle tennis"); a phoneme may persevere ("I can't cook worth a cam" instead of "I can't cook worth a damn"), or two segments may be transposed ("Yew Nork" instead of "New York"). Such segmental errors can involve vowels as well as consonants ("budbegs" instead of "bedbugs"). Moreover, two consonants that form a cluster can be either split or moved as a unit ("tendahl" instead of "Stendahl" and "foon speeding" instead "spoon feeding") [see top illustration on page 155]. Such errors demonstrate that even though we do not produce discrete elements of sound at the stage of muscular movement in speech, discrete segments do exist at some earlier stage.

It is not the phonetic properties of sounds alone that determine the more abstract representation of phonemes. Sounds such as those represented by the "ch" in "church" and the "j" and "dge" in "judge" are clusters of two consonants on the phonetic level. This is shown by the fact that in the regular tempo of conversation the following two sentences will be pronounced identically by most people: " 'Why choose,' she said" and " 'White shoes,' she said." Yet linguists have posited that in words such as "choose," "church," "chain" and "judge" these phonetic clusters are single phonemes. The fact that the "ch" and "j" sounds in such words are never split in

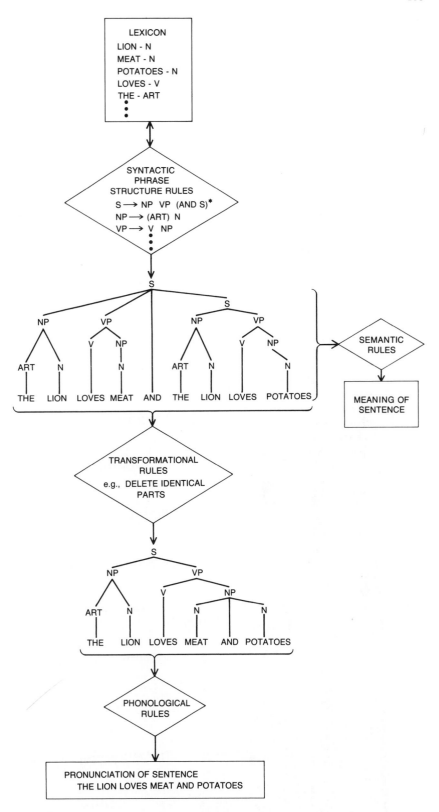

GRAMMAR OF A LANGUAGE consists of a finite set of basic elements (lexicon) and a finite set of rules for combining the basic elements such as nouns (N), verbs (V), articles (ART) and so forth. In order to generate a sentence (S), noun phrases (NP) and verb phrases (VP) are combined according to syntactic rules. The semantic rules determine whether or not the sentence generated is meaningful. Transformational rules enable a speaker to permute the sentence without altering its meaning. Phonological rules determine how the sentence is articulated. Errors at various stages can result in production of a deviant sentence, for example "The meat loves lion and potatoes" or "The lion loves peat and motatoes."

SENTENCE	[THE WILLOWY LIONESS LOVES THE WIRY LION]
PHRASES	[[THE WILLOWY LIONESS] [LOVES [THE WIRY LION]]] NOUN PHRASE VERB PHRASE NOUN PHRASE
WORDS	[[[THE] [WILLOWY] ᐧNESS]] [[LOVES] [[THE] [WIRY] [LION]]]] ARTICLE ADJECTIVE ᴗUN VERB ARTICLE ADJECTIVE NOUN
MORPHEMES	[[[THE] [WILLOW + Y] [LION + NESS]] [LOVE + S] [[THE] [WIR + Y] [LION]]]
PHONEMES	TH + E + W + I + LL + OW + Y + L + I + O + NN + E + SS + L + O + VE + S + TH + E + W + I + R + Y + L + I + O + N

HIERARCHY OF LINGUISTIC ELEMENTS is depicted. A sentence is composed of noun phrases and verb phrases. Phrases are made up of phrases or individual words and words in turn consist of morphemes, the basic units of meaning. Morphemes are made up of discrete elements of sound called phonemes. Spelling of the phonemes does not represent their sounds in a one-to-one fashion.

speech errors, although other consonant clusters such as "sp" and "gl" are, bears out this analysis. When these sounds are involved in speech errors, they always move as a single unit, as in "chee cane" instead of "key chain" and "sack's jute" instead of "Jack's suit." In cases where they represent two discrete phonemes, however, they can be independently disordered as in "Put the white boos in the shocks" for "Put the white shoes in the box." Speech errors therefore support the abstract analysis of linguists.

Segmental errors are constrained by rules of grammar that dictate the allowable sequence of sounds. Although "slips of the tongue" can be incorrectly uttered as "stips of the lung," it cannot be uttered as "tlip of the sung" because the sound "tl" is not allowed as the beginning of an English word. It is not the inability to say "tl" that inhibits such errors; we can say it easily enough. Rather it is a grammatical constraint in the English language. It is in this sense that speech errors are predictable and nonrandom.

Phonemic segments have been classified into intersecting sets dependent on shared properties. Thus the sounds that are produced by a closure of the lips, such as /p/, /b/ and /m/ (the diagonals are used to distinguish the sounds from the alphabetic letters), are classified as labials. The sounds produced by raising the tip of the tongue to the top of the teeth, such as /t/, /d/ and /n/, are alveolars. The sounds produced by raising the back of the tongue to the soft palate, such as /k/, /g/ and the /ng/ in "sing," are velars.

Such classes have been used to describe the sounds of all languages, but they had no basis in linguistic theory until recently. Roman Jakobson suggested a set of universal features that could be used to describe the sound system of all languages. These features, somewhat revised, were then incorporated into the theory of generative phonology by Morris Halle, who developed them further in collaboration with Noam Chomsky. It was shown that if segments are not viewed as being composites of features

in the grammar of a language, certain regularities would be obscured, and the grammar written by the linguist would fail to correctly model a speaker's linguistic knowledge.

There has been some debate in linguistic circles over whether or not these universal phonetic features have any psychological reality. Some argue that they merely provide an elegant description of the sound system and do not exist as elements in the mental grammar of speakers. Just as speech errors show that discrete segments are real units, so also do they attest to the reality of phonetic features. Among the features posited in the universal set are the binary-valued features: voiced/voiceless and nasal/oral. Sounds produced with vocal-cord vibrations are voiced; sounds produced with an open glottis are voiceless. Nasal sounds are produced by lowering the soft palate to allow some air to escape through the nose while making a sound; oral sounds are produced by raising the soft palate to block off the nasal passage. In speech errors a single feature can be

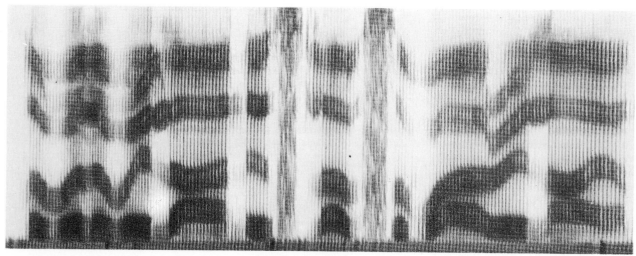

THE WILLOW-Y-LI O N E SS LO VE STHE W I R Y L I O N

SOUND SPECTROGRAM of the utterance "The willowy lioness loves the wiry lion" shows the speech sounds as a series of bands with the lowest sound frequencies at bottom and the highest frequencies at top. Note that the acoustical signal is semicontinuous.

disordered while all other features remain as intended; for example, "clear blue sky" was transposed to "glear plue sky." There was a voicing switch: the voiceless velar /k/ became a voiced /g/ and the voiced labial /b/ became a voiceless /p/ [*see bottom illustration at right*].

Unless the individual features have an independent existence in the mental grammar such errors cannot be accounted for. Prior to or simultaneous with the stage in the production process when neural signals are sent to the appropriate muscles, the specifications for voicing or not voicing must have been disordered. Similar transpositions can occur with nasal/oral features.

Speech errors involve more than sound units. In all languages different meanings are expressed by different strings of phonemes. That is, knowing a language enables one to associate certain sounds with certain meanings. One learns the vocabulary of the meaningful units of a language by learning not only the sounds but also what the sounds mean. Since the words of a language can consist of more than one meaningful element, words themselves cannot be the most elemental units of meaning. "Tolerant," "sane," "active" and "direct" are all English words; so are "intolerant," "insane," "inactive" and "indirect." The latter set includes the meanings of the former plus the meaningful unit "in-," which in these instances means "not."

In learning a language we learn these basic meaningful elements called morphemes and how to combine them into words. Speech errors show that there can be a breakdown in the application of the rules of word formation. The result is an uttered word that is possible but nonexistent. For example, "groupment" was said instead of "grouping," "intervenient" for "intervening," "motionly" for "motionless," "ambigual" for "ambiguous" and "bloodent" for "bloody." It is clear from such examples that rules for word formation must exist; otherwise there is no way to explain the deviant word forms. Obviously we do not have such words stored in our mental dictionary. Speech errors suggest that we learn morphemes as separate items and the rules for their combination. This ability enables us to create new words.

Many morphemes have alternative pronunciations depending on their context. The indefinite-article morpheme in English is either "a" or "an" depending on the initial sound of the word that follows: a coat, a man, an orange coat, an old man. This rule of language depends

ERRORS	EXAMPLES	
CONSONANT ERRORS		
ANTICIPATION	A READING LIST	A LEADING LIST
	IT'S A REAL MYSTERY	IT'S A MEAL MYSTERY
PERSEVERATION	PULLED A TANTRUM	PULLED A PANTRUM
	AT THE BEGINNING OF THE TURN	AT THE BEGINNING OF THE BURN
REVERSALS (SPOONERISMS)	LEFT HEMISPHERE	HEFT LEMISPHERE
	A TWO-PEN SET	A TWO-SEN PET
VOWEL ERRORS		
REVERSALS	FEET MOVING	FUTE MEEVING
	FILL THE POOL	FOOL THE PILL
OTHER ERRORS		
ADDITION	THE OPTIMAL NUMBER	THE MOPTIMAL NUMBER
MOVEMENT	ICE CREAM	KISE REAM
DELETION	CHRYSANTHEMUM PLANTS	CHRYSANTHEMUM P ANTS
CONSONANT CLUSTERS SPLIT OR MOVED	SPEECH PRODUCTION	PEACH SEDUCTION
	DAMAGE CLAIM	CLAMMAGE DAME

SEGMENTAL ERRORS IN SPEECH can involve vowels as well as consonants. Some typical types of substitution of sounds are shown. Such errors provide evidence that the discrete phonetic segments posited by linguistic theory exist in the mental grammar of the speaker.

	VOICED ORAL	VOICED NASAL	VOICELESS ORAL
LABIALS	BAT	MAT	PAT
	TAB	TAM	TAP
	BEAT	MEAT	PEET
	BEST	MESSED	PEST
	LIB	LIMB	LIP
	CAB	CAM	CAP
	AMBLE	AMBLE	AMPLE
ALVEOLARS	DIP	NIP	TIP
	CAD	CAN	CAT
	CANDOR	CANNER	CANTOR
	DOLE	KNOLL	TOLL
	DOOR	NOR	TORE
	RAID	RAIN	RATE
	RIDE	RHINE	RIGHT
VELARS	GIRL	*	CURL
	GREASE	*	CREASE
	GUARD	*	CARD
	LUG	LUNG	LUCK
	SAG	SANG	SACK
	ANGLE	ANGLE	ANKLE
	FINGER	SINGER	SINKER

LANGUAGE SOUNDS are categorized by certain universal features such as voiced/voiceless and nasal/oral. Some examples of voiced, oral, nasal and voiceless sounds are shown here. In speech errors a single feature may be disordered while the other features remain as intended. For example, when a person says "cedars of Lemadon" instead of "cedars of Lebanon," the nasality features of the /b/ and the /n/ are reversed. The intended oral labial /b/ becomes a nasal labial /m/ and the intended nasal alveolar /n/ becomes an oral alveolar /d/. Such reversal suggests that these features must also exist in mental grammars.

on the morpheme and not on the sound. We do make the "a" sound before a vowel ("America is") and the "an" sound before a consonant ("Roman court"). But errors such as "an istem" for "a system" or "a burly bird" for "an early bird" show that when segmental disordering occurs that changes a noun beginning with a consonant to a noun beginning with a vowel, or vice versa, the indefinite article is also changed so that it conforms to the grammatical rule. The rule also operates when entire words are disordered, as when "an example of courage" was produced as "a courage of example."

This operation is accomplished automatically, and such errors tell us something about the ordering of events in the brain. The disordering of the words or the phonemic segments must occur before the indefinite article is specified, or alternatively the rule that determines the indefinite article must reapply or feed back after the disordering has occurred. Furthermore, the monitoring function of the grammatical rule must specify the sounds of the indefinite article prior to the stage where neural signals are sent to the vocal muscles, since the rule does not change a structure such as "Rosa is" to

"Rosan is." The existence of similar rules, called morphophonemic rules, and the ordering of their application are shown over and over again in speech errors.

The errors I have cited show that when we speak, words are structured into larger syntactic phrases that are stored in a kind of buffer memory before segments or features or words are disordered. This storage must occur prior to the articulatory stage. We do not select one word from our mental dictionary and say it, then select another word and say it. We organize an entire phrase and in many cases an entire sentence. This process can be demonstrated by the examination of errors in disordered phrases and sentences: "Nerve of a vergeous breakdown" instead of "Verge of a nervous breakdown"; "Seymour sliced the knife with a salami" instead of "Seymour sliced the salami with a knife"; "He threw the window through the clock" instead of "He threw the clock through the window"; "I broke the whistle on my crotch" instead of "I broke the crystal on my watch."

If these phrases had not been formed in some buffer storage, the transpositions could not have occurred. Furthermore, the intonation contour (stressed syllables and variations in pitch) of the utterance often remains the same as it is in the intended phrase even when the words are disordered. In the intended utterance "Seymour sliced the salami with a knife" the highest pitch would be on "knife." In the disordered sentence the highest pitch occurred on the second syllable of "salami." The pitch rise is determined by the grammatical structure of the utterance. It must be constructed prior to articulation and is dependent on the syntactic structure rather than on the individual words. Thus syntactic structures also are shown to be units in linguistic behavior.

When words are exchanged, they are usually exchanged with words of the same grammatical category; nouns are exchanged with nouns, adjectives with adjectives and so on. This phenomenon shows that words are represented in memory along with their grammatical characteristics. Indeed, when different grammatical classes are involved in a speech error, there is often a restructuring of the words to correct what otherwise would be syntactically incorrect. "I think it is reasonable to measure with care" was not transformed into "I think it is care to measure with reasonable" but rather into "I think it is careful to measure with reason." Such corrections

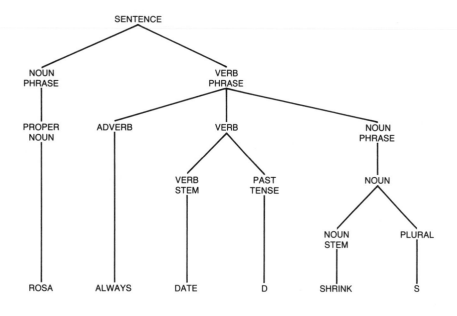

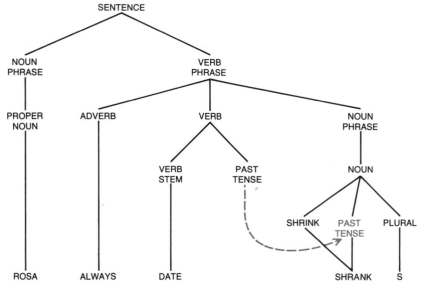

DISORDERING OF SYNTACTIC ELEMENTS can result in transformation of a sentence such as "Rosa always dated shrinks" into "Rosa always date shranks." The syntactical hierarchical structure of the intended sentence is shown in the top diagram. The error seems to have been caused by a disordering of the past-tense element, which mistakenly became attached to the noun node, as the bottom diagram illustrates. The shift probably occurred because "shrink" is a verb as well as a noun. After the disordering the phonological rules produced "shrank" and since the plural element was not disordered, "shranks" resulted.

reveal that there is constant monitoring at different stages of the speech-production chain. Although some errors emerged, a compounding of errors does not usually occur. In speech errors we never find a total disruption of the permissible syntactic structure, such as "Breakdown nervous a of verge."

But syntactic rules can be broken or misapplied, and syntactic elements can be disordered. Misstatements such as "If he swimmed in the pool nude" and "The last I knowed about it" indicate that words are stored in a basic form. To produce a past tense we do not select a stored past-tense form of a word but apply the rule of past-tense formation to the elemental morpheme. The regular rule for past-tense formation must have been wrongly applied to produce "swimmed" and "knowed." In these two instances the mistakes recorded were made by university professors who do not regularly say "swimmed" or "knowed." The reality of such rules is also shown by the forms produced by children before they have learned that there are exceptions to the rules they have generalized. Children regularly say "swimmed," "knowed," "bringed" and "singed" even though they have never heard these words spoken. Language acquisition involves constructing rules rather than merely imitating what one hears. It is these rules that may be wrongly applied in speech errors [*see illustration on preceding page*].

The negation element in sentences is another example of mistaken rule application: "I regard this as imprecise" came out "I disregard this as precise." The error shows that in producing a negative sentence a speaker must generate an abstract negative element that is ordered in the string according to the rules of the language. The negative element in this sentence is independent of the particular words and can be disordered just as other units can be disordered. The sentence also shows that phonologically the negative element must be determined after the structure of the sentence is imposed. Only then can the negative plus "regard" be realized as either "do not regard" or as "disregard." A model of linguistic performance cannot posit a chain process of word selection; a hierarchical order exists.

Speech errors can involve entire words. A common type of error is a blend of two words: "shrig soufflé" for "shrimp and egg soufflé," "prodeption of speech" for "production and perception of speech." A more interesting blend, called a portmanteau word by Lewis Carroll, combines two words with similar meanings into one: "instantaneous" and "momentary" into "momentaneous," "splinters" and "blisters" into "splisters," "shifting" and "switching" into "swifting" and "edited" and "annotated" into "editated." This type of error reveals that the idea of the message is generated independently of the particular words selected from the mental dictionary to represent these concepts. A speaker seems to match the semantic features of words with the semantic notion to be conveyed. When there are alternatives, synonyms or near-synonyms, the speaker may be unsure of what word will best express his thoughts and in the moment of indecision may select two words and blend them.

The involuntary substitution of one word for the intended word shows that the meaning of a word is not an indissoluble whole. The semantic representation of a word is a composite of hierarchically ordered semantic features. In word selection one finds that the substituted and the original word often fall into the same semantic class: "blond eyes" for "blond hair," "bridge of the neck" for "bridge of the nose," "When my tongues bled" for "When my gums bled," "my boss's husband" for "my boss's wife" and "There's a small Chinese—I mean Japanese—restaurant."

Some errors show that antonyms are substituted: "like" for "hate," "big" for "small," "open" for "shut" and "hot" for "cold." Whatever the psychological causes of such slips, they show the ways we represent language in our stored mental grammar. The person who substituted "dachshund" for "Volkswagen" apparently selected a word with the semantic features "small, German." In the selection he underspecified the features to be matched.

There are many other varieties of speech error. All of them must be accounted for in a model of speech production. By positing the same units and rules required in a linguistic grammar, many of the errors can be categorized and explained. Speech therefore does provide a window into the cerebral life. By carefully studying speech errors we can get a view of the discrete elements of language and can see the grammatical rules at work. We also can look into the mental dictionary and get some notion of the complexity of the specifications of words and how the dictionary is organized. Throughout history men have speculated, theorized and conjectured about the nature of human language. Speech errors provide good data for testing some of these theories.

The Synthesis of Speech

by James L. Flanagan
February 1972

*Electronic speaking machines capable of synthesizing
output speech with no recourse to any vestige of human
speech are in the process of development. They may
provide articulate voices for computers*

If computers could speak, they could be given many useful new tasks. The telephone on one's desk might then serve as a computer terminal, providing automatic access to such things as airline and hotel reservations, selective stock market quotations, inventory reports, medical data and the balance in one's checking account. In principle such information could be provided by recordings of an actual voice, just as telephone companies already provide weather reports and other repetitive messages. Prerecording is not practical, however, if the information desired is only a small extract from a voluminous file, if the information changes rapidly (as stock market prices do) and particularly if the information must be gathered to order. Although one might assemble verbal messages of any complexity from a prerecorded vocabulary of speech fragments, the result would be highly unsatisfactory. Thus if a computer is to speak with a large, sophisticated vocabulary, and if it is expected to frame messages in many contexts, the simple technique of prerecording actual speech is ruled out. The alternative is to develop a mechanism, basically electrical, that is capable not only of synthesizing speech but also of introducing the various inflections characteristic of natural spoken language. There are other important motivations for attempting to synthesize speech. One is learning how speech is produced in the human vocal tract. Another is applying such knowledge to the reduction of the amount of information needed to transmit speech signals.

Human speech is remarkable in many ways, not the least of which is that it employs a physiological apparatus designed for other purposes: breathing and eating. The specialized acoustic code we call speech must have developed slowly over aeons. At least one speculation holds that early man's first means of communication were hand signals. Speech perhaps evolved when man discovered he could supplement his hand signals by grunts and other distinctive "gestures" of his vocal tract. "What drove man to the invention of speech," Sir Richard Paget has suggested, "was ...not so much the need of expressing his thoughts as the difficulty of 'talking with his hands full.' It was the continual use of man's hands for craftsmanship, the chase, and the beginnings of art and agriculture, that drove him to find other methods of expressing his ideas—namely, by a specialized pantomime of the tongue and lips."

The Origin of Speech Sounds

The fundamental principles of sound generation in the vocal tract and the acoustic filtering that takes place in the tract are now understood in considerable detail. The main gaps in knowledge have to do largely with nonlinearities in the generation of sound in the vocal tract and with certain interactions, still obscure, between the sound sources and the soft-walled pipe of the vocal tract. Apart from such details, however, enough is known about human speech production to allow the design of successful speech synthesizers. On the other hand, comparatively little is known so far about the linguistic rules that dictate the ordered activities of the vocal system. Much fundamental study is currently being devoted to speech prosody: the way the speaker unconsciously introduces stresses and pauses and alters the pitch of his voice. These factors are closely related to the dynamical properties of vocal-tract motion, another aspect of current study.

The human vocal tract is an acoustic tube of variable cross section about 17 centimeters long, extending from the vocal cords to the lips [*see illustration on page 160*]. The cross-sectional area of the vocal tract can be varied from zero (complete closure) to about 20 square centimeters by the placement of the lips, the jaw, the tongue and the velum: the flexible tissue—the soft palate—attached to the back of the roof of the mouth. The trapdoor action of the velum couples the vocal tract proper to a secondary cavity involved in speech production: the nasal tract. The nasal cavity is about 12 centimeters long and has a volume of about 60 cubic centimeters.

The vocal system can produce three basic kinds of sounds: voiced sounds, fricative sounds and plosive sounds. Voiced sounds, exemplified by the vowels, are produced by raising the air pressure in the lungs and forcing air to flow through the glottis (the orifice between the vocal cords), causing the vocal cords to vibrate. The vibrations interrupt the airflow and generate quasi-periodic broad-spectrum pulses that excite the vocal tract. The vibrating ligaments of the vocal cords are some 18 millimeters long and the glottal opening typically varies in area from zero to about 20 square millimeters.

Fricative sounds, exemplified by the consonants *s*, *sh*, *f* and *th*, are generated when the vocal tract is partly closed at some point and air is forced through the constriction at high enough velocity to produce turbulence. Plosive sounds, typified by the consonants *p*, *t* and *k*, are produced when the vocal tract is closed completely (usually with the lips or tongue), allowing air pressure to build up behind the closure, and is then abruptly opened. The sharp sound produced when the air is released is often followed by a fricative sound or aspiration. All these vocal sources, whether for periodic voiced sounds or for aperiodic voiceless (fricative or plosive) sounds, have a fairly broad spectrum of frequencies extending over the voice-frequency range from about 100 cycles per second to more than 3,000. The vocal system acts as a time-varying filter to impose its resonant characteristics on the sound waves generated by the broad-spectrum sources. Operation of the voiced and voiceless sources is not mutually exclusive. For some sounds, such as the voiced fricative consonants v and z, two sound sources act in combination.

Because the interaction between the sound sources and the vocal system is fairly loose, the two can be represented diagrammatically as being linearly separable [*see top illustration on page 161*]. The sound radiated from the mouth has a frequency spectrum that, to a first approximation, can be considered the mathematical product of the source spectrum and the transmission characteristics of the vocal system (the combination of the vocal and nasal tracts).

For voiced sounds the excitation source is the volume velocity of air passing the vocal cords. The flow is typically

pulsive and periodic, with a spectrum whose harmonics diminish in amplitude approximately as 1 over the frequency squared. The vocal tract acts on this source as a filter with transmission "poles," or favored frequencies, corresponding to the acoustic resonances of the vocal tract. These resonances are often referred to as formants. It happens that, at the usual frequencies of speech, sound has a wavelength comparable to the length of the vocal tract. The tract is open at the mouth end and essentially closed at the glottal end. Therefore its resonant frequencies correspond roughly to the odd quarter-wave resonances of a pipe 17 centimeters long. For a straight pipe of this length the first three resonant frequencies are 500, 1,500 and 2,500 cycles per second.

For vowel sounds, in which the nasal tract is closed off, there are no additional resonances in this frequency range and thus the transmission filter operates to emphasize just these three frequencies. When the nasal tract is made part of the transmission system, another resonant pole is typically introduced at about 1,000 cycles per second adjacent to an antiresonance, or "zero," also near 1,000 cycles. The voiced sound that issues

from the mouth is therefore a line spectrum that has imposed on it an envelope that reflects the resonances produced by passage through the vocal transmission system. The various voiced sounds of speech are produced by changing the shape of the vocal tract, thereby changing its resonances. In a similar manner the unvoiced sounds are excited from a noise source that has a fairly broad, uniform spectrum. Because the source is typically positioned at some point along the tract it alters the length of pipe acting as a resonance system so that the resonances and antiresonances now fall at different frequencies. Again the radiated sound reflects the frequencies that are favored or suppressed by the resonant system.

In continuous speech the formant resonances move around as the vocal tract changes shape. Because the tongue, the jaws, the lips and the velum have significant mass their accelerations are limited by the forces that the articulatory muscles can generate. Thus the vocal tract changes shape rather slowly compared with the rate of pressure fluctuations in the speech wave. When the speech wave is recorded in a sound spectrogram, which shows the changes

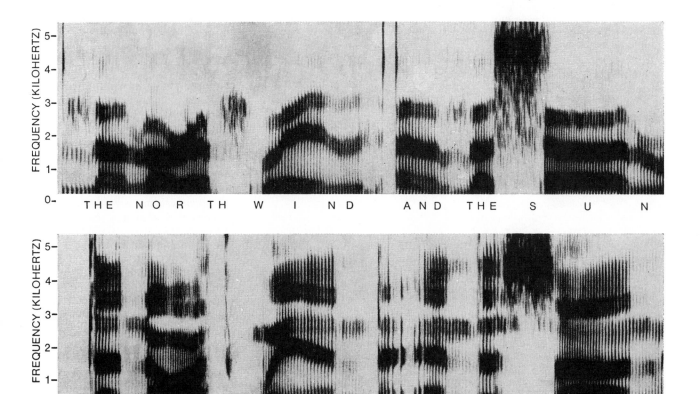

SOUND SPECTROGRAM of a spoken sentence synthesized from printed text by a computer-controlled electronic speaking machine designed and built at the Bell Telephone Laboratories is shown at top. A comparable spectrogram for a human utterance of the same sentence is shown at bottom. At the present stage of development the machine's intelligibility is just beginning to be acceptable.

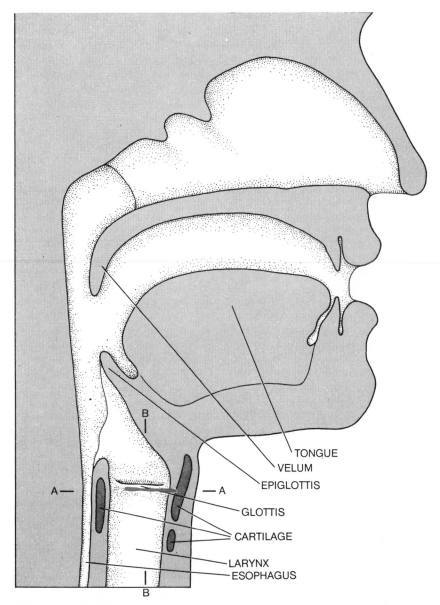

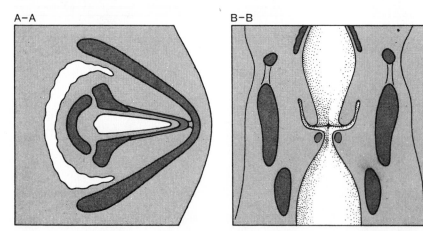

HUMAN VOCAL SYSTEM consists of two main parts: the vocal tract proper, an acoustic tube of variable cross section extending from the vocal cords to the lips, and the nasal tract, a secondary cavity coupled to the vocal tract proper by means of the trapdoor action of the velum. View at top is a median sagittal section of the entire system; views at bottom are a transverse section (*A–A*) and a vertical section (*B–B*) of the vocal-cord region. The vocal system can produce three basic kinds of sounds: voiced sounds (such as vowels), fricative sounds (such as the consonants *s*, *sh*, *f* and *th*) and plosive sounds (such as *p*, *t* and *k*).

in sound frequency and intensity with time, one can see the relatively slow rates at which formants change their frequency [*see bottom illustration on opposite page*].

Mechanical Speaking Machines

Just as some early inventors attempted to build flying machines with wings that flapped like a bird's, others tried to build speaking machines by crudely duplicating the physiology of the human vocal tract. On the whole the second group of inventors had somewhat greater success than the first.

One of the earliest efforts at speech simulation was made by Christian Gottlieb Kratzenstein, who won a prize offered in 1779 by the Imperial Academy of St. Petersburg. For its scientific competition that year the academy posed the following two questions: "(1) What is the nature and character of the sounds of the vowels *a, e, i, o, u* [that make them] so different from one another? (2) Can an instrument be constructed like the *vox humana* pipes of an organ, which shall accurately express the sounds of the vowels?"

Kratzenstein's winning solution consisted of a set of acoustic resonators somewhat similar in form and dimension to the human mouth [*see top illustration on page 162*]. He activated the resonators with a vibrating reed that mimicked the human vocal cords by interrupting an airstream. (Apparently Kratzenstein invented this particular type of reed, subsequently used in the harmonica.) It is reported that Kratzenstein's mechanism imitated the five vowels "with tolerable accuracy."

A machine that not only more successfully imitated the vowel sounds and several consonants but also connected speech utterances was built a dozen years later by Wolfgang von Kempelen of Vienna. His device was not taken seriously by his scientific colleagues, however, because he had earlier exhibited a fake chess-playing machine. The "machine," which won many games, concealed a legless Polish army officer named Worouski who was a master chess player.

Von Kempelen's speaking machine was nevertheless a completely legitimate device. It had a bellows to supply air to a reed that in turn excited a single, hand-controlled resonator that imitated voiced sounds. Consonants, including nasals, were simulated by four separate constricted passages, which the operator controlled with the fingers of his other

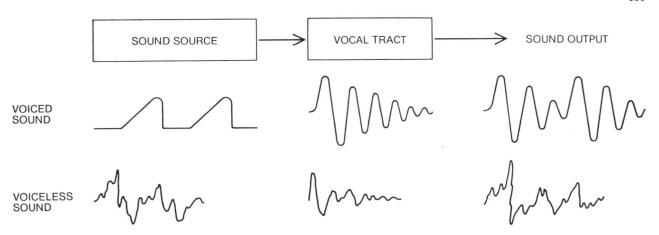

MODEL OF HUMAN SPEECH PRODUCTION represents the sound sources for periodic voiced sounds and for aperiodic voiceless sounds as being linearly separable from the vocal system, which acts as a time-varying filter to impose its resonant characteristics on the sound waves generated by the broad-spectrum sources.

According to this model, the frequency spectrum of the sound radiated from the mouth is the mathematical product of the source spectrum and the transmission characteristics of the vocal system. Equivalently, the output sound wave is the convolution of the source wave form with the impulse response of the vocal system.

hand [*see bottom illustration on next page*].

Von Kempelen's ingenious device had a more far-reaching influence than he could have suspected. When Alexander Graham Bell was a boy in Edinburgh in the 1850's, he was greatly impressed by a reproduction of von Kempelen's machine that had been built by Sir Charles Wheatstone, a maker of musical instruments who later contributed to the development of electric telegraphy. Young Alexander was encouraged by his father, who was an elocutionist, to construct a speaking automaton of his own.

Assisted by his brother Melville, Alexander attempted to copy the vocal organs by making a cast of a human skull. The boys used gutta-percha and other simple materials to represent the lips, tongue, palate, teeth, pharynx and velum. The lips were a framework of wire covered with rubber that had been stuffed with cotton batting. The cheeks were made of rubber; the tongue was simulated by wooden sections surrounded by batting and covered with rubber skin. There was a sheet-metal box for a larynx and a flexible tube for a windpipe. A vocal-cord structure consisted of a slotted rubber sheet stretched over metal supports. The various parts were activated by levers controlled from a keyboard. Bell recalled that the device

produced both vowels and nasals and could even be manipulated to emit a few simple utterances.

More than 100 years later, even with the great progress in electronics and computational methods, there are still a number of speech and acoustic questions that are best approached through mechanical models of the vocal tract. These questions relate particularly to nonlinear properties of turbulent flow, and mechanical analogues can provide data about the location, intensity, spectrum and internal impedance of the sound sources for unvoiced sounds. All these factors are difficult to measure in the human vocal tract.

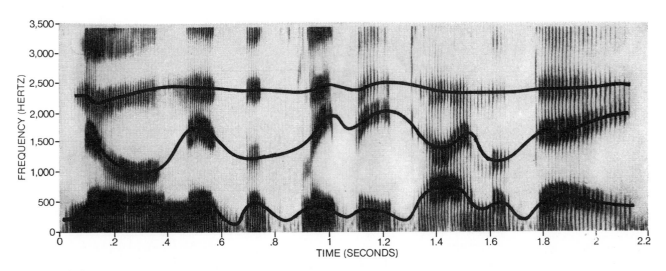

FIRST THREE FORMANTS, or natural acoustic resonances of the human vocal tract, occur at frequencies of approximately 500, 1,500 and 2,500 hertz (cycles per second). In this sound spectrogram of a short sentence ("Noon is the sleepy time of day") the relatively slow rates at which these formants change their frequency with time (*solid black curves*) are evident. The vocal tract changes rather slowly compared with the rate of pressure fluctuations in the speech wave, because the tongue, the jaws, the lips and the velum have significant mass and their accelerations are accordingly limited by the forces that the articulatory muscles can generate.

The ability to send spoken words over wires, dating from Bell's invention of the telephone in 1876, has provided a continuing motivation to learn how words are generated, how they can be electrically transmitted with economy and how they can be synthesized with fidelity. Modern developments in electronic technology have therefore shifted the emphasis in speech synthesis from mechanical and semimechanical methods to all-electrical systems.

Electrical Speech Synthesis

One of the first electrical synthesizers that attempted to produce connected speech was the Voder ("voice-operation demonstrator"), which was exhibited at the New York world's fair in 1939 and a year later at the San Francisco world's fair. The Voder employed two sound sources: a wide-band noise source and a periodic buzz oscillator [*see illustration on opposite page*]. These sounds were modified by passing them through a "resonance control" box (the "vocal tract") containing 10 contiguous band-pass filters that spanned the frequency range of normal speech. The outputs of the band-pass filters were modulated by gain controls individually operated by 10 finger keys. Three additional keys provided a transient excitation of selected filters to simulate three types of plosive sound: *t-d, p-b* and *k-g*. The operator had a wrist bar for selecting either the noise or buzz source and a foot pedal for controlling the pitch of the buzz oscillator. The operators who demonstrated the Voder at the two world fairs required a year or more of training, but eventually they learned to "play" the Voder much as if it were an organ or a piano, and they were able to produce intelligible speech with considerable facility.

The Voder and related developments led to other analogue electronic synthesizers of speech. The devices ranged from analogue circuitry that duplicated the vocal resonances to electrical simulation of the vocal tract as a bilateral transmission line. The efforts had the two motivations of gaining fundamental knowledge of speech production and of finding new ways to transmit the voice with high efficiency. The technological

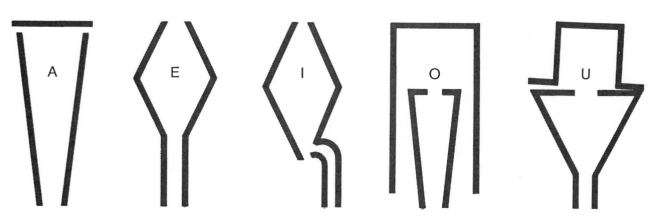

ACOUSTIC RESONATORS somewhat similar in form and dimension to the human mouth were devised by Christian Gottlieb Kratzenstein in 1779 for the synthesis of vowel sounds. The resonators were activated with a vibrating reed that mimicked the human vocal cords by interrupting an air stream. Kratzenstein's novel mechanism reportedly imitated the five vowels "with tolerable accuracy."

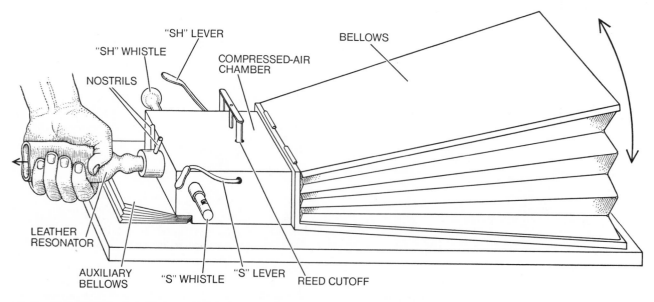

MORE SUCCESSFUL SPEAKING MACHINE was designed in 1791 by Wolfgang von Kempelen. The device had a bellows to supply air to a reed that in turn excited a single, hand-controlled resonator that imitated voiced sounds. Consonants, including nasals, were simulated by four separate constricted passages, which the operator controlled with the fingers of his right hand. The illustration shows a reconstruction of von Kempelen's original speaking machine described by Sir Charles Wheatstone in 1837.

goal, drawing on techniques of both speech analysis and speech synthesis, was to effect a significant reduction in the bandwidth needed to transmit speech signals.

On the fundamental side good progress continued to be made in the understanding of speech production. On the technological side complete band-compression systems were devised and tested. The most notable early system was the Vocoder, invented by Homer Dudley at about the same time that the Voder was being demonstrated. It is fair to say that the Vocoder spawned an entire new subfield of communication study, one having as its principal aim the efficient coding and transmission of speech signals. The Vocoder samples the amplitude spectrum of a speaker's voice at a number of different frequencies and derives electrical voltages that describe the relatively slow fluctuations of these samples. It also derives a voltage that represents the voice pitch and whether a sound is voiced or unvoiced. Since only these slowly changing quantities are transmitted over the communication channel, they require less bandwidth than a normal voice channel. At the receiving end the transmitted quantities are used to resynthesize the original frequency range of the speaker's voice.

Although the Vocoder and its many relatives cannot reproduce all the subtle qualities of the human voice, they can usually indicate such things as whether the speaker is male or female and whether he or she has a distinctive accent. The Vocoder and similar systems have been used for a number of years in special applications where bandwidth is at a premium, but no such system has yet been introduced into civil telephony. In its transoceanic telephone facilities the Bell system has achieved useful savings in bandwidth in a different way, by a time-division switching method.

This system, called TASI (for Time Assignment Speech Interpolation), exploits the fact that in ordinary two-way telephone conversations each speaker is silent roughly half the time. In addition, normal speech has many pauses and silent intervals. A given talker therefore transmits a signal only 35 or 40 percent of the total time. In long-distance communication, where amplification of the signal is necessary, the two-way communication channels are normally four-wire circuits—or two unilateral transmission paths. Each party has a transmit circuit and a receive circuit. Because of the relative inactivity of each talker, a single one-way channel is not used 60

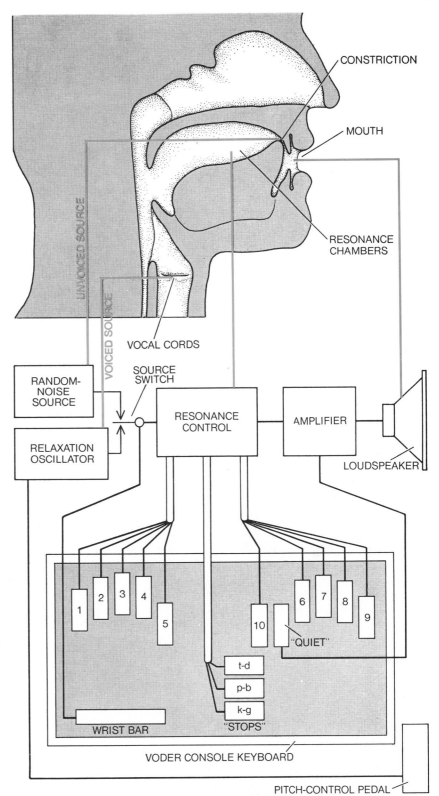

VODER ("voice-operation demonstrator"), an all-electrical speech synthesizer exhibited at the New York world's fair in 1939, was one of the first electrical synthesizers to produce connected speech. The Voder employed two sound sources: a wide-band random-noise source and a periodic buzz oscillator. These sounds were modified by passing them through a "resonance control" box containing 10 contiguous band-pass filters that spanned the frequency range of normal speech. The outputs of the band-pass filters were modulated by gain controls individually operated by 10 finger keys. Three additional keys provided a transient excitation of selected filters to simulate three kinds of plosive sounds: *t-d*, *p-b* and *k-g*. A wrist bar was used to select either noise or buzz and a foot pedal to control the pitch of the buzz oscillator. Analogies to human speech-production components are in color.

or 65 percent of the time. When a large group of such connections is accessible from single transmit and receive locations, as is the case for an undersea cable, the statistical properties of the conversation ensemble make a significant amount of time and bandwidth available for signal transmission, and the system can serve a number of talkers greater than the number of unilateral circuits. The incoming transmit circuit of each talker is equipped with a fast-acting speech detector, or voice switch. When the detector indicates the presence of speech on its line, an automatic electronic switch connects the line to an available transmit path of the TASI group.

During pauses and silent intervals a given talker loses his priority on the transmit link. He is reassigned a channel—often a different one—when he again becomes active. The TASI switch must consequently keep track of who is

talking to whom, and it must identify the recipient of each signal presented for transmission. This "message-addressing" information can be transmitted in the form of a very short identification signal, either before each talk spurt or over an auxiliary channel that serves the entire system.

A limit obviously exists to the number of incoming signals that can be transmitted by a given group of transmit paths before some "freeze-out," or loss of speech signals, occurs. Among other things, this limit is a function of the size of the cable group, the circuit signal-to-noise ratio and the sensitivity of the speech detectors. Several TASI systems have been put into practical operation on undersea cables. On a 36-channel cable, for example, the effective increase in transmission bandwidth is roughly two or three times the bandwidth of the physical circuit.

With the advent of digital computers,

low-cost integrated circuits and sophisticated understanding of sampled-data theory, the techniques of speech analysis and synthesis have acquired new attractiveness. Sampled-data theory tells one how to represent the behavior of continuous physical systems (for example the vocal tract) in terms of discrete numerical operations. Computers are able to perform the arithmetic of these operations quickly and accurately; associated memory devices are able to store large quantities of numbers that can represent speech signals. Advances in integrated circuitry enable one to build small, inexpensive, complex electrical components, including the digital circuits needed in computers.

Talking Computers

Along with these developments, and with the still growing understanding of speech acoustics, the foci of fundamental

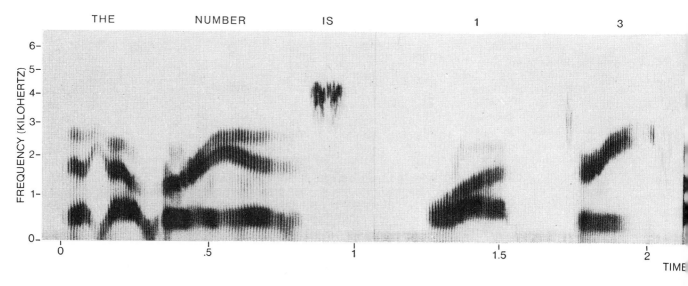

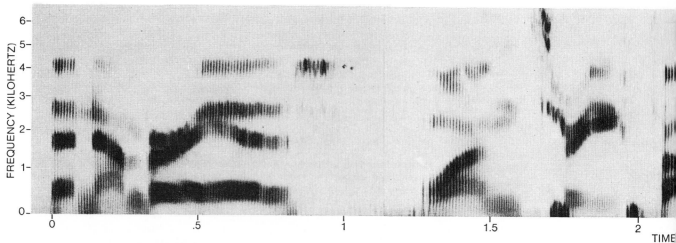

SEVEN-DIGIT TELEPHONE NUMBER synthesized by a computer-controlled formant-synthesis system at Bell Laboratories is represented by a sound spectrogram (*top*) that closely resembles a spectrogram of the same message spoken by a human (*bottom*).

and applied research have shifted somewhat. On the fundamental side linguistic and semantic problems of speech are coming under scrutiny through the power of digital computers. On the applied side two notable goals have emerged. One is to raise the quality of Vocoder-like systems by exploiting the complex digital processing made possible by low-cost integrated circuitry. Bandwidth savings achieved in this way would be highly desirable in satellite communication, deep-space exploration and mobile radiotelephony. A second, and perhaps more compelling, goal is to provide voices for computers, thus opening up new possibilities in automatic information services, computer-based instruction and the design of simple, inexpensive terminals. If computers could voice their answers, as well as print them on a typewriter or display them on a cathode ray tube, their capabilities could be applied in many new ways.

Let us consider what is required to give a computer a voice. Synthesis of a meaningful speech signal requires a description, in some form, of the vocal-tract resonances corresponding to that signal and suitable sound sources for exciting these resonances. A digital synthesis system may therefore operate as follows. A random-number generator simulates the source for voiceless sounds; its variance is controlled as a function of time by a noise-amplitude signal. A digital counter simulates the vocal-cord source for voiced sounds and produces pulses at the required pitch frequency. The amplitude of the voiced source is altered as required by an input designated the voicing-intensity parameter. The two sources—one for voiced sounds, the other for voiceless sounds—are then applied to a recursive filter whose coefficients are determined by the speech resonances and antiresonances as they change with time. Three variable reso-

nances are typically used for voiced sounds and a combination of resonances and antiresonances for voiceless sounds. The digital output of the system is converted to analogue form to give the synthetic signal an audible form.

The recursive filter generates quantized samples, expressed in binary numbers, of the synthetic speech signal. The filter can be organized to operate digitally in a number of ways. A particularly convenient approach is to represent the resonances and antiresonances individually by second-order difference equations. The recursion relations can be programmed directly in the computer that is doing the "talking" or they can be accomplished by special digital circuitry—in effect a hardware digital filter that is controlled by the computer.

The control functions that specify the resonances, the antiresonances and the excitation of the filter must be supplied by the computer. Two computer tech-

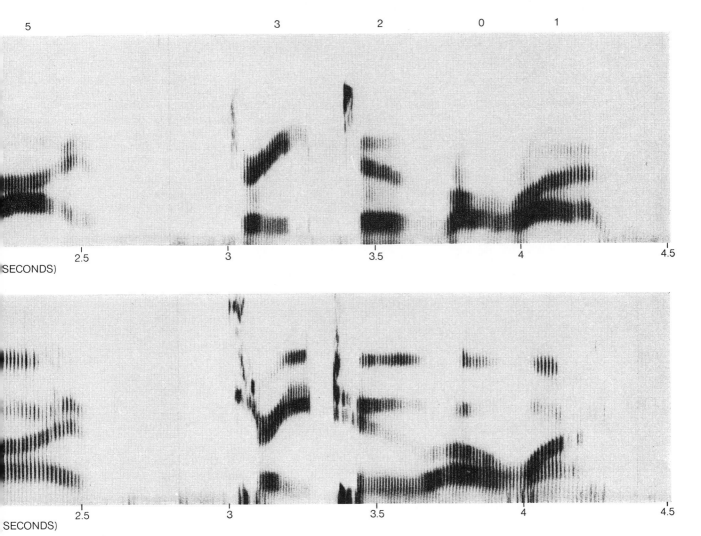

The formant-synthesis method employs a computer program that analyzes natural speech to obtain the variation of three formants and the voice pitch. The particular system used to make the top spectrogram is implemented on a Honeywell DDP-516 computer.

niques for providing the control functions are available. In one technique, called formant synthesis, the control values are measured directly from human speech and are stored in the machine. In another, called text synthesis, the control values are calculated solely from programmed knowledge of the speech process.

Formant Synthesis

The formant-synthesis method employs a computer program that analyzes natural speech to obtain the variation of three formants and the voice pitch.

When data so derived are provided to a synthesizer, they produce speech that closely resembles the original utterance.

Economical storage and flexibility of vocabulary are achieved by storing a library of formant-coded words. Individual, naturally spoken words are analyzed for formants and the formant functions so obtained are stored. Only 530 bits (binary digits) per second are needed to record the formant-coded data, whereas about 50,000 bits per second would be needed to record and store the complete wave form of natural speech. When the computer is instructed to articulate a particular word sequence, or

message, by the "answer back" program, it turns to its library of formant functions and looks up the required functions in the prescribed sequence. By means of a stored program it calculates the duration and the pitch inflection for each word to fit the prescribed context. It then calculates smooth transitions of the formant functions at the word boundaries to produce a realistic concatenation of the words in the message. Finally, the computer issues the resulting control functions to a digital speech synthesizer.

The system described has been implemented at the Bell Telephone Laboratories on a Honeywell DDP-516 computer. In this case the speech synthesizer is a hardware digital filter, external to the computer. The program that creates the control functions for the hardware synthesizer runs about 10 times faster than is necessary to generate speech at the normal word rate, thus making it possible for one computer to serve up to 10 external synthesizers. The system has been applied experimentally to the automatic generation of seven-digit telephone numbers and to the synthesis of spoken instructions for the production-line wiring of telephone circuits. A spectrogram of a typical message synthesized by the computer system ("The number is 135–3201") closely resembles a spectrogram of the same message spoken by a human [see illustration on preceding two pages].

Formant synthesis offers sufficient economy of storage and flexibility of vocabulary to make it attractive for "middle-sized" vocabularies such as inventory reporting, flight information and computer instruction. If, however, a computer is expected to compose messages from encyclopedic amounts of information, a more economical storage system is required. This can be provided by the text-synthesis technique.

Mimicking the Vocal Tract

In text synthesis the computer stores a pronouncing dictionary that contains essentially what one finds in an ordinary desk dictionary: a phonemic transcription of each word, an indication of syllable stress, some rudimentary grammatical information (whether the word is a noun, a verb, an adjective and so on) and information about endings and derived forms. The message to be converted into speech is supplied as the printed English text. Each word is looked up in the dictionary, and the resulting information is passed on to a

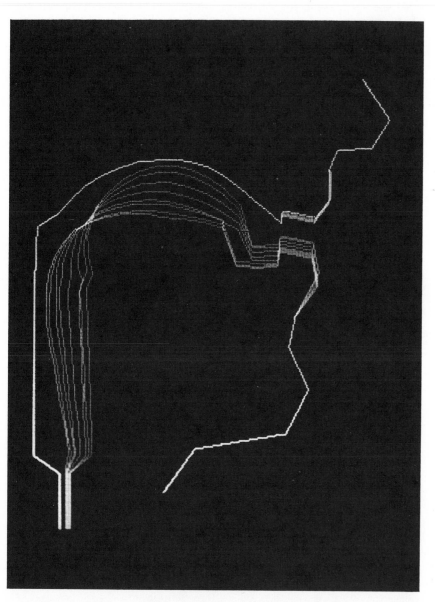

OSCILLOSCOPE DISPLAY of a model of the human vocal tract changes shape with each sound uttered by the associated printed-text speech synthesizer at Bell Laboratories. An expanded set of phonemes, with their individual pitch and duration calculated to satisfy the context of the message, constitutes "commands" that are given to the computer-programmed model of the vocal tract, which simulates the shape of the actual human vocal tract. The photograph shown here is a multiple exposure of the actual oscilloscope display.

program that incorporates linguistic and syntactic rules for English. In this program a strategy is formed for the stress and phrasing of each sentence, pauses are inserted where necessary, and the duration and pitch of individual phonemes are assigned. The result is an output of discrete symbols representing the sequence of phonemes, with their individual pitch and duration calculated to satisfy the context of the message. This string of symbols represents an expansion of two or three times over the input of discrete alphabetic symbols. (Thus, for example, the English-text message "the north wind and the sun" becomes "4dh 4a 6n $4aw 2er 6th 6w *qq5i 4n-4d 4aa -n -d -dh 4a 6s *qq5uh 6n.")

The expanded set of symbols constitutes "commands" that are given to a programmed dynamic model of the vocal tract that simulates the shape of the human vocal tract. The DDP-516 computer programmed for text synthesis at Bell Laboratories also provides an oscilloscope display of the vocal tract showing how it changes shape with each sound uttered by the associated speech synthesizer [see illustration on page 166]. The shape of the vocal tract is defined by seven articulatory parameters. They assume values dictated by the expanded set of phonetic symbols but in responding to these discrete commands they impose their own time constants, governed by physiological constraints. About 100 times per second the formants of the model vocal tract are computed as the tract deforms; the results, along with calculated excitation information, are issued to an external speech synthesizer similar to the one described above.

In this scheme the machine synthesizes the output speech with no recourse to any vestige of human speech. The storage economy in text synthesis approaches 1,000 to one when compared with a facsimile recording of the speech wave form. Comparison spectrograms of synthesized speech and natural speech give an idea of what can be achieved with text synthesis [see illustration on page 159]. As might be expected, the machine displays its own distinctive accent and the accent can be varied by changing the linguistic rules. At the present stage of development the machine's intelligibility is beginning to be acceptable. It is "learning" the rules of speech generation as fast as investigators can formulate, quantify and interpret them for the digital computer. Ultimately both the text-synthesis technique and the formant-synthesis method may provide articulate voices for computers.

18

Speech Recognition by Computer

by Stephen E. Levinson and Mark Y. Liberman
April 1981

Designing a machine that listens is much more difficult than making one that speaks. Significant improvements in automatic recognition may come only with a better understanding of human speech patterns

Modern computers have prodigious powers, but they would be still more useful if more natural ways of communicating with them were possible. The evolution of spoken language has made it well adapted to the needs of human communication. It is fast and nearly effortless. It requires neither visual nor physical contact and it places few restrictions on the mobility of the body or on the use of the hands. A machine capable of recognizing human speech could combine these advantages with the quite different powers of the computer. Such a machine could provide universal access to large data bases through the telephone network. It could provide for the control of complex machines by vocal command and make possible sophisticated prosthetic devices for the handicapped.

After more than 40 years of research, however, the automatic recognition of natural or conversational speech remains a utopian goal. Current speech-recognition devices have small vocabularies and little ability to deal with fluent sequences of words; usually they must be trained to recognize only one speaker's voice. Even so, the advantages of automatic speech recognition are so great that devices capable of recognizing isolated words or short phrases from a vocabulary of between 10 and 30 words are commercially available and are economically practical in some applications. In research laboratories there are speech recognizers with vocabularies of up to 1,000 words, systems that recognize limited-vocabulary sentences with brief pauses between the words and systems that recognize connected speech with fair accuracy if the vocabulary is small, the syntax is limited and the speaker is careful.

The interaction of technology and economics will undoubtedly lead to speech-recognition systems of greater capability. We cannot accurately predict the pace of such development. We are certain, however, that mere elaboration and extrapolation of current technology will not lead to the development of machines that match the human capacity for recognizing speech. Major progress depends on new discoveries.

Why is the problem of recognition so hard? The core of the difficulty is the complex and variable way linguistic messages are encoded in speech. Spoken language enables people to express their thoughts in sound and to recover messages from the sounds produced by others. This curious two-way mapping between concepts in the mind and vibrations in the air presupposes the participants have some common conceptual framework, so that the message received is at least approximately equivalent to the one that was sent. It is not enough, however, to share knowledge of the things one might want to say. Monolingual speakers of English and of Finnish may have many potential messages in common without being able to understand each other's utterances at all. In order to speak and to understand, people must share a system for encoding messages in sound and for decoding speech sounds to yield meanings. In other words, they have to know the same language.

Speech communication with a computer can be understood in an analogous way. The computer "knows" (in some extended sense of the word) about a domain its users also know about. It is useful for information in this domain to be exchanged, and speech happens to be the chosen medium of communication.

Consider a conversation between a computer and its users concerning the inventory of a warehouse. The computer "knows" how many of each item are on hand and where each article is stored. Its data base also lists costs and suppliers. People probably think about the warehouse and its contents in many ways, but the structure of the computer data base is sufficiently similar to one mode of human thought for certain kinds of communication to be possible. The users have questions that the computer can answer, at least in principle, such as, "Do we have any blue pencils in stock?" The users also have things to say that the computer can profitably "understand," such as, "There is no more room in bay 13." If such communication is to be accomplished through the medium of speech, the computer and its users must agree on how to encode such messages in sound and how to reverse the process. They have to "know" the same language.

We are mainly interested in languages such as English, which are called natural because they are defined implicitly by the everyday usage of ordinary people. Computers now function with formal languages such as FORTRAN, which are defined by an explicit set of rules consciously established by specialists. At least for now, computers do only what they are specifically programmed to do. They do not live in the world of people and learn from everyday experience. Hence for a computer to "know" a natural language, it must be provided with an explicit and precise characterization of the language, or at least with a characterization of what the programmer takes the language to be. In all existing and currently conceived speech-recognition systems the formal description of a natural language covers only a fragment of the language, and the formalism reconstructs the fragment in ways that are probably quite different from the implicit knowledge of a native speaker. Even imperfect linguistic abilities on the part of a computer, however, are enough to make possible useful communication with people.

It will help in understanding various approaches to natural-language recognition if we begin by considering some aspects of language and speech in their own terms. We shall then discuss methods of recognizing isolated words and review some procedures for analyzing connected speech. Finally we shall describe a speech-recognition system developed at Bell Laboratories that attempts to combine the major elements of human speech communication into a single operating unit.

At the center of human language is the word. Sequences of words are generally arranged into phrases according to principles of combination known as syntax; moreover, such sequences are usually intended to mean something. The fact that words are ordinarily part of coherent discourse can help in the recognition of the words themselves by providing a context in which some words are likelier than others. Arranging for a computer to act as if it could "understand" word sequences is formidably difficult. The problem involves not only relations among words but also knowledge and reasoning about the nature of the world.

Although a capacity for understanding language may be the ultimate goal, the enterprise of speech recognition is really founded on the identification of words. The aspect of words that concerns us here is their sound. In this sense a word is an equivalence class of noises: the set of all sounds, however distinct in other ways, that represent (in the context of their utterance) the same lexical unit. The problem in word recognition is to find a mathematically defined space in which such a set of sounds can be effectively delimited. Because the amount of variation within the set of sounds corresponding to a given word is quite large, because the acoustic distinc-

tion between words can be quite small and because an adult speaker may know 100,000 words or more, the problem is a difficult one.

In order to understand the sources of variation in the sound of a word and the nature of the distinction between one word and another, it is necessary to grasp two things. First one must understand the basic medium of spoken communication: the ways in which acoustic disturbances of the air can be produced by the human vocal apparatus and perceived by the human auditory system. Second, one has to recognize that speech sounds are elements of a phonological system peculiar to a given language. The

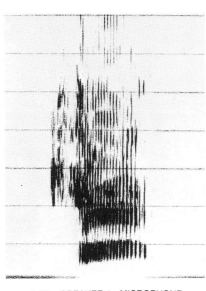

"CAT" SPEAKER 1 MICROPHONE

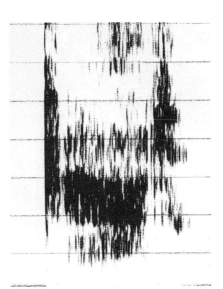

"CAT" SPEAKER 1 WHISPERED

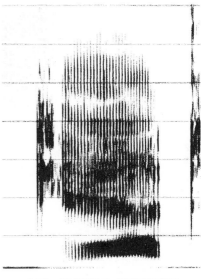

"CAT" SPEAKER 2 MICROPHONE

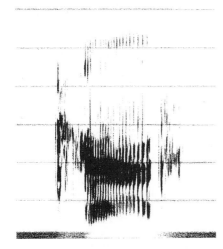

"CAT" SPEAKER 1 TELEPHONE

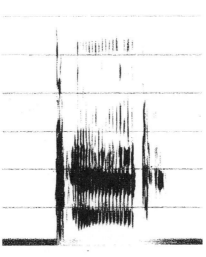

"PAT" SPEAKER 1 TELEPHONE

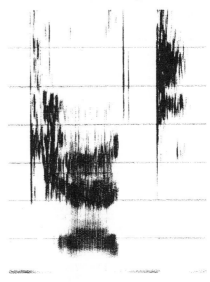

"CAT" SPEAKER 3 MICROPHONE

VARIABILITY OF HUMAN SPEECH, illustrated here by means of sound spectrograms, is one of the principal difficulties encountered in building an automated system for speech recognition. Spectrograms of distinct but acoustically similar words may be more alike than spectrograms of the same word pronounced under various conditions by different speakers. Automatic speech recognition must **be able to attend only to relevant spectral differences (when they exist) and must disregard apparent differences that are linguistically irrelevant. The sound spectrogram represents a series of amplitude spectra over time. Time varies along the horizontal axis and frequency varies along the vertical axis. The darker the mark on the graph, the greater the amplitude of the waveform at that frequency and time.**

```
NFRAM=  396
NO. OF WORDS=  5
CANDIDATES FOR WORD NO.  1  20 FRAMES
WHAT          1    .180
CANDIDATES FOR WORD NO.  2  29 FRAMES
IS            1    .270
CANDIDATES FOR WORD NO.  3  24 FRAMES
NINE          1    .343
ONE           1    .278
SIX           1    .370
SEVEN         1    .242
THE(ALT)      1    .314
CANDIDATES FOR WORD NO.  4  24 FRAMES
SOME          1    .296
FLIGHT        1    .341
ONE           1    .414
THREE         1    .390
CANDIDATES FOR WORD NO.  5  28 FRAMES
NINE          1    .378
OH            1    .390
TIME          1    .291
ONE           1    .411
SEVEN         1    .396
TIMES         1    .315
WHAT IS SEVEN SOME TIME
METRIC=  .1279442E 01
WHAT IS THE FLIGHT TIME
METRIC=  .1396801E 01
THE FLIGHT TIME IS FIVE HOURS AND TWENTY-FIVE MINUTES
```

Machine:	This is the Bell Laboratories flight information system. May I help you?
User:	I want one first-class seat on flight number three one to Denver on Sunday.
Machine:	I am sorry the flight is not available on Sunday.
User:	I would like to leave on Saturday.
Machine:	Flight number three one leaves New York at nine forty-five A.M.; arrives in Denver at one ten P.M.
User:	What is the flight time?
Machine:	The flight time is five hours and twenty-five minutes.
User:	How many stops are there on the flight?
Machine:	This flight makes one stop.
User:	I want a nonstop flight.
Machine:	I am sorry there are no nine A.M. nonstop flights.
User:	I want to go at four P.M.
Machine:	Flight number one six leaves New York at four fifty P.M.; arrives in Denver at seven P.M.
User:	What stops are there on the flight?
Machine:	This flight makes no stops.
User:	Is a meal served on the flight?
Machine:	Dinner is served.
User:	How much is the fare?
Machine:	The round-trip first-class fare is three hundred sixty dollars.
User:	What plane is on the flight?
Machine:	The aircraft is a Douglas DC ten.
User:	I prefer the Boeing seven four seven.
Machine:	The aircraft is a Douglas DC ten.
User:	Please repeat the departure time.
Machine:	The departure time is four fifty P.M.
User:	I will take flight number six five.
Machine:	I am sorry there is no flight six five to Denver.
User:	Please repeat the flight number.
Machine:	The flight number is one six.
User:	I want flight one six.
Machine:	Your reservation on flight number one six to Denver on Saturday is confirmed. Thank you.

TELEPHONE CONVERSATION between man and machine proceeds according to steps that can be displayed on the screen of a computer terminal. The computer counts the number of words in each sentence to be recognized and also divides the entire utterance into "frames" by taking a spectral sample every 15 milliseconds. "NFRAM" is the number of frames in the sentence. It exceeds the number of frames occupied by individual words because the speaker must pause briefly between the words. The candidate words listed for each position in the sentence have been found by comparison with word templates stored in the computer. Only those candidates appear that are grammatically possible in a given position and similar in spectral structure to the spoken word. Not all the candidates to be considered are listed. The numbers following each candidate word are measures of the distance between the word's template and the utterance. The shorter the distance is, the more similar the template is to the utterance. "METRIC" is the unrounded sum of the distance measures for a particular string of words. If the smallest possible METRIC (which necessarily consists of the most likely word in each position) is not allowed by the internal grammar, the grammatically correct string with the smallest METRIC is substituted. A synthetic-voice response to the question by the user is given over the telephone. The complete conversation is transcribed in the computer printout.

phonological system limits the ways in which the various words of the language can differ and controls in part the ways in which the pronunciation of any specific word in the language can vary.

During speech a flow of air from the lungs passes through the larynx, or voice box, into the throat and out through the mouth. If the velum (the flap of soft tissue at the rear of the palate) is lowered, the airflow also proceeds out through the nose; if the velum is raised, the nasal passages are blocked. The airflow can also be obstructed by closing the lips, by pressing the tongue against the palate or by closing the glottis, which consists of two parallel folds of soft tissue (the vocal cords) within the larynx.

The flow of air through the vocal tract can give rise to sound in three main ways. First, the vocal cords can be made to vibrate in somewhat the same manner as the double reed of an oboe or a bassoon. When the vocal cords are brought together, they stop the passage of air from the lungs, and so pressure builds up below them. The pressure forces the vocal cords apart, but the velocity of the rushing air then reduces the pressure in the space between them. The reduction in pressure and the elasticity of the tissues bring the vocal cords together again, in position for another buildup of pressure. The rate at which this cycle is repeated is the fundamental frequency of the voice, which is heard as pitch.

The second way of generating sound in the vocal tract is to form a constriction in the airway narrow enough to cause turbulence. For example, forcing air past a close contact between the upper teeth and the lower lip causes a turbulent flow that is perceived as the sound "f." Unlike the periodic sounds created by vibration of the vocal cords, the sounds generated by turbulent flow are aperiodic, or noiselike. It is possible for the vocal tract to create both periodic and aperiodic sounds at the same time. Combining vocal-cord vibration with the noise source of an "f" gives rise to the sound perceived as a "v."

A third kind of sound generation takes place when pressure built up behind a closure is abruptly released. Such bursts of acoustic energy occur in the pronunciation of consonants such as "p," "t" and "k."

These three sources of speech sound are shaped acoustically by the changing physical shape of the vocal tract. If the vibrations of the vocal cords were somehow vented directly to the outside air without first passing through the throat, mouth and nose, they would sound rather like a door buzzer and not like speech at all. On passing through the throat, mouth and nose cavities, however, the quality of the buzz is changed profoundly. It is the shape of the vocal tract, including the positions of the larynx, the tongue, the lips and the velum, that distinguishes (for example) the "ee" sound in "me" from the "oo" sound in "you."

One way of understanding this acoustic transformation is the mathematical technique called Fourier analysis. In 1822 the French mathematician Jean Baptiste Joseph Fourier showed that any periodic waveform can be represented as the sum of an infinite series of sine waves. A periodic waveform is one that is repeated at uniform intervals. If the interval of repetition is t seconds, the fundamental frequency of the waveform is $1/t$ hertz. In the Fourier series for a periodic waveform, the frequencies of the component sine waves are harmonics, or integral multiples, of the fundamental frequency of the waveform being analyzed, and they must be assigned appropriate amplitudes and phases. The Fourier transform is a generalization of the Fourier series; it allows analysis of aperiodic waveforms. Thus the noisy hiss of an "f" sound can be represented as a sum of sinusoidal components all along the frequency continuum.

The most obvious way to represent sound waves is to graph the variation of air pressure with time. Fourier's result implies that the same information can also be displayed by a graph that shows amplitude and phase as a function of the frequency of the sinusoidal components. Because phase differences are of little perceptual significance, a speech sound can be represented in practice by its amplitude spectrum, a graph that shows the amplitude of the sine-wave component at each frequency.

What is the acoustic effect of the shape of the vocal tract on the sound emitted? When the sounds are represented by their amplitude spectra, the effects are clear [*see illustration on next page*]. The vocal tract acts as a filter on the spectrum of the sound source, enhancing some frequencies and diminishing others. The selective filtering can be described by a mathematical expression called a transfer function; a separate transfer function is associated with each position assumed by the organs of the vocal tract. The transfer function usually has several well-defined frequency peaks, called formants, in which most of the energy from the sound source is concentrated.

It is now possible to state with some precision why it is hard for a computer to make the translation from sounds to words, from an acoustic characterization of an utterance to a linguistic characterization of the intended message. One source of difficulty is that the organs of speech do not take up a series of fixed configurations corresponding to units of the message. Instead parts of the vocal tract are in constant motion along smooth trajectories. Some investigators

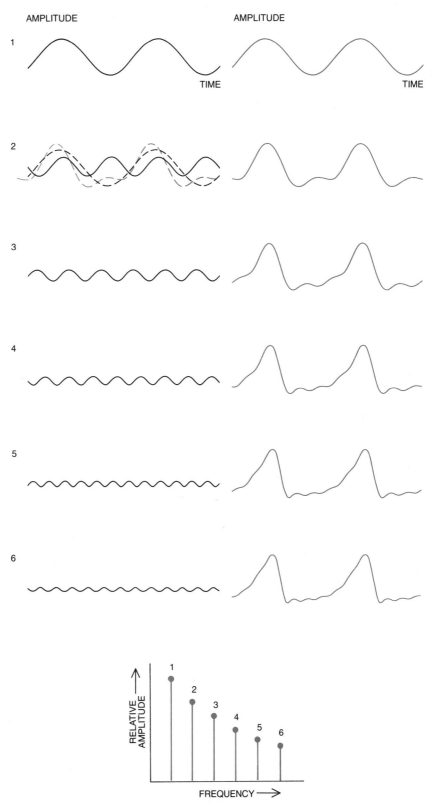

PRINCIPLE OF SUPERPOSITION allows temporal variation in the sound pressure of the signal to be represented as a spectrum of sound amplitude, or energy, at different frequencies. The amplitude spectrum is generally a more useful way of displaying acoustic information. The waveform (here a glottal wave) can be treated mathematically as a pattern that repeats indefinitely in the past and the future at a fundamental frequency. As the French mathematician Jean Baptiste Joseph Fourier showed, any such waveform can be decomposed into a series of sine waves at integral multiples of the fundamental frequency, with various amplitudes and phases. When the sine waves are combined by adding the amplitudes at each point, the result is the original waveform. When the amplitude of each sine wave that makes up the decomposition is graphed as a function of its frequency, the result is an amplitude spectrum.

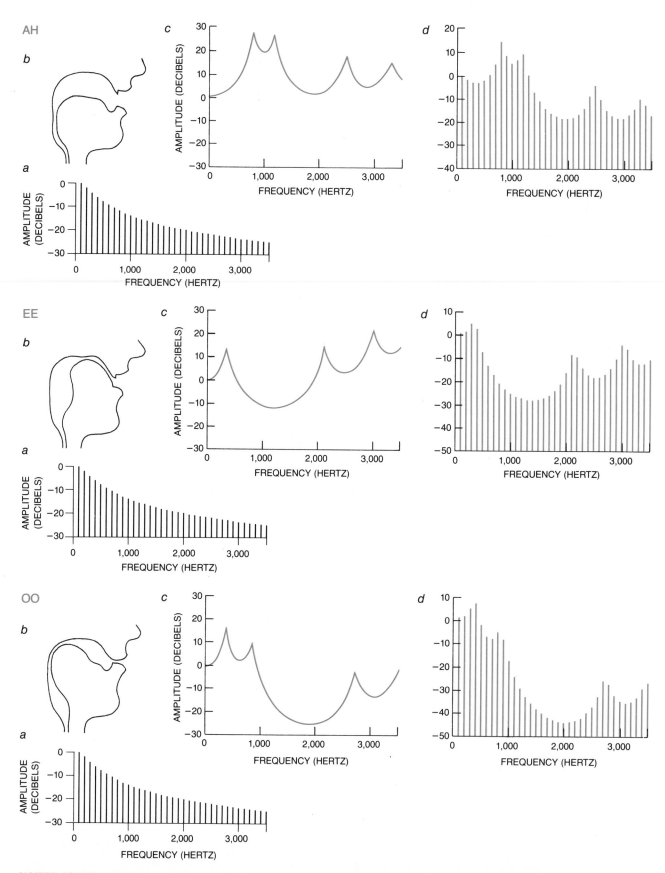

VOWEL SOUNDS result from various configurations of the mouth, lips, tongue and velum (soft palate). The resulting shape of the vocal tract can be modeled by a series of resonating cavities that enhance energy at some frequencies and diminish it at others in predictable ways. Such filter-response characteristics can be represented by a transfer function (c) for each position of the model of the vocal tract (b). When the input sound energy is periodic (which is almost the case for vocal-cord vibration), both the input spectrum (a) and the output spectrum (d) are line spectra. In a line spectrum the sound energy is concentrated at harmonics, or integral multiples, of the vocal-cord frequency. An aperiodic sound source such as a whispered vowel has no discrete lines in its spectrum, but the shape of the output spectrum still matches that of the transfer function. Model vocal-tract configurations for vowels "ee," "ah" and "oo" are shown.

believe these motions "flow" through a sequence of target positions defined by linguistic units such as consonants and vowels. Others think even the simplest linguistic units are inherently dynamic. In any case the result is a complex and continual motion, which is inherited by the emitted sound in the form of a constantly changing amplitude spectrum. Such patterns of changing sound quality can conveniently be represented by a sound spectrogram, a graph in which time proceeds from left to right, frequency increases from bottom to top and amplitude increases from white through shades of gray to black.

Motions of the vocal tract that correspond to linguistic units usually overlap and combine with their neighbors. For instance, in saying "coo" the lip-rounding of the vowel "oo" usually precedes the tongue motion of the initial consonant. Hence the acoustic effects of the two motions are combined from the beginning of the word. In fluent speech such amalgamation also applies between one word and the next. The effects are sometimes quite plain to the ear. When the "t" of "cat" combines with the "y" of "your," it makes the phrase "You gave the cat your dinner" sound like "You gave the catcher dinner."

Other variations in the sound of a word result from its position in a phrase, from its degree of emphasis and from the rate at which it is pronounced. The size and shape of the vocal tract vary from individual to individual, and habits of speech differ widely according to age, sex, geographic region and social background. Furthermore, the signal that reaches a speech-recognition device is influenced by various circumstances in addition to the sounds made by the speaker, such as room acoustics, background noise and the characteristics of the transmission channel.

For these reasons it is hard to divide a speech signal into chunks corresponding to the elements of the message the signal conveys, and it is difficult to translate pieces of acoustic information into information about the identity of pieces of the message. People find speech easy to understand, and so the needed information must be present in the signal. The trick is to find it.

A natural starting place is the recognition of words. Words are generally distinct from one another as elements of a linguistic system, and they constitute natural and relatively stable patterns for an automated speech-recognition system. Although speech is more than a sequence of words, it is at least such a sequence, so that a crucial function of a speech recognizer is identifying words. If a speech-recognition system can recognize words accurately, it will succeed; if it cannot, it will fail.

Most speech recognizers now in use are not capable of recognizing words in

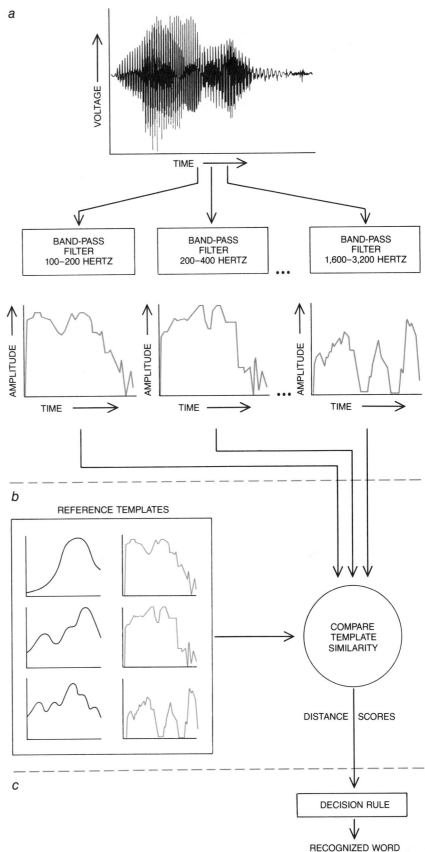

STANDARD METHOD OF WORD RECOGNITION employs the basic principles of pattern recognition to discriminate among acoustic patterns. The speech waveform is measured and analyzed (*a*), in this case by filters that divide the signal into frequency bands, each band being an octave wide. The output of each filter is the energy in its band. The outputs are compared with stored reference templates, and distance scores are assigned to each template (*b*). A decision procedure then classifies the input utterance on the basis of the distance scores (*c*).

connected speech. Instead recognition is carried out on isolated words by a process of acoustic pattern recognition. Generally the user must "train" the machine by speaking into a microphone all the words the system is to recognize. In some cases the training is limited to one utterance of each word by a few of the speakers who will use the system. In other applications every potential user must say each word several times. The result of this training process is a set of stored "templates," which represent typical acoustic patterns for the words in the vocabulary.

When a word is presented for recognition, the machine analyzes the acoustic signal, compares the results of the analysis with the stored templates and decides which one of the templates most closely resembles the spoken word. The machine may also list other possible matches in decreasing order of similarity. Once a classification has been made the machine can respond to the user's utterance or issue an appropriate signal to some other device. Each stage of the template-matching procedure (analysis of the speech signal, comparison with the template and classification of the signal) can be carried out by a variety of techniques.

The aim of all methods of analyzing the speech signal is to characterize the temporal variation of the signal's amplitude spectrum. Perhaps the simplest method of estimating the spectrum is the zero-crossing count. This method consists in counting the number of times the voltage analogue of the speech signal changes its algebraic sign (from plus to minus or from minus to plus) in a fixed interval. The number of such axis crossings is related to the frequency.

One refinement of the zero-crossing method filters the speech signal into three frequency bands. The zero crossings are measured separately in each band to give rough estimates of the first three formant frequencies. Such measurements are useful in classifying vowel sounds, and for small vocabularies of easily distinguished words these measurements alone are sufficient for discrimination. The zero-crossing method is economically attractive because it can be accomplished by simple electronic devices.

A more elaborate procedure for spectral estimation is the filter-bank method. The speech signal is divided by filtering into between 20 and 30 frequency bands, covering the frequency range of human speech. The output of each filter is a measure of the energy in that frequency band. The energy levels are suitable for direct comparison with those of a template. The Fast Fourier Transform provides a general, computationally efficient method for estimating the amplitude spectrum of a signal from its time-domain waveform. This algorithm

provides one of several ways to obtain filter-bank information in purely digital form.

Recently a new method for estimating the amplitude spectrum of speech, called linear predictive analysis, has been introduced. Actually statisticians have employed the method for some time under the name autoregressive analysis. The method predicts the amplitude of a speech wave at a given instant from a weighted sum (or linear combination) of its amplitudes at a small number of earlier instants. The coefficients, or weights, that give the best estimate of the true speech wave can then be mathematically converted into an estimate of the amplitude spectrum. For the analysis of speech linear predictive analysis is particularly appropriate because it is mathematically equivalent to treating the vocal tract as a pipe of varying circular cross section, or in other words as a sequence of resonant cavities. The model is quite faithful for nonnasalized, voiced speech. Because it is a model of the vocal-tract resonances and not of vocal-cord vibration, the linear-prediction spectrum is smooth. None of the pitch harmonics are in evidence. Consequently the formant structure of the speech wave, which is important for speech recognition, is brought clearly to the fore.

During the comparison, or template-matching, stage the phonological structure of a word can be exploited in an indirect way. A spoken word consists of a sequence of vocal gestures, which gives rise to a time-varying pattern of sound. The parts of the sound pattern rarely have the same durations in different utterances of the same word, but their sequence is more nearly constant. For example, the word "fable" begins with an "f" noise, which is followed by a pattern of moving formants that show the lips opening out from the "f" and closing again for the "b" while the tongue is moving through the first vowel; next there is a "b" lip closure, and finally there is another pattern of spectral motion as the lips open and the tongue moves into the final "l." On different occasions the timing of these patterns may vary considerably, but they must all be

present in the described order if the utterance is to count as a reasonable rendition of the word "fable."

Because of differences in timing, the various parts of a word may be badly out of alignment with the corresponding parts of the template it is to be matched against. Since the order of events is fairly constant, the misalignment can be corrected by stretching the template in some places and compressing it in others so that a mathematically optimum match is found. Nonuniform temporal alignment is accomplished by means of a procedure called dynamic programming. Dynamic programming was developed by Richard E. Bellman of the University of Southern California School of Medicine for solving problems in the design of servomechanisms. It is a technique for mathematical optimization that is often carried out with the aid of a computer, but it should not be confused with computer programming itself.

Comparison implies some estimate of the degree of similarity between the sound of the input and the sound represented by the stored template. The final aspect of processing common to all word recognizers is a decision strategy, which is usually based on a statistical measure of closeness of fit. Each template is assigned a point in an abstract space; the position of the point is defined by the spectral characteristics of the template. The utterance to be classified is represented as a point in the same space. The recognizer calculates the distance in the space between the utterance and each of the templates. It then picks either the template closest to the utterance or the equivalence class of templates that is closest to the utterance in a statistical sense.

The performance of automatic recognition systems in identifying isolated words is poor compared with that of people. Even for the most powerful word recognizers the number of errors rises rapidly as the vocabulary increases to more than a few hundred words. The error rates get worse still when unknown speakers and acoustic conditions are introduced. In a recent experiment isolat-

METHODS OF ESTIMATING the amplitude spectra of short intervals of a word (here the word "language") all seek to highlight linguistically relevant information in a computationally efficient way. Zero-crossing counts exploit the fact that as the frequency increases, the number of times the voltage analogue of the acoustic signal changes its sign increases as well. In the band-pass-filter method the signal is divided into several frequency bands and the amount of energy in each band is measured. These measurements yield an amplitude spectrum for the interval. The Fast Fourier Transform is a general, computationally efficient algorithm for estimating the amplitude spectrum of the signal from its time-domain waveform. It is one of several ways of computing filter-bank information in digital form. The rough appearance of the spectrum is caused by pitch harmonics or other fine structure in the spectrum. The fourth method of spectral estimation, called linear predictive analysis, employs a model of the vocal tract to generate successive frequency spectra. Its advantage is that a smooth, continuous spectrum is generated for each sample. The spectra in dark color are all constructed from the same interval of the time-varying signal. Several other methods of spectral estimation are also in use.

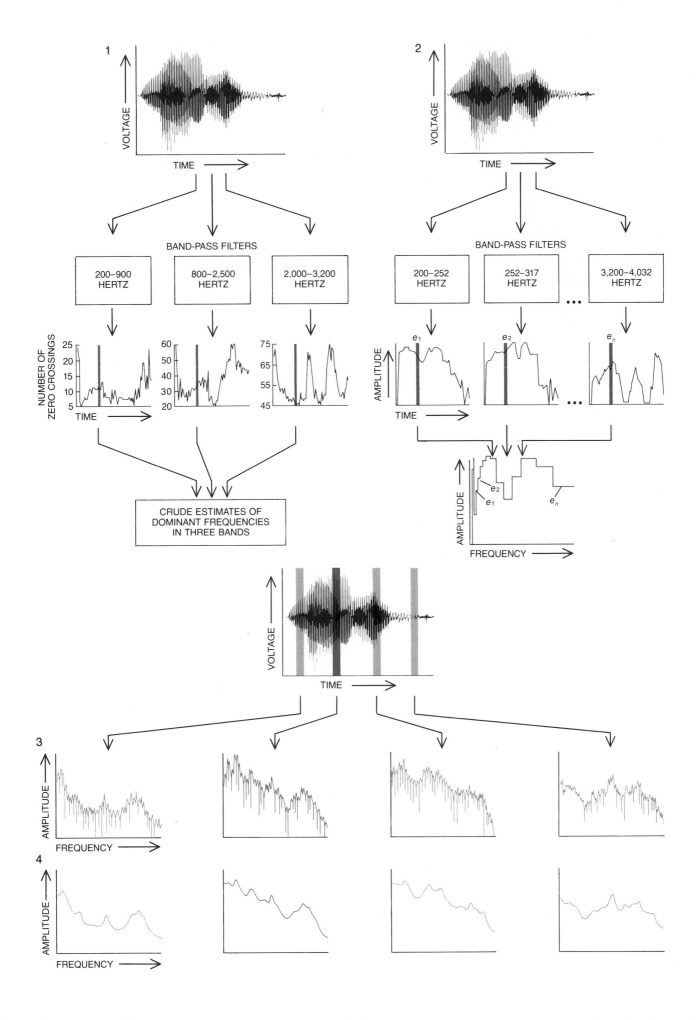

ed words from a 26,000-word vocabulary were spoken by a variety of speakers unknown to the listener; the words were identified with an error rate of less than 3 percent. Human word-recognition abilities are also remarkably tolerant of background noise: conversation can be understood even at a noisy party. No existing recognition system can approach this level of performance.

In attempts to recognize continuous speech the disparities between human and computer performance are even more evident. People generally find it easier to recognize words in context, but for an automated system the recognition of fluent speech is far more difficult than the recognition of words in isolation. One of the crucial problems is coarticulation, which causes the blending at the boundaries between words and makes the spectral patterns to be recognized highly complex and unstable. In fluent

speech there are no clear acoustic signs of word boundaries and direct template-matching becomes extremely difficult. In essence every template must be aligned with every possible interval of the utterance by means of a variant of the dynamic-programming method.

The computational burden is somewhat reduced by the requirement that the intervals be contiguous, so that the end of one word meets the beginning of the next. Still, the combinatorial complexity of the process increases too fast for it to be considered a practical solution to the general problem of recognizing continuous speech. Direct template-matching can be useful only where the range of possible utterances is small. With present technology the technique can work in real time (that is, as fast as the utterance is spoken) for sequences as many as five words long, drawn from a vocabulary of about 20 words.

Instead of looking for every possible pattern everywhere in the signal, a continuous-speech-recognition system can search for linguistic units in a more constrained way, such as in sequence from the beginning of the utterance to the end. The speech signal is divided into intervals that correspond to specific acoustic patterns, and the intervals are classified in a way that matches the categories of a potential linguistic message as closely as possible. We shall call such techniques segmentation and labeling. The processes of segmentation and labeling can be carried out in many ways, and the intervals to be found can correspond to words or to smaller linguistic units such as syllables, phoneme pairs or phonemes.

The easiest way to achieve automatic segmentation and labeling is to require the user to pause briefly between words. The pauses that appear as intervals of

DIRECT MATCHING

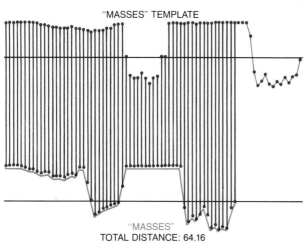

"MASSES" TEMPLATE

"MASSES"
TOTAL DISTANCE: 64.16

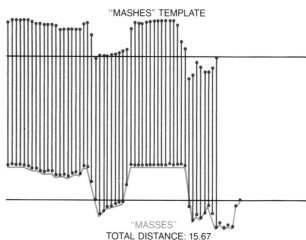

"MASHES" TEMPLATE

"MASSES"
TOTAL DISTANCE: 15.67

MATCHING BY DYNAMIC PROGRAMMING

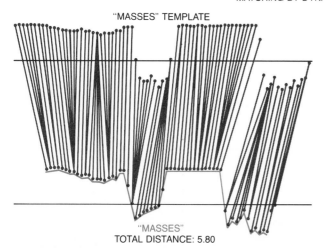

"MASSES" TEMPLATE

"MASSES"
TOTAL DISTANCE: 5.80

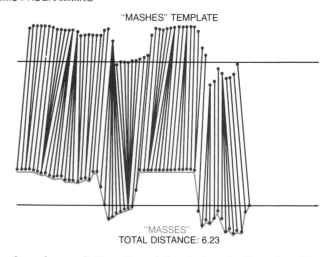

"MASHES" TEMPLATE

"MASSES"
TOTAL DISTANCE: 6.23

COMPARISON STAGE of word recognition is carried out by compressing and stretching stored templates according to an optimization process called dynamic programming. For each stored template, dynamic programming seeks to associate every frame of the input word with some frame of the template in such a way that a distance measure of overall fit between the input and the template is minimized. The nonuniform time alignment of the stored template with the spoken word allows for variations in the rate of speech and in the relative lengths of the vowels and consonants in a word. Here matching the templates (*black*) to the input (*color*) without dynamic programming yields a misidentification, indicated by the distance scores, that is corrected when the compression and expansion procedure is applied. Dynamic programming is often done with the aid of a computer but should not be confused with computer programming.

low sound energy are a reliable indication of word boundaries. Once the words have been segmented they can be analyzed independently. Although this method works well, it does not really address the question of fluent speech recognition. Other methods of segmentation and labeling are available.

Discontinuities in the spectrum, peaks and valleys in the energy of certain frequency bands and other acoustic signs provide clues to articulatory events: the closing or opening of the vocal tract or the beginning or ending of laryngeal vibration. This suggests that segmentation and labeling might be carried out on the basic phonological units of which words are constructed.

Blending and the diffusion of acoustic information across boundaries affect the acoustic shape of the smaller speech units even more than they affect words. As a result such units are difficult to identify by template-matching, and segmentation errors would probably be at least as frequent for the smaller speech units as they would be for words. Nevertheless, there may be reason to favor segmentation into smaller units as the vocabularies of speech recognizers become larger.

There are some 300,000 words in English, far too many for all of them to be tested by template-matching. Moreover, it is difficult to allow for the effects of blending at the boundaries of words when word templates are employed. English syllables number some 20,000, which is still too many for them to be identified easily and reliably. In addition the effects of blending at boundaries are even more disruptive to template-matching with syllables than they are with words. In contrast, there are only about 40 English phonemes (basic linguistic elements such as consonants or vowels), and the phonemes can be further decomposed into about a dozen phonological features that specify distinctive characteristics of vocal-tract shape and larynx control. Such features can also be combined directly into syllable-like units. As the set of linguistic units is reduced in number, however, the relation of the units to patterns of sound becomes more abstract, more complex and less well understood. Segmenting and labeling such small speech units by currently available techniques leads to high error rates. Still, if constraints imposed by the linguistic code can compensate for the errors, or if more reliable methods of analysis can be found, the small number of the basic phonological units will give them a decided advantage as the fundamental elements of a recognition system.

There is one difficulty that is common to all segmentation and labeling procedures: the probability of error is much higher in making a number of independent classifications than it is in making

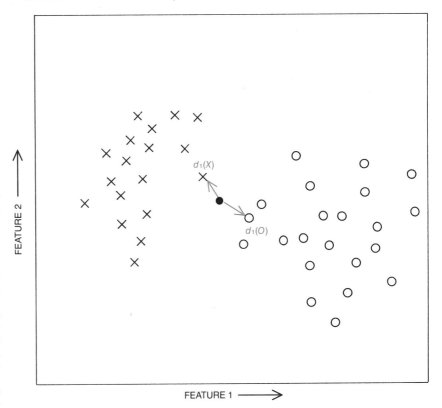

CLASSIFICATION OF AN INPUT SOUND consists in finding the shortest distance in a space of acoustic features from the input (represented by a dot) to a stored template or class of templates (represented by X's and O's). The simplest decision strategy picks the closest template (*upper graph*), and so the input is classified as the sound "ah" (an X). When several templates represent linguistically equivalent sounds (as when the computer must recognize the voices of several speakers), the decision strategy may take account of entire classes of templates. One method calculates the distance from the input to the third-nearest neighbor in each class (*lower graph*); here the input is classified as the sound "aw" (an O). Under certain conditions it is possible to draw equal-density contours along which the number of template samples per unit area is constant. The highest-density contour that passes through the input can then be found; because $p_1(X)$ is greater than $p_1(O)$ the input is classified as the sound "ah" (an X).

a single classification. In a three-word phrase, even if the probability of recognizing the correct word in any given position is .8, the probability of recognizing the entire phrase correctly is only about one-half (.8 × .8 × .8).

One way of offsetting this effect is to introduce constraints imposed by the linguistic code, such as allowable sequences of words in a sentence or allowable sequences of syllables in a word. An area of mathematics called formal-language theory provides several methods for specifying and using such constraints. By applying some of the elementary principles of formal-language theory it is possible to write precise and efficient descriptions, or formal grammars, of linguistically possible sequences of sounds and words. One can also write computer programs that utilize these grammars to recognize formally correct linguistic sequences.

One simple way of exploiting grammatical structure makes use of a mathematical construction called a state diagram. A state diagram defines every possible sentence the machine can recognize. Each path from the starting point of the diagram to the end points represents an acceptable sentence. From acoustic measurements the recognizer assigns a probability to each transition in the diagram. A probability can then be calculated for each path by forming the product of the probabilities of all the transitions that make up the path. The sentence chosen is the one represented by the path with the highest probability. This technique can significantly reduce the error rate in sentence recognition: it can choose a word with a relatively low probability in a given position in order to enhance the likelihood that the overall transcription is correct.

Such a reduction in the error rate was demonstrated in a phoneme-based system for the recognition of fluent Japanese, which was tested at Bell Laboratories and at the Nippon Telegraph and Telephone Electrical Communication Laboratories. The segmentation and labeling of phonemes was correct only 60 percent of the time. Syntactic processing, however, led to a 70 percent success rate for the recognition of sentences with an average length of 25 phonemes. Although 70 percent recognition is not adequate for reliable communication, the result is remarkable in view of the small probability of finding a correct sentence without syntactic processing: it comes to about one chance in three million.

A state diagram can also improve the efficiency of continuous-speech recognition by nonlinear time alignment. Instead of matching every template to every interval in the input sentence, the recognition system tests only those templates that fit admissible sequences described by the state diagram. This procedure eliminates much wasted computation, since only a small subset of the words in the vocabulary can appear at a given position in a sentence. A device employing syntax-directed time alignment can recognize connected sentences of more than 20 words composed from a vocabulary of more than 100 words.

So far we have described the phonological symbols that correspond to the acoustic reality of speech and the grammatical organization of the symbols into words and phrases. These form the linguistic code of speech. The purpose of the linguistic code is to convey meaningful messages: semantic information. Hence semantic information imposes additional constraints on the way the symbols of a language can be combined to form messages.

A machine that processes the semantic information encoded in speech attempts a much more complex and subtle task than a machine that merely recognizes words. In order to deal with meaning a machine not only must recognize acoustic patterns but also must manipulate abstract representations of reality. In other words, it must simulate at least some important aspects of human intelligence.

At Bell Laboratories we have incorporated a rudimentary semantic proc-

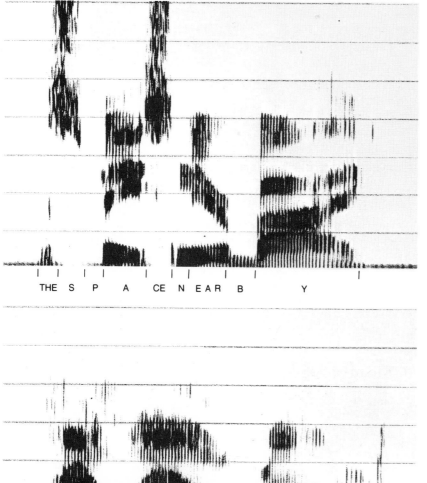

THE   S   P   A   CE N E AR   B   Y

THE   A   R   E   A   AR   OU   N   D

SEGMENTATION OF ACOUSTIC PATTERNS into words or other linguistic units is difficult because of the temporal smearing of speech sounds. Certain sounds, however, exhibit more spectral discontinuity than others. The alternation of the consonants and vowels in the phrase "The space nearby" shows up in relatively clear discontinuities. The smooth sequence of blended vowels in the phrase "The area around" makes segmentation more difficult.

essor in a system designed to emulate the entire process of human speech communication. The user communicates with the system by telephone. The computer, which is intended to function as an airline ticket agent, responds in a synthetic voice. The integration of the necessary functions into a single device has enabled us to study the interaction of the subsystems and their control.

As a complete simulation of human communication the Bell Laboratories machine is the most advanced system known to us. The individual components, however, are less advanced than those of experimental systems in other laboratories. There are speech-recognition systems that work with vocabularies much larger than the 127 words our machine recognizes, and there are systems with a more flexible syntax. There are more sophisticated semantic processors that accept typed input instead of speech. There are processors that respond faster than ours does. A question that is asked in 10 seconds receives a reply on our system after about 50 seconds. We hope to improve the performance of all the building blocks of our system.

In the airline-information system the acoustic processor and the syntactic parser are coupled, so that the acoustic processor tests each hypothetical word-identification made by the parser for agreement with spectral information. The rest of the system, with the exception of two memory units that are shared by all the components, is devoted to semantic processing.

The semantic processor incorporates a world model, whose state can be changed as a conversation progresses, and a memory module, which cannot be altered. The world model is based on a set of concepts, each of which can take on a number of values. Among the concepts are "destination," "departure day" and "departure time." During a particular conversation these categories might be assigned the values "Boston," "Tuesday" and "5:00 P.M.," whereas another state of the world model might correspond to the values "Chicago," "unknown" and "unknown." The semantic processor determines a new state from its present state, from the words in the input sentence and from the transitions in the state diagram that were employed in generating the sentence. The need for the latter two sources of information reflects the fact that semantic content is a function both of the words and of their relations in a sentence.

The memory units store two kinds of information: facts and procedures. Facts are of two types. Airline schedules are stored as a portion of the *Official Airline Guide,* but relations among the concepts in the *Airline Guide* must also be stored. If the system is asked the elapsed time of a flight, it can calculate

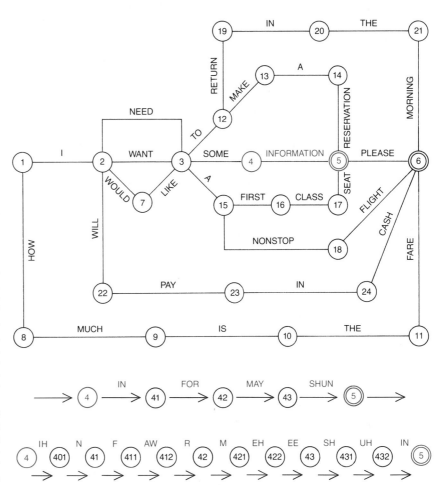

FINITE-STATE GRAMMAR is computationally the most straightforward means of imposing syntactic (or word-order) constraints on the recognition of sentences. The grammar diagrammed here would force the computer to classify every sequence of acoustically possible words as one of the 26 sentences that can be traced through the state diagram, starting at state 1 and ending at state 5 or 6. For instance, one possible sentence is "I would like a first-class seat, please." The principles of the diagram can also be extended to levels of analysis lower than the level of the word, such as the syllabic and phonemic analyses of the word "information." The grammars of experimental recognition systems allow for billions of sentences.

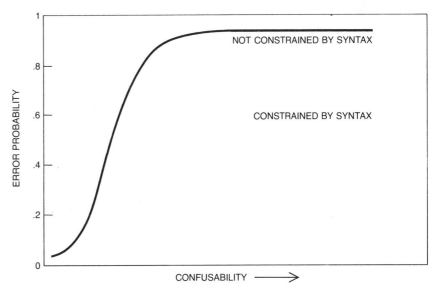

CONFUSABILITY OF A SPEECH SIGNAL is a complex function of the size of the input vocabulary, the acoustic similarity of the elements to be discriminated, the number of speakers to whom the system must respond and the amount of noise in the communication channel. Errors tend to become more frequent as confusability increases. Syntactic contraints can significantly reduce the effect. This error pattern is as true for human listeners as it is for machines.

the time from the listed departure and arrival times; for it to do so, however, the time zone of each city must be available. (In the *Official Airline Guide* all times are local.)

Procedures are special-purpose programs that use stored facts to derive new information from an input and from the current state of the world model. For example, one program is a perpetual calendar, which can find the day of the week for any given date. The conversion is needed because a question may specify only a departure date, whereas the *Official Airline Guide* is organized by day of the week.

When an internal instruction calls for a reply to the user, the system activates a linguistic encoder. The semantic analyzer tells the encoder what concepts are to be communicated from the world model. Then the encoder retrieves grammar and vocabulary from memory and transforms the concepts into a sequence of symbols. The speech synthesizer transforms the sequence into speech [see "The Synthesis of Speech," by James L. Flanagan; beginning on page 158].

In what ways can the art of speech understanding be advanced? We see two basic aims. For the near term it is important to seek a better grasp of the fine structure of speech communication. This should include detailed information about the kind of signal analysis done by the human ear and a better understanding of the relation between sound symbols (such as phonemes and syllables) and actual sounds. More efficient ways of exploiting this information must be developed and incorporated into recognition systems.

For the long term several areas of investigation may bring significant advances. We have stressed that the speech code includes a number of coexisting kinds of structure, such as phonology, syntax and semantics. A general theory of such complex codes is needed, particularly so that the interactions of the levels can be coordinated and controlled. It is also desirable to gain a better understanding of the processes by which people acquire a language. Although present speech recognizers are "trained," the training is rudimentary and cannot be altered through "experience." We believe this lack of adaptive abilities is a serious disadvantage. The best design strategy is not to program a computer directly with the wealth of descriptive detail that constitutes a natural language but rather to give it the basic set of expectations and abilities that are needed to learn a language.

It is hard to predict how well these investigative strategies can ultimately succeed in approximating natural speech communication. Whatever the rate of progress, this goal will continue to be pursued. Some success is guaranteed, and wisdom will be required in its application.

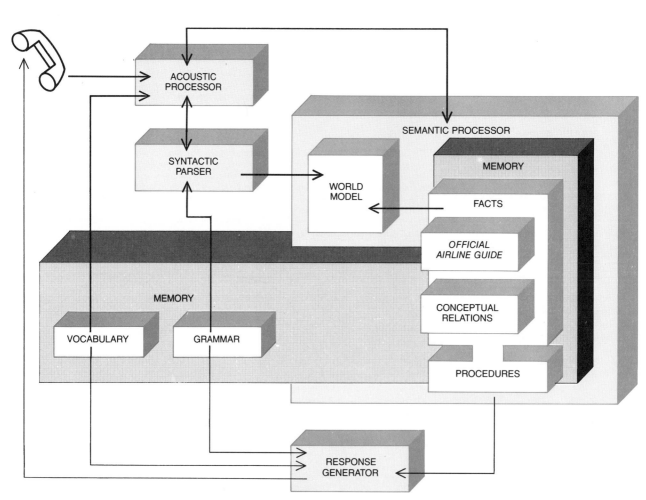

COMPLETE SIMULATION of human speech communication is attempted by an automated system constructed by the authors and their colleagues at Bell Laboratories. Functional relations among major parts of the system are shown here in a block diagram. The user asks for information about airline timetables over the telephone, and the computer replies in a synthesized voice. Heavy arrows trace the flow of information related to speech recognition. The generation of a response is traced by lighter arrows. Memory modules concerned with semantic processing include facts and procedures related to flights and reservations. Nonsemantic memory stores vocabulary templates and grammatical rules used both in speech recognition and in speech synthesis. The semantic processor also includes a world model, which is constantly updated with data based on the user's questions and on the information in the semantic memory.

BIBLIOGRAPHIES

I HUMAN LANGUAGE AND ANIMAL COMMUNICATION

1. The Origin of Speech

A COURSE IN MODERN LINGUISTICS. Charles F. Hockett. Macmillan Company, 1958.

ANIMAL "LANGUAGES" AND HUMAN LANGUAGE. C. F. Hockett in *The Evolution of Man's Capacity for Culture*, arranged by J. N. Spuhler, pages 32–38. Wayne State University Press, 1959.

BEES: THEIR VISION, CHEMICAL SENSES, AND LANGUAGE. Karl von Frisch. Cornell University Press, 1950.

LANGUAGE: AN INTRODUCTION TO THE STUDY OF SPEECH. Edward Sapir. Harcourt, Brace & Company, 1921.

2. Dialects in the Language of Bees

COMMUNICATION AMONG SOCIAL BEES. Martin Lindauer. Harvard University Press, 1961.

THE DANCING BEES. Karl von Frisch. Harcourt, Brace, 1955.

"SPRACHE" UND ORIENTIERUNG DER BIENEN. Karl von Frisch. Verlag Hans Huber, 1960.

3. Mimicry in Parasitic Birds

CHARACTER DISPLACEMENT. W. L. Brown, Jr., and E. O. Wilson in *Systematic Zoology*, Vol. 5, pages 49–64; 1956.

HOMAGE TO SANTA ROSALIA, OR WHY ARE THERE SO MANY KINDS OF ANIMALS? G. E. Hutchinson in *The American Naturalist*, Vol. 93, No. 870, pages 145–159; May–June, 1959.

EVOLUTION IN CHANGING ENVIRONMENTS. Richard Levins. Princeton University Press, 1968.

ON THE METHODS OF RESOURCE DIVISION IN GRASSLAND BIRD COMMUNITIES. Martin L. Cody in *The American Naturalist*, Vol. 102, No. 924, pages 107–147; March–April, 1968.

4. Teaching Language to an Ape

SYNTACTIC STRUCTURES. Noam Chomsky. Mouton & Co., 1957.

THE GENESIS OF LANGUAGE. Edited by F. Smith and G. A. Miller. The M.I.T. Press, 1966.

BEHAVIOR OF NONHUMAN PRIMATES: Vols. III–IV. Edited by Fred Stollnitz and Allan M. Schrier. Academic Press, 1971.

LANGUAGE IN CHIMPANZEE? David Premack in *Science*, Vol. 172, No. 3985, pages 808–822; May 21, 1971.

A FIRST LANGUAGE: THE EARLY STAGES. Roger Brown. Harvard University Press, 1973.

II LANGUAGES AND DERIVATIVE SYSTEMS

5. The Indo-European Language

DIE HEIMAT DER INDOGERMANISCHEN GEMEINSPRACHE. P. Thieme. Wiesbaden, 1954.

6. The American Languages

A WORD GEOGRAPHY OF THE EASTERN UNITED STATES. Hans Kurath. University of Michigan Press, 1949.

7. The Chinese Language

A Grammar of Spoken Chinese. Yuen Ren Chao. University of California Press, 1968.

CLIBOC: Chinese Linguistics Bibliography on Computer. William S-Y. Wang and Anatole Lyovin. Cambridge University Press, 1970.

The Computer in Chinese Linguistic Research. William S-Y. Wang, Stephen W. Chan and Benjamin K. Tsou in *Proceedings of the USA–Japan Computer Conference*, 1972.

DOC, 1971: A Chinese Dialect Dictionary on Computer. Mary L. Streeter in *Computers and the Humanities*, Vol. 6, No. 5, pages 259–270; May, 1972.

A Synchronic Phonology of Mandarin Chinese. Chin-Chuan Cheng. Mouton Publishers, 1973.

8. The Spread of the Bantu Language

Zur genetischen Gliederung der Bantu-Sprachen. Bernd Heine in *Afrika und Übersee*, Vol. 56. No. 4, pages 164–185; April, 1972.

The Chronology of the Iron Age in Bantu Africa. D. W. Phillipson in *The Journal of African History*, Vol. 16. No. 3, pages 321–342; 1975.

The Prehistorical Implications of Guthrie's Comparative Bantu, Part I: Problems of Internal Relationship. David Dalby in *The Journal of African History*, Vol. 16, No. 4, pages 481–501; 1975.

Linguistic Evidence and Its Correlation with Archaeology. Christopher Ehret in *World Archaeology*, Vol. 8. No. 1, pages 5–18; June, 1976.

The Later Prehistory of Eastern and Southern Africa. D. W. Phillipson. Heinemann Educational Books. 1977.

9. Pidgin Languages

Hands Off Pidgin English! Robert A. Hall, Jr. Pacific Publications Pty. Ltd., 1955.

10. The Earliest Precursor of Writing

An Operational Device in Mesopotamian Bureaucracy. A. Leo Oppenheim in *Journal of Near Eastern Studies*, Vol. 17, pages 121–128; 1958.

Glyptique Susienne. Pierre Amiet in *Mémories de la Délégation archéologique en Iran*, Vol. 43; 1972.

An Archaic Recording System and the Origin of Writing. Denise Schmandt-Besserat in *Syro-Mesopotamian Studies*, Vol. 1, No. 2; July, 1977.

11. Zapotec Writing

Sculpture and Mural Painting of Oaxaca. Alfonso Caso in *Handbook of Middle American Indians*, edited by Robert Wauchope and Gordon R. Willey. University of Texas Press, 1965.

Monte Albán: Settlement Patterns at the Ancient Zapotec Capital. Edited by Richard E. Blanton. Academic Press, 1978.

The Cloud People: Evolution of the Zapotec and Mixtec Civilizations of Oaxaca, Mexico. Edited by Kent V. Flannery and Joyce Marcus. University of New Mexico Press, in press.

III LANGUAGE AS BIOLOGICAL AND SOCIAL BEHAVIOR

12. Specializations of the Human Brain

Emotional Behavior and Hemispheric Side of the Lesion. G. Gainotti in *Cortex*, Vol. 8, No. 1, pages 41–55; March, 1972.

Selected Papers on Language and the Brain. Norman Geschwind. D. Reidel Publishing Co., 1974.

The Integrated Mind. Michael S. Gazzaniga and Joseph E. Ledoux. Plenum Press, 1978.

Right–Left Asymmetries in the Brain. Albert M. Galaburda, Marjorie LeMay, Thomas L. Kemper and Norman Geschwind in *Science*, Vol. 199, No. 4311, pages 852–586; February 24, 1978.

13. The Acquisition of Language

The Acquisition of Language: The Study of Developmental Psycholinguistics. David McNeill. Harper & Row, Publishers, 1970.

Language, Structure and Language Use: Essays by Charles A. Ferguson. Selected and introduced by Anwar S. Dil. Stanford University Press, 1971.

A First Language: The Early Stages. Roger Brown. Harvard University Press, 1973.

One Word at a Time. Lois Bloom. Mouton, 1975.

14. The Visual Characteristics of Words

The Similarity of Lower-Case Letters of the English Alphabet. Peter Dunn-Rankin in *Journal of Verbal Learning and Verbal Behavior*, Vol. 7, pages 990–995; 1968.

VISUAL INTERFERENCE IN THE PARAFOVEAL RECOGNITION OF INITIAL AND FINAL LETTERS OF WORDS. Herman Bouma in *Vision Research*, Vol. 13, pages 267–282; 1973.

THE RESOURCES OF BINOCULAR PERCEPTION. John Ross in *Scientific American*, Vol. 234, No. 3, pages 80–86; March, 1976.

15. Bilingualism and Information Processing

LANGUAGES IN CONTACT: FINDINGS AND PROBLEMS. Uriel Weinrich. Linguistic Circle of New York, 1953.

PROBLEMS OF BILINGUALISM. Edited by John Macnamara. *The Journal of Social Issues*, Vol. 23, No. 2; April 1967.

READING AND TALKING BILINGUALLY. Paul A. Kolers in *The American Journal of Psychology*, Vol. 79, No. 3, pages 357–376; September, 1966.

WORDS AND THINGS. Roger Brown. Free Press, 1958.

16. Slips of the Tongue

THE NON-ANOMALOUS NATURE OF ANOMALOUS UTTERANCES. Victoria A. Fromkin in *Language*, Vol. 47, No. 1, pages 27–52; March, 1971.

LANGUAGE AND MIND. Noam Chomsky. Harcourt Brace Jovanovich, 1972.

SPEECH ERRORS AS LINGUISTIC EVIDENCE. Edited by Victoria A. Fromkin. Mouton, 1973.

17. The Synthesis of Speech

THE VOCODER. Homer Dudley in *Bell Laboratories Record*, Vol. 18, No. 4, pages 122–126; December, 1939.

SYNTHETIC VOICES FOR COMPUTERS. J. L. Flanagan, C. H. Coker, L. B. Rabiner, R. W. Schafer and N. Umeda in *IEEE Spectrum*, Vol. 7, No. 10, pages 22–45; October, 1970.

SPEECH ANALYSIS, SYNTHESIS AND PERCEPTION. James L. Flanagan. Springer-Verlag, 1971.

COMPUTER SYNTHESIS OF SPEECH BY CONCATENATION OF FORMANT-CODED WORDS. L. R. Rabiner, R. W. Schafer and J. L. Flanagan in *The Bell System Technical Journal*, Vol. 50, No. 5, pages 1541–1558; May-June, 1971.

18. Speech Recognition by Computer

ON HUMAN COMMUNICATION: A REVIEW, A SURVEY AND A CRITICISM. Colin Cherry. The MIT Press, 1966.

TRENDS IN SPEECH RECOGNITION. Edited by W. A. Lea. Prentice-Hall, Inc., 1980.

INDEX

Italic page numbers indicate material in illustrations.